Recruiting *the* Ancients
for the Creation Debate

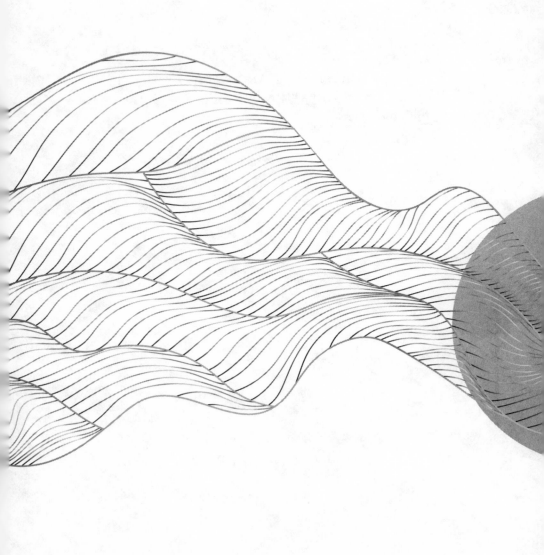

RECRUITING *the* ANCIENTS
for the CREATION DEBATE

Andrew J. Brown

WILLIAM B. EERDMANS PUBLISHING COMPANY
GRAND RAPIDS, MICHIGAN

Wm. B. Eerdmans Publishing Co.
4035 Park East Court SE, Grand Rapids, Michigan 49546
www.eerdmans.com

Published 2023

Book design by Lydia Hall

Printed in the United States of America

29 28 27 26 25 24 23   1 2 3 4 5 6 7

ISBN 978-0-8028-7459-7

Library of Congress Cataloging-in-Publication Data

A catalog record for this book is available from the Library of Congress.

For my family

CONTENTS

CONTENTS

PREFACE

Welcome to this study. Let me make a few comments about how it is meant to work. It is related to my first book, *The Days of Creation: A History of Christian Interpretation of Genesis 1:1–2:3* (Deo/Brill), first published in 2014, which was a revised version of my doctoral thesis with the University of Queensland (2011). My narrower goal in this work is to arbitrate on the use of ancient Christian interpretations of Genesis 1 in modern debates over creation in Genesis, especially in relation to the creation week of Genesis 1. My driving concern is that Christian interpreters of the past have been lassoed at times against their wills into supporting various modern stances on the question with inherent problems of superficiality, inaccuracy, and anachronism. I hope not to discourage exploration of ancient Christian interpretations but to discipline its methods in this department, taking lessons in good methodology from other historical fields as well as those earned by experience in this discussion.

So, I am operating here in somewhat of a historical research mode, specifically in the history of interpretation or history of exegesis. I do not really have a specific stance on Genesis 1 to push for here, and in my view that should help me to evaluate various treatments of ancient interpretations of Genesis 1 fairly objectively rather than targeting any one party for criticism. For those who want to ask me, as others have, "But what do *you* think about the creation week?" I have to rather apologetically say that explaining Genesis is a good project for a book, but that this is not really that book, and indeed so many of that kind of book have been written that I am not sure another one is needed. But what we have not done enough of yet is include in our conversations about the meaning of such critical biblical texts the giants of the Christian past whose wealth of wisdom lies readily at our disposal if we just take the trouble to look into it. This book is necessary because we do not do that enough.

My focus, therefore, is on past Christian figures you probably have heard of rather than the more obscure ones, as interesting as they might be. It is the more prominent figures whose legacies are contested. For accessibility, I try to point out available English translations while also looking out for the latest and best quality critical editions. Those who can reference the original languages will find those editions pointed out for consultation. One unfortunate factor for the monolingual of us, and that is very much my background, is that historical Christian interpretation has often been better studied outside of English-speaking circles. This forces me to consult and cite works in French and German. If I have found something important in their work, academic honesty requires me to cite them, and they are important for readers who can utilize them, but this is not meant to be obscure or elitist. Church roots run deep in continental Europe, naturally, so that is where the conversations have happened, although English is the scholarly *lingua franca* today. I usually give Latin and Greek primary documents English titles in the main text unless the sense of the original is obvious or it is well known. Important Latin and Greek terms are transliterated in the main text when it is necessary to mention them.

Access to ancient sources is better than ever, having been completely revolutionized by the advent of the internet and mass digitization programs by major companies. Multiple editions of virtually any publication relevant to us from the advent of printing in Europe are normally accessible online in digital repositories such as Google Books, Internet Archive, or Christian Classics Ethereal Library. Some repositories such as Early English Books Online or Classic Protestant Texts involve paywalls and might be best sought out via a public or university library service. I will not normally indicate the use of digital channels to access such sources in the footnotes unless there is no print equivalent. I have likewise eliminated most URLs and DOIs from my footnotes in consideration of space limitations. I trust that you will be able to successfully find the pertinent references within these digital repositories using inbuilt search functions.

I hope I inspire you to revisit the ancients as you follow this conversation.

AB

Acknowledgments

Writing a book is like running a marathon. You enjoy the first three miles and the final lap around the track inside the stadium. The rest of the time, you wonder why you keep doing this sort of thing to yourself. But marathon runners, like writers, keep doing their thing. It somehow all looks worth it from the finish line.

I wish I could thank all the people who read the manuscript through and spotted errors. If only I had left time for that part. I would, however, sincerely like to thank my acquisitions editor at Eerdmans, Andrew Knapp, who has shown extraordinary patience. He faced a marathon when he had bargained on a modest steeplechase, but he did not lose faith, nor did his Eerdmans colleagues. Like an old-time prisoner whose cell looks out on the gallows, I always worried that my time would come. It is due to their patience, Andrew's in particular, that it never did. Thank you, indeed. I trust this final product repays you in some way. Let me add my thanks to Blake Jurgens for his careful and systematic work as copyeditor. His efforts greatly improved the clarity of my writing here. He has done you a service, dear reader.

Commencement and completion of this project were made possible through two semesters of study leave, one at either end, granted by my teaching institution, Melbourne School of Theology (MST) in Melbourne, Victoria, Australia. Because MST is a small theological institution, faculty study leave costs it dearly in resource terms, especially when I constitute the English department, Old Testament, and Biblical Hebrew faculty in its entirety. Thank you again for permitting me this time. MST operates under the auspices of the Australian College of Theology, and this publication therefore counts in the research output of that parent body also.

To my family: Naomi my wife, and my teenage children, Gil, Tim, and Kyria: you don't have much idea what I wrote about, just that it took practically forever. Virtually all of your teenage years, Gil! But we kept doing things together as a family, because those memories will last better than books ever do. Thank you all for your patience too. I love watching you all thrive and live—my beloved anothers.

Thanks be to God for his inexpressible gift(s)! (2 Cor. 9:15, ESV).

ABBREVIATIONS

GENERAL

AM	*Anno mundi*, "year of the world"
ANE	Ancient Near East(ern)
BCE	Before Common (or Christian) Era (= BC)
ca.	circa (approximately)
CE	Common (or Christian) Era (= AD)
ET	English translation
Gk.	Greek
Heb.	Hebrew
Lat.	Latin
LXX	Septuagint (Greek translation of the Old Testament)
NT	New Testament
OT	Old Testament/Hebrew Bible
r.	reigned
v(v).	verse(s)

PREMODERN NONBIBLICAL SOURCES

Early Jewish Texts and Apostolic Fathers

Alleg. Interp.	Philo, *Allegorical Interpretation*
Ant.	Josephus, *Jewish Antiquities*

Barn.	Epistle of Barnabus
Creation	Philo, *On the Creation of the World*
1 En.	1 Enoch
2 En.	2 Enoch
4 Ezra	4 Ezra
Jub.	Jubilees
Sib. Or.	Sibylline Oracles

Church Fathers and Medieval Authors

1 Apol.	Justin Martyr, *1 Apology*
C. Ar.	Athanasius, *Orations against the Arians*
Cels.	Origen of Alexandria, *Against Celsus*
C. Gent.	Aquinas, *Summa contra Gentiles*
Chron.	Julius Africanus, *Chronography*
Civ.	Augustine, *City of God*
Comm. Dan.	Hippolytus, *Commentary on Daniel*
Comm. Gen.	Ephrem, *Commentary on Genesis*
Comm. Sent.	Aquinas, *Commentary on the Sentences*
Conf.	Augustine, *Confessions*
De Trin.	Hilary of Poitiers, *On the Trinity*
Dial.	Justin Martyr, *Dialogue with Trypho*
Div. quaest. LXXXIII	Augustine, *Eighty-Three Different Questions*
Enarrat. Ps.	Augustine, *Enarrations on the Psalms*
Ep.	Augustine, *Letters*; Jerome, *Epistles*
Gen. imp.	Augustine, *On the Literal Interpretation of Genesis (Unfinished)*
Gen. litt.	Augustine, *On Genesis Literally Interpreted*
Gen. Man.	Augustine, *On Genesis against the Manichaeans*
Haer.	Irenaeus, *Against Heresies*
Hex.	Ambrose, *Hexaemeron*; Basil, *Hexaemeron*
Hom. Gen.	John Chrysostom, *Homilies on Genesis*; Origen of Alexandria, *Homilies on Genesis*
Hymn. Nativ.	Ephrem, *Hymns on the Nativity*
Hymn. Parad.	Ephrem, *Hymns on Paradise*
In Gen.	Bede, *On Genesis*

Inst.	Lactantius, *Divine Institutes*
Moral.	Gregory the Great, *Moralia in Job*
Myst.	Hilary of Poitiers, *Tractatus mysteriorum*
Princ.	Origen of Alexandria, *On First Principles*
Retract.	Augustine, *Retractations*
Sent.	Peter Lombard, *Sentences*
ST	Aquinas, *Summa theologiae*
Strom.	Clement of Alexandria, *Stromateis*
Symp.	Methodius, *Symposium*

REFERENCE WORKS, SERIES, DATABASES, AND JOURNALS

Works listed here are not duplicated in the bibliography.

ACW	Ancient Christian Writers
AHBI	*A History of Biblical Interpretation.* Edited by Alan J. Hauser and Duane F. Watson. 2 vols. Grand Rapids: Eerdmans, 2003, 2009
ANF	*The Ante-Nicene Fathers.* Edited by Alexander Roberts and James Donaldson. 10 vols. 1885–1887. Repr., Peabody, MA: Hendrickson, 1994. Available online via Christian Classics Ethereal Library (ccel.org)
ATTA	*Augustine through the Ages: An Encyclopedia.* Edited by Allan D. Fitzgerald, O.S.A. Grand Rapids: Eerdmans, 1999
BAC	The Bible in Ancient Christianity
BZNW	Beihefte zur Zeitschrift für die neutestamentliche Wissenschaft
CAH 12	*The Cambridge Ancient History.* 2nd ed. Vol. 12. *The Crisis of Empire, AD 193–337.* Edited by Alan Bowman, Peter Garnsey, and Averil Cameron. Cambridge: Cambridge University Press, 2005
CAH 13	*The Cambridge Ancient History.* 2nd ed. Vol. 13. *The Late Empire, AD 337–425.* Edited by Averil Cameron and Peter Garnsey. Cambridge: Cambridge University Press, 1997
CBQ	*Catholic Biblical Quarterly*
CHLGEMP	*The Cambridge History of Later Greek and Early Medieval*

	Philosophy. Edited by A. H. Armstrong et al. Cambridge: Cambridge University Press, 1967
CO	John Calvin, *Opera quae supersunt omnia.* Edited by Guilelmus Baum, Eduardus Cunitz, and Eduardus Reuss. Brunsvigae: Schwetschke and Sons, 1882
CSEL	Corpus Scriptorum Ecclesiasticorum Latinorum
DECL	*Dictionary of Early Christian Literature.* Edited by Siegmar Döpp and Wilhelm Geerlings. New York: Crossroad, 2000
DMBI	*Dictionary of Major Biblical Interpreters.* Edited by Donald K. McKim. Downers Grove, IL: InterVarsity Press, 2007
DOC	*The Days of Creation: A History of Christian Interpretation of Genesis 1:1–2:3.* Andrew J. Brown. Leiden: Brill, 2012; Blandford Forum: Deo, 2014
DTC	*Dictionnaire de théologie catholique.* Edited by Alfred Vacant et al. 15 vols. Paris: Letouzey et Ané, 1908–1950
EBR	*Encyclopedia of the Bible and Its Reception.* Edited by Hans-Joseph Klauck et al. Berlin: de Gruyter, 2009–
FC	Fathers of the Church: A New Translation
GCS(NF)	Die griechischen christlichen Schriftsteller der ersten [drei] Jahrhunderte (Neue Folge)
HBI	*History of Biblical Interpretation.* Henning Graf Reventlow. Translated by Leo G. Perdue et al. 4 vols. RBS 50, 61–63. Atlanta: Society of Biblical Literature, 2009–2010
HB/OT	*Hebrew Bible/Old Testament: The History of Its Interpretation.* Edited by Magne Sæbø. 3 vols. in 5 parts. Göttingen: Vandenhoeck & Ruprecht, 1996–2015
HHMBI	*Historical Handbook of Major Biblical Interpreters.* Edited by Donald K. McKim. Downers Grove, IL: InterVarsity Press, 1998
HTR	*Harvard Theological Review*
IA	Internet Archive (https://archive.org/)
JECS	*Journal of Early Christian Studies*
JETS	*Journal of the Evangelical Theological Society*
JSOTSup	Journal for the Study of the Old Testament Supplement Series

JSNT	*Journal for the Study of the New Testament*
LCL	Loeb Classical Library
LW	*Luther's Works*. American Edition. Edited by Jaroslav Pelikan and Helmut T. Lehman. 55 vols. Philadelphia: Muehlenberg and Fortress; St. Louis: Concordia, 1955–
NIDCC	*The New International Dictionary of the Christian Church.* Edited by J. D. Douglas and Earle E. Cairns. 2nd ed. Grand Rapids: Zondervan, 1978
NPNF¹	*The Nicene and Post-Nicene Fathers.* Series 1. Edited by Philip Schaff. 14 vols. 1886–1889. Repr., Peabody, MA: Hendrickson, 1994. Available online via Christian Classics Ethereal Library (ccel.org)
NPNF²	*The Nicene and Post-Nicene Fathers.* Series 2. Edited by Philip Schaff and Henry Wace. 14 vols. 1890–1900. Repr., Peabody, MA: Hendrickson, 1994. Available online via Christian Classics Ethereal Library (ccel.org)
ODCC	*The Oxford Dictionary of the Christian Church.* Edited by F. L. Cross and E. A. Livingstone. 2nd rev. ed. Oxford: Oxford University Press, 1983
OECS	Oxford Early Christian Studies
OTP	*The Old Testament Pseudepigrapha.* Edited by James H. Charlesworth. 2 vols. Garden City, NY: Doubleday, 1983, 1985
PG	Patrologia Graeca [= Patrologiae Cursus Completus: Series Graeca]. Edited by Jacques-Paul Migne. 162 vols. Paris, 1857–1886
PL	Patrologia Latina [= Patrologiae Cursus Completus: Series Latina]. Edited by Jacques-Paul Migne. 217 vols. Paris, 1844–1864
PSCF	*Perspectives on Science and Christian Faith*
RAC	*Reallexikon für Antike und Christentum.* Edited by Theodor Klauser et al. Stuttgart: Hiersemann, 1950–
RBS	Resources for Biblical Study
RCS	Reformation Commentary on Scripture
SC	Sources chrétiennes
STAC	Studies and Texts in Antiquity and Christianity

VC	*Vigiliae Christianae*
VCSup	Supplements to Vigiliae Christianae
VT	*Vetus Testamentum*
VTSup	Supplements to Vetus Testamentum
WA	*D. Martin Luthers Werke: Kritische Gesamtausgabe: Schriften.* 65 vols. Weimar: Böhlau, 1883–2009. Available at Internet Archive
WTJ	*Westminster Theological Journal*
ZAC	*Zeitschrift für antikes Christentum*

Introduction

THE PROBLEM AND THE PURPOSE OF THIS BOOK

"Go read the church fathers for yourself. Read Augustine and Basil. Read John Chrysostom and the Eastern Fathers. See what each had to say about the Flood and about Creation."[1] This is a great suggestion, and at first glance creation-related Christian literature seems to be doing just that. If you could have a dollar for every time Saint Augustine is mentioned in a book about Christianity and science from the past forty years or so, you might supplement the weekly grocery budget quite nicely. That is not bad for someone who has been dead for more than one and a half millennia. Augustine is not the only dead Christian thinker cited as a model for our own thinking. Also high on the podium would be John Calvin, the sixteenth-century French reformer; his German predecessor, Martin Luther; and the pioneering Italian astronomer Galileo Galilei. Some believing writers lionize Calvin or Luther for their fidelity to the faith. Secular writers might praise Galileo for gallantly resisting the institutionalized church. Many ancient figures of repute are effectively "recruited" for the modern writer's theological or ideological cause in the manner of a celebrity endorsement. The surface message might be, "We ought to side with Augustine on this," but the undertone is something like, "Augustine is dead, admittedly, but if he were alive, I am fairly sure he would agree with me on this."

---

1. Paul Nelson and John Mark Reynolds, "Young Earth Creationism," in *Three Views on Creation and Evolution*, ed. J. P. Moreland and J. M. Reynolds (Grand Rapids: Zondervan, 1999), 74. The names of Basil and Chrysostom are mentioned nowhere else in that volume, and Augustine only superficially.

This fixation with the glorious dead in creation-related Christian writing is a little unexpected. As a teacher in an evangelical Protestant theological college in the English-speaking sphere, I see many students' eyes glaze over when they suspect I am talking about the distant past. History has an unfortunate reputation; many Westerners have a hard time believing that much worthy of attention happened before the advent of Facebook or, more generously, powered flight. Western Protestant Christians make an exception for Jesus Christ, the Apostle Paul, and perhaps a favorite patron such as Calvin or Luther. The average twenty-first-century Westerner does not take much interest in those centuries when kings and nobles wore strangely elaborate wigs, let alone in ancient history. So whence this sudden focus on not just Reformers and Puritans, but also the early church fathers when it comes to books about Genesis, or Christianity generally, and science?

Let us admit first that not every modern Christian has been in the habit of neglecting Christian tradition. For Orthodox scholars such as Peter Bouteneff and Andrew Louth or for Hungarian Catholic priest and physicist Stanley Jaki (1924–2009), the recourse to ancient theological precedent is familiar and instinctive.[2] Likewise, Calvin, Luther or the Westminster Divines possess acknowledged authority and form a natural locus for study for the Protestant denominations that look back to them. For lower-church strands of Christianity, this turn to the ancients amounts to a rediscovery and a new exploration into the past. Speaking as an Australian Baptist, and thus having distant roots in the radical wing of the Reformation, I would characterize my own cultural tradition as forgetful, unappreciative, and uncritical of its spiritual and ecclesial ancestry. For me as a young adult to read an ancient author was to pull out a dusty copy of C. S. Lewis's *Mere Christianity*. I did not realize what a rich backstory I was missing.

There is a determined movement now to rediscover our theological and ecclesial past, more so for the Evangelicals who forgot it than for those Catholics, Orthodox, and Presbyterians who never did. Within Catholicism, the *ressourcement* movement—helmed by Henri de Lubac, Yves Congar and M.-D. Chenu[3]—began to call attention back to the church's historic theological heritage. Andrew

2. Stanley Jaki, *Genesis 1 through the Ages*, 2nd ed. (Royal Oak, MI: Real View, 1998).

3. Marie A. Mayeski, "Catholic Theology and the History of Exegesis," *Theological Studies* 62.1 (2001): 141–44; John Webster, "Theologies of Retrieval," in *The Oxford Handbook to Systematic Theology*, ed. John Webster, Kathryn Tanner, and Iain Torrance (Oxford: Oxford University Press, 2008), 590.

Louth, editor of *Genesis 1–11* in the Ancient Christian Commentary on Scripture series, is a good example of an Orthodox voice in this sphere. In the more recent evangelical sphere this increasing impetus might be represented by the works of Daniel H. Williams and others in Baker Publishing's Evangelical Ressourcement series or by Gavin Ortlund's *Theological Retrieval for Evangelicals*.[4] Many works are calling for a "retrieval" of patristic theology or spirituality as a normative guide.[5] A few of these studies point to medieval figures,[6] while for my own church context some reacquaintance with its own Reformation ancestors might be a first step.[7] This movement is often cast as *theological* retrieval,[8] or in terms of reviving a sacramental spirituality.[9] But the most relevant strand of this movement for our conversation is where earlier Christian exegetical *outcomes*, or more basically, interpretive *methods* are advocated.[10] The whole conversation about the theological

4. Daniel H. Williams, *Retrieving the Tradition and Renewing Evangelicalism: A Primer for Suspicious Protestants* (Grand Rapids: Eerdmans, 1999); D. H. Williams, *Evangelicals and Tradition: The Formative Influence of the Early Church*, Evangelical Ressourcement (Grand Rapids: Baker Academic, 2005); D. H. Williams, *Tradition, Scripture, and Interpretation: A Sourcebook of the Ancient Church* (Grand Rapids: Baker Academic, 2006); Gavin Ortlund, *Theological Retrieval for Evangelicals: Why We Need Our Past to Have a Future* (Wheaton, IL: Crossway, 2019); as well as Robert Webber, *Ancient-Future Faith* (Grand Rapids: Baker, 1999), and others.

5. Paul M. Blowers, *Drama of the Divine Economy: Creator and Creation in Early Christian Theology and Piety*, OECS (Oxford: Oxford University Press, 2012); W. David Buschart and Kent Eilers, *Theology as Retrieval: Receiving the Past, Renewing the Church* (Downers Grove, IL: IVP Academic, 2015); Christopher A. Hall, *Learning Theology with the Church Fathers* (Downers Grove, IL: InterVarsity Press, 2002).

6. Norman Geisler, *Thomas Aquinas: An Evangelical Appraisal* (Eugene, OR: Wipf and Stock, 2003).

7. Timothy George, *Reading Scripture with the Reformers* (Downers Grove, IL: InterVarsity Press, 2011) and see the Reformation Commentary on Scripture series.

8. Webster, "Theologies of Retrieval," 583–99.

9. Hans Boersma, *Heavenly Participation: The Weaving of a Sacramental Tapestry* (Grand Rapids: Eerdmans, 2011).

10. Hans Boersma, *Scripture as Real Presence: Sacramental Exegesis in the Early Church* (Grand Rapids: Baker Academic, 2017); Craig A. Carter, *Interpreting Scripture with the Great Tradition: Recovering the Genius of Premodern Exegesis* (Grand Rapids: Baker, 2018); Christopher Hall, *Reading Scripture with the Church Fathers* (Downers Grove, IL: InterVarsity Press, 1998); Ronald E. Heine, *Reading the Old Testament with the Ancient Church*, Evangelical Ressourcement (Grand Rapids: Baker Academic, 2007); John L. Thompson, *Reading the Bible with the Dead: What You Can Learn from the History of Exegesis That*

interpretation of Scripture and finding Christ in the Old Testament tends to be involved with this retrieval push too.

Do I see this book as part of this retrieval effort? My answer is a qualified yes. My teaching career has involved much retrieving of the Old Testament with my generally evangelical Christian students, and likewise my research continues to involve retrieving the wealth of interpretive history for the current church. This book will focus on well-known figures who feature in creation debates but will also retrieve forgotten, less accessible, or less orthodox voices for critical re-examination, although not necessarily as models for belief. Yet while we have much to emulate and learn from Christian believers and thinkers from the past, there is a time traveler's truth to be faced. We cannot go back in an absolute sense. The world has changed since those days; we will not be able to fully regenerate the philosophies or ancient Christian theologies in their ancient forms. Retrieval will also involve thoughtful and determined work to bring the ancient gems, the positive recoveries, back into *this* world and *this* age.

Some of the books and articles focused on Genesis 1–3 that will most engage us here are birthed out of this concern for theological and hermeneutical retrieval, while others are driven more by modern differences over creation or by the authority claims of a debate opponent concerning one of these figures.[11] The latter are more like special ops hostage retrievals than long backpacker stays or permanent migration. The quest for authoritative ancient precedents for modern interpretive positions is prone to surgical excision and even distortion of the sources found. The title *Recruiting the Ancients for the Creation Debate* alludes to this error, where the notables of church history and their writings are prooftexted to gain the upper hand in some current polemic. John Thompson complains:

You Can't Learn from Exegesis Alone (Grand Rapids: Eerdmans, 2007); David P. Parris, *Reading the Bible with Giants* (London: Paternoster, 2006).

11. Craig D. Allert, *Early Christian Readings of Genesis One: Patristic Exegesis and Literal Interpretation* (Downers Grove, IL: InterVarsity Press, 2018); for theological retrieval, Peter C. Bouteneff, *Beginnings: Ancient Christian Readings of the Biblical Creation Narratives* (Grand Rapids: Baker Academic, 2008); Kyle R. Greenwood, ed., *Since the Beginning: Interpreting Genesis 1 and 2 through the Ages* (Grand Rapids: Baker Academic, 2018); Andrew Louth, "The Fathers on Genesis," in *The Book of Genesis: Composition, Reception, and Interpretation*, ed. David L. Petersen, Craig A. Evans, and Joel N. Lohr, VTSup 152 (Leiden: Brill, 2012), 561–78.

Sometimes readers have entered into the theological past in order to recruit allies or to find and vilify opponents. In this way, historical figures are pressed into service as proxies for present-day conflicts that may or may not genuinely pertain to the distant past. All too often, Christian writers of bygone days are valued only for the sake of some supposedly clever quotation or sound bite, which is then hauled back to the present, stripped of its original context.[12]

We are about to see how easy it is to recruit ancient figures superficially, selectively, or carelessly. To line up church fathers or Reformers like NBA draft picks and thrust them forward in support of some current creation stance trivializes their personal distinctiveness and historical distance from us and from one another. Ancient figures are glamorized ("Galileo had the courage . . . to read the Bible with sensitivity toward its various genres")[13] or disparaged ("Many of the . . . leading geologists of the 1820s and 1830s were . . . anti-Christian")[14] to suit. Calvin takes "our side" in one dispute says one writer;[15] another announces that their perspective is "the view that Maimonides . . . and Saint Augustine would espouse today" if they were presented with the evidence.[16] Sweeping generalizations[17] and slanted assessments[18] are disappointingly common. His slumber

12. John Thompson, ed., *Genesis 1–11*, RCS 1 (Downers Grove, IL: InterVarsity Press, 2012), xlvi.

13. Charles Halton, ed., *Genesis: History, Fiction, or Neither: Three Views on the Bible's Earliest Chapters* (Grand Rapids: Zondervan, 2015), 15.

14. Terry Mortenson, "'Deep Time' and the Church's Compromise: Historical Background," in *Coming to Grips with Genesis: Biblical Authority and the Age of the Earth*, ed. Thane H. Ury and Terry Mortenson (Green Forest, AR: Master Books, 2008), 92.

15. Jonathan D. Sarfati, *Refuting Compromise* (Green Forest, AR: Master Books, 2004), 124.

16. Francis Collins, *The Language of God: A Scientist Presents Evidence for Belief* (New York: Free Press, 2006), 199–200.

17. Hugh Ross, *Creation and Time* (Colorado Springs, CO: Navpress, 1994), 25. "Throughout the Dark and Middle Ages, church scholars maintained the tolerant attitude of their forefathers toward differing views and interpretations of the creation time scale." This is such a broad, unsubstantiated statement that it has little meaning, especially when the terms of discussion were so different from present-day ones.

18. Collins, *Language of God*, 175. "To Saint Augustine, and to most other interpreters throughout history, until Darwin put believers on the defensive, the first chapters of Genesis had much more the feel of a morality play than an eyewitness report on the evening news."

disrupted like Samuel's grumpy ghost at Saul's séance (1 Sam. 28:15), Augustine often reluctantly follows some modern author around in clanking chains.[19] This reverses the master-disciple relationship most appropriate in this situation. We are still talking about people like Augustine, Aquinas, Calvin, or Wesley because their ideas and their personal gravitas and caliber of thinking as people of God have stood the test of time. We should neither recruit them to our retinue nor ignore them at the cost of limiting our own thinking.

My goal in this book, then, is to trace these now overgrown paths back to the lives and the learning of these saints (and sinners!) of the past in order to learn from them. But we ought to do this carefully, honestly, objectively, and humbly. Sometimes we will find out what we should think, and at other times we will find their example dated or even detrimental. We might find the present intellectual and theological climate so changed that the questions these historic thinkers were so determined to answer no longer seem pressing or even comprehensible. Even then, we can still discover how they, as people of God, confronted the challenges of *their* thought-world and culture. Their apologetic and interpretive strategies might remain relevant even when their particular interpretations are passé. There is always value in exploring our spiritual and intellectual past.

WHY THE ANCIENTS ARE RECRUITED IN CREATION DEBATES

Background Issue: The Relationship of Biblical and Natural Truth

Some writers have sought ancient precedents for integrating their reading of biblical creation texts such as Genesis with a scientific understanding of the natural world. Genesis 1–3 and the hard sciences are understood to be speaking essentially the same kind of language about the same, real, physical world and its past, and therefore these writers would argue that this information from these two sources should be integrated to achieve one consistent picture of the world's origin. Where both sources are regarded as offering reliable information is usually called "concordism" or referred to as a harmonizing approach. Hugh Ross's day-

19. As one example among others, see Darrel Falk, *Coming to Peace with Science: Bridging the Worlds between Faith and Biology* (Downers Grove, IL: InterVarsity Press, 2004), 34, 169–70, 199, 201, 214.

age approach is certainly of this type and governs his best-known book, *Creation and Time* (1994).

Two other options view biblical and scientific information as being of the same kind and therefore directly comparable (or commensurable) but with a different outcome due to the conclusion that the two are *not* compatible but are in conflict. These opposing approaches are those of young-earth creationism and naturalistic evolutionism, the latter commonly associated with Richard Dawkins. Francis Collins appropriately calls these two positions "when faith trumps science" and "when science trumps faith," respectively.[20] What these apparently polar opposite positions share with each other and with the concordist is the idea that Genesis and science speak the same kind of language about the same kinds of things, and so can legitimately be compared and found either to agree or to disagree. Both of these conflict positions find that Genesis and science disagree and force the onlooker to choose sides.

Other works on science and Christianity represent the more recent mood swing against such a zero-sum game position. This standpoint in its strong form involves a denial that Genesis and science are even talking about the same thing, claiming that the Bible is related to spiritual matters and science to physical matters. More moderately, it might say that Genesis speaks about the "why" of creation while science addresses the "how" of creation, with little overlap. A softer form might agree that the origin of the physical world is the common topic of the "two books," Scripture and nature, but that they speak in such different languages that direct agreement or conflict is hardly possible. A nonconcordist model that is systematically argued and much discussed in the evangelical world currently is John Walton's claim that Genesis 1 concerns functional rather than material origins. The opening chapter of his *Lost World of Genesis 1* clearly frames his entire argument in contrast to concordist explanations.[21]

There are nonconcordist, concordist, and conflict positions that seek to find historical precedent in ancient figures, and their contrasting stances on how we

20. Collins, *Language of God*, 159, 171.

21. John H. Walton, *The Lost World of Genesis One: Ancient Cosmology and the Origins Debate* (Downers Grove, IL: IVP Academic, 2009), 14–21. I will often speak of Genesis 1 as shorthand for Gen. 1:1–2:3, without meaning to diminish the place of day seven in the creation framework.

should relate information from the Bible to discoveries from the world of nature will affect our study without constituting its primary focus.

Foreground Issue: A Literal or Nonliteral Creation Week

Most recruitment of the ancients in creation debates is intended to show either that the dominant or even the exclusive interpretation of the days of creation in Genesis 1 was literal, or that literal interpretation of the days is by no means the exclusive pattern and therefore does not represent a unitary, authoritative precedent for our interpretation of Genesis today. The dominance of this interpretive criterion as a motivator for recruitment will mean that certain famous figures who appear frequently in science and religion tomes, such as Copernicus or Galileo, but who do little direct interpretation of Genesis 1 themselves do not get much airplay here. That being said, tracking this presenting issue will offer us insights into the more fundamental science and Scripture issues that inject energy into the debate.

The Heart of Recruitment: An Appeal to Authority

Our present-day Western culture admires empirical knowledge—"seeing is believing"—understanding this as the scientific ideal. Mikael Stenmark introduces his argument in *How to Relate Science and Religion* (2004) with a summary of Stephen Jay Gould's *Rocks of Ages*:

> Gould contrasts the different ways in which the disciple Thomas's request for evidence is evaluated.... When the other disciples told Thomas that they had met the resurrected Jesus, Thomas responded by saying, "Unless I see the nail marks in his hands and put my finger where the nails were, and put my hand into his side, I will not believe" (John 20:25). A week later Jesus reappeared and this time Thomas was also present. Jesus let Thomas put his finger where the nails had been and put his hand into his side, and then Thomas believed and said to Jesus, "My Lord and my God." Jesus responded by saying, "Because you have seen me, you have believed: blessed are those who have not seen and yet have believed" (John 20:29). Gould accepts this as a proper epistemic norm of religion but also writes that he "cannot think of a statement more foreign to the norms of science.... A skeptical attitude toward appeals based

only on authority, combined with a demand for direct evidence . . . represents the first commandment of proper scientific procedure."[22]

Such is the scientific (or positivist) ideal, and whether or not you are a scientist, this ideal of self-checking all facts before believing them probably influences your own approach to knowledge.

However, in the real world of knowledge, it is not only religious people who accept things on faith or authority. Stenmark goes on to argue that when we inform ourselves properly about social behaviors, we realize that "assignments of authority are important also in science. Science could not be done unless scientists were prepared to take some matters on trust. In science just as in any other human context, we believe on authority."[23] In the philosophy of logic, too, despite the dangers, "an appeal to *reliable* authority is generally appropriate."[24] This is the basic motive for having footnotes in a book like this. Like our learning and our writing, "our lives would be intolerable if we were never to rely upon authorities. The reason we consult lawyers, doctors, architects, and engineers, is that we have to rely upon their advice on matters about which we lack knowledge."[25] As one student's guide to research points out, "No one knows everything . . . you included. It stands to reason, then, that if you want to make good arguments, you will need to rely on the arguments, ideas, and expertise of other authors."[26] Stenmark would add that no one, the scientist included, has the time available in their life span to find everything out experimentally.[27]

If appeal to authority is a practical necessity as well as a sociological reality, let us briefly consider how it counts in the search for truth. What are the factors

22. Mikael Stenmark, *How to Relate Science and Religion: A Multidimensional Model* (Grand Rapids: Eerdmans, 2004), 2–3; summarizing Stephen Jay Gould, *Rocks of Ages: Science and Religion in the Fullness of Life* (New York: Ballantine, 1999), 12–16.

23. Stenmark, *Science and Religion*, 19, and see whole section, 16–27.

24. Frances Howard-Snyder, Daniel Howard-Snyder, and Ryan Wasserman, *The Power of Logic*, 5th ed. (New York: McGraw-Hill Education, 2012), 182.

25. Jonathan Lavery, William Hughes, and Katheryn Doran, *Critical Thinking: An Introduction to the Basic Skills*, 6th ed. (Peterborough: Broadview, 2009), 157.

26. Richard A. Holland Jr. and Benjamin K. Forrest, *Good Arguments: Making Your Case in Writing and Public Speaking* (Grand Rapids: Baker Academic, 2017), 91.

27. "Scientists . . . have neither the time nor the resources to check every scientific theory and method in their field or even all those which form the basis of their own research." Stenmark, *Science and Religion*, 20.

that might give someone authority in our minds? One writer refers to a classical "Roman distinction between *potestas* as the power of the office and *auctoritas* as personal power," a distinction that helps us to understand the workings of leadership in churches, organizations, and governments.[28] Many writers on this topic mention and develop pioneer sociologist Max Weber's threefold division of "traditional, rational-legal, and charismatic legitimations of authority."[29] Leaving aside labels for how authority is *given* to someone in a social setting, we might synthesize ideas like these to say that authority might be *perceived* or felt as:

1. Personal *gravitas*, the quality best suiting the term "charisma"
2. Prophetic gifting: being the channel of divine or spiritual communication, employing another meaning of "charisma"
3. Persuasive power, the ability to sway a person or crowd through rhetoric or reasoning
4. Position or office
5. Projected competence or expertise
6. Personal relationship, like the authority of a parent or older sibling

My sense is that a potential seventh category, traditional authority, is really a development of some combination of these; the person or text or doctrine recognized as bearing authority on account of one or more of these factors then acquires a kind of communally shared recognition that proves durable over time. Thus, traditional authority seals the original, inherent authority with sociological and chronological confirmation, a combination we might sum up as "canonization."

This process of canonization of authority "into" a tradition explains why the same names keep recurring in the turn to the ancients in creation debates. Figures such as Augustine, Calvin, and Luther who gained recognition as authorities in their own day for some of the above reasons achieve "canonical" status and

28. Rolf Schieder, "Authority. II. History and Theology," in *Religion Past and Present*, ed. Hans Dieter Betz et al., 4th ed. (Leiden: Brill, 2006), 1:519.

29. James R. Lewis, "How Religions Appeal to the Authority of Science," in *Handbook of Religion and the Authority of Science*, ed. Olav Hammer and James R. Lewis (Leiden: Brill, 2010), 24; see also Schieder, "Authority," 520; and especially Inger Furseth and Pål Repstad, *An Introduction to the Sociology of Religion: Classical and Contemporary Perspectives* (Aldershot: Ashgate, 2006), 145–48.

resonate with many listeners or readers who are attuned to the heritage of past Christian thought and biblical interpretation, like so many well-recognized medals in the display cabinet of a war veterans' association. This is a social reality and plays a legitimate part, with suitable protections, in our knowledge formation.

A standard of protection we should look for here is that the authorities we listen to most closely are Christian thinkers who were skilled in biblical interpretation and well credentialed in the personal Christian spirituality that could make their biblical insights both practical and pastoral. Because they have demonstrated competence interpreting our authoritative biblical documents, these figures become authoritative conduits of spiritual interpretation to present audiences. Their perceived authority in modern creation debates can be legitimate so long as it is correctly employed in terms of good use of historical sources, which raises the question of what our study has to do with historiography, or the practice of doing history.

WHAT SORT OF STUDY ARE WE DOING HERE?

Utilizing History of Interpretation Scholarship

Forays into the past looking for interpretive precedents concerning the biblical text are exercises in the history of interpretation, a field of study that has its own specialists, theory, and literature. Surprised? That might be because there is little evidence that creation debate recruiters are familiar with this field of study and its theory and methods. Now I defend the right of the thinking person to be a self-starter in any area of knowledge and not wait humbly at the gate to be invited in and shown around. We cannot remain at the mercy of the academic elite. But when I suspect something is wrong with my car, I could prop up the hood and, with my limited insight into automotive engineering, begin to unplug anything that looks plugged in, clean anything that looks dirty, and pour some liquid into any convenient-looking opening. It would be better to open a service manual for the car before attempting any remedies beyond checking the oil level. Even better, I could consult my local mechanic, tap into his years of practical experience, and learn some of the "theory" of car repair and maintenance.

Why then do writers who are intelligent and skilled in other areas jump into interpreting the thought and commentary of past Christian scholars with little or no preparation in the theory or methods that belong to the field of study involved? Otherwise competent and informative works in this field sometimes begin with hardly a sentence on why they have undertaken the task and how they mean to go about it as if these things are self-explanatory. Now it is true that some church, intellectual, and general historians are wary of spending much time talking about method and worry that it might ideologically skew or simply delay real historical work.[30] Yet the risk of superficial recruitment of past figures as authorities for present debates is elevated by ignorance of historical methodology (historiography). Neighboring fields of research have long wrestled with legitimacy in historical method; it seems shortsighted not to try to learn their lessons and avoid the long route of trial and error.[31]

History of Interpretation and Reception History

History of interpretation is a subfield of biblical studies that analyzes and looks for patterns in the ways in which human interpreters have understood the biblical texts. When individual interpretations are gathered according to shared features or attached to trends over time that would permit location on a timeline, we have a history of interpretation. Rather than directly study the Bible, the history of interpretation approach looks at the Bible through the lenses of its interpreters to see what they saw and why. This requires understanding not only the biblical text in view but also what colors a past viewer's lenses: his or her own thinking, learning, inclinations, and environment. This makes it quite interdisciplinary, residing at the boundary of biblical exegesis, hermeneutics, historical theology, church history, and even the history of philosophy and of science. Today there exists a range of good general treatments of this topic, some quite affordable and compact, and some in a form too vast and expensive for the individual but more likely to be found in your nearest theological library.[32]

30. A good example is Carl R. Trueman, *Histories and Fallacies: Problems Faced in the Writing of History* (Wheaton, IL: Crossway, 2010), 22, 55. This comes in a whole book about historical methodology!

31. An excellent guide, though directed in the first instance to church history, is James E. Bradley and Richard A. Muller, *Church History: An Introduction to Research Methods and Resources*, 2nd ed. (Grand Rapids: Eerdmans, 2016).

32. Some examples of the more recent, general literature include the works edited by Sæbø, Hauser and Watson, McKim, and the four-volume *History of Biblical Interpretation* of H. G. Reventlow. See also Gerald Bray, *Biblical Interpretation: Past and Present*

While vigorous study continues in the history of biblical interpretation (or history of exegesis), a new umbrella discipline has emerged that has absorbed history of interpretation, known as reception history. Its greater scope is apparent in this definition from Jonathan Roberts: "The reception of the Bible comprises every single act or word of interpretation of that book . . . over the course of three millennia."[33] With roots in the thought of German philosopher Hans-Georg Gadamer (1900–2002) and literary theorist Hans Robert Jauss (1921–1997), reception history extends beyond biblical commentaries and theological works to seek out echoes of biblical texts in a much wider range of genres, such as plays, musical pieces, works of art, movies, and so forth, often being attracted to the more whimsical, subversive, or unconscious echoes of Scripture.[34] And where history of interpretation generally retains an interest in clarifying the meaning of the biblical text, reception history sometimes reflects its associations with reader-response theory by resigning any quest for inherent meaning and exploring instead the kinds of meanings that readers have made of the biblical text. Therefore, while history of biblical interpretation generally belongs close to biblical studies along with historical theology, reception history in spirit often resides nearer to the field of cultural studies, being more interested in the text's readers than the text itself.[35] What we are about to undertake here does relate, therefore, to the

---

(Downers Grove, IL: InterVarsity Press, 1996), and the anthology W. Yarchin, *A History of Biblical Interpretation: A Reader* (Peabody, MA: Hendrickson, 2004). There is a vast amount of learning to be tapped also in works such as the massive *Dictionnaire de théologie catholique* (1899–1950) and similar continental resources.

33. Jonathan Roberts, "Introduction," in *The Oxford Handbook of the Reception History of the Bible*, ed. Michael Lieb, Emma Mason, and Jonathan Rowland (Oxford: Oxford University Press, 2006), 1.

34. David P. Parris, *Reception Theory and Biblical Hermeneutics* (Eugene, OR: Pickwick, 2009).

35. For further explanation, see Jonathan Roberts and Christopher Rowland, "Introduction," *JSNT* 33.2 (2010): 131–36; John F. A. Sawyer, "The Role of Reception Theory, Reader-Response Criticism and/or Impact History in the Study of the Bible: Definition and Evaluation" (paper presented at the Society of Biblical Literature Annual Meeting, San Antonio, Texas, 2004). Mark Knight, "Wirkungsgeschichte, Reception History, Reception Theory," *JSNT* 33.2 (2010): 137–46; Susan Gillingham, "Biblical Studies on Holiday? A Personal View of Reception History," in *Reception History and Biblical Studies: Theory and Practice*, ed. Emma England and William John Lyons (London: Bloomsbury, 2015), 19–22, 26–27.

reception history of the creation week of Genesis 1 as its parent category but relates more strictly to the history of interpretation of that passage. I would not want to cordon off the possibility or importance of learning about the meaning of Genesis 1 itself in favor of learning purely about its readers!

What Do You *Think about the Creation Week?*

Upon publication of my earlier book, *The Days of Creation*, a broader effort in the history of biblical interpretation, people asked me, "What do *you* think about the creation week? Is it meant to be literal or not?" Now my primary task had not been to study the text directly but to study interpretations of the text. One motivation for me was to raise awareness that studying worthy interpretations of the biblical text can add to our understanding of the text itself and that past interpretations *do* influence our own, whether we like it or not. Our "recruiters" have made it that far at least; by seeking them out, they recognize the authority and influence of past interpreters. Telling you how to read Genesis 1 is a bit like training a budding artist to paint a single portrait. It is important, but another good way is to take the trainee through an art gallery and see how some of the past masters painted portraits. Good reading of past readers of the Bible can teach us how to read our Bibles better; it is bad reading of these past readers that misleads and obscures discussion of the Bible, and it is those bad readings that we want to correct here. New readings of Genesis 1 itself, as you will know, are not in short supply.

Who Else Has Studied Past Interpretation of Genesis 1?

Good work has already been done on the history of interpretation of the early chapters of Genesis, particularly Genesis 1, though it is often overlooked. Some is virtually lost to modern Christian consciousness; for example, Otto Zöckler's *History of the Relationship between Theology and Natural Science* (1877–1879) is comprehensive and informative.[36] Works like this capped off a long line of tradi-

---

36. Otto Zöckler, *Geschichte der Beziehungen zwischen Theologie und Naturwissenschaft: Mit besonderer Rücksicht auf Schöpfungsgeschichte*, 2 vols. (Gütersloh: Bertelsmann, 1877). The last direct echo of his creation scholarship in the English-speaking world was probably Otto Zöckler, "Creation and Preservation of the World," in *The New Schaff-Herzog Encyclopedia of Religious Knowledge*, ed. Samuel Macauley Jackson (Grand Rapids:

tional ecclesiastical scholarship on the European continent where the best biblical commentaries covered the preceding history of interpretation exhaustively.[37] Medieval, Renaissance, and Enlightenment biblical commentaries regularly drew deeply, though critically, from traditional sources. In this sense, the history of interpretation is nothing new except in being extracted from the larger task of biblical interpretation. An important survey covering interpretation of Genesis 1 in the patristic and early medieval eras was Frank Robbins, *The Hexaemeral Literature* (1912).[38] This raises a point I need to clear up: the Greek word for the six-day unit in early church conversation about Genesis 1 was *hexaemeron*, becoming *hexameron* in Latin. This word could be used either as the name of a *text* or of a commentary on that text. We will stick with the Greek spelling since the key early examples were in Greek.

Such older surveys are now dated, difficult to access, and often locked up in languages we do not read. As one historian comments on the resulting deficit: "No adequate book-length general historical survey of hexameral interpretation exists."[39] One fairly recent attempt was Stanley Jaki's *Genesis 1 through the Ages* (1992), which offers access to a wide range of traditional sources easily missed by the non-Catholic. My *The Days of Creation* (2014) was another attempt to fill this gap, striving for better objectivity than Jaki achieved yet somewhat hobbled by space constraints.

More recent books and articles on the topic are narrower in scope. Many focus purely on the patristic period, such as Peter Bouteneff's *Beginnings* (2008) and Allert, *Early Christian Readings of Genesis One* (2018).[40] A number of studies

---

Baker, 1963), 3:298–304. Other good studies exist in French and German from about this time, but this example might suffice.

37. So the practice of the "history of interpretation" is not new at all; it is more a case of rediscovery. But the present focus on reception history means that more theoretical work is being done on the process of crafting such a history. Scholars are thinking more about how and why they are studying the history of interpretation of a text like Gen. 1:1–2:3, and that attention can have great benefit.

38. F. Robbins, *The Hexaemeral Literature: A Study of the Greek and Latin Commentaries in Genesis* (Chicago: University of Chicago Press, 1912).

39. K. V. Magruder, "Theories of the Earth from Descartes to Cuvier: Natural Order and Historical Contingency in a Contested Textual Tradition" (PhD diss., University of Oklahoma, 2000), 73.

40. See above and also Andrew Louth, "The Six Days of Creation according to the Greek Fathers," in *Reading Genesis after Darwin*, ed. Stephen C. Barton and David Wilkin-

narrow their focus down to a single figure, such as Augustine's view of creation. Others look instead at the creation teaching of the Reformers or early modern scientists. The topical focus might be narrowed to a single day of creation, the opening two or three verses of Genesis, or even a single line of the text.[41] So while we lack any other current and comprehensive histories of interpretation of the creation week in English, we have to keep an eye out for a wide range of more specific, high-quality studies.

The quality of historical discussion in creation debate literature varies. Some writers are evenhanded and fair in their presentation while others have an axe to grind or are there to recruit ancient interpreters to their cause. In between are the writers who would like to prove a point but are still trying to be objective. Some are experts in a scientific field and are not as competent in a humanities field such as the history of interpretation, while others make such a cross-disciplinary move quite well. This variety in quality means that some publications will be sources for reliable information while others will serve as negative examples of recruiting past giants of the faith to their present-day creation cause.

Learning from the Historiographers

History of interpretation is, as the name suggests, a historical kind of research. It bears the same relation to biblical studies and biblical hermeneutics as historical theology does to theology, the history of philosophy does to philosophy, or the history of science does to science. It is also related to a discipline known as the history of ideas or intellectual history. The field of intellectual history has in recent decades intently discussed how to faithfully represent the past in the present. Because this is exactly what we want modern creation debates to do with our great Christian thinkers of the past, a nutshell view of this field and the lessons learned in the past century is one final piece needed for our preparation.

"Intellectual history" and the "history of ideas" are sometimes treated as synonyms for the discipline. The history of ideas has ancient precedents but came to

---

son (Oxford: Oxford University Press, 2009), 39–55. If German is an option for you, most thorough is J. C. M. van Winden, "Hexaemeron," *RAC* 14:1250–69.

41. E.g., "Be fruitful and increase" at the opening of Gen. 1:28; see Jeremy Cohen, *Be Fertile and Increase, Fill the Earth and Master It: The Ancient and Medieval Career of a Biblical Text* (Ithaca, NY: Cornell University Press, 1989).

prominence in the twentieth century, as epitomized by US scholar A. O. Lovejoy's *The Great Chain of Being* (1936). This study explored the history of the idea that the cosmos is fully populated on an ontological scale ascending from the lowest, humblest inanimate entity right up to God himself.[42] This ancient scale placed plants and then animals below humans, who occupy the central level in the hierarchy, while angels and (in some systems) any divine or quasi-divine beings come between humans and God. Lovejoy's work has been criticized for treating ideas as if they had an independent existence outside of personal or social context, but it remains a watershed example of the development of the field.

Meanwhile, on the other side of the Atlantic, British scholar Herbert Butterfield was warning his fellow historians in his *The Whig Interpretation of History* (1931) regarding the tendency to write history as if it led naturally and almost inevitably to the zenith of one's own kind of thinking.[43] This sort of smug historiography is what is wrong with two works already mentioned—Farrar's *History* and, when this lesson should already have been learned, Stanley Jaki's *Genesis 1 through the Ages*. Butterfield's slim book is more of a lengthy opinion piece than a research project, with hardly a footnote to be seen, but is a lyrical and effective put-down of historical triumphalism and the "we won" attitude to history, which tends to mash the past into prefabricated conceptual boxes fashioned from the present. More on this in a moment.

Another important piece represents something of a natural heir to Butterfield's book. Some regard it as the death knell of the older history of ideas and the harbinger of its replacement, intellectual history, if indeed these terms are to be distinguished. In his essay, "Meaning and Understanding in the History of Ideas," Cambridge scholar Quentin Skinner also targeted what Butterfield had named a "Whiggish" or triumphalist approach to history. A related problem is the selective cherry-picking of useful-looking texts from their textual, historical, and intellectual context to prove a present-day point. Such prooftexting is an inherent part of what I am calling recruitment. Otherwise, Skinner complains, where past figures are praised, this kind of history becomes "a means to fix one's own prejudices on to the most charismatic names," and where they are condemned, erring writers forget "the question of whether any of these writers ever intended,

42. A. Lovejoy, *The Great Chain of Being* (Cambridge: Harvard University Press, 1936).
43. Herbert Butterfield, *The Whig Interpretation of History* (London: Bell and Sons, 1931).

or even could have intended, to do what they are thus castigated for not having done" (as Jaki so frequently does).[44]

For Skinner, the key question for the historian to ask is "what its author, in writing at the time he did write for the audience he intended to address, could in practice have been intending to communicate."[45] Context is critical. We risk applying categories of thought to those we are studying that are more comfortable for us than they actually correspond to the thinker's situation.[46] Richard Muller emphasizes, for example, that careful study of a figure like Calvin in his context will reveal a figure "both less original than . . . typically admitted and less amenable" to present-day use.[47]

This is one of the dominant messages from "contextualists" like Skinner: we must have the historical honesty to allow past figures to be "foreign" and conditioned by their immediate intellectual circumstances.[48] The false alternative is to "plunder only those extracts that serve [our] present-minded purposes."[49] Ancient heroes are often not interested in answering the questions we would like to ask them. Muller feels that the problem of poor historiography will not be solved until theologians put more effort into reading the relevant historical documents and "develop competency in the various cognate disciplines." [50] Intellectual history and its cousin, the history of interpretation, are by nature interdisciplinary activities. In the spirit of this admonition, we will bring the input of neighboring fields such as church history, patristics, intellectual history, and the history of science, as well as the scholarship specific to the history of biblical interpretation and reception history, to the task of evaluating the use of famous Christian thinkers of the past in creation debates.

44. Quentin Skinner, "Meaning and Understanding in the History of Ideas," *History and Theory* 8.1 (1969): 13, 16.

45. Skinner, "Meaning and Understanding," 49.

46. Skinner, "Meaning and Understanding," 26–27.

47. Richard A. Muller, "Reflections on Persistent Whiggism and Its Antidotes in the Study of Sixteenth- and Seventeenth-Century Intellectual History," in *Seeing Things Their Way: Intellectual History and the Return of Religion*, ed. Alister Chapman, John Coffey, and Brad Stephan Gregory (Notre Dame: University of Notre Dame Press, 2009), 138.

48. Trueman, *Histories and Fallacies*, 109–19.

49. Stefan Collini, "The Identity of Intellectual History," in *A Companion to Intellectual History*, ed. Richard Whatmore and Brian Young (Chichester: Wiley & Sons, 2015), 14.

50. Muller, "Reflections on Persistent Whiggism," 137, 142, 149; Trueman, *Histories and Fallacies*, 140.

WHAT ARE WE TRYING TO ACHIEVE?

The Umpire's Call: Fair Ball or Foul in the Use of an Interpretation

The first purpose of this study is to adjudicate between the contested claims to authoritative precedent in historical Christian interpretation of the creation week narrative. This means making a call on which ancient Christian thinkers (or specific texts) really count as precedents for, say, either a literal or a figurative interpretation of the creation days. The tone should be irenic and nonpartisan with regard to the current debate positions, but I intend to "call them as I see them" as fair or foul employment of the historical evidence.[51] If I feel obliged to call foul on your favorite pitch, it is nothing personal. I will try to explain why I consider a particular claim about the interpretive record to be valid or not.

The Coach's Correction: Training the Pitcher's Technique

We can do better than simply spotting flawed interpretations; we can look for the source of the problem, as the pitching coach in baseball might look for the cause of repeated foul balls in the pitcher's technique. Thus, where present-day commentators are drafting ancient voices to their cause in a superficial or unsatisfactory way, we will look for a cause in their method of using those sources—a problem of historiographic technique. This would be like a coach's encouragement to lift our historiographic game. We all need to remember that when we are studying the interpretive models of past thinkers, we are doing rather technical historical work as well as literary and theological work. We will need to inform ourselves about how this can be done well. We need to continue refining our method to bring about the best results as we study the history of interpretation, avoiding superficial research, biased reading, prooftexting, or selective use of sources.

The Final Score: Evaluating the Testimony of Interpretive History on the Creation Week

Interpretive history has yielded many distinct strategies for interpreting the creation week so that it makes good sense in the reader's world. Some of these strat-

---

51. See the helpful taxonomy of positions in Gerald Rau, *Mapping the Origins Debate* (Downers Grove, IL: IVP Academic, 2012).

egies were eccentric, fly-by-night options. Others were so obvious or derivative from previous efforts that they were forgotten. Some were serious, persuasive options in their day, achieving a special status as the point of reference for other approaches. Augustine's unique, literal-but-instantaneous creation in *The Literal Meaning of Genesis* is the standout example and has been cited and critiqued ever since his death. All these offerings have been tested at the bar of history. Some of the Genesis and science alternatives that we encounter today turn out to have already been stress-tested, such as the day-age (or periodic day) theory, the gap theory (or ruin-restitution hypothesis), and something like the framework hypothesis. While taking note of Butterfield's objection that history has no final "verdict" while it continues, we might still be positioned to differentiate stronger from weaker interpretive options when it comes to the seven-day framework of Genesis 1:1–2:3.[52]

The Plan of Attack

Guided as we will be by the prominence of ancient interpreters in modern books discussing biblical creation, the church fathers loom large in this treatment and occupy the first six chapters. This indicates just how seminal they are for contemporary creation discussions.[53] It seems sensible to move in chronological order without seeking to provide a full, connected account or intellectual history of each period. Within each chapter, I begin by introducing key figures before turning to the relevant written works and some of the popular claims made about the creation week (and creation more generally) on the basis of these writings. I then attempt to explain carefully the meaning and importance of the most pertinent passages in the context of the larger work (literary context), the thinker (intellectual and personal context), and the period in which they were written (intellectual and cultural context). Then I return to evaluate how that figure's contribution has been utilized and perhaps too hastily recruited in current debates

---

52. Butterfield, *Whig Interpretation of History*, 64–66, 107–10, 130–32.

53. Jewish interpretation will have to be largely overlooked, since it only occasionally features in these creation debates, but is well covered in *HB/OT* and the relevant essays in Craig A. Evans, Joel N. Lohr, and David L. Petersen, eds., *The Book of Genesis: Composition, Reception, and Interpretation*, VTSup 152 (Leiden: Brill, 2012). For the early period, a valuable volume is M. J. Mulder, ed., *Mikra: Text, Translation, Reading and Interpretation of the Hebrew Bible in Ancient Judaism and Early Christianity* (Assen: Van Gorcum, 1988).

on the creation week. I finally suggest the true value of that individual's thinking for teaching us about the creation week and creation more generally along with broader issues surrounding our interpretation of the Bible, our thinking about science and religion, and our living as Christian believers.

Why Is This Study Important?

The potential benefits of this approach extend well beyond simply helping us to decide whether or not we will interpret the days of Genesis 1 figuratively, or whether or not our preferred interpretation has good company in church history. Richard Hess has suggested that Genesis 1 is "arguably the single most reflected upon written text ever written in human history."[54] It is tied to one of the headline doctrines of Christianity, the doctrine of creation, so it promises to be an enlightening case study in the history of Christian theology. Its pivotal role at the junction of biblical revelation and natural philosophy (or the study of the natural world) also makes its history of interpretation an informative study in the history of philosophy and, as we approach modern times, the history of science. The intellectual path by which Western society reached its present attitudes and worldview, I would suggest, cannot be fully understood without a solid grasp of the contribution of Genesis 1. And as we study this, we learn the ancestry of our own perspectives on the Bible:

> [A] text's reception history exposes the reader to the great repository of understanding and significance that other Christians have found in the Bible. It allows us to learn from previous interpretations and may also reveal to us why we read a particular Bible passage in the way we do. History reveals to us what we owe to those who preceded us. . . . We are like dwarves standing on the shoulders of giants.[55]

54. Richard S. Hess, "God and Origins: Interpreting the Early Chapters of Genesis," in *Darwin, Creation and the Fall: Theological Challenges*, ed. R. J. Berry and T. A. Noble (Downers Grove, IL: InterVarsity Press, 2009), 86.

55. Parris, *Reading the Bible with Giants*, xviii; See also Thompson, *Reading the Bible with the Dead*, 224–27; Richard A. Muller and John L. Thompson, "The Significance of Precritical Exegesis: Retrospect and Prospect," in *Biblical Interpretation in the Era of the Reformation: Essays Presented to David C. Steinmetz in Honor of His Sixtieth Birthday*, ed. Richard A. Muller and John L. Thompson (Grand Rapids: Eerdmans, 1996), 335–45.

As we bring an outsider's eyes to the way other leading Christian readers made sense of Genesis within their own unique spiritual, intellectual, and cultural settings, we begin to see how we, too, bring our own contexts into play when we read. We have the chance to become more self-aware as Bible readers, not so that textual meaning dissolves in cultural relativity but that we might become better self-checkers and read our Bibles, including Genesis 1, more maturely and more effectively.

Chapter One

EARLY ALEXANDRIAN INTERPRETATION
OF GENESIS 1

We have all seen those mysterious twin volumes sitting on a neglected rear shelf in our Christian bookstore, accessible only by weaving through hundreds of colorful repackaged Bibles and Christian self-help books. Philo's and Josephus's works sit side by side, faithfully reprinted for hundreds of years, their purpose for the Christian reader still unclear, but their evident value attested by their continued presence. Well, we can think of Josephus (ca. 37–ca. 100 CE) as a notable Jewish historian living in the generation following Jesus, a one-time resistance fighter who managed to enter high circles of influence in the Roman administration and is best known for isolated (and debated) references to Jesus in his *Jewish Antiquities*.[1] Josephus offers only a brief treatment of Mosaic creation in his *Antiquities*, promising a more philosophical treatment that, as far as we know, he never completes.[2] In any case, he appears to depend on his philosophically better-equipped Jewish predecessor, Philo.

1. The discussed passage about Jesus is *Ant.* 18.63–64. See Flavius Josephus, *Jewish Antiquities Books XVIII–XIX*, trans. Louis H. Feldman, LCL (Cambridge: Harvard University Press, 2000), 48–51. On Josephus's life, see J. N. Birdsall, "Josephus Flavius (A.D. 37–Post 100)," *NIDCC*, 549; *ODCC*, "Josephus, Flavius (*c.* 37–*c.* 100)," 759.

2. *Ant.* 1.25, 29. Josephus's straightforward, abbreviating paraphrase of the creation week at the opening of his *Jewish Antiquities* tantalizes his reader with the hint that he could well explain why Moses used the enigmatic phrase "one day" (Gen. 1:5) rather than "first day," but states he would save that venture for another day. When he reaches Gen. 2:4, Josephus alludes to a change in discourse style from Moses, as "Moses begins

Philo (ca. 20 BCE–ca. 50 CE) was Josephus's senior and a contemporary of Jesus, and while Josephus was based ultimately in Rome, Philo's base was the Roman Empire's intellectual capital at the time: Alexandria in Egypt.[3] If Josephus was the Jewish nation's contribution to classical history writing, Philo was its contribution to Hellenistic philosophy. Although not a church father himself, Philo often features in debates over creation week precedents because his influential writings about the early chapters of Genesis provided the early church with one of its preferred interpretive approaches to creation texts and to biblical texts generally. We return to Philo shortly, but first let us take one step back to contextualize Genesis 1 among other OT creation texts.

CREATION IN GENESIS 1 AND ITS EARLIEST BIBLICAL AND EXTRABIBLICAL PARALLELS

Innerbiblical Relations of Creation Texts

Genesis 1 integrates a key biblical theme with a noteworthy ancient Near Eastern (ANE) literary motif. The theme is God's creation of the world, and the motif is the listing of items or events in a stock number with a superlative final item that represents the culmination of the series.[4] The number chosen does not have to be, but often is, seven, and the unit is often the day. This motif is not limited to the Bible but is common to ANE literature more generally; we find flood events described in a seven-day sequence in the *Gilgamesh Epic*, a Mesopotamian story with close affinities to the Genesis flood story.[5] Focusing on the number seven,

---

to interpret nature [φυσιολογεῖν]," very likely reflecting influence from Philo's "double-creation" interpretation (*Ant.* 1.34). Text and translation from Flavius Josephus, *Jewish Antiquities Books I–IV*, trans. Henry St. J. Thackeray, LCL (Cambridge: Harvard University Press, 1995). On this passage from Philo, see David T. Runia, *On the Creation of the Cosmos according to Moses: Introduction, Translation and Commentary*, Philo of Alexandria Commentary Series (Leiden: Brill, 2001), 37 and n. 107.

3. See *HBI* 1:41.

4. Roth called this the X/X + 1 numerical sequence: W. M. W. Roth, "The Numerical Sequence X/X+1 in the Old Testament," *VT* 12 (1962): 300–311. See also S. E. Loewenstamm, "The Seven-Day Unit in Ugaritic Epic Literature," *Israel Exploration Journal* 15 (1965): 122–33.

5. See *Gilgamesh Epic* 11.127–131, 140–146, 215–218, 225–228. Other examples include *Enuma Elish* 5.16–17; *Atrahasis Epic* 3.4.24–25; *Eridu Genesis* 3.203; *Tale of Aqhat* A.I.1–

this literary pattern appears in the Bible most obviously in the description of Moses's ascent of Sinai to meet God (Exod. 24:15–18) and at the conquest of Jericho in Joshua 6:1–21, a passage dense with sevens.[6]

Switching from a structural to a thematic track, we may trace creation themes through the OT and compare them with Genesis 1. Some of the most important OT creation texts are Psalms 104 and 148 and parts of Psalms 33, 95–100, and 136; Proverbs 8:22–31; and Isaiah 40:12–31, followed by frequent recurrence of creation themes in short compass throughout Isaiah 40–48. Nearly all of the creation vocabulary seen in Genesis 1 can be found in one or other of these creation texts.[7] Sometimes this language is found in such abundance that the reader is tempted to think not just of a shared worldview or theology but of conscious literary dependence, though that is difficult to prove.[8] More important for our study of the interpretation of the creation week would be any correspondence in the *order* of creation acts. Of most interest here is Psalm 104, since there is a strong correlation between the order of creation found there and in Genesis 1. Notice that the Lord wraps himself in light in Psalm 104:2a, stretches out the heavens in verse 2b, and structures the heavenly realm and upper waters in verse 3a. The earth (or land; Heb. *'ereṣ*) comes into focus in verse 5, while in a passage that may meld ideas about the primordial deep of Genesis 1:2 and the flood of Genesis 6–8, the waters that initially covered the land here in verses 6–9

17; 2.30–40; *Baal Cycle* 6.22–33; *Keret Epic* A.3.103–109, 114–120; 4.194–195, 207–211; 5.218–222. You can read these texts in collections such as W. W. Hallo and K. L. Younger, eds., *The Context of Scripture*, 4 vols. (Leiden: Brill, 1997–2016). The Gilgamesh example is from A. Heidel, *The Gilgamesh Epic and Old Testament Parallels*, 2nd ed. (Chicago: University of Chicago Press, 1949), esp. 85–86.

6. The flood story features several sevens without the obvious culminating structure: Gen. 7:4, 10; 8:10, 12. For a study connecting this biblical phenomenon with later Jewish traditions, see Robert Gordis, "The Heptad as an Element of Biblical and Rabbinic Style," *Journal of Biblical Literature* 62.1 (1943): 17–26.

7. Samuel D. Giere, "A New Glimpse of Day One: An Intertextual History of Genesis 1.1–5 in Hebrew and Greek Texts up to 200 CE" (PhD diss., The University of St. Andrews, 2007), 19–48; since published as S. D. Giere, *A New Glimpse of Day One: Intertextuality, History of Interpretation, and Genesis 1.1–5*, BZNW 172 (Berlin: de Gruyter, 2009). I worked with the thesis document.

8. E.g., for Isaiah 40–48, see the comments in Michael A. Fishbane, *Biblical Interpretation in Ancient Israel* (Oxford: Clarendon, 1985), 324–26. He also agrees with the suggestion that Deut. 4:16–19 shows deliberate connections with Genesis 1 (319–21).

are regulated by coastal boundaries, reminding us of the work of day three of creation. Birds, animals, and humans, along with vegetation, feature in verses 10–18, deviating from the order found in Genesis 1, though the sun and moon preside over the natural schedule in verse 19 in a similar way to their roles on day four in Genesis 1. So there is a partial parallel here but no systematic adoption of the Genesis 1 pattern.[9]

The only other OT texts where the seven-day motif and the creation theme coincide are in Exodus, and this is not accidental. Exodus concludes with the construction of the tabernacle according to God's exact instructions (e.g., Exod. 39:42–43) on the first day of the first month (40:17), a construction task that is only fulfilled when the Lord indwells the completed structure (40:34). Thus, the author of these chapters deliberately establishes a correspondence between God's creation of the (macro)cosmos in Genesis 1 and Israel's fabricating of the tabernacle as a corresponding microcosmos in Exodus 35–40.[10] The Sabbath, as the enshrinement of the culminating seventh day of God's creative work, is mandated in Exodus 20:8–11 within the Ten Commandments, and again in Exodus 31:14–17. These two passages mandate the defining Jewish Sabbath observance and both explicitly recall the creation narrative of Genesis 1:1–2:3. In this twofold respect they are unique in the entire OT. Both statements seem to speak plainly of a creative period of six familiar days, though the wording of Exodus 31:17 represents a subtle warning against taking anthropomorphic representations of God in the Bible too literally, reading "and on the seventh day he rested and was refreshed." "Refreshed" represents a scarce Hebrew verb (*nāpaš*) whose only other occurrences are in Exodus 23:12, another Sabbath commandment context where the Sabbath is intended for the refreshment of all levels of society, and in 2 Samuel 16:14 where David's exhausted party fleeing a coup in Jerusalem is finally able to stop and rest. It is a very human term with the connotation of "catching

9. Tremper Longman III, "What Genesis 1–2 Teaches (and What It Doesn't)," in *Reading Genesis 1–2: An Evangelical Conversation*, ed. J. Daryl Charles (Peabody, MA: Hendrickson, 2013), 114; Giere, "New Glimpse," 21–22.

10. Michael Fishbane, *Biblical Text and Texture: A Literary Reading of Selected Texts* (Oxford: Oneworld, 1998), 12–13; Moshe Weinfeld, "Sabbath, Temple, and the Enthronement of the Lord: The Problem of the Sitz im Leben of Genesis 1:1–2:3," in *Melanges bibliques et orientaux en l'honneur de M. Henri Cazelles*, ed. Andre Caquot and Mathias Delcor (Kevelaer: Butzon and Bercker, 1981), 501–5; M. Welker, "Creation, Big Bang or the Work of Seven Days?," *Theology Today* 52.27 (1995): 182–83.

one's breath."[11] We will entangle ourselves in theological problems if we cannot recognize that statements like this are anthropomorphic and speak of God and the things of God using human analogies.

Intertestamental Reception

There is some reuse of Genesis 1 in intertestamental literature, as Jewish writers began to paraphrase and expand the biblical text in order to enhance its relevance for present concerns.[12] We see a developing interest in mystical exploration of numbers, especially the number seven, for instance in a fragment from Aristobulus that was preserved by the patristic church historian Eusebius.[13] When this is combined with a worldview that was highly attuned to correspondences between the various planes of reality, this begins to yield a divine program for history measurable in regular periods.[14] Some church fathers would expand this into a full-fledged "dispensational" plan of seven thousand years of redemptive history, one for each day of creation.[15]

Another important development was the translation of the Old Testament from Hebrew into Greek, a work now known as the Septuagint (LXX). Completed sometime during the second century BCE, the Septuagint represented the first translation of the OT writings into another language, and every translation naturally had its impact on what readers understood Scripture to be saying to them. Yet the creation day framework in Genesis 1 was not materially affected by the translation of the Hebrew Bible into Greek or its subsequent translation into Latin (the Old Latin from the LXX, and later Jerome's Vulgate from the Hebrew), save for one or two important exceptions affecting Genesis 2:4–5 (see below).

---

11. William L. Holladay, ed., *A Concise Hebrew and Aramaic Lexicon of the Old Testament* (Grand Rapids: Eerdmans, 1988), 242.

12. This genre of extrabiblical literature therefore sometimes goes by the label "rewritten Bible."

13. For a translation see *OTP* 2:841–42. For other examples, see Jub. 2:1–33 (*OTP* 2:841–42); 4 Ezra 6:38–54 (*OTP* 1:536). 4 Ezra already belongs to the first century of the Christian era according to the Charlesworth edition. See also the retelling of creation in the Christian expansion of the Sibylline Oracles in Sib. Or. 1:1–24 (*OTP* 1:335).

14. This appears vaguely in 2 En. 33:1–2, in what might be a Christian expansion (*OTP* 1:356); also the Qumran scroll 4QWords of the Heavenly Lights (4Q504). For a translation of the latter see Geza Vermes, *The Complete Dead Sea Scrolls in English* (London: Penguin, 2004). See also Jub. 4:29–30.

15. See chapters 2 and 3 below.

New Testament Appropriation of Old Testament Creation Themes

Our NT authors clearly draw on important creation themes from Genesis 1:1–2:3, such as when recording Jesus's teaching about marriage (Matt. 19:4; Mark 10:6) or when they make theological points about the image of God in man or in Christ (1 Cor. 11:7; Eph. 4:24; Col. 1:15; 3:10; Jas. 3:9), creation out of nothing (Heb. 11:3), the creation and flood as counterparts to the eschatological judgment (2 Pet. 3:5–7), the creation of light as a type of spiritual enlightenment of the heart (2 Cor. 4:6), or the spiritual Sabbath that the believer in Christ must be sure to appropriate (Heb. 4:10). Ira Driggers highlights the significance of the timing of Jesus's healings on the Sabbath: "people *receive rest* from the physical, emotional, and social labors that their maladies have forced on them," and thus gain a fore-taste of the benefits of the imminent kingdom announced by Jesus.[16] From a different angle, the Gospels of Matthew, Mark, and John allude to the early chap-ters of Genesis in their beginning statements. Matthew 1:1, in the Greek phrase translated "An account of the genealogy" (*biblos geneseōs*), deliberately reuses the heading terminology found in Genesis 2:4 and 5:1 in the LXX. Mark 1:1 and John 1:1 both use the first Greek noun found in the LXX, *archē*, "beginning," at the head of their respective Gospels in what looks like an intentional move to offer a new covenant story that can act as a counterpart to the existing OT Scriptures. John 1 goes on to speak explicitly about creation and explain how Jesus himself is the new covenant light corresponding to the light of creation. The reference to the incarnation in John 1:14 recalls human creation in Genesis 2:7.[17]

So, creation remains an important theological theme in the NT, and Genesis 1 is clearly part of the scriptural deposit being accessed here, but we do not see any meditation on the length of time creation took, as if it does not yet seem to be an arresting fact that creation occupied six days. One feature we will explore later, though, is the way Matthew 1:1–17 divides the genealogy of Jesus into three sets

16. Ira Brent Driggers, "New Testament Appropriations of Genesis 1–2," in *Since the Beginning: Interpreting Genesis 1 and 2 through the Ages*, ed. Kyle R. Greenwood (Grand Rapids: Baker Academic, 2018), 52.

17. Calum Carmichael's thesis is that the narration of the whole first five chapters of the Gospel of John is at its base an allegorization of the creation week. Notice how the Sabbath issue rises to prominence in chapter 5. Calum M. Carmichael, *The Story of Cre-ation: Its Origin and Its Interpretation in Philo and the Fourth Gospel* (Ithaca, NY: Cornell University Press, 1996), 36–37; Jeannine K. Brown, "Creation's Renewal in the Gospel of John," *CBQ* 72.2 (2010): 275–77.

of fourteen generations, equivalent to six lots of seven generations leading from Abraham to Christ. This might be a milder version of the numerological interest that is so obvious in the book of Jubilees and presages a future tactic of allocating biblical history into redemptive periods or epochs of equal length.

PHILO OF ALEXANDRIA

Importance

Philo of Alexandria holds an odd position in our discussion. Because Hugh Ross includes Philo (and Josephus) in his chapter "Interpretations of Early Church Leaders" in *Creation and Time*—albeit under the subheading "First-Century Jewish Scholars"—Sarfati protests "that Philo and Josephus were non-Christian Jews, not church fathers."[18] True, and clear enough in Ross's original text, too. But this raises the question: why mention Philo in a treatment of the Christian interpretation of the creation week, which is already a massive task?[19] Moreover, the Christian reader might be more interested in the church's own interpretive legacy. Yet Philo's barnstorming interpretation of the creation narratives of Genesis represents a *tour de force* of integration of biblical origins teaching and contemporary Hellenistic thought. Many leading patristic thinkers were deeply impressed and treated Philo's creation interpretation as a reference point for their own interpretive efforts.[20] A moment of our attention to his writings is warranted.

Philo was a true boundary rider; his home city of Alexandria was a meeting place of Greco-Roman and eastern Mediterranean cultures and the effective

---

18. Hugh Ross, *Creation and Time* (Colorado Springs, CO: Navpress, 1994), 16–17; Hugh Ross, *A Matter of Days: Resolving a Creation Controversy* (Colorado Springs, CO: Navpress, 2004), 42–43; Jonathan D. Sarfati, *Refuting Compromise* (Green Forest, AR: Master Books, 2004), 109.

19. Brevard Childs limits his study to Christian interpretation for this very reason in Childs, *The Struggle to Understand Isaiah as Christian Scripture* (Grand Rapids: Eerdmans, 2004), xi.

20. Gregory E. Sterling, "Philo," in *Dictionary of New Testament Background*, ed. Craig A. Evans and Stanley E. Porter (Downers Grove, IL: InterVarsity Press, 2000), 791; Runia, *On the Creation of the Cosmos*, 37–38. Folker Siegert, "Early Jewish Interpretation in a Hellenistic Style," *HB/OT* 1.1:188. David Runia made Philo's interpretive legacy the focus of his study *Philo in Early Christian Literature* (Assen: Van Gorcum; Philadelphia: Fortress, 1993).

capital of diaspora Judaism in his day.[21] Philo marketed Torah theology to the Hellenistic world. Indeed, he presented the Mosaic law as the embodiment of the divinely conceived inner structure of the universe, a structure whose comprehension lay at the heart of the philosophical quest of the Hellenistic mind.[22] To live in conformity with this law would be to live in keeping with the deep workings of the world. To understand its written form in the Torah in its deepest sense, accessed through allegorical reading, would be to approach an understanding of God.[23] The book of Genesis held a great fascination for Philo, and he left a written deposit on this single biblical book that would exceed any other single repository of commentary on a biblical book for centuries to come.[24] Philo's influence can be detected in later Christian interpretation of Genesis, particularly where his allegorical method of reading was adopted. So, we begin our evaluation of the "recruitment of the ancients" with this figure from outside the Christian church.

Philo's Allegorical Hermeneutic

Explaining allegory is like describing your mystery illness to a medical specialist. You know what it is but putting it into words is a whole new challenge. Early Christians and Jews like Philo shared a strong sense of the divine inspiration of Scripture. In the NT, words from the Psalms (Ps. 95:7–11 in Heb. 3:7), Isaiah (Isa. 6:9–10 in Acts 28:25), and Jeremiah (Jer. 31:33–34 in Heb. 10:15) are cited as oracles from the Holy Spirit. The intended meaning of the human OT author involved in the text's composition, so important in modern biblical scholarship, clearly played a subsidiary role for these readers to what God intended to say through the text. Along with this went a perception that the text could readily speak to an audience beyond its original one, even primarily so, with a kind of eschatological priority such that its relevance was not limited to its historical situation.

21. Frederick Copleston, SJ, *Greece and Rome*, vol. 1 of *A History of Philosophy* (Westminster, MD: Newman, 1946), 457.

22. Peder Borgen, "Philo of Alexandria as Exegete," *AHBI* 1:118–21.

23. Gregory E. Sterling, "When the Beginning Is the End: The Place of Genesis in the Commentaries of Philo," in *The Book of Genesis: Composition, Reception, and Interpretation*, ed. Craig A. Evans, Joel N. Lohr, and David L. Petersen, VTSup 152 (Leiden: Brill, 2012), 440. See below on allegorical reading.

24. Sterling, "Beginning Is the End," 444.

Ancient thinkers also perceived the world as heavily "networked," that is, as having multiple levels of reality that were interlinked by meaningful correspondences. Astrology might be a helpful example. Belief that the stars could influence human affairs was tempting if you saw the motion of the stars and planets as woven into the same reality that calendrical time measured and into which human lives were connected by virtue of birth. One planet's behavior could relate to a certain day of the week (which is how we get "Sunday," "Monday," and "Saturday"), to a certain system of the body, to a certain natural element, or to a certain political power. In contrast to our rather physical or dual physical-spiritual view of the world, classical thought saw reality as multilayered from the lowest, most trivial, most decay-prone entities up to a transcendent God or divine reality. The most important, highest layers were not physical at all but spiritual and accessible only to the suitably prepared mind, if at all. Numbers were one "conceptual elevator" that might provide meaningful connections between levels of reality. We might think of it as a "hall of mirrors" view of reality. Whereas for us the world is a set of opaque doors bearing names like science, history, psychology, or theology, an ancient thinker saw a world made of mirrored glass where different disciplinary domains might be looked at in their own right but also constantly refer the viewer to other domains.

Read in these terms, a biblical text was expected to refer beyond its immediate historical situation to other important realities such as virtues of character or to the quest for a spiritual ascent to God. The process of reading to find these alternate meanings is known as allegorical interpretation.[25] This process assumes that God has more to say than the sometimes rather trivial or time-bound meaning of an OT text. Paul is thinking in this manner when he reads "Do not muzzle an ox while it is treading out the grain" (Deut. 25:4) and responds, "Is it about oxen that God is concerned?" (1 Cor. 9:9). It is clear to him that there must be some spiritual significance that extends beyond an earthy point of Jewish law.[26] The

---

25. Major alternative terms are "spiritual" or "figurative" reading. Like any important conceptual label, the meaning and even viability of the label "allegory" for a historic interpretive approach is highly contested. See for example Craig D. Allert, *Early Christian Readings of Genesis One: Patristic Exegesis and Literal Interpretation* (Downers Grove, IL: InterVarsity Press, 2018), 123–25. Rather than abandon the term, I am attempting here to cultivate in the reader an appreciation for the ancient reader's sensitivity to correspondences between the orders of reality s/he perceived, that is, the mindset that made allegory viable.

26. The best known and clearest example of Paul's use of allegory is where he interprets

"mirrored glass" illustration highlights the fact that a more spiritual meaning was usually not meant to exclude the literal sense, though occasionally Philo or Origen might rule out the value of the literal meaning of certain troublesome texts. Philo wanted to show that the philosophical truths that he could acknowledge in his surrounding, Hellenistic intellectual culture were in fact embedded in the OT in cryptic fashion but accessible to the enlightened reader. He was an apologist for the Jewish Scriptures, and his allegorical approach carries over into apologists for Christianity and Christian Scripture such as Origen.

Looking forward to patristic Christian interpretation, we may anticipate a somewhat more restrained form of figurative interpretation of Scripture, known as typology, as well as the stronger form known as allegory. The perceived correspondences in typology operate on the plane of redemptive history: Adam might prefigure Christ (Rom. 5:12–21) as might David (Luke 20:41–44)[27] or Moses (implicit in Acts 7:35–37). Jonah's fish-based voyage could prefigure Jesus's death and resurrection (Matt. 12:39–40). These and other perceived connections were all located in the same flow of redemptive history, just at different temporal points. These interpretations grade into allegory with no distinct break, but allegory in Christian practice might as easily find reflections in a biblical text of moral virtues and vices or ascending stages of spiritual contemplation of God. That is, we can think of typology as operating on a horizontal historical plane, whereas allegory includes but goes beyond typology and applies to the vertical spiritual axis between God and humanity.[28] Examples of these approaches will come along regularly as we look at interpretation of the creation week.[29]

---

the stories about Abraham's slave-concubine Hagar and his wife Sarah as symbols of the old and new covenants and thence (via Mt. Sinai) of the earthly (enslaved) Jerusalem and the heavenly (free) Jerusalem. See Gal. 4:21–31.

27. Note that Jesus in this context is undercutting the received wisdom regarding this typology.

28. See the discussion in relation to Origen in Henri Crouzel, *Origen*, trans. A. S. Worrall (Edinburgh: T&T Clark, 1989), 79–84.

29. There is no end to scholarship on the contentious topic of allegorical interpretation in the ancient church, and whether allegory differs from typology, but you might start with Frances Young, "Alexandrian and Antiochene Exegesis," *AHBI* 1:335–38; *HBI* 1:41–42; Siegert, "Early Jewish Interpretation," *HB/OT* 1.1:182–89; Joseph W. Trigg, "Introduction," in *Allegory and Event: A Study of the Sources and Significance of Origen's Interpretation of Scripture* (Louisville: Westminster John Knox, 2002), xiv–xxiv; Gerald Bray, *Biblical Interpretation: Past and Present* (Downers Grove, IL: InterVarsity Press, 1996), 99–103.

Philo's Writings on Genesis

Philo's interpretation of the creation account in Genesis 1:1–2:3 is hinted at in the first two questions of his *Questions and Answers on Genesis*, covered in more detail in *Allegorical Interpretation* 1.1–10 (though this latter work concentrates on Gen. 2:4–3:24), and treated quite extensively in *On the Creation of the World* 1.1–16.130.[30] Philo famously explains that God's creation is logically prior to earthly time and does not require, *could* not require, its solar time divisions:

> It would be a sign of great simplicity to think that the world was created in six days, or indeed at all in time; because all time is only the space of days and nights, and these things the motion of the sun as he passes over the earth and under the earth does necessarily make. But the sun is a portion of heaven, so that one must confess that time is a thing posterior to the world. Therefore it would be correctly said that the world was not created in time. . . . When, therefore, Moses says, "God completed his works on the sixth day," we must understand that he is speaking not of a number of days, but that he takes six as a perfect number. (*Alleg. Interp.* 1.2.2 [Yonge])

Philo cannot imagine that God, with infinite power at his command and beginning his creation in any case with the invisible, fundamental "forms" of reality, would take time to create. To treat the creation week as a period of ordinary history would, for Philo, be a categorical error that misconstrues the genre of Genesis 1. The framework of the creation week is an ideal schema, and even where Philo understands visible and tangible entities to be in view, as with the second mention of "heaven" and of "earth" on days two and three, respectively, statements such as the one quoted above make it clear that these entities are produced without the passage of time. The elements of creation that Philo does treat as physical, such as trees, appear full-grown with ripe fruit (*Creation* 42).

30. I use the translation of *On the Creation of the World* from Runia's recent critical edition published in the Philo of Alexandria Commentary Series (Brill) cited earlier in the chapter. See also the sections "Questions and Answers on Genesis, I," 791, "Allegorical Interpretation," 25–27, and "On the Creation," 3–18 in the more accessible reprint edition of C. D. Yonge, trans., *The Works of Philo: Complete and Unabridged*, rev. ed. (Peabody, MA: Hendrickson, 1993).

Such sudden creation action seems initially friendly to a young-earth concept of creation, but Philo's intellectual world is in fact a very different one. Our modern writers acknowledge that Philo's interpretation of the creation week conceives of an instantaneous creation by God. Those who prefer to see the creation week as a conceptual framework tend to mention him, while those who prefer literal interpretive models often direct their attention to more suitable figures.[31] Perhaps the key question about Philo is whether he can be taken as an example of symbolic interpretation of the creation days within an overall literal interpretation of the passage. Forster and Marston assert, "Philo is quite explicit. Genesis 1–3 is about real events, not myths, but God has chosen through Moses to use figurative or 'allegorical' language to speak to us."[32] Once we are convinced, as Bouteneff comments, that Philo "completely detemporalizes the six days of creation,"[33] we are inclined to agree that Philo must be consciously reading Genesis 1 in an allegorical mode.

Philo's Hermeneutic in Genesis 1–2

As we just saw, asking whether Philo is speaking allegorically about Genesis 1 in *On the Creation* is not all that helpful. A better question to ask is which of the two worlds he is speaking about. Philo is a dyed-in-the-wool Platonist. Much as Plato did, Philo believes that behind the world that we perceive with our physical senses lies an invisible world, a fabric of "ideas" or logical realities that actually make the world of visible forms possible. In *On the Creation* 17–21, Philo explains this concept clearly: the architect who designs a city must first have a complete conception of that city in mind. Then the physical city is constructed in keeping with the detailed concept. So it is with the visible world. It has a logically prior existence in the mind of God, and in some sense that conceptual existence, al-

---

31. For the former, see, e.g., John Lennox, *Seven Days That Divide the World: The Beginning according to Genesis and Science* (Grand Rapids: Zondervan, 2011), 40–41. Representing the latter approach, Sarfati mentions Philo in passing but focuses instead on Josephus; see Sarfati, *Refuting Compromise*, 110–12. A more even-handed creationist treatment is Andrew Kulikovsky, *Creation, Fall, Restoration: A Biblical Theology of Creation* (Fearn: Mentor, 2009), 60–61. Kulikovsky wants to challenge Roger Forster and Paul Marston, *Reason, Science and Faith* (Crowborough: Monarch, 1999).

32. Forster and Marston, *Reason, Science and Faith*, 193–94.

33. Peter C. Bouteneff, *Beginnings: Ancient Christian Readings of the Biblical Creation Narratives* (Grand Rapids: Baker Academic, 2008), 28.

though intangible, is more "real" than the physical manifestation. This intelligible world is the basis for the existence of the "sensible" or sense-perceptible world.

Philo brings this dualistic Platonic principle to his interpretation of Genesis 1. You may have noticed that "heaven" seems to be created twice in Genesis 1, first with the earth in 1:1, and then as the "firmament" on day two (1:6–8). This and the other famous Genesis 1 conundrum of the creation of light before the sun, as well as the appearance of the earth on day three, all fall neatly into this dual scheme for Philo.

> First, therefore, the maker made an incorporeal heaven and an invisible earth and a form of air and of the void. To the former he assigned the name darkness, since the air is black by nature, to the latter the name abyss. . . . Then he made the incorporeal being of water and of spirit, and as seventh and last of all light, which once again was incorporeal and was also the intelligible model of the sun and all the other light-bearing stars which were to be established in heaven. (*Creation* 29 [Runia])

Seven great conceptual entities are made; seven "ideas" from the one great Idea of creation in the mind of God, which Philo normally equates to the "Logos" (Gk. word, logic, reason, plan, applied in time by some Christian writers to Christ as the Word of God, following John 1:1–14). Therefore the day devoted to these "ideal" creations is not called the "first day" but "one day," because it is a class apart, an archetypal day (*Creation* 35). Once we reach days two through six it feels as if we are dealing with our familiar, physical creation (*Creation* 36–68). Yet even then, as Bouteneff notices, the creation of humanity in the image of God in Genesis 1:26–27 is described by Philo as another ideal creation, because the real, physical creation of the first human is yet to come in Genesis 2:7.[34] After Philo explains why the Greek text of Genesis 2:5 states that God created vegetation before it sprang up from the earth (*Creation* 129)[35] he asserts that every tangible thing in creation requires its antecedent form. Thomas Tobin, in a thorough study, argues that here Philo begins a second explanation of the "double creation" of the world where the transition from the creation of the ideal realm to the perceptible realm

---

34. Compare *Creation* 76 and 134; Bouteneff, *Beginnings*, 29–30.

35. The relevant prepositional phrases in the Septuagint are πρὸ τοῦ γενέσθαι ἐπὶ τῆς γῆς καὶ . . . πρὸ τοῦ ἀνατεῖλαι.

now comes at Genesis 2:5 rather than after the "one day" in 1:5.[36] Paul Blowers follows this understanding of Philo's presentation while David Runia disagrees and thinks Philo remains consistent and restricts ideal creation to day one.[37]

It is true that Philo presents a seven-part ideal creation as occupying (without taking any time) one day, which is a conceptual container or philosophical principle for him rather than a period of time. But notice in the block quote above how basic those seven entities are. Having ideal heaven and earth as initial creations (i.e., thoughts in the creative mind of God) can help Philo explain why another, more physical heaven will turn up in Genesis 1:6 and land or earth in verses 9–10. But what about plants, animals, and humans? They are first mentioned during creation days two through six, but then are described as being created again at points in Genesis 2. Philo has a ready explanation at hand: a twofold creation, the first of ideals and the second of concrete reality. But he will now map out this distinction differently. For these less fundamental parts of creation, the (first) ideal description does not come in Genesis 1:1–5 but rather through creation days two through six, and is then followed by a sense-perceptible creation in what we call the Eden narrative in Genesis 2. Philo has different overlays for the creation narrative depending on which created beings we have in mind. That is as deep as we need to go right now; the key idea is that Philo tells a generation that still loves Plato's view of the world that Genesis 1–2 competently narrates both the creation of the ideal forms and the physical objects of creation based on those forms, as the dual references in Genesis to the creation of heaven, earth, light and luminaries, plants, animals, and humans seem to show.

All of this largely vindicates Forster and Marston. Philo might seem to be speaking very abstractly, but he is speaking about "real creation," keeping in mind

---

36. Thomas H. Tobin, *The Creation of Man: Philo and the History of Intepretation*, Catholic Biblical Quarterly Monograph Series (Washington, DC: Catholic Biblical Association of America, 1983), esp. 129. Devoted almost entirely to this question and in more compact form is Tobin, "Interpretations of Creation in Philo of Alexandria," in *Creation in the Biblical Traditions*, ed. Richard J. Clifford and John J. Collins (Washington, DC: Catholic Biblical Association of America, 1992), 108–28. He explains that this is driven by Philo's anthropology, drawing on Gen. 1:26–27 and 2:7.

37. Paul M. Blowers, *Drama of the Divine Economy: Creator and Creation in Early Christian Theology and Piety*, OECS (Oxford: Oxford University Press, 2012), 54–57. See Runia, *On the Creation of the Cosmos*, 19, 223–24, 310–11.

that the ideal things—the invisible entities of one day—and the ideal human of day six are "real" in Philo's terms. The details of Genesis 1 are rarely allegorized in *On the Creation*.[38] But does Philo become an interpretive example for us to imitate? I frankly think that the very distinctive (Middle) Platonic worldview that allowed his impressive scheme to make sense has passed, and without it his particular scheme seems needlessly complex or philosophically pretentious. Note, however, that occasional modern Christian writers still offer rather Platonic proposals, such as the "upper register cosmogony"[39] model of Meredith Kline, a well-known advocate of the framework hypothesis.[40]

Yet I do not think that the question of whether the creation week should be taken literally stands or falls purely based on sympathy with a Platonic worldview or its lack. Philo's protest that the Creator cannot require time to create still holds weight for the Christian theist, making his understanding of the creation week as a conceptual framework a significant early precedent for a modern framework understanding. Does Philo accommodate his intellectual culture too much? Later Jewish tradition did not follow him, and his scheme remained influential only as long as the late antique, Neoplatonic philosophical synthesis did (i.e., long enough to influence Augustine).

Perhaps Philo was too accommodating, tying his conceptual life raft to the Titanic of the then-dominant worldview, only to eventually go down with it, despite the power and sophistication of his interpretation. Yet he was the first ancient thinker to leave a discrete commentary on the creation week. Philo's creation explanation is original in its integration of Hellenistic and Jewish strands of thought into an original explanation of biblical creation.[41] In proposing a rather thoroughgoing integration of biblical teaching and contemporary intellectual thought, he may provide us with a yardstick by which we measure how far we would like to go in achieving coherence with or even just comprehensibility in our own intellectual culture.

---

38. Bray, *Biblical Interpretation*, 116–17.

39. A cosmogony is an account of the origin (etymologically, the "birth") of the world or cosmos.

40. We will discuss the framework hypothesis below; see the glossary for a short definition. See Meredith G. Kline, "Space and Time in the Genesis Cosmogony," *PSCF* 48.1 (1996): 2–6.

41. J. C. M. van Winden, "Hexaemeron," *RAC* 14:1257–58.

The Alexandrian Christian Allegorists

Between Philo, who lived until about the midpoint of the first century CE, and the early Alexandrian church father Clement (ca. 155–ca. 220), whose career belongs at the turn of the third century, we face a discontinuity in our historical knowledge. Philo's hermeneutical legacy in the thought and interpretation of Clement and of Origen (ca. 185–ca. 254) is widely acknowledged, but how that legacy was transmitted is not easy to establish.[42] Historical sources are also scant when it comes to answering the parallel questions of (1) the fortunes of Alexandrian Jewry in the second and third centuries; and (2) the rise of the Christian community in Alexandria in which Clement and Origen emerged. While the oral Torah of rabbinic Judaism in Judea may have experienced its first codification in the form of the Mishnah despite the disasters of the unsuccessful Jewish Revolt (66–70 CE) and Bar Kokhba Rebellion (132–135 CE), Alexandrian Judaism, as far as surviving witnesses go, falls silent. A popular theory is that another Jewish revolt that occurred between the two mentioned above brought devastation on the Jewish community in Alexandria. This revolt under Emperor Trajan (115–117 CE) spread to several parts of the eastern Roman Empire rather than being concentrated solely in Judea. But it is known only from isolated references so the details remain uncertain.[43]

Equally obscure is the rise of Alexandrian Christianity. Eusebius of Caesarea's *Ecclesiastical History* (5.10.1–4) claims that a Christian catechetical school existing in late second-century Alexandria was headed by a philosophically trained Christian called Pantaenus, though recent scholarship has read this as a less formal arrangement than "school" might imply. Alexandria had its first Christian bishop in the final decades of the second century, Bishop Demetrius, and Origen would head the city's catechetical school from about 204 CE until his departure to live

42. J. N. B. Paget, "The Christian Exegesis of the Old Testament in the Alexandrian Tradition," *HB/OT* 1.1:479; Borgen, "Philo of Alexandria as Exegete," 136–38; F. Robbins, *The Hexaemeral Literature: A Study of the Greek and Latin Commentaries in Genesis* (Chicago: University of Chicago Press, 1912), 28.

43. Paget, "Alexandrian Tradition," 479; David Brakke, "The East (2): Egypt and Palestine," in *The Oxford Handbook of Early Christian Studies*, ed. Susan Ashbrook Harvey and David G. Hunter (Oxford: Oxford University Press, 2008), 346–47; James D. G. Dunn, *Neither Jew nor Greek*, vol. 3 of *Christianity in the Making* (Grand Rapids: Eerdmans, 2015), 616–17.

in Caesarea Palestina in coastal Palestine around 231 CE. This departure came on account of conflict with Demetrius, which was provoked by Origen's ordination as priest in the Caesarea bishopric without his approval.[44] Alexandria would remain an important center of Christianity for centuries and host Nicene stalwart Athanasius (ca. 296–373) as well as theological hard man Cyril of Alexandria (d. 444).

Clement of Alexandria

Our understanding of both Clement and Origen is hindered by the loss of the majority of their writings. (Ironically, the writings of Philo were probably safer in that they would probably have been suspected of heresy and destroyed had they been Christian writings.) What does remain evinces a heavy debt to Philo's synthesis. Whereas Philo defends the intellectual credibility of Judaism and the Jewish Scriptures in his Hellenistic intellectual milieu, Clement defends the intellectual credibility of a young and embattled Christianity in that same environment. Clement faced the additional challenge of contesting several gnostic sects claiming to possess true illumination and to represent authentic Christianity. Clement uses gnostic terms and ideas, often derived from the smorgasbord of existing Greek philosophies, to either capture gnostic concepts with true definitions or refute them entirely. I will not try to explain gnostic beliefs here, as that is its own massive field of research. But the largest known trove of gnostic writings, the Nag Hammadi library, arose during this period but was only discovered in 1945 in central Egypt.[45] A mystical movement combining pagan thought, Greek philosophy, and Jewish and Christian ideas, Gnosticism seriously distorted key early Christian doctrines and advocated a complex and abstract mythology. Attracted by a sense of their metaphysical importance, gnostic writers often turned to the creation narratives in Genesis but showed little interest in the creation week as any record of the production of the physical world and often viewed its creation and its creator deity, whom they distinguished from the ultimate God, negatively.

The writing of Clement of Alexandria that is most interesting for us is his *Stromateis*, which Crouzel translates as "Tapestries" but is traditionally known in English as the "Miscellanies."[46] Acknowledged to be "a difficult and enigmatic

---

44. *HBI* 1:174–78; Crouzel, *Origen*, 1–36; Trigg, "Introduction," ii–iv.
45. E.g. *ODCC*, "Gnosticism," 574.
46. Crouzel, *Origen*, 39.

work" even by experts, the *Stromateis* is not easy reading.[47] Andrew Louth's words have never been more applicable: "It is indeed a foreign country that we enter when we read the fathers; they do things differently there."[48] There are a few references to Genesis 1–2 scattered through this work, but Clement clearly begins to adopt and expound Philo's rendition of creation in *Stromateis* 5.14.93–94, offering "a Platonizing interpretation of Genesis" that relies on Philo's and Plato's dualistic concept of an invisible, ideal, "noetic" world and its realization in the visible, sense-perceptible world.[49] This concept underlies the passage most often cited for its clear presentation of Clement's instantaneous creation stance:

> For the creative operations followed in grand succession, according to the different days, heirs as it were to the honor of the firstborn, all present at once, created together intellectually, but not sharing the same dignity. . . . For it was necessary to name something first. Therefore the first things were declared from which the second things came, although all things came from one essence by one power. . . . Since how could creation occur in time when time was born along with the other things that exist? (*Strom.* 6.16.142.2–4)[50]

A little later follows a statement that confirms the impression that Clement wishes to affirm a nonchronological creation:

> So, therefore, we might learn that the universe had an origin, and yet not suppose that God made it in time, the prophecy adds: "This is the book of the generation: and also of the things in them, when they came into being, in the day that God made heaven and earth." For the expression "when they came into being" indicates an undefined and dateless production. But the expression "in the day that God made," that is, in and by which God made "all things," and "without which not even one thing was made," points out

47. D. Wyrka, "Clement of Alexandria," *DECL*, 131.

48. Andrew Louth, "The Six Days of Creation according to the Greek Fathers," in *Reading Genesis after Darwin*, ed. Stephen C. Barton and David Wilkinson (Oxford: Oxford University Press, 2009), 39.

49. A. van den Hoek, *Clement of Alexandria and His Use of Philo in the Stromateis* (Leiden: Brill, 1988), 196. For the Greek see Otto Stählin, Ludwig Früchtel, and Ursula Treu, eds., *Stromata Buch I–VI*, 4th ed., GCS 52 (Berlin: Akademie, 1985), 388.

50. My translation from the Greek text of Stählin, Früchtel, and Treu.

the activity of the Son. . . . For the Word that brings the concealed things to light and by whom each created thing came into life and being, is called day. (*Strom.* 6.16.145.4–6)[51]

Annewies van den Hoek has proven that Clement consciously interacts with Philo and adopts his timeless creation, particularly from the beginning of his *Allegorical Interpretation.*[52] When comparing these texts with Philo's *On the Creation*, as van den Hoek does, Clement seems to share the same cosmogony but avoids referring directly to the days of creation in places where Philo does.[53] By passing over the creation process that Philo perceives as happening on days two through six, Clement's creation is more abstract than Philo's.[54] His concise reference to the "monad" as relating to the ideal realm and the "six" as relating to the sense-perceptible world is compatible with, and probably derives from, Philo's earlier "double creation" interpretation, which devoted day one of creation to the "noetic" creation and related the remaining creation days to the origin of the world we see.[55] But let's remember that Clement is a Christian thinker, and "remodels Philo's cosmology in a Christological, Gnostic and eschatological sense."[56] The way that impetus shows up here is that "day" in Genesis 2:4 is interpreted allegorically to signify Christ, and heaven and earth is made "in" Christ.

Among our "recruiters," Clement's interpretation, representing an instantaneous creation, is naturally more favorably received by those who celebrate figurative interpretations than those supporting a literal viewpoint. J. Ligon Duncan III and David Hall, in their answer to Hugh Ross and Gleason Archer in

51. My revision of the translation from *ANF* 2:514 in consultation with Stählin, Früchtel, and Treu.

52. Van den Hoek, *Clement of Alexandria*, 202–5.

53. The best example applies to the first quotation above, *Strom.* 6.16.142.2–4, where the parallel text in Philo, *Alleg. Interp.* 1.2, makes such reference.

54. This may be a function of the loss of some of Clement's creation writings.

55. See Stählin, Früchtel, and Treu, *Stromata Buch I–VI*, 387; Blowers, *Drama of the Divine Economy*, 145; Paul M. Blowers, "Creation," in *The Oxford Handbook of Early Christian Biblical Interpretation*, ed. Paul M. Blowers and Peter W. Martens (Oxford: Oxford University Press, 2019), 515. This differs from Chadwick, who sees the conceptual division falling between the creation week and the Eden narrative, i.e., Philo's "second" version as described by Tobin and Blowers. See Henry Chadwick, "Philo and the Beginnings of Christian Thought," *CHLGEMP*, 170.

56. Van den Hoek, *Clement of Alexandria*, 145–46.

The Genesis Debate (2001), protest, "If Ross and Archer believe that Clement of Alexandria explicitly endorses 'six consecutive thousand-year periods for the Genesis creation days' (which, incidentally, is not what they say about Clement at the location cited), we urge them to read Clement's bizarre numerology in its entirety to an audience."[57] We might take this as a valid warning against cherry-picking the parts we like from the quite complex and rather foreign thinking of a figure like Clement. However, we should still aspire to continue deepening our understanding even of such a foreign text as the *Stromateis* in its cultural and intellectual context.

Origen the Scholar

Origen is a contentious figure in church history. He has been both loved and hated, sometimes it would seem by the same person (e.g., the church father Jerome).[58] Interpreting the creation days nonchronologically in line with Philo and Clement before him, Origen becomes a kind of ambiguous pin-up boy for non-literal interpretations of the creation week in the present day. On the other hand, in his *Against Celsus*—written between 244 and 249 CE to refute the skepticism of the second-century Middle Platonist scholar Celsus[59]—Origen allows that according to the Mosaic creation account, "the world is not yet ten thousand years old but is much less than this."[60] So young-earth creationists love to (counter)cite him on this point in order to deny his support to opponents who believe in "deep time" and align him instead with a long list of advocates for a traditional biblical chronology.[61] Others want to emphasize that Origen is so doctrinally suspect that his support is fatally compromised: "Considering Origen's record, it does not really matter what he believed about the Creation days."[62] Yet we can hardly

57. David Hagopian, ed., *The Genesis Debate: Three Views on the Days of Creation* (Mission Viejo, CA: Crux, 2001), 101, citing 69.

58. Crouzel, *Origen*, 23, 36.

59. Crouzel, *Origen*, 47–48; R. P. C. Hanson, *Allegory and Event: A Study of the Sources and Significance of Origen's Interpretation of Scripture* (Louisville: Westminster John Knox, 2002), 159–60; Copleston, *Greece and Rome*, 455–56.

60. *Cels.* 1.19. English translation from Origen, *Contra Celsum*, trans. Henry Chadwick (Cambridge: Cambridge University Press, 1953), 20. See also *ANF* 4:404.

61. E.g., Sarfati, *Refuting Compromise*, 117–18.

62. Mark Van Bebber and Paul S. Taylor, *Creation and Time: A Report on the Progres-*

ignore him. "Origen," Stephen Presley reminds us, "was the towering figure of this period and is essential for understanding the early Christian reception of Gen. 1–2."[63] Let's try to understand Origen's sophisticated thinking about creation a little better and evaluate how seriously we should take his example.

Origen is widely acknowledged as the greatest scholar to emerge in the Christian church between the apostle Paul and Augustine, rivaled perhaps only by his Latin counterpart Jerome. Our primary source for his life story is the sympathetic treatment in the *Ecclesiastical History* of Eusebius of Caesarea. Origen's father, Leonides, died around 203 CE in the persecution overseen by Roman emperor Septimius Severus (r. 193–211), and one famous story told by Eusebius is that the young and keen teenage Origen would have joined his father at the chopping block had his mother not hidden all of his clothes (proving that dying of shame is worse than beheading).[64] Origen, again, was based in Alexandria in Egypt until his move to Caesarea in Palestine (ca. 231). There, with local support and a patron, Ambrose, who evidently expected consistent written output, Origen had his most fruitful phase of scholarship.[65] His death in 253 or 254 is attributed to his sufferings during the persecution of Emperor Decius (249–51).[66]

Origen developed a devoted personal following particularly in Palestine, Arabia, and many of the Eastern churches in his own time.[67] Yet the academic theological freedom he exercised did face increasing condemnation in the vexed and

---

sive Creationist Book by Hugh Ross (Mesa, AZ: Eden Productions, 1994), 96; and see also James R. Mook, "The Church Fathers on Genesis, the Flood, and the Age of the Earth," in *Coming to Grips with Genesis: Biblical Authority and the Age of the Earth*, ed. Terry Mortenson and Thane H. Ury (Green Forest, AR: Master Books, 2008), 34–35.

63. Stephen O. Presley, "Interpretations of Genesis 1–2 among the Ante-Nicene Fathers," in *Since the Beginning: Interpreting Genesis 1 and 2 through the Ages*, ed. Kyle R. Greenwood (Grand Rapids: Baker Academic, 2018), 100.

64. For the broader chronology, see the table in Margaret M. Mitchell, Frances M. Young, and K. Scott Bowie, eds., *Origins to Constantine*, vol. 1 of *The Cambridge History of Christianity* (Cambridge: Cambridge University Press, 2006), xxii–xxiii. The biographical details here and following may be found in brief in Trigg, "Introduction," iii–iv. For the long version, see Crouzel, *Origen*, 4–36.

65. *HBI* 1:176–78; Crouzel, *Origen*, 27.

66. Trigg, "Introduction," iv.

67. Crouzel notes that four regions, Palestine, Arabia, Phoenicia, and Greece, continued to acknowledge Origen's priestly qualifications when Alexandria, with eventual Roman imprimatur, declared them void. See Crouzel, *Origen*, 22.

heresy-torn centuries to follow until many of his writings were purged and lost. Regarding his scholarship, it is common to hear accolades such as "As a Christian expounder of Scripture, Origen towers like a giant above his predecessors and contemporaries." Its author, R. P. C. Hanson, regards Origen as the founder of Christian biblical commentary as we understand it.[68] Origen was also the first great Christian textual critic, creating a six-column parallel Bible that featured a Hebrew text, the same text transliterated into Greek, and the classic Greek translation of the OT that we call the Septuagint alongside three subsequent Greek editions labeled Aquila, Symmachus, and Theodotion, all for the sake of cross-checking and evaluating textual differences.[69] In his personal life, Origen's credentials in self-denial and hard work were acknowledged by contemporaries, capped off by his torture under Decius, and students such as Gregory Thaumaturgus speak of his personal devotion, pastoral concern, and spiritual influence.[70]

Yet after his death Origen became an increasingly contentious figure. The first Origenist controversy saw Origen's former advocate Jerome (ca. 345–ca. 419) switch sides to join Epiphanius of Salamis (ca. 315–403) in seeking the censure of Origen's works in the 390s, with ecclesiastical and monastic politics entangled in the affair, especially in Palestine and Egypt. Controversy resurfaced in the sixth century, culminating in Origen's condemnation at the Fifth Ecumenical Council of Constantinople under the Byzantine Emperor Justinian I in 553, though Origen was being interpreted via the writings of an older supporter, Evagrius of Pontus (345–399) and current monastic supporters known as the Isochristoi.[71] This was the so-called second Origenist controversy. Sometimes it was Origen's Christology that most offended theologians, at other times his anthropology, and at others his biblical hermeneutic.

At the center of Origen's thought was his ontology, that is, his concept of ultimate reality, a concept framed under the influence of his early immersion in the incipient Neoplatonism of the Alexandrian intellectual scene, his exposure to the interpretive legacy of both Philo and Clement, and the rival beliefs of Judaism, pagan or Greco-Roman polytheism, and Gnosticism. His concept is that

68. Hanson, *Allegory and Event*, 360.
69. E.g., *ODCC*, "Hexapla," 645.
70. Crouzel, *Origen*, 25–29; Henry Chadwick, "The Early Christian Community," in *The Oxford Illlustrated History of Christianity*, ed. John McManners (Oxford: Oxford University Press, 1990), 52–53.
71. E. M. Harding, "Origenist Crises," in *The SCM Press A–Z of Origen*, ed. John Anthony McGuckin (London: SCM, 2006), 162–66.

everything that exists, especially all personal beings, have come forth from God in creation in a descending hierarchical series starting with the Logos, Christ, who defines and expresses the very mind of God. "The final procession within the Godhead is the Holy Spirit," and thence, from the Godhead, all of creation, with angelic beings highest in dignity and the devil and demons as the lowest.[72] All human souls have preexisted their earthly embodiment and are, like angelic souls, immortal. Origen believed that Scripture warranted such a belief, even in enigmatic hints in Genesis itself, although this is not obvious to us today.[73]

Most controversially, if God is to be "all in all" (1 Cor. 15:28, the pivotal verse for Origen's concept), then all things that emerged from God in creation must be restored to union with God in redemptive return. This teaching of Origen is known as *apokatastasis*.[74] If taken to its logical conclusion, as nearly happens in his *On First Principles* and which Jerome claimed that Origen in fact did, *apokatastasis* would imply that every personal being—the devil and demons included—must ultimately submit to God and be restored to God.[75] The Christian doctrines most obviously at risk here were (1) the status of Christ in relation to the Father, where Christ, though highly dignified, was in fact the first step down the hierarchy from the true God; (2) God's freedom in creation, since in Origen's mind God, as the almighty ruler and creator, could not be without a created order to rule; (3) the eternal reprobation of the devil; and (4) the future physical resurrection of human beings.[76]

Origen's Interpretation of Creation in Genesis 1

Before we try to finalize our own stance toward Origen, however, let us first identify his creation teaching. There are two or three tracts from Origen's writings that

---

72. Frederick Copleston, SJ, *Augustine to Scotus*, vol. 2 of *A History of Philosophy* (New York: Doubleday, 1950), 27–28.

73. Peter Martens, "Origen's Doctrine of Pre-Existence and the Opening Chapters of Genesis," *ZAC* 16.3 (2012): 516–49. See esp. 518.

74. Blowers, *Drama of the Divine Economy*, 91–92; David Fergusson, *Creation*, Guides to Theology (Grand Rapids: Eerdmans, 2014), 45.

75. See the prevarication in *Princ.* 1.6.3; 7.5. Translation from Origen, *On First Principles*, ed. Paul Koetschau, trans. George William Butterworth (Gloucester, MA: Smith, 1973), 53–55, 65 and 55 n. 1.

76. Copleston, *Augustine to Scotus*, 27–28; Christopher Hall, *Reading Scripture with the Church Fathers* (Downers Grove, IL: InterVarsity Press, 1998), 52–53; Anders Lund Jacobsen, "Genesis 1–3 as Source for the Anthropology of Origen," *VC* 62.3 (2008): 222–23, 227–31.

commonly appear in creation discussions. Of the commentary that Origen wrote on the first four chapters of Genesis, sadly, only fragments preserved in later quotations remain. Origen repeatedly refers the reader of his *Against Celsus*—much of which was preserved in the *Philocalia*, a patristic collection of extracts from Origen—to this lost commentary concerning his stance on creation in Genesis.[77] His comment in *Against Celsus* 6.51 that "the natures of the days" have been divided between "intelligible and sensible things,"[78] which comes immediately after a list of the creations of the different creation days and a strong emphasis on the singular "day" in "In the day in which God made heaven and earth" (Gen. 2:4b), suggests that his interpretation ran very close to the lines of Philo's *On the Creation*.[79] But Origen shows his hand a little more clearly when, in *Against Celsus* 6.10, he makes another reference to his Genesis commentary: "In what we said earlier we criticized those who follow the superficial interpretation and say that the creation of the world happened during a period of time six days long."[80]

So, along with Philo, Origen sees the singular day in Genesis 2:4 as signifying the "one day" of Genesis 1:5, an archetypal "day" of creation that embraces the whole preceding creation. And in line with Philo's *On the Creation*, Origen can say in his homily on Genesis 1 that "one day" designates a "time before time," where the physical world and its history are not yet in view: "But time begins to exist with the following days. For the second day and the third and the fourth and all the rest begin to designate time."[81] The dividing line within the "double creation" apparently falls not between Genesis 1:1–2:3 and 2:4–25 but between 1:1–5 and 1:6–2:3, as seen in Philo's first (and primary) interpretation.[82] This reading differs

77. E.g., *Cels.* 6.49, 51 (Chadwick); and see Crouzel, *Origen*, 44, 46.

78. See the earlier note on the meaning of "sensible" when referring to Platonist philosophy.

79. See Chadwick, *Contra Celsum*, 366–67.

80. This is Chadwick's wording. I would translate "superficial" as "plain" or "apparent," which rightly connotes a surface-level meaning but which might even for Origen seem too dismissive of the literal sense. The Greek term is τὴν προχειροτέραν ἐκδοχὴν, lit. "the most ready-to-hand interpretation." Text from PG 11:1389. See also Origen's *Princ.* 4.2.4 for similar wording.

81. Origen, *Hom. Gen.* 1.1. Translation from Origen, *Homilies on Genesis and Exodus*, trans. Ronald E. Heine, FC 71 (Washington, DC: Catholic University of America Press, 1981), 48.

82. Blowers, "Creation," 3–4; Blowers, *Drama of the Divine Economy*, 91, 145–46; Presley, "Interpretations of Genesis 1–2," 104–5; Charlotte Köckert, *Christliche Kosmologie und*

cautiously from Mark Scott when he says, "Origen interprets the two creation narratives in Genesis 1–2 as two separate creations: immaterial/incorporeal and material/corporeal." Notice that later in his treatment of Origen's *Homilies on Genesis* 1.2 Scott distinguishes the "heaven" of day one from the "firmament" of day two, which implies that the break falls between days one and two of Genesis 1: "And, therefore, that first heaven indeed, which we said is spiritual, is our mind, which is also itself spirit, that is, our spiritual man which sees and perceives God. But that corporeal heaven, which is called the firmament, is our outer man which looks at things in a corporeal way."[83]

The same distinction holds in parts of Origen's most systematic work on biblical interpretation, *On First Principles* (2.3.6; 2.9.1), but his most-cited passage in this connection makes clear that while days two through six of creation begin time, they do not indicate distinctions of time between themselves:

> Now what man of intelligence will believe that the second and the third day, and the evening and the morning existed without the sun and moon and stars? And that the first day, if we may so call it, was even without a heaven? And who is so silly as to believe that God, after the manner of a farmer, 'planted a paradise eastward in Eden' . . . And when God is said to 'walk in the paradise in the cool of the day' . . . I do not think anyone will doubt that these are figurative expressions which indicate certain mysteries through a semblance of history and not through actual events. (*Princ.* 4.3.1 [Butterworth])

The twofold exegetical issue turning Origen toward a figurative understanding here, to the extent that it is not just his idealist worldview talking, is that on the one side the plain reading of the chapter leads to physical implausibilities such as the earth experiencing a day with no sky above, and on the other side that God is represented in very anthropomorphic terms. It is not too much of a stretch to begin thinking of the creation week as an anthropomorphism akin to God's breathing into the man to bring him to life in Genesis 2:7, or God walking in the

---

kaiserzeitliche Philosophie: Die Auslegung des Schöpfungsberichtes bei Origenes, Basilius und Gregor von Nyssa vor dem Hintergrund kaiserzeitlicher Timaeus-Interpretation, STAC 56 (Tübingen: Mohr Siebeck, 2009), 239–40.

83. Mark Scott, "Origen: Decoding Genesis," Henry Center for Theological Understanding (blog), April 26, 2017, http://henrycenter.tiu.edu/2017/04/origen-decoding-genesis/.

garden in Genesis 3:8, as C. John Collins does.[84] But can the fan of nonliteral interpretation safely rally Origen to his cause, as we see with Denis Alexander, John Lennox, and, with reservations, Robert Letham?[85]

Origen does offer a serious precedent for a figurative interpretation of the creation days, with the proviso that we should study his interpretive stance and decide how closely we identify with it. Origen held that this world is one of a succession of worlds extending before and after ours, as Young and Stearley note while adding that this is dissimilar to modern belief in the ancient beginning of our present creation.[86] Is Origen interpreting the days allegorically? This is not easy to finally determine. He is, after all, mostly interpreting the Genesis 1 creation narrative as referring to cosmic creation prior to implementing his allegorical readings, although the difficulty of literal "upper waters" in day two of creation, among other difficulties, drives him to a purely spiritual interpretation of those waters as representing unseen heavenly beings (i.e., angels).[87] While Origen does not abandon all interest in the literal sense of Scripture, for him it is a kind of early stage of reading for the inexperienced Christian, and one should move on to deeper things as soon as one is mature enough.[88] When he says of elements of Genesis, such as the days of creation, that "these are figurative expressions which indicate certain mysteries through a semblance of history," we are faced rather clearly with a test case for our own strategies for interpreting Scripture. Do we agree that there is often more to be discovered in a biblical (especially Old Testament) text than its baldly literal sense, or does treating what look like units of history, "days," as a figure play too freely with the sense of the text?

84. C. John Collins, *Genesis 1–4: A Linguistic, Literary, and Theological Commentary* (Phillipsburg, NJ: P&R, 2006), 230; C. John Collins, "How Old Is the Earth? Anthropomorphic Days in Genesis 1:1–2:3," *Presbyterion* 20 (1994): 109–30.

85. Denis Alexander, *Creation or Evolution: Do We Have to Choose?* (Oxford: Monarch, 2008), 155–56; Lennox, *Seven Days*, 41–42; Robert Letham, "'In the Space of Six Days': The Days of Creation from Origen to the Westminster Assembly," *WTJ* 61.2 (1999): 151.

86. Davis A. Young and Ralph Stearley, *The Bible, Rocks and Time: Geological Evidence for the Age of the Earth* (Downers Grove, IL: InterVarsity Press, 2008), 40.

87. Adam Rasmussen, *Genesis and Cosmos: Basil and Origen on Genesis 1 and Cosmology*, BAC 14 (Leiden: Brill, 2019), 7–8, 143–44.

88. Stephen Westerholm and Martin Westerholm, *Reading Sacred Scripture: Voices from the History of Biblical Interpretation* (Grand Rapids: Eerdmans, 2016), 81–88.

What was Origen trying to do? A standout Christian thinker of profound intelligence and the first great Christian biblical commentator, he occupied a delicate apologetic position. His educational work in Caesarea Palestina served educated students, whom Crouzel thinks were not necessarily yet baptized into the faith, who needed a robustly philosophical explanation of the Christian faith to win their confidence that Christianity was not a "check your brains at the door" religion. Rival gnostic explanations competed for the inquiring mind, and Martens suggests that Origen's challenge was to supply a more true and insightful natural philosophy in response.[89] Yet the pastoral demands of his preaching meant that Origen could not afford to stray too far into rarified academic air and become irrelevant for the saints that he wanted to see ascending ever greater spiritual heights toward God.[90] Origen synthesized a sophisticated worldview, as *On First Principles* makes clear, that integrated (1) what he understood of seen and unseen reality (i.e., the metaphysics he had been steeped in growing up in Alexandria); with (2) his conscious and consistently lived Christian theology (i.e., the "Rule of Faith"); and (3) his engagement with the biblical text. How these three strands are unified into a single worldview in Origen's mind is endlessly discussed.[91] But no Christian thinker up to this time had formulated such a sophisticated Christian worldview.

On the other hand, Origen's worldview was clearly of his time and governed by the Platonic "exemplarist" perspective that saw behind visible reality an invisible, divine archetypal design, and beneath every written word of sacred text an "under-meaning" available to the truly spiritual reader.[92] So in terms of the delicate balancing of the scales between a *relevant* explanation of Christianity and a *durable* explanation, Origen's relative success at achieving cutting-edge intellectual coherence and relevance was attained at the cost of offering a view that would not long outlive its Neoplatonist and Stoic philosophical underpinnings. We might find fault at a second point, in that this intellectual system required some rather serious theological concessions that seemed a bridge too far for other leading Christians. There are signs that Origen battled the skepticism

---

89. Martens, "Origen's Doctrine of Pre-Existence," 543–48.

90. Crouzel, *Origen*, 27.

91. Paget, "Alexandrian Tradition," 532–34; Trigg, "Introduction," xv–xvi; Hanson, *Allegory and Event*, 235–58.

92. Crouzel, *Origen*, 78–79.

of everyday believers who found his explanations too clever.[93] Origen sought to lead his ecclesiastical horse to exegetical water, but in the long run might only have brought the head. While his moral allegories probably seemed very relevant to his ordinary Christian listeners, his undergirding hermeneutic was really only accessible to an educated elite. This is a difficult gulf to bridge in the church, ancient or modern, but the ordinary person does have a nose, I believe, for an interpretation that is one step too clever. Nevertheless, Origen exemplifies the reader who believes that Genesis 1–3 contains enough *internal* clues to indicate that something beyond the simplest historical or chronological reading is warranted. Talking snakes, anyone?

Successors to Origen in the Alexandrian School

Origen's influence was considerable, waxing and waning region by region and century by century. In Egypt and Palestine and their surrounding environment he developed a loyal following, and his timeless interpretation of the creation week reappears with some provisos in the writings of Didymus the Blind and then, briefly but clearly, in Athanasius's *Orations against the Arians*, who says that the days of creation indicate differing degrees of dignity in created things, perhaps, but not any distinction in time of origin.[94] On the other hand, a reaction against this Alexandrian exegetical method developed among the Eastern churches, notably in the important Syrian city of Antioch.[95] Somewhere between these two interpretive poles of Alexandria and Antioch belong the influential Cappadocian Fathers, Basil the Great, Gregory of Nazianzus, and Gregory of Nyssa, who gathered and transmitted ideas and materials from Origen and yet did so with increasing critical reserve. We will see that Basil's treatment of the "hexaemeron" or creation week consciously steps away from Origen's; the less familiar *Apologia in Hexaemeron* of Gregory of Nyssa is more sympathetic to it. Origen's legacy also entered the Western sphere through substantial tracts of his work being translated into Latin by his supporter Rufinus of Aquileia (ca. 345–411/412) and through

---

93. Hanson, *Allegory and Event*, 149–54.

94. *C. Ar.* 2.48–49, 60 (*NPNF*[2] 4:374–75, 381; PG 26:251–52, 276).

95. I will have more to say on this shortly, but see Young, "Alexandrian and Antiochene Exegesis," *AHBI* 1:334–54; Sten Hidal, "Exegesis of the Old Testament in the Antiochene School with Its Prevalent Literal and Historical Method," *HB/OT* 1.1:543–68.

emulation by two influential Western fathers: Ambrose of Milan (ca. 339–397) and Hilary of Poitiers (ca. 315–367).

Hilary was a stout defender of eastern father Athanasius and of the Nicene orthodoxy that he represented. For this stance, Hilary underwent exile in the regime of the eastern emperor Constantius II.[96] Hilary acted as a conduit for Alexandrian (notably Origenist) perspectives into the Western church. Like Athanasius, he appears at one point to sympathize with an instantaneous creation teaching. The passage in question is from the closing paragraphs of Hilary's *On the Trinity*, where he argues for the preexistent and uncreated status of the Son of God:

> Even if, according to Moses, the strengthening of the firmament, the laying bare of the dry land, the gathering of the waters, the arrangement of the stars, and the generation of the water and the earth in sending forth living beings from themselves are done according to their proper order, there is not even a moment of time discernible in the work of creating the heavens, the earth, and the other elements, because their preparation has been brought about as the result of a like infinity of eternity with God. (*De Trin.* 12.40)[97]

Whether the passage that climaxes with this reading teaches an instantaneous creation depends greatly on whether by "elements" Hilary means the raw materials of creation, as it were, or rather the different parts of creation, and whether it is their *individual* creation that is seen as instantaneous or their *collective* creation. It is difficult to tell for sure, though we might suspect that Philo's list of "day one" instantaneous productions of a matrix is in view, leaving room for possible temporal progression in the appearance of the details of creation. Hilary's interest here is christological and he treats creation theology only as a means to that end. Luther understood Hilary to be advocating an instantaneous creation of the cosmos,[98] while Luther's near contemporary, the well-regarded Jesuit scholar Francisco Suarez, took Hilary to mean the instantaneous creation of the raw

---

96. Henry Chadwick, "Orthodoxy and Heresy from the Death of Constantine to the Eve of the First Council of Ephesus," *CAH* 13:569–70.

97. Translation of Hilary of Poitiers from Stephen McKenna, trans., *The Trinity*, FC 25 (Washington, DC: Catholic University of America Press, 1968), 529. See also *NPNF*² 9:228; PG 10:457a–459a.

98. Martin Luther, *Lectures on Genesis Chapters 1–5*, trans. George V. Schick, LW 1 (St. Louis: Concordia, 1958), 4, 37, 69.

forms of matter ready for their shaping through six days, which we will find was a rather common creation belief in the patristic period.[99] The question receives only a few contemporary comments, most of which assess Hilary as teaching an instantaneous creation.[100] However, rereading the prior context leads me to agree, tentatively, with the assessment of Young and Stearley:

> [A] close examination of what Hilary said indicates that he was establishing the point that God had a single plan prior to creation rather than that he created all things at once. What Hilary denied was that God created the Earth, then thought out the next step, then created the waters . . . and so on.[101]

Hilary, then, emphasizes that although created things "had a beginning in so far as their creation is concerned, they did not have a beginning in so far as the knowledge or power of God is concerned." It is possible that while for Hilary, the true, noetic scheme or Platonic plan of creation exists eternally in the mind of God, its physical realization might unfold in time. But it is not absolutely clear. It would fall to Augustine, protégé of Ambrose and a generation younger than Hilary, to decide what to do with Origen's legacy of an instantaneous creation as it affected creation week interpretation.

99. LW 1:4, 37–38, 69; Francisco Suarez, "Tractatus de opere sex dierum," in *Francisci Suarez opera omnia*, ed. D. M. André (Paris: Vivès, 1856), 3:55a.

100. E.g., E. Mangenot, "Hexaméron," *DTC* 6:2338; Forster and Marston, *Reason, Science and Faith*, 205; Jack P. Lewis, "The Days of Creation: An Historical Survey of Interpretation," *JETS* 32 (1989): 448 rather blindly following the (in)famous A. D. White at this point.

101. Young and Stearley, *Bible, Rocks and Time*, 41–42 n. 44.

Chapter Two

THE MILLENNIAL ROOTS OF THE WORLD-WEEK
APPROACH TO GENESIS 1

This chapter is designed to clear up one common misunderstanding of patristic creation week interpretation. This requires us to expand our field of view beyond creation alone to the structure of human history (as the history of redemption) and right up to eschatology, belief about final things. Put succinctly, some ancient Christian writers concluded that as creation was completed in six days, God's plan for history would be executed in the course of six thousand years, because after all, a thousand years were just like a single day to God (Ps. 90:4; 2 Pet. 3:8). This viewpoint has been called world-week typology or belief in the "cosmic week."

Patristic Christian thought, like ancient thought more generally, was thoroughly attuned to finding correspondences between different spheres of reality, so it is not surprising that Christian thinkers should readily conclude that God's creative purposes might manifest themselves in history, as the object of God's providential governance, before finding final realization at the end of the age and the new world inaugurated by Christ's return. And if history was destined to play out under God's guidance over six thousand years, then, the seventh-day rest of God might find its typological fulfillment either in an earthly millennium as featured in Revelation 20 or in an endless, heavenly Sabbath such as might find support in Hebrews 3:7–4:11. Dispute over the expectation of a millennium was stormy in the patristic period and continues today, albeit usually disconnected from world-week belief.

This typological understanding that the creation narrative, besides describing actual creation, also has a prophetic role, indicating the outlines of human redemption history in six stages or across six thousand years, has sometimes been confused with the day-age or periodic-day interpretation of the creation week. This is a relatively modern concordist interpretation, where each day of the creation narrative corresponds to a long phase of prehuman, geological history. While there is a genetic relationship between the two ideas, a thoughtless equation of the two is misleading. This misunderstanding surfaced in a claim made by Hugh Ross, a day-age scheme advocate, first in his *Creation and Time* (1994) and then still in *A Matter of Days* (2004): "The earliest-known Christian writings on the meaning of the creation days date back to the second century. Justin Martyr ... and Irenaeus ... drew support from Psalm 90:4 and 2 Peter 3:8 to suggest that the 'days' could be epochs, perhaps thousand-year-long creation periods."[1] In *Creation and Time*, Ross elaborates, "Writing later in the third century, Lactantius, ... Victorinus of Pettau, and Methodius of Olympus, all concurred with Justin Martyr's and Irenaeus's view of the creation days as thousand-year epochs."[2] A similar statement appeared in Ross's contribution to *The Genesis Debate* (2001).[3] In the same volume, debate opponents J. Ligon Duncan III and David W. Hall protested vigorously against this characterization with good reason.[4] Ross had given the impression that many church fathers were advocates of something resembling a modern day-age or concordist view of the creation week. That impression was misleading and represented a superficial, prooftexting approach to these ancient witnesses, possibly reflecting a poor understanding of what their claims really meant and how they made sense in the context of their broader thinking.

Ross softened his statement about Lactantius, Victorinus, and Methodius in *A Matter of Days*, improving the accuracy of the impression given to the reader: "Writing later in the third century, Lactantius, ... Victorinus of Pettau, and Methodius of Olympus all indicated in their writings that many of their contemporaries espoused the idea that just as there were seven days of creation, so there would

1. Hugh Ross, *A Matter of Days: Resolving a Creation Controversy* (Colorado Springs, CO: Navpress, 2004), 43; Hugh Ross, *Creation and Time* (Colorado Springs, CO: Navpress, 1994), 17–18.

2. Ross, *Creation and Time*, 19.

3. Nominally Hugh Ross with Gleason Archer, though we see little sign of the better awareness of patristic theology that we might have expected from Archer, a recognized OT scholar. See their responses in *The Genesis Debate: Three Views on the Days of Creation*, ed. David Hagopian (Mission Viejo, CA: Crux, 2001), 69 and 125–26, 205.

4. Hagopian, *Genesis Debate*, 99–101.

follow thereafter seven days of human history in which each such day would last for 1,000 years."[5] The new inclusion of the phrase "*human* history" was a significant improvement. The key is that the "typological mind" of the church fathers is at work in this view. It is not that each creation day lasts for a thousand years, but that each creation day *corresponds* to a thousand-year epoch of human (i.e., redemptive) history. It is not an either/or, but a both/and with room for more correspondences besides. I illustrated this mindset as a hall of mirrors in talking about Philo previously; for the church fathers, a biblical text can mean more than just one thing and operate on more than one level. So can persons and events and things in the natural world. The fathers looked around and saw a symbolic universe full of meaning, with one thing related to another and everything ultimately referring upward to Christ, his bride the church, and ultimately to God the Father.[6] So Ross was right to introduce the "just as/so" language into his statement. We will see how this multilevel interpretive consciousness surfaces in some patristic explanations of this fascinating interpretation of the creation week before posing the question how this ancient Christian belief relates to modern questions around biblical creation.

CLASSICAL AND JEWISH PRECEDENTS FOR THE WORLD-WEEK SCHEME

I will merely touch on the roots of the view that finds in the creation week a master framework for a seven-thousand-year plan of God for human history. The demarcation of history by the hegemony of successive kingdoms in Daniel 2 and 7 and then the dividing up of prospective time by groups of seven years in Daniel 9:24–27 provide our clearest OT examples of what is called the "periodization of history."[7] Classical Greco-Roman mythology of origins also divided the past into separate eras, often beginning with a golden age (as Daniel 2 does) and declining in quality by successive periods.[8] Societies east of Israel could have influ-

---

5. Ross, *Matter of Days*, 45.

6. It was also possible for words and things and persons to symbolize what was sinful and evil, all the way down to the devil or antichrist. See the opening comments regarding Satanic symbolism in Tyconius's *Book of Rules* in W. Yarchin, *A History of Biblical Interpretation: A Reader* (Peabody, MA: Hendrickson, 2004), 51–53.

7. James D. Tabor, "Ancient Jewish and Early Christian Millennialism," in *The Oxford Handbook of Millennialism*, ed. Catherine Wessinger (Oxford: Oxford University Press, 2016), 255–56.

8. Arnaldo Momigliano, "The Origins of Universal History," in *The Poet and the His-*

enced early Jewish ideas of marking out history too. Persian culture had a scheme breaking history down into four sets of three thousand years, and Mesopotamian astrology encouraged the division of time into sets of seven corresponding to the seven planets.[9]

Early Jewish literature now found in the Pseudepigrapha reveals further explorations of ways to divide up the time of the (human) world's existence under the influence of the seven-unit week and Sabbath and of the forty-nine-part jubilee (Lev. 25:8–55). The book of Jubilees portrays the number seven as built into the cosmos in the creation week, so that the earliest history of the world up to Joshua's conquest unfolds by means of these intrinsic sevens, that is, in forty-nine jubilees of forty-nine years plus a culminating fiftieth jubilee. World history is also alluded to as God's "week" and defined as seven thousand years long in 2 Enoch 33:1–2.[10] A similar enumeration is hinted at in the Testament of Abraham 7:16.[11] Perhaps the most significant and earliest example in this literature is the pre-Maccabean (i.e., pre-170 BCE) Apocalypse of Weeks now found embedded in the composite book of 1 Enoch (91:12–17; 93:1–10).[12] Given that Enoch appears at the end of the first set of seven or "week," Tabor concludes that each week in the Apocalypse of Weeks probably equates to a set of seven centuries. The full set of ten weeks would thus represent "for the first time . . . a complete seven-thousand-year scheme of human history."[13] Later rabbinic tradition as preserved in the Babylonian Talmud records several models of historical subdivision, two of the clearest appearing in Sanhedrin 97a–b:

---

torian: *Essays in Literary and Historical Biblical Criticism*, ed. R. E. Friedman (Chico, CA: Scholars, 1983), 133–35, 145.

9. Jonathan Z. Smith, "Ages of the World," in *The Encyclopedia of Religion*, ed. Mircea Eliade (New York: Macmillan, 1987), 1:129–30; Garry W. Trompf, *The Idea of Historical Recurrence in Western Thought: From Antiquity to the Reformation* (Berkeley: University of California Press, 1979), 201–4 and n. 109; Jean Daniélou, "La typologie millénariste de la semaine dans le Christianisme primitif," *VC* 2.1 (1948): 5.

10. This rather vague reference, possibly a Christian insertion, occurs only in the longer manuscript tradition entitled J by Charlesworth. For his explanation, see *OTP* 1:92–94, 98–99, 156.

11. *OTP* 2:898; see also A. Wikenhauser, "Weltwoche und Tausendjähriges Reich," *Theologische Quartalschrift* 127 (1947): 400.

12. *OTP* 1:7, 73–74.

13. Tabor, "Millennialism," 257.

1. Six thousand years of history followed by one or perhaps two thousand years of lying essentially fallow in a kind of Sabbath year rest for the earth and for God

2. Two thousand years lacking the Torah, two thousand years with the Torah, and a two-thousand-year messianic era for a total of six thousand years, a scheme that receives the comment that it has been broken due to the sin of the nation.[14]

Such Jewish schemes are likely to have been known in some form by many of the early church fathers, who nevertheless heavily adapted them to the needs of Christian theology, as we will see.

A Seminal Text in the Apostolic Fathers: The World-Week in Barnabas

Despite such important precedents, Scripture was the foundation upon which any convincing Christian scheme of periodizing history had to be built, or at least the standard by which it had to be justified. But it would be Scripture seen through typological eyes where the surface meaning foreshadowed a deeper or longer range scheme. In this case we are talking about a historical typology primarily based on Genesis 1:1–2:3. This creation week typology first appears in Christian patristic literature in the letter of Barnabas, which belongs to the earliest collection of Christian writings to follow the New Testament: the Apostolic Fathers:

> He speaks of the sabbath at the beginning of the creation: "And God made the works of his hands in six days, and finished on the seventh day, and rested on it, and sanctified it." Observe, children, what "he finished in six days" means. It means this: that in six thousand years the Lord will bring everything to an end, for with him a day signifies a thousand years. And he himself bears me witness when he says, "Behold, the day of the Lord will be as a thousand years." Therefore, children, in six days—that is, in six thousand years—everything

14. Given how close most Hebrew chronological schemes went to positing four thousand years before the era of Jesus Christ, any such belief existing in the time of Jesus must have fed messianic expectations among his audiences.

will be brought to an end.... Finally, he says to them: "I cannot bear your new moons and sabbaths." You see what he means: it is not the present sabbaths that are acceptable to me, but the one that I have made; on that Sabbath, after[15] I have set everything at rest, I will create the beginning of an eighth day, which is the beginning of another world. (Barn. 15.3–4, 8)[16]

The context of this clear and seminal world-week teaching is an assertion by the writer that just as there is a true heavenly temple that is superior to the physical one recently destroyed (in 70 CE) in Jerusalem, there is also a spiritual Sabbath to be enjoyed, not the Jewish observance rejected by God through the prophet Isaiah (Isa. 1:13 being alluded to in the quotation above), but the "rest" at the end of history brought about when Christ asserts his full authority and quells all opposition, especially that of the "lawless one" (Barn. 15:5). The influence of Hebrews 4:1–11 is clear, though the literal, earthly millennium of Revelation 20:1–6, where the saints rule with Christ, remains absent.[17] In fact, an earthly millennium is not really compatible with the author's thinking, despite the confusion created when he harnessed a seventh-day/world Sabbath typology and subordinated it to Christian teaching of the "eighth day" of perfected future eternity. Against the expectation of the modern reader that an eighth day ought to follow a seventh day in sequence, the two days coincide in Barnabas 15, precluding the conclusion some earlier scholars reached that the author was a chiliast teaching a physical, earthly, thousand-year reign of Christ.[18]

15. This is a questionable translation of the Greek phrase ἐν ᾧ in my view. In Liddell and Scott, *An Intermediate Greek-English Lexicon* it receives the definition "while," and "when" might be the simplest translation here. "After" implies the completion of an intervening period in a way the Greek phrase does not seem to justify and raises questions of the back-influence of expectations of a millennial teaching here.

16. Translation from Michael W. Holmes, ed., *The Apostolic Fathers*, rev. ed. (Grand Rapids: Baker, 1999), 315, 317.

17. J. Daniélou, *The Theology of Jewish Christianity*, trans. John A. Baker (London: Darton, Longman and Todd, 1964), 398; Auguste Luneau, *L'histoire du salut chez les pères de l'église: La doctrine des âges du monde* (Paris: Beauchesne, 1964), 84–85.

18. Albert Hermans, "Le pseudo-Barnabé est-il millénariste?," *Ephemerides Theologicae Lovanienses* 35.4 (1959): 849–76; K.-H. Schwarte, *Die Vorgeschichte der augustinischen Weltalterlehre* (Bonn: Habelt, 1966), 86–105, following Hermans's treatment and summarizing it succinctly on 96–97; Craig D. Allert, *Early Christian Readings of Genesis One: Patristic Exegesis and Literal Interpretation* (Downers Grove, IL: InterVarsity Press,

In this passage from Barnabas, the principle enunciated in 2 Peter 3:8, "With the Lord a day is like a thousand years, and a thousand years are like a day," where it is only a correction of perspective, here is utilized as a hermeneutical key to unlock the meaning ostensibly concealed in the creation week narrative. Psalm 90:4, "A thousand years in your sight are like a day that has just gone by, or like a watch in the night," upon which 2 Peter 3:8 is based, served the same purpose. This was typological interpretation at work, with roots in Jewish interpretive methodology, bringing a second biblical text into play with the primary one like a catalyst to an idle chemical mixture to yield greater meaning. We will see other biblical texts unlocked in similar ways in connection with world-week belief as we continue. We have visited the Epistle of Barnabas first not because it is much discussed in creation debates,[19] but simply because his is the pioneering Christian presentation of six day/six millennium historical typology.[20]

CREATION AS WORLD-WEEK IN THE SECOND-CENTURY APOLOGISTS

We turn next to a trio of famous second-century apologists: Justin Martyr (100–ca. 165), Irenaeus of Lyons (d. 202), and Tertullian (ca. 160–ca. 220).[21] We could think of these men as representing the next generation or two of Christian thinking about this correspondence between creation and history. They each played a significant role in the development of Christian theology of creation more generally. First, they sought to establish a clear role for Christ in creation, seeking to prove that Christ was God's indispensable agent of creation, rather than an object of God's creation. Second, moving from Justin to Tertullian we see signs of the development

---

2018), 255–56; Charles E. Hill, *Regnum Caelorum: Patterns of Millennial Thought in Early Christianity*, 2nd ed. (Grand Rapids: Eerdmans, 2001), 77.

19. See James R. Mook, "The Church Fathers on Genesis, the Flood, and the Age of the Earth," in *Coming to Grips with Genesis: Biblical Authority and the Age of the Earth*, ed. Terry Mortenson and Thane H. Ury (Green Forest, AR: Master Books, 2008), 41; Davis A. Young and Ralph Stearley, *The Bible, Rocks and Time: Geological Evidence for the Age of the Earth* (Downers Grove, IL: InterVarsity Press, 2008), 34–35.

20. Monique Alexandre, *Le commencement du livre Genèse I–V: La version grecque de la Septente et sa réception*, Christianisme Antique 3 (Paris: Beauchesne, 1988), 98–99.

21. A fourth second-century figure sometimes grouped with them, Theophilus of Antioch, warrants separate mention below for his balancing of literal and allegorical interpretations.

of an *ex nihilo* (out of nothing) creation doctrine; Justin is content to view creation as performed on preexisting, featureless matter, while Tertullian clearly renounces this possibility.[22] Third, the writings of these three figures shared the purpose of Christian self-definition in distinction from Judaism (especially Justin), various versions of Gnosticism, from the particular second-century threat of Marcion's teaching (Irenaeus and Tertullian) and from pagan religion and philosophy.[23]

But while biblical creation looms as quite important across large tracts of Irenaeus's *Against Heresies* and Tertullian's *Against Hermogenes* in particular, the time period that God's creative work occupied is not yet on the radar.[24] This concern will come later. We do, however, find in these apologists' writings, following earlier leads, further development in belief about the final millennium and the world-week (or cosmic week) scheme where history divides into periods corresponding to the days of creation.

The Millennium of Justin Martyr and Tertullian

One of the most famous and early church fathers living just a couple of generations after New Testament times, Justin lived in the dangerous days when Rome

22. E.g., Paul M. Blowers, *Drama of the Divine Economy: Creator and Creation in Early Christian Theology and Piety*, OECS (Oxford: Oxford University Press, 2012), 170–73; G. T. Armstrong, *Die Genesis in der alten Kirche: Die drei Kirchenväter, Justinus, Irenäus, Tertullian*, Beiträge zur Geschichte der Biblischen Hermeneutik 4 (Tübingen: Mohr, 1962), 102–5.

23. Andrew Louth, "The Six Days of Creation according to the Greek Fathers," in *Reading Genesis after Darwin*, ed. Stephen C. Barton and David Wilkinson (Oxford: Oxford University Press, 2009), 41–43; Peter C. Bouteneff, *Beginnings: Ancient Christian Readings of the Biblical Creation Narratives* (Grand Rapids: Baker Academic, 2008), 91–93. Multiple essays on the early church's task of self-definition as against these religious (and social) alternatives are found, for example, in Margaret M. Mitchell, Frances M. Young, and K. Scott Bowie, eds., *Origins to Constantine*, vol. 1 of *The Cambridge History of Christianity* (Cambridge: Cambridge University Press, 2006); Susan Ashbrook Harvey and David G. Hunter, eds., *The Oxford Handbook of Early Christian Studies* (Oxford: Oxford University Press, 2008).

24. See Anders-Christian Jacobsen, "The Importance of Genesis 1–3 in the Theology of Irenaeus," *ZAC* 8.2 (2004): 299–316; Thomas Holsinger-Friesen, *Irenaeus and Genesis: A Study of Competition in Early Christian Hermeneutics*, Journal of Theological Interpretation Supplements 1 (Winona Lake, IN: Eisenbrauns, 2009); Armstrong, *Die Genesis in der alten Kirche*, esp. 62–73, 102–11.

was becoming aware of the existence of Christians as a group distinct from Judaism and was prepared to test their conformity to imperial values by requiring a gesture of worship to the emperor.[25] Justin's refusal to do so would bring about his death in around 165 CE during the co-regency of Marcus Aurelius and Lucius Verus. Justin converted to Christianity following a long quest for truth that exposed him to a range of philosophies.[26] Rather than renouncing all philosophical learning, he vetted and retained those elements of his education that proved consistent with his Christian faith.[27]

Justin's *Dialogue with Trypho* is addressed nominally to a non-Christian Jewish conversation partner and explores many of the issues affecting the self-definition of Christianity vis-à-vis Judaism. Justin alludes to the dramatic defeat of the last great Jewish revolt against Rome, the Bar Kokhba rebellion (132–135 CE), and the subsequent barring of all Jews from Jerusalem, while nations who believe the gospel of Jesus are summoned to assemble there.[28] As chapter 80 opens, Trypho feels driven to ask Justin, "Do you really believe that this place Jerusalem shall be rebuilt, and do you actually expect that you Christians will one day congregate there to live joyfully with Christ?" Justin replies affirmatively (80.2), admitting, however, "that there are many pure and pious Christians who do not share our opinion," showing that a literal future millennial kingdom presided over in person by Christ is not universally held in the church of the day. Moreover, gnostic sects were naturally opposed to such a teaching, holding the material world to be inherently contaminated (80.3, cf. 35.5–6), as were "nominal Christians" who wished to deny a physical resurrection (80.4). Justin concludes this chapter by extending the orthodox high ground he claims: "Whereas I, and all other wholeheartedly orthodox Christians, feel certain that there will be a resurrection of the flesh, fol-

---

25. Daniel N. Schowalter, "Churches in Context: The Jesus Movement in the Roman World," in *The Oxford History of the Biblical World*, ed. Michael D. Coogan (Oxford: Oxford University Press, 2001), 518, 547–49.

26. See, e.g., *ODCC*, "Justin Martyr, St. (*c.* 100–*c.* 165)," 770.

27. Allert, *Early Christian Readings*, 67–68.

28. *Dial.* 16.2 and 24.3, respectively. Unless otherwise noted, translation of Justin Martyr taken from Michael Slusser, ed., *Dialogue with Trypho*, trans. Thomas B. Falls and Thomas P. Halton, Selections from the Fathers of the Church 3 (Washington, DC: Catholic University of America Press, 2003), 27, 39. See also Oskar Skarsaune, "The Development of Scriptural Interpretation in the Second and Third Centuries—Except Clement and Origen," *HB/OT* 1.1:403.

lowed by *a thousand years in the rebuilt, embellished, and enlarged city of Jerusalem*, as was announced by the prophets Ezekiel, Isaiah and the others" (80.5).[29]

Next, in *Dialogue with Trypho* 81, Justin undergirds this millenarian position utilizing the entirety of Isaiah 65:17–25 from "there shall be a new heaven and a new earth" to the wolf lying down with the lamb, which he understands as describing millennial conditions (*Dial.* 81.1–2). As a Greek writer, Justin naturally quotes the Greek OT, the Septuagint. Now the Hebrew (or Masoretic) text tradition supports our English Bible versions, where Isaiah 65:22 reads along the lines of the NIV, "For as the days of a tree, so will be the days of my people," rhetorically indicating the enjoyment of full lifespans uninterrupted by premature death. But the Septuagint version of the same text includes an extra term, yielding, "For as the days of *the tree of life*," changing a general figure of speech into a direct allusion to the Eden narrative of Genesis. Justin latches on to this (81.3): "Now, by the words, *For as the days of the tree [of life]* . . . we understand that a period of one thousand years is indicated in symbolic language."[30]

Jean Daniélou brings out the logic here: Justin and his circle regard "the messianic reign as a return to Paradise," so that "it was natural that in it the length of life should be the same as Adam's ought to have been."[31] This helps explain how the divine threat is fulfilled that Adam will die "in the day" he eats the fruit (Gen. 2:17), since he dies within a thousand-year time span.[32] And as we saw with Barnabas, "The day of the Lord is as a thousand years" (Ps. 90:4; 2 Pet. 3:8). Finally, Justin adds fresh testimony (*Dial.* 81.4): "Moreover, a man among us named John, one of Christ's apostles, received a revelation and foretold that the followers of Christ would dwell in Jerusalem *for a thousand years*, and that afterwards the universal and, in short, *everlasting resurrection and judgment* would take place."

29. Charles Hill calls this statement "enthusiastically chiliastic." See Hill, *Regnum Caelorum*, 24.

30. The editors have bracketed the words "of life" as additional compared to the Hebrew OT, but Justin's Greek gives no indication of any distinction. For the Greek text of the *Dialogue*, see Miroslav Marcovich, ed., *Apologiae pro Christianis. Dialogus cum Tryphone*, Patristische Texte und Studien (Berlin: de Gruyter, 2005), 210.

31. Daniélou, *Jewish Christianity*, 392–93; Daniélou, "La typologie millénariste," 8–9.

32. The Hebrew expression rendered "in the day," *bayôm*, is best translated "when," since it often does not denote a precise day.

We recognize this as Revelation 20:4–6, in a letter destined for NT canonical status but not yet widely received at this point.[33]

So, Justin's millennial passage here represents the convergence of several lines of scriptural evidence for a concrete, earthly, millennial reign of Christ.[34] Still absent is the idea of six historical periods corresponding to six creation days that was seen in Barnabas. It is an error on Hugh Ross's part to assume that Justin's millennial teaching extends explicitly to the other days of creation, as Duncan and Hall gleefully retorted.[35] At this point in the mid-second century, these two ideas—a firm this-worldly millennium and redemptive history periodized according to the creation week—have yet to coalesce, but their natural compatibility is already clear.[36] Retention of such a millennium by the early Latin father Tertullian is clear in this passage from his polemic work *Against Marcion*:

> But we do confess that a kingdom is promised to us upon the earth, although before heaven, only in another state of existence; inasmuch as it will be after the resurrection for a thousand years in the divinely-built city of Jerusalem, "let down from heaven" . . . This both Ezekiel had knowledge of and the Apostle John beheld. . . . We say that this city has been provided by God for receiving the saints on their resurrection, . . . After its thousand years are over . . . there will ensue the destruction of the world and the conflagration of all things at the judgment: we shall then be changed in a moment into the substance of angels, even by the investiture of an incorruptible nature, and so be removed to that kingdom in heaven. (*Marc.* 3.24.3–6)[37]

33. Bernard McGinn, "Turning Points in Early Christian Apocalypse Exegesis," in *Apocalyptic Thought in Early Christianity*, ed. Robert J. Daly (Grand Rapids: Baker Academic, 2009), 86.

34. Daniélou, *Jewish Christianity*, 393. Justin's realistic, literal millennium has Jewish precedent in the book of Jubilees (4:29–30; 23:27) and Christian roots as early as Papias (c. 60–130), the bishop of Hierapolis in Asia Minor. Holmes, *Apostolic Fathers*, 581; Daniélou, "La typologie millénariste," 5, 7, 9, 16; Daniélou, *Jewish Christianity*, 380–84, 391–93; Luneau, *Âges du monde*, 82–83; Tabor, "Millennialism," 262.

35. Ross, *Creation and Time*, 17–18; Ross, *Matter of Days*, 43; Hagopian, *Genesis Debate*, 69, 99.

36. Luneau, *Âges du monde*, 83–85, 93; Daniélou, *Jewish Christianity*, 378–85.

37. Translation from *ANF* 3:342–43. The critical edition is René Braun, ed., *Contre*

Irenaeus's World-Week

Irenaeus of Lyons (or Lugdunum, a provincial capital in Roman Gaul) is widely reckoned to be the most significant Christian theologian of the second century. Known to have traveled to Rome in 178 CE to meet Bishop Eleutherus, he is supposed to have lived until about 200.[38] Irenaeus was one of the most influential theological pioneers of the early church and articulated a theology of redemptive history that placed creation and redemption into a grand symmetry labeled "recapitulation" in English discussion. The burgeoning stock of books and articles concerning Irenaeus's teaching on creation demonstrates both his theological status and the importance of creation in his scheme.[39]

Irenaeus's greatest surviving written work, *Against Heresies*, occupied primarily in refuting gnostic beliefs, attracts our attention for its historical typology of the creation week. The important role of both millennialism and world-week typology in his theological schema means that his name often appears in our modern creation discussions. Irenaeus's chief motivations in grounding this entire antiheretical work on near-constant exegesis of Genesis 1–3 are theological; he seeks to craft a biblical "anthropology, soteriology and eschatology" to pit against equivalent gnostic doctrines.[40] Thus his primary texts from this part of the Bible are Genesis 1:26–27 and 2:7, the two most relevant texts for the formation of a biblical view of humanity.[41] Moreover, Irenaeus periodically mentions Genesis 1 because of the strong interest of many gnostic teachers in this seminal biblical origins text. Blowers explains that Irenaeus's task was to portray the true, inherent power of the redemptive story in a way that would trump the mythical visions of Gnosticism.[42]

Marcion, 5 vols., SC 365, 368, 399, 456, 483 (Paris: Cerf, 1990–2004), 3:204–7. See also Daniélou, *Jewish Christianity*, 389–90.

38. U. Hamm, "Irenaeus of Lyons," *DECL*, 301.

39. Recent books in English include Holsinger-Friesen, *Irenaeus and Genesis*; Stephen O. Presley, *The Intertextual Reception of Genesis 1–3 in Irenaeus of Lyons*, BAC 8 (Leiden: Brill, 2015); Matthew Steenberg, *Irenaeus on Creation: The Cosmic Christ and the Saga of Redemption*, VCSup 91 (Leiden: Brill, 2008). Irenaeus is also a central figure in the highly relevant eschatological study of Hill, *Regnum Caelorum*.

40. Jacobsen, "Importance of Genesis 1–3," 314; Presley, *Genesis 1–3 in Irenaeus*, 25–26, 39–40.

41. Thus each warrants its own chapter in the discussion in Holsinger-Friesen, *Irenaeus and Genesis*, 104, 145; Jacobsen, "Importance of Genesis 1–3," 304–6.

42. Blowers, *Drama of the Divine Economy*, 82–85.

Two separate ideas already introduced, belief in a physical and temporal millennial kingdom on the one side and the typological analogy between the six days of creation and a six-thousand-year present age on the other, appear jointly in Irenaeus's *Against Heresies* without being properly integrated. First, Justin's position that Adam died on the very day he ate the fruit (Gen. 2:17) if "a day of the Lord is as a thousand years" reappears as one of two alternative explanations of that verse in *Against Heresies* 5.23.2. According to Irenaeus, if Adam died on the same day of the week that he ate the fruit (i.e., on a Friday), then appropriately Christ died on the same day of the week, the day before the Sabbath, to remedy the effects of that first sin. Thus far Irenaeus sounds like a reader of Justin Martyr, but a little noncommittal on the millennial idea.[43] He sounds much more committed in 5.33.2–4 as he relates traditions, understood to come from the apostle John himself via Papias, of incredible peace and fruitfulness in nature to be expected in the "seventh day" or world-sabbath of the millennial kingdom.[44] For instance, every grain of wheat upon planting would yield ten thousand new ears, and each ear another ten thousand wheat grains. It must be pretty good wheat, Irenaeus comments as he closes the section, if its chaff is of sufficient quality to feed lions (Isa. 65:25)! This is the earthly and literal millennium already noted by Justin and by Irenaeus's younger contemporary, Tertullian.

But in *Against Heresies* 5.28.3 comes a clause often cited by our modern debaters:

The world will come to an end in as many millennia as the days in which it was made. And therefore the scripture of Genesis says, "And heaven and earth and all their adornment were finished. God finished on the sixth day all his works that he made, and he rested on the seventh day from all his works that he made" (2:1–2). This is an account of past events as they took place and a prophecy of the future. For if "a day of the Lord is like a thousand years" (2 Pet. 3:8), and if the creation was finished in six days, it is clear that the end of things will be the 6,000th year.[45]

43. U. Hamm, "Irenaeus of Lyons," 302.

44. See also *Haer.* 5.30.4.

45. The translation is from Robert M. Grant, *Irenaeus of Lyons*, Early Christian Fathers (London: Routledge, 1997), 176. Examples of modern citations include Mook, "Church Fathers," 41–42; Young and Stearley, *Bible, Rocks and Time*, 35; Jonathan D. Sarfati, *Refuting Compromise* (Green Forest, AR: Master Books, 2004), 116.

Now this is clearly the world-week typology based on Genesis 1, first seen in Barnabas in the corpus of Christian writings.[46] However, there is as of yet no assignment of specific figures, redemptive events, or historical developments to the individual "days" of world history. Irenaeus's scheme is still essentially binary: there is ordinary present time, lasting six thousand years, followed by the ideal millennial Sabbath.[47] Yet the world-week and a material and earthly millennium come into close proximity within the same theological framework for the first time here. The seventh-day "rest" for creation and redeemed humanity is no longer simply the open-ended rest of eternity here, but a specific period of earthly history (not yet explicitly one thousand years)[48] in which the kingdom of Christ presides on earth.

Importantly, contrary to some older scholarship on Irenaeus's theology, Irenaeus's millennialism does not represent an awkward final addition to Irenaeus's scheme for redemptive history. His task of refuting Gnosticism and his entire theology of creation renewed and fulfilled in Christ really demand that this final kingdom include rather than avoid physical creation and present history. The temporality and tangibility of Christ's kingdom remains integral to the completeness of redemption and the value of physical creation in contrast to gnostic belief. The importance of the integration of this eschatology of physical creation redeemed into Irenaeus's grand theological proposal can hardly be overemphasized.[49]

Hiatus: The Nature of the Misunderstanding

There is more yet to tell of this story of a growing theology of history in the early church that looks for the connection between creation's intention, corruption through the fall, and final redemption, sometimes seen in terms of a physical, millennial kingdom, and sometimes in terms of a more immediate and spiritual return to an ideal state where the saints enjoy perfect communion with God. This theology matters! But at this juncture, let us recall our motivation for this inquiry:

46. Daniélou, "La typologie millénariste," 10.

47. Luneau, *Âges du monde*, 95; Schwarte, *Vorgeschichte*, 109, 116.

48. See especially Christopher R. Smith, "Chiliasm and Recapitulation in the Theology of Ireneus," *VC* 48.4 (1994): 315–16.

49. Steenberg, *Irenaeus on Creation*, 49–53; Smith, "Chiliasm and Recapitulation," 313–31; Hill, *Regnum Caelorum*, 254–59; Gerald Hiestand, "'And Behold It Was Very Good': St. Irenaeus' Doctrine of Creation," *Bulletin of Ecclesial Theology* 6.1 (2019): 15–24.

it is to highlight the common misunderstanding of this typological interpretation of the creation week and its Sabbath as a prophecy of the course of redemptive history. Discussing Justin's millennial interpretation in his *Dialogue with Trypho*, Forster and Marston say that Justin offers us "a kind of early 'age-day' theory," but this is misleading.[50] Not only did Justin not exemplify the six-day/six-thousand-year typology of Barnabas and Irenaeus, but upcoming figures who do are *not* offering a scheme for understanding the rise of our physical world or the life that inhabits it *before* human history. Instead, they offer a scheme for understanding the structure *of* human history understood as guided providentially by God and punctuated by identifiable biblical episodes, such as the call of Abraham or the rise of David. That is a major difference. It means that these patristic schemes bear only a superficial resemblance to day-age or periodic-day explanations of prehuman creation in connection with Genesis 1. In the meantime, however, let us see where this interpretive trend in the early church finally leads.

THE CONTRIBUTION OF EARLY CHRISTIAN BIBLICAL CHRONOLOGY

Pioneering Christian Chronologists

We cannot make sense of the world-week belief without mentioning early Christian chronological works, for the two would occasionally become enmeshed despite their largely discrete beginnings.[51] It is hard to tell whether world-week belief gave rise to chronologies that placed the birth of Christ on or near year 5500 of the world's existence, as Landes and Hughes think, or whether it was instead the mathematical exercise of toting up the generational numbers found in the Septuagint, the OT version universally read in the early church that yielded numbers in this vicinity.[52] The latter, mathematical approach seems to drive the outcomes of the earliest Christian chronological efforts.

50. Roger Forster and Paul Marston, *Reason, Science and Faith* (Crowborough: Monarch, 1999), 201.

51. Martin Wallraff, "The Beginnings of Christian Universal History. From Tatian to Julius Africanus," *ZAC* 14.3 (2011): 554. Wallraff emphasizes the independence of these ideas as the norm.

52. Richard Allen Landes, "Lest the Millennium Be Fulfilled: Apocalyptic Expectations and the Pattern of Western Chronography 100–800 CE," in *Use and Abuse of Eschatology in the Middle Ages*, ed. Werner Verbeke, Daniel Verhelst, and Andries Welken-

The earliest known calculation of the world's age from year zero to the writer's time, a goal that partly defines the genre "universal history," concludes the early work *To Autolycus* written by Theophilus of Antioch.[53] Writing retrospectively of the death of Roman emperor Marcus Aurelius, and thus not long after 180 CE (our only clue to his time of death),[54] Theophilus calculates that the world has existed 5,695 years from creation (i.e., since 5515 BCE).[55] Within a few decades of Theophilus, Clement of Alexandria (d. ca. 220 CE) offered a chronological scheme toward the end of book 1 of his titanic *Stromateis* that put the birth of Christ 5,592 years after creation.[56] There are no surviving Christian chronologies prior to Theophilus's, though Josephus's works (*Jewish War*, *Jewish Antiquities*, and *Against Apion*) are a probable source of much of his chronological information.[57] Despite the suspicions already mentioned, there is no real proof that world-week belief played any part in the chronological calculations either of Theophilus or of Clement.

Earliest Possible Contacts of Biblical Chronology with World-Week Typology and Millennialism

We are here compelled to tread carefully in historical terms. Two separate literary traditions, Christian biblical chronologies and world-week typology, were naturally compatible and eventually became acquainted. Belief in an earthly millen-

---

huysen (Leuven: Leuven University Press, 1988), 141–43. As Jeremy Hughes writes, "Early Christian interpretations of Biblical chronology were strongly influenced by the belief that the history of the world would last for six millennia corresponding to the six days of the world's creation, and that this would be followed by a seventh sabbatical millennium paralleling the day on which God rested from his creation." See Hughes, *Secrets of the Times: Myth and History in Biblical Chronology*, JSOTSup 66 (Sheffield: Sheffield Academic, 1990), 258.

53. See chapter 4 for more detail on Theophilus. See also Wallraff, "Christian Universal History," 545.

54. P. Pilhofer, "Theophilus of Antioch," *DECL*, 573.

55. *Autol.* 3.28. Translation by Robert M. Grant, *Ad Autolycum* (Oxford: Clarendon, 1970), 142–45. See also *ANF* 2:120.

56. John Ferguson, *Clement of Alexandria* (New York: Twayne, 1974), 117; Wallraff, "Christian Universal History," 547–49.

57. Hughes, *Secrets of the Times*, 245; Wallraff, "Christian Universal History," 553; Landes, "Apocalyptic Expectations," 144 n. 25.

nium, a third member of this delicate dance, was deliberately introduced into a world-week scheme by Irenaeus, since the earlier proposal in Barnabas 15 involved a transcendent, not earthly, millennium. But Irenaeus did not subdivide the six thousand years into epochs; his world-week scheme remained binary, divided into a six-thousand-year block covering present history and a final millennium.[58] Although a world-week version of biblical chronology seems inevitable, it had not yet arrived during this period. We will see Hippolytus and Julius Africanus taking the first tentative steps in that direction.

Hippolytus

Hippolytus of Rome (d. 235) was an influential presbyter in the Roman church scene around the final decade of the second century and left a range of significant writings, including a lost hexaemeron, although his relative antiquity and involvement in early christological controversies challenged the survival of many of his works.[59] Thankfully, we do possess his important commentary on Daniel that provides clear evidence of world-week belief that seems indebted to Irenaeus.[60] Hippolytus wrote his *Commentary on Daniel*, "the oldest surviving commentary on the Bible," during the outbreak of persecution against the church under Emperor Septimius Severus between 201 and 203.[61] Bardy is among those who see this persecution as a primary factor in forming the character of the commentary, while Schwarte is not sure it was widespread and comprehensive enough to warrant such consideration; he looks to the dubious apocalyptic movements of the times that saw bishops leading their flocks into the desert to await Christ's return.

---

58. Luneau, *Âges du monde*, 95 and compare the similar statement about Hippolytus on 211.

59. For his hexaemeron, see F. Robbins, *The Hexaemeral Literature: A Study of the Greek and Latin Commentaries in Genesis* (Chicago: University of Chicago Press, 1912), 37, 39. In general, see Skarsaune, "Development of Scriptural Interpretation," 434. For biographical introduction, see B. R. Suchla, "Hippolytus," *DECL*, 287.

60. David G. Dunbar, "The Delay of the Parousia in Hippolytus," *VC* 37.4 (1983): 313 and see quotation below.

61. B. R. Suchla, "Hippolytus," 288; Brian Daley, *The Hope of the Early Church: A Handbook of Patristic Eschatology* (Grand Rapids: Baker Academic, 2010), 39. See also G. Bardy's introduction in G. Bardy and M. Lefèvre, eds., *Commentaire sur Daniel*, SC 14 (Paris: Cerf, 1947), 17; Dunbar, "Parousia in Hippolytus," 315.

In any case there is general agreement that pastoral concerns are uppermost in Hippolytus's mind as he writes.[62]

In the passage most relevant to us, Hippolytus finds help for understanding the church's present historical situation in the vision of the four beasts in Daniel 7. It is much in the spirit of Daniel to frame present suffering within an orderly scheme that clarifies the ultimately good intentions of God for his people, and so Hippolytus inserts his world-week chronology into his exposition:

> For the first, embodied appearance [*parousia*] of our Lord, involving his birth in Bethlehem, took place before the eighth of January, on a Wednesday, in the forty-second year of Augustus' reign, and 5,500 years after Adam. . . . Six thousand years have to be completed in order for the Sabbath to arrive, the rest, the holy day, in which God "rested from all his works. . . ." The Sabbath is a type and symbol of the coming kingdom of the saints, when they will reign with Christ after he appears from heaven, as John explains in [the book of] Revelation. A day of the Lord is "like a thousand years." Since, therefore, God made everything in six days, the six thousand years have to be completed. For they are not yet completed, as John says, "The five have fallen, one is," that is, the sixth; "the other has not yet come," by which 'other' he means the seventh, in which the rest will come. (*Comm. Dan.* 4.23.3–6)[63]

This is the first clear combination of a world-week scheme based on a typological understanding of the creation week with an AM 5500 advent chronology.[64] It appears later than Irenaeus's *Against Heresies* by more than a decade and, given the influence of the latter work, presumably in full awareness of it, as the similarity of the core statements of the two men suggests.[65] Thus Hippolytus

62. Bardy and Lefèvre, *Commentaire sur Daniel*, 15–18. See also Schwarte, *Vorgeschichte*, 140–43. The dispute over whether we are dealing with a single Hippolytus or instead have the works of two different figures combined under this name is too involved to treat here. See Suchla, "Hippolytus," 287; McGinn, "Turning Points," 90.

63. My translation of the Greek text of Bardy and LeFèvre, *Commentaire sur Daniel*, 306–9. See also *ANF* 5:179, under "On Daniel."

64. AM = *anno mundi*, "year of the world" (i.e., a date from creation).

65. U. Hamm, "Irenaeus of Lyons," 301–2. Luneau cites debate over whether Hippolytus really follows in Irenaeus's footsteps (*Âges du monde*, 212). Compare Irenaeus's statement in *Haer.* 5.28.3 with Hippolytus's *Comm. Dan.* 4.23.6. For the former, see the

lays the groundwork, at least, for the integration of world-week typology with biblical chronology.

Hippolytus also buttresses his world-week concept with fresh biblical arguments. The quoted section features his application of the words of Revelation 17:10 about five past kings, one present ruler, and one yet to come to these periods of world history. If that already seems tenuous, immediately afterward he finds the 5,500-year period preceding Christ's advent suggested in the fact that the three dimensions of the ark of the covenant design in Exodus 25:10 add up to 5.5 cubits. Furthermore, if a day equals a thousand years, we may take the reference to the sixth hour of the day in which Jesus is judged before Pilate (John 19:14) as another subtle allusion to the location of Jesus's redemptive career at the 5,500-year mark in history.[66]

Whether or not we find Hippolytus's scriptural arguments convincing, we should observe the process by which he steadily reinforces this interpretation of history with biblical prooftexts. This use of Genesis 1 and other biblical texts (including early use of NT ones) does not preclude those texts having their own literal meaning.[67] Hippolytus was certainly no ultra-conservative apocalyptic prophet here. His calculation of a five-hundred-year gap between the advent of Christ and the end of the age at this point in history, just after 200 CE, amounts not to apocalyptic frenzy but a considerable defusing of the apocalyptic expectations inflamed by the persecution occurring at the time.[68] This eschatological tactic is Hippolytus's gift to chronologist Julius Africanus.[69] In turn Hippolytus produced

translation by Adelin Rousseau, Louis Doutreleau, and Charles A. Mercier, eds., *Contre les hérésies*, 10 vols., SC 100, 152–53, 210–11, 263–64, 293–94 (Paris: Cerf, 1965–1982), 2:383. For the latter text, see Bardy and LeFèvre, *Commentaire sur Daniel*, 306, 308.

66. *Comm. Dan.* 4.24 (Bardy and LeFèvre); Daniélou, *Jewish Christianity*, 402; Luneau, *Âges du monde*, 210–11.

67. Hippolytus is satisfactorily summarized in Mook, "Church Fathers," 42–43; Young and Stearley, *Bible, Rocks and Time*, 39. Allert's criticism of Mook here for not detailing Hippolytus's allegorical/typological arguments for his position seems overcritical on this occasion; Allert, *Early Christian Readings*, 89–91.

68. Daniélou, "La typologie millénariste," 13; Landes, "Apocalyptic Expectations," 147; Schwarte, *Vorgeschichte*, 140–45; Luneau, *Âges du monde*, 211; and especially Dunbar, "Parousia in Hippolytus," 315–16.

69. Martin Wallraff and William Adler, eds., *Iulius Africanus Chronographiae: The Extant Fragments* (Berlin: de Gruyter, 2007), xxviii; G. Broszio, "Julius Africanus," *DECL*, 354.

his own chronological work, the *Chronicon*, in about 235 CE, which probably draws on Africanus's *Chronography* and manifests subtle world-week shades.[70]

Julius Africanus

The world-week idea does not manifest itself in surviving fragments of the highest profile early Christian systematic chronology, the *Chronography* of Julius Africanus (ca. 160–240). Written around 220 CE, this chronology became the standard reference for those following Africanus, including his contemporary Hippolytus of Rome (ca. 170–235) and later the church historian Eusebius of Caesarea (265–340).[71] Julius Africanus was a respected scholar who studied at Origen's catechetical school in Alexandria and later served the Severan dynasty in Rome.[72] Africanus credits Jewish tradition (rather than Irenaeus) with having "handed down a period of 5500 years up to the advent of the Word of salvation," while his own calculations lead him to a date very close to Theophilus's: "From Adam to the death of Peleg there are, then, 3000 years. Up to the *Parousia* of the Lord and his resurrection there are 5531 years."[73] The latter figure, apparently applying to Christ's death and resurrection, results in a date for Christ's parousia or first advent around AM 5500. Observing alongside this figure the calculation of a three-thousand-year period from Adam to Peleg, one might easily conclude that Africanus has a world-week scheme in mind.

Unfortunately, Africanus's work only survives in fragments quoted within other works, and it can be quite unclear which words in those later sources (such as the chronological work of the Byzantine historian George Syncellus) belong to the original source. Africanus's original wording might have been retouched to strengthen its world-week associations.[74] The more overt world-week language that follows in fragment 94 might belong to the reporting text, Pseudo-

70. Wallraff, "Christian Universal History," 553; Schwarte, *Vorgeschichte*, 154–55.
71. Broszio, "Julius Africanus," 354.
72. Broszio, "Julius Africanus," 354.
73. *Chron.* fragments 15 and 94 (trans. Wallraff and Adler, 24–25, 290–91). See also *ANF* 6:131, 138. The *ANF* reading lacks reference to the resurrection, although for what reason why I have not discovered, leaving the chronology less clear. It is present not only in the Wallraff and Adler edition but also in Julius Africanus, "Chronica," in *Reliquiae Sacrae*, ed. M. J. Routh, 5 vols. (Oxford: E Typographeo Academico, 1846), 2:306.
74. Wallraff and Adler, *Chronographiae*, 291 n. 1; Routh, "Chronica," 2:493–95.

Eustathius's *Hexaemeron*, rather than to Africanus.[75] The fact that Africanus's chronology was *compatible* with a world-week scheme leads Daniélou to conclude overconfidently, "He makes the seven millennia the basis of his universal chronicle," while others are more cautious.[76] However, that Africanus locates Peleg neatly at a three-thousand-year halfway mark suggests some contact between these two initially independent Christian approaches to biblical history.[77] Yet Africanus clearly has reasons for producing chronological scholarship that do not ostensibly rely on such a rational *pro forma*. Perhaps he sought to confirm Hippolytus's advent date by means of an independent line of evidence. But such hypotheses about motives must remain very tentative.

Christian Chronologies That Avoided World-Week Associations

Eusebius of Caesarea, whose famous *Ecclesiastical History* pioneered the genre of church history, makes clear by his comments about Papias and other early believers in an earthly millennium to come that he does not share their view.[78] Eusebius followed Origen's teachings and worldview and believed that the biblical millennium, or the seventh day of creation, spiritually understood, referred to an elevated spiritual existence that could be enjoyed by the believer in the present.[79] Origen had already written against belief in a physical millennium in his *Commentary on John*.[80] Moreover, we recall that Barnabas's world-week scheme, rightly understood, did not encourage this belief either, belonging as it does to the same Alexandrian milieu as Clement and Origen.[81] Written in the early 300s, Eusebius's chronology of history concentrates on Abraham rather than Adam as its point of departure and, in proposing that Christ arrived in AM 5228, Eusebius

---

75. Wallraff and Adler, *Chronographiae*, 290–91.

76. Daniélou, *Jewish Christianity*, 402; Schwarte, *Vorgeschichte*, 150–52. Wallraff and Adler, *Chronographiae*, xxi, xxiii, are a little more cautious than Daniélou, but more confident than I am.

77. Wallraff, "Christian Universal History," 551.

78. *Hist. eccl.* 3.28.1–6; 3.39.11–12; 7.24.1–5. For a translation, see Jeremy M. Schott, *The History of the Church: A New Translation* (Berkeley: University of California Press, 2019), 151–52, 164, 366. Also in *NPNF²* 1:160–61, 172, 308.

79. Tabor, "Millennialism," 262; Daniélou, "La typologie millénariste," 1.

80. Daniélou, "La typologie millénariste," 11.

81. Daniélou, *Jewish Christianity*, 396–99.

was effectively offering a history that postponed the end of any sixth age of the world that existed in the minds of believers for quite some centuries.[82]

Eusebius's alternative to Julius Africanus's chronology would eventually become enshrined in Western tradition when Jerome translated it into Latin and updated it to reach his own time. Jerome's adjusted date for Christ's advent in world years, AM 5199, would enshrine what was really Eusebius's scheme in Western Christian tradition for centuries to come. Jerome, too, was an anti-millennialist and was probably pleased to support a scheme that did not support apocalyptic fervor, though his translation work on what became known as the Vulgate, which would reveal the shorter OT chronology of the Hebrew Masoretic tradition, undercut his own chronological scheme, which was based on the longer time scale derived from Septuagint dates. It would await (the Venerable) Bede's new chronological proposal in *On Times* (703 CE) for this contradiction to be resolved, as Bede offered a much lower chronology with Christ's advent in AM 3952, the third and last major Christian *anno mundi* historical chronology to appear.[83]

82. Peter Darby, *Bede and the End of Time* (London: Routledge, 2016), 28–29, 32; Landes, "Apocalyptic Expectations," 149–50.

83. Darby, *Bede and the End of Time*, 29–32; Landes, "Apocalyptic Expectations," 151.

Chapter Three

THE WORLD-WEEK SCHEME HISTORICIZED
IN AUGUSTINE

The third century of the present era was a period of newfound strength and importance for the Christian church. However, the years between the end of the Severan dynasty (193–235) and the beginning of the rule of Diocletian (284–305) constituted a period that was "among the most disruptive ever experienced by the Roman empire."[1] As the empire struggled for survival, some in power who concluded that Rome's true integrity and continued strength depended on a restoration of its spiritual identity through the worship of the traditional gods initiated Christian persecution. If it was not conformity to the worship of the gods that was being enforced, it was often deference to the cult of the emperor, and both amounted to compulsion to identify as sincere citizens of the Empire.[2] The Christian insistence that the world had room for only one Lord made Christianity the most difficult religion for Roman civilization to assimilate. It is not surprising that this century opened with the persecution that saw Origen's father Leonidus martyred, featured the persecution of Decius (249–251) at its centerpoint, and ended with the Great Persecution of Diocletian beginning in 303.[3]

1. John Drinkwater, "Maximinus to Diocletian and the 'Crisis,'" *CAH* 12:28.
2. Drinkwater, "Maximinus," 12:61.
3. *ODCC*, "Origen (*c.* 185–*c.* 254)," 1008; Garth Fowden, "Late Polytheism: Public Religion," *CAH* 12:559; Graeme Clarke, "Third-Century Christianity," *CAH* 12:625–35, 647–57.

Forerunners to Augustine

It is characteristic of this historical setting that many of the figures mentioned in our modern debates were both leaders of the church, with pastoral responsibility to go with their scholarly publications, and politically involved with the Empire. Passing over the martyred bishop Cyprian of Carthage (d. 258), who makes isolated mention of the world-week scheme in his *Exhortation to Martyrdom*, we meet two other bishops reputed to have died in the Diocletian persecution, along with a Christian scholar who, like Eusebius, lived to narrate it afterward.[4] This third-century trio is commonly mentioned in modern "recruiting drives" thanks to their world-week comments, sometimes giving the misleading impression that they represent a day-age viewpoint (e.g., "Lactantius, . . . Victorinus of Pettau, and Methodius of Olympus all concurred with Justin Martyr's and Irenaeus's view of the creation days as thousand-year epochs").[5]

Victorinus

Victorinus of Pettau (d. ca. 304) presided as bishop in Roman Pannonia (now Slovenia) and died in the Diocletian persecution. He is described as "the first exegete to write in Latin."[6] Schwarte also credits him as the "founder of the Lat[in] reception of Origen," so we are not too surprised to find that his *De fabrica mundi* (*On the Creation of the World*) approaches the days of the creation week from a numerological point of view in an Alexandrian mode, such as we saw in Philo. While the treatment of creation here, which begins only with the fourth day, does retain a place for the production of the physical elements of the world, Mook's categorization of Victorinus as a literalist about the creation week ought to be treated cautiously, given what he as an Origenist probably had in mind when speaking of the days (i.e., a logical rather than chronological distinction), even though God's

---

4. *ANF* 5:503; *ODCC*, "Cyprian, St. (d. 258), Bp. of Carthage," 367. A. Wikenhauser, "Weltwoche und Tausendjähriges Reich," *Theologische Quartalschrift* 127 (1947): 401.

5. See the response of Hugh Ross and Gleason Archer in "Part Three: The Framework View," in *The Genesis Debate: Three Views on the Days of Creation*, ed. David Hagopian (Mission Viejo, CA: Crux, 2001), 205.

6. Jack P. Lewis, "The Days of Creation: An Historical Survey of Interpretation," *JETS* 32 (1989): 445; *ODCC*, "Victorinus, St. (d. *c.* 304)," 1438; K.-H. Schwarte, "Victorinus of Pettau," *DECL*, 596.

creation of light defines the prototypical diurnal day.[7] We saw already in Philo that an apparently physical creation week (after day one) might still be described as atemporal. We lack any explicit statement from Victorinus that would settle the question either way here. Yet the symbolic significance of the numbers involved clearly dominates Victorinus's interest, and it is in the context of exploring the meaningfulness of the number seven that he explains that Jesus demotes the importance of the Sabbaths of present practice (Matt. 12:3–8) in order that

> that true and just Sabbath should be observed in the seventh millenary of years. Wherefore to those seven days the Lord attributed to each a thousand years; for thus went the warning: "In Thine eyes, O Lord, a thousand years are as one day." Therefore in the eyes of the Lord each thousand of years is ordained, for I find that the Lord's eyes are seven. Wherefore, as I have narrated, that true Sabbath will be in the seventh millenary of years, when Christ with His elect shall reign.[8]

This is akin to Cyprian's passing world-week reference and appears in a similar numerological context. We see neither the emphasis on the physical presence of the millennial kingdom nor any allocation of redemptive-historical events into separate millennial stages in what is, after all, quite a brief reference. Significantly, Schwarte's close study suggests that Victorinus's mediation of the world-week scheme by virtue of the potency of the number seven opens up the possibility of a historical scheme whose seven periods do not have to be of equal length, making possible the kind of scheme shortly to be offered by Lactantius.[9]

7. Translation from Robert Ernest Wallis, "A Fragment on the Creation of the World," in *The Writings of Quintus Sept. Flor. Tertullianus: Vol. 3, with the Extant Works of Victorianus and Commodianus*, Ante-Nicene Christian Library 18 (Edinburgh: T&T Clark, 1870), 341; James R. Mook, "The Church Fathers on Genesis, the Flood, and the Age of the Earth," in *Coming to Grips with Genesis: Biblical Authority and the Age of the Earth*, ed. Terry Mortenson and Thane H. Ury (Green Forest, AR: Master Books, 2008), 29; Mark Van Bebber and Paul S. Taylor, *Creation and Time: A Report on the Progressive Creationist Book by Hugh Ross* (Mesa, AZ: Eden Productions, 1994), 94.

8. Translation from Wallis, "Creation of the World," 342. See also Victorinus of Petau, "De fabrica mundi," in *Victorini Episcopi Petavionensis opera*, ed. Johannes Haussleiter, CSEL 49 (Vienna: Tempsky, 1916), 6.

9. K.-H. Schwarte, *Die Vorgeschichte der augustinischen Weltalterlehre* (Bonn: Habelt, 1966), 220–26, esp. 226. For a careful analysis of his teaching about the millennium, see

Methodius

The world-week reference of Methodius of Olympus (d. ca. 311), a bishop in Lycia in modern Turkey, appears in his lone writing that has survived in its entirety: the *Symposium*, or *Banquet of the Ten Virgins*. Methodius is a unique writer who is difficult to characterize theologically, and he attempts in the *Symposium* a unique literary undertaking in patristic literature: an ambitious meditation on Christian virtues—especially self-control and above all chastity or virginity—while using (or, as Alexander Bril says, deliberately abusing) the literary model of Plato's *Symposium*.[10] Since the fictional setting is a formal dialogue between ten virgin women who at times disagree or correct one another, we take Mejzner's point up front about the inherent risk of taking any one speaker's words automatically as representing Methodius's own attitude: "One must exercise extreme caution when attributing to Methodius all the thoughts and concepts presented."[11] We should check subsequent passages for refutation or qualification of the passages that most concern us.

Like his late third-century colleague Victorinus, Methodius had to take a position on the current and powerful hermeneutic of Origen. Methodius is known for being strongly influenced by that hermeneutic and yet resisting some of Origen's doctrinal stances, particularly by defending bodily resurrection.[12] Though happy to do so elsewhere, Methodius shows reluctance to take an allegorical approach

Bernard McGinn, "Turning Points in Early Christian Apocalypse Exegesis," in *Apocalyptic Thought in Early Christianity*, ed. Robert J. Daly (Grand Rapids: Baker Academic, 2009), 101–4.

10. Translation of Methodius of Olympus from Herbert Musurillo, trans., *The Symposium: A Treatise on Chastity*, ACW 27 (Westminster, MD: Newman, 1958); see also Musurillo's comment at 3, 16–17, 21–22, 37; Alexander Bril, "Plato and the Sympotic Form in the Symposium of St Methodius of Olympus," *ZAC* 9.2 (2005): 280–81, 293, 299–302; McGinn, "Turning Points," 98–99.

11. Mirosław Mejzner, "Methodius: Millenarist or Anti-Millenarist," in *Methodius of Olympus. State of the Art and New Perspectives*, ed. Katharina Bracht (Berlin: de Gruyter, 2017), 65. E.g., after the first speech praising virginity, speech 2 features Theophila defending the spiritual value of marriage and procreation.

12. Peter C. Bouteneff, *Beginnings: Ancient Christian Readings of the Biblical Creation Narratives* (Grand Rapids: Baker Academic, 2008), 121; Brian Daley, *The Hope of the Early Church: A Handbook of Patristic Eschatology* (Grand Rapids: Baker Academic, 2010), 62; Ernesto Buonaiuti, "The Ethics and Eschatology of Methodius of Olympus," *HTR* 14.3 (1921): 260–62.

to the Genesis creation narratives in discourse three, entitled "Thaleia": "For it is a precarious procedure to disregard utterly the actual meaning of the text as written, particularly in the book of Genesis which contains God's immutable decrees on the constitution of the universe."[13] Methodius evidently regarded Origen's timeless creation as taking liberties with the text, though he happily allegorizes Genesis 2:23–24 in the preceding chapter, following Paul's lead in Ephesians 5:31–32. Yet he speaks very literally of the antediluvians as "neighbors to the great six days of creation" who could actually recall "that God fashioned His creation in six days," notwithstanding the difficulties of such literal recollection (*Symp.* 7:5 [Musurillo]).

Methodius's *Symposium* sees speaker number two, Theophila, advocate a unique kind of *creatio continua*, emphasizing the present aspect of creation: "God, like a painter, is at this very time working in the world" (cf. John 5:17). Rivers still flow to the sea and the dry land keeps producing vegetation in obedience to the third day's command; therefore marriage is still justified, since "at present man must cooperate in the forming of the image of God, while the world exists and is still being formed." But once creation is complete, so will be human reproduction (i.e., in the world's Sabbath), thus exalting the ideal of virginity.[14] This creation teaching comes out more fully in discourse 9, "Tusiane," where Methodius sees the true significance of the Feast of Tabernacles, celebrated in the middle of the seventh month of the Jewish calendar, as its typological representation of the resurrection of believers, which is realized at the culmination of the world-week in its seventh day:

> In the Seventh Millennium we shall celebrate the great Feast of the true Tabernacle in that new creation where there shall be no pain, when all the fruits of the earth will have been harvested, and men will no longer beget or be begotten, and God will rest from the work of His creation.
>
> For God made heaven and earth and completed the entire universe in six days: *And on the seventh day He rested from the works which He had done....* Thus under a figure we are bidden to celebrate a feast in honor of the Lord *in the seventh month* ... when this world shall come to an end at the time of

---

13. *Symp.* 3.2 (Musurillo, 60). For critical editions see H. Musurillo and V.-H. Debidour, eds., *Le Banquet*, SC 95 (Paris: Cerf, 1963); Saint Methodius, "Symposion," in *Methodius*, ed. G. Nathanael Bonwetsch, GCS 27 (Leipzig: Hinrichs, 1917), 1–142. Also *ANF* 6:317.

14. *Symp.* 2.1 (Musurillo); *ANF* 6:313.

the Seventh Millennium, when God will really have finished the world and will rejoice in us.

For even now He is still creating by His omnipotent will and inscrutable power; the earth still yields its fruit, the waters still gather together into their receptacles, light is still being divided from the darkness, and the number of men is still growing through creation, the sun still rises to rule over the day and the moon over the night, and four-footed creatures and beasts and creeping things are still being brought forth by the earth, as are winged things and fish by the watery element. But when the days shall be accomplished and God shall cease to work in this creation of His in that Seventh Month, the great day of the resurrection, then will our Feast of Tabernacles be celebrated to the Lord. (*Sym.* 9.1 [Musurillo])[15]

This treatment of the creation process of Genesis 1 as occupying the present span of world history rather than preceding it is unique for the era to my knowledge.[16] It blends type and antitype within the world-week scheme, so that the six days of creation are equivalent to present history, although Methodius does not refer to the six thousand years directly.

Nevertheless, he certainly singles out the seventh day here in Tusiane's discourse, and Methodius's later statements (in *Symp.* 9.5) on the model of Israelite shelters in the Sinai prior to reaching the promised land (and particularly commemoration of this through the Feast of Tabernacles) show that he has a definite temporal millennium spent on earth in view, though it is less "materialistic" than in some other patristic descriptions and is the subject of hot debate in scholarship.[17] The millennium or seventh day is the part of world-week teaching that interests Methodius almost exclusively, and retaining the millennium in a carefully

15. Italics original, indicating biblical quotations. See also *ANF* 6:344.

16. Musurillo, *Symposium*, 133 n. 9. Mejzner, "Methodius," 71; J. Daniélou, *The Theology of Jewish Christianity*, trans. John A. Baker (London: Darton, Longman and Todd, 1964), 395.

17. Musurillo, *Symposium*, 20–22, 36, 139–40; G. Nathanael Bonwetsch, *Die Theologie des Methodius von Olympus*, Abhandlungen der Königlichen Gesellschaft der Wissenschaften zu Göttingen. Philologisch-Historische Klasse. Neue Folge 7 (Berlin: Weidmannsche, 1903), 124–25; Buonaiuti, "Methodius of Olympus," 263; Daniélou, *Jewish Christianity*, 382, 394–95, 400; Charles E. Hill, *Regnum Caelorum: Patterns of Millennial Thought in Early Christianity*, 2nd ed. (Grand Rapids: Eerdmans, 2001), 39–41, 68; Mc-

nuanced form allows him to defend the theological value of physical creation and physical embodiment by protecting its redemption rather than idealizing escape from the body and all that is physical. Note that although the eighth speaker, Thecla, receives the highest final praise for her role in the dialogue, Tusiane's millennial explanation is permitted to stand unqualified by anything that follows. By the way, Methodius's insertion of the seventh-month Feast of Tabernacles into the already-established typological relationship between the seventh day of creation and the millennium of Revelation 20 is a distinctly new contribution to the world-week interpretation.

This brings us to one curious passage preserved from a lost work of Methodius by the ninth-century Byzantine politician and academic Photius. The work is *De creatis* (*On the Created Things*), and the passage inspires the curious comment by Forster and Marston that according to Methodius, "There are six [days of creation] before Adam, and six from Adam until the present (the seventh day being the day of judgement), making thirteen millennia in all," which they conclude is "far from what we today would call a 'literal' interpretation."[18] This would make Methodius the only church father clearly to include a substantial prehuman history in a creation scheme. But although this text does refer to "thirteen days . . . from the creation of the world,"[19] we face a challenge to identify the speaker. Photius is quoting Methodius, who, in turn, is expressing opinions that may or may not be his own through "the saint," one of the speakers in a dialogue.[20] And "the saint" is quoting Origen disapprovingly while Origen, finally, is quoting "some" with whom he disagrees concerning creation.

So, there are four links in the chain of quotation, aside from the fact that we lack the dialogue framework so critical to making sense of the content of the original work![21] We are poorly placed to tell whose opinion occupies the body of

---

Ginn, "Turning Points," 98–99; Mejzner, "Methodius," 72–74, 78 who references substantial Italian-language literature.

18. Roger Forster and Paul Marston, *Reason, Science and Faith* (Crowborough: Monarch, 1999), 205.

19. See *ANF* 6:381; Saint Methodius, "De creatis," in *Methodius*, ed. G. Nathanael Bonwetsch, GCS 27 (Leipzig: Hinrichs, 1917), 491–500.

20. "The saint" is last identified in the preceding fragment 8 in *ANF* 6:381 and fragment 10 in Bonwetsch, 498.

21. L. G. Patterson, *Methodius of Olympus: Divine Sovereignty, Human Freedom, and Life in Christ* (Washington, DC: Catholic University Press of America, 1997), 200–203.

this fragment, though it seems to spoof world-week belief with a creation week made of thousand-year epochs fused to the standard world-week with the seventh day of creation acting as the weld. Young and Stearley, along with Forster and Marston, take it as Methodius's own opinion, but this misses the "chain of quotation" situation just mentioned.[22] This might not be Methodius or even Origen speaking for themselves. The final comment of the fragment, where Methodius is apparently speaking through "the saint," might represent Methodius's own sympathies: "These are the things that Origen earnestly says, but notice the game he is playing."[23] If this is reliable, Methodius might be taking Origen to task for frivolously mocking world-week belief along with a creation in time. In that case, the thirteen-millennia idea was never a serious proposal.

Lactantius

Many of the thinkers mentioned so far have been leaders in the church, and as we move toward the fourth century, church leaders tend more and more to be politically involved. Lactantius (ca. 240–ca. 320) was an educator familiar to more than one Roman imperial administration. Like Augustine a century later, Lactantius's training was in rhetoric. He was summoned by the eastern Roman emperor Diocletian to teach in the eastern capital Nicomedia some years prior to the emperor's initiation of the Great Persecution of Christians in 303 CE. Losing his prestigious position but preserving his life in the turbulent years following, he was restored to his former glory when recruited by the newly victorious Constantine to tutor his eldest son Crispus at the imperial residence in Trier about 315.[24]

Lactantius's epic seven-volume *Divine Institutes* was designed to fill the lack of a systematic explanation of Christian belief for educated non-Christians.[25] Written during his time away from the halls of power, it incorporates a thor-

---

22. Davis A. Young and Ralph Stearley, *The Bible, Rocks and Time: Geological Evidence for the Age of the Earth* (Downers Grove, IL: InterVarsity Press, 2008), 36; Forster and Marston, *Reason, Science and Faith*, 205.

23. My translation of the Greek at Bonwetsch, 500.

24. For these biographical details see Averil Cameron, "The Reign of Constantine," *CAH* 12:90; *ODCC*, "Lactantius (*c.*240–*c.*320)," 791–92; K.-H. Schwarte, "Lactantius," *DECL*, 366; C. Peter Williams, "Lactantius (c.240–c.320)," *NIDCC*, 575.

25. Auguste Luneau, *L'histoire du salut chez les pères de l'église: La doctrine des âges du monde* (Paris: Editions Beauchesne, 1964), 229.

ough Christian philosophy of history as would Augustine's *City of God* later. Importantly, Lactantius includes a strong statement of the world-week historical principle (*Inst.* 7.14) accompanied by a physical, earthly millennium (7.24–26), though whether he actually frames his presentation of history using the world-week schema must be clarified. In a work that describes the original Adamic era and the coming millennium in "age of gold" terms reflecting classical influences such as Hesiod and Ovid,[26] Lactantius offers the fullest and clearest surviving statement of world-week belief since Irenaeus's *Against Heresies*, in response to other traditional claims for an age of up to 470,000 years for the (human) world. Having repeated what is by this time a trope in Christian writing, "that the six thousandth year has not yet been concluded," Lactantius continues:

> God completed the world . . . in the space of six days . . . and the seventh day, on which He rested from His labors, He sanctified. . . . Therefore, since all the works of God were completed in six days, the world must continue in its present state through six ages, that is, six thousand years. For the great day of God is limited by a thousand-year cycle as the prophet indicates, who says "In your sight, Lord, a thousand years are like one day." And as God worked during those six days to make such things, so true worship of Him and true belief in Him must toil for these six thousand years, when evil prevails and dominates. Then since God, having finished His works, rested the seventh day and blessed it, at the end of the six thousandth year all evil must be abolished from the earth, and righteousness reign for a thousand years; and there must be tranquility and rest from the toil which the world now has long endured. . . .
>
> For just as, once He had finished making everything suitable for human use, God finally made the human himself on the sixth day and brought him into this world as into a by now well-prepared home, so now on the great sixth day the true human is being shaped by the word of God, that is, a holy people is formed for righteousness by the doctrine and precepts of God. And just as then a mortal and imperfect human was shaped from earth, that he might live

---

26. Luneau, *Âges du monde*, 234; Garry W. Trompf, *The Idea of Historical Recurrence in Western Thought: From Antiquity to the Reformation* (Berkeley: University of California Press, 1979), 210; Jonathan Z. Smith, "Ages of the World," in *The Encyclopedia of Religion*, ed. Mircea Eliade (New York: Macmillan, 1987), 1:130; Jean Daniélou, "La typologie millénariste de la semaine dans le Christianisme primitif," *VC* 2.1 (January): 15.

a thousand years in this world, so now from this earthly age a perfect human is being shaped, so that brought to life by God he might rule this same world for a thousand years. (*Inst.* 7.14)[27]

Lactantius's millennium, described a few chapters later, proves to be of the very literal, earthly kind, a millennium of untold fruitfulness, prosperity, and prolific reproduction in the families of the righteous (*Inst.* 7.24). This was a view of the millennium that most Greek-speaking church fathers, such as Origen, Eusebius, and Gregory of Nazianzus, found offensively materialistic for a people seeking a holy detachment from worldly things.[28] We recall that Methodius acknowledged a real millennium but was quite reserved about describing its conditions in any detail, while the seventh day in world-week schemes derived from Barnabas 15 was purely a symbol of a spiritual plane of existence.[29] So Lactantius is an enthusiastic millennialist, "the highpoint of chiliasm in the West," expecting the end of the age and the inauguration of the reign of Christ in no more than two hundred years.[30] The basis for this expectation of Lactantius's was not merely the world-week concept articulated most clearly hitherto by Irenaeus.[31] He also drew on the biblical-chronological work of Theophilus of Antioch and, given his two-hundred-year statement, also the conclusion of Hippolytus and Julius Africanus

27. My translation. Compare Mary Francis McDonald, trans., *The Divine Institutes. Books I-VII*, FC 49 (Washington, DC: Catholic University of America Press, 1955), 510–11; *ANF* 7:211–12. The Latin passage is identical in Lactantius, *Divinae institutiones et Epitome divinarum institutionum*, ed. Samuel Brandt, CSEL 19 (Vienna: Tempsky, 1890), 629–30; Lactantius, *Divinarum institutionum libri septem*, ed. Eberhard Heck and Antonie Wlosok, Bibliotheca Scriptorum Graecorum et Romanorum Teubneriana (Berlin: de Gruyter, 2011), 4:695–96.

28. Daniélou, *Jewish Christianity*, 394; Daniélou, "La typologie millénariste," 15–16; Luneau, *Âges du monde*, 109–11, 153.

29. Luneau, *Âges du monde*, 108, 110, 162.

30. *Inst.* 7.25. See Hill, *Regnum Caelorum*, 41–42 (source of quote); Daley, *Hope of the Early Church*, 67; Bernard McGinn, "Augustine's Attack on Apocalypticism," *Nova et Vetera* 16.3 (2018): 781–82.

31. For Irenaeus the typological fulfilment of human formation on the sixth day of creation is the incarnation of Christ; for Lactantius the "perfect human" formed on the sixth cosmic day is now the Christian church. The best on this point is Schwarte, *Vorgeschichte*, 165, 167. See also Daniélou, "La typologie millénariste," 16; Trompf, *Historical Recurrence*, 209.

that put the incarnation of Christ at about AM 5500, creating an expectation of the onset of the millennium at about 500 CE.

Lactantius's *Divine Institutes* demonstrates the potential for a world-week schema to become attached to history writing.[32] Yet so far, the six millennia pertaining to present history had not been subdivided into their individual millennia. Nor had biblical chronologies been made to conform to a millennium-by-millennium, world-week framework, aside from dating the incarnation to AM 5500. Lactantius came close, featuring both impulses within the same work, impressing Nicholson as a noteworthy new venture in this direction: "Lactantius' system is unique in combining Theophilus' dates with the pattern of the cosmic week."[33] However, Trompf rightly observes that although Lactantius explains the world-week system, "he neither documented it from biblical history, as [would] Augustine, nor interwove it carefully into his more classically-derived model." In fact, "the millennial stages could not be readily justified by known historical facts."[34] Schwarte emphasizes that Lactantius develops no historical periodization *within* the world-week scheme and simply juxtaposes the two approaches to history without integrating them, because in fact they were mutually exclusive![35] The rigidity of a chain of millennia did not allow for the messy details of actual history. We will see that a new approach would be needed if the schema of seven ages was to accommodate the reality of history.

Lactantius's exposure in modern creation debates relates either to (1) the clarity and fullness of his world-week explanation; (2) his firm defense of creation out of

32. From a historical point of view, Lactantius acted alongside Eusebius as the church historian of the Diocletian persecution and the Constantinian supremacy. On Lactantius as historian, see Alan K. Bowman, "Diocletian and the First Tetrarchy," *CAH* 12:85; Cameron, "The Reign of Constantine," 12:91; and Clark, "Third-Century Christianity," 12:650, 663.

33. Oliver P. Nicholson, "The Source of the Dates in Lactantius' 'Divine Institutes,'" *Journal of Theological Studies* 36.2 (1985): 308; Luneau, *Âges du monde*, 234; Daniélou, "La typologie millénariste," 15.

34. Trompf, *Historical Recurrence*, 211, 209 n. 132.

35. Schwarte, *Vorgeschichte*, 167, 226, 269. Nicholson's more optimistic reading of the integration involves the point that the world-week scheme seems to draw significant dates within biblical history toward the edges or centers of millennia arranged from an AM 5500 creation, leading Lactantius to place the exodus from Egypt at about 2100 BCE and emphasize the construction of Solomon's temple around 1000 BCE, among other dates: Nicholson, "Dates in Lactantius," 307–10.

nothing; or (3) his general literalism in *Divine Institutes* 2.9–11.[36] The key point to remember, as Sarfati rightly points out, is that we are dealing with typology, a both/and relationship between the creation week and periodized redemptive history.[37] Hugh Ross's early misunderstanding on this point in *Creation and Time* and *The Genesis Debate*[38] was corrected in his later statements where he acknowledges this typological relationship, such as his chastened description in *A Matter of Days*: "Lactantius was the earliest church father on record to infer from Genesis, based on the thousand-year-day view, that the creation was less than six thousand years old."[39] Meanwhile Lactantius's "young world" belief (*Inst.* 7.14) goes much earlier and wider in the church than Lactantius. The more *avant-garde* Origen himself confesses that according to Genesis, "the world is not yet ten thousand years old but is much less than this."[40] Young and Stearley rightly admit Lactantius as another example of widespread young-earth belief,[41] and James Mook can rightly claim Lactantius as advocate of a detailed premillennial eschatology alongside it.[42]

Whether Lactantius's view is suitable for imitation today is a different matter. For example, his overt flat-earth belief, though seemingly a viable option at the time, is defended with a smugness that belies the tenuousness of his evidence and the looming obsolescence of his view, which became a minority view even in the Middle Ages.[43] Yet Duncan and Hall are able to deny his support to their opponents too: "Lactantius may be mocked as a young-earth creationist [or] as a literalist . . . but he assuredly did *not* explicitly endorse 'six consecutive thousand-

36. Stephen O. Presley, "Interpretations of Genesis 1–2 among the Ante-Nicene Fathers," in *Since the Beginning: Interpreting Genesis 1 and 2 through the Ages*, ed. Kyle R. Greenwood (Grand Rapids: Baker Academic, 2018), 104 n. 29, 108.

37. Jonathan D. Sarfati, *Refuting Compromise* (Green Forest, AR: Master Books, 2004), 114; Young and Stearley, *Bible, Rocks and Time*, 34.

38. Hugh Ross, *Creation and Time* (Colorado Springs, CO: Navpress, 1994), 19; Hagopian, *Genesis Debate*, 69, 205. The latter location repeats the statement from *Creation and Time* verbatim.

39. Hugh Ross, *A Matter of Days: Resolving a Creation Controversy* (Colorado Springs, CO: Navpress, 2004), 45.

40. *Cels.* 1:19 (Chadwick), see also *ANF* 4:404; PG 11:693–94.

41. Young and Stearley, *Bible, Rocks and Time*, 33, 35.

42. Mook, "Church Fathers," 43–45.

43. See *Inst.* 3.24 (*ANF* 7:94–95); F. Robbins, *The Hexaemeral Literature: A Study of the Greek and Latin Commentaries in Genesis* (Chicago: University of Chicago Press, 1912), 61; Jeffrey B. Russell, *Inventing the Flat Earth* (New York: Praeger, 1991), 23–24.

year periods for the Genesis creation days," that is, he did not present anything like a day-age concordist scheme.[44] Judged within his own intellectual context, Lactantius's *Divine Institutes* emerges as an ambitious, if uneven, *tour de force*, a grand apologetic theology of history cast in good Ciceronian Latin and designed to appeal, in a period of transition from the last great persecution of the church by Diocletian into the Constantinian *détente*, to the cultured despisers of Christianity.

Hilary of Poitiers

Hilary's (ca. 315–367) fondness for world-week interpretation is not mentioned often by creation debaters, perhaps because it does not come embedded in a Genesis commentary or accessibly in English translation. But as Young and Stearley notice, Hilary continues the pattern of combining a world-week schema of history with the AM 5500 model established by Julius Africanus and introduces fresh typological support for it from the New Testament. The OT types appear in a work devoted to uncovering such types, the *Tractatus Mysteriorum*, discovered only in 1887.[45] Hilary reads the six days of marching around Jericho and its fall on the seventh (Joshua 6)[46] as a type of the cycling of six millennia of world history before the "trumpet call" brings it all to an end with the preservation, like Rahab and her family, of the righteous alone.[47] A little earlier, the collection of manna by the Israelites in the desert (Exod. 16:22) supplies a moral application: the collection of manna in double quantity the day before the Sabbath signifies the earnest preparation needed by their saints in the present age to be ready for the coming Sabbath of final rest (*Myst.* 1.41).

Now that the church's NT canon was becoming settled and its authority more certain than in Irenaeus's time, Hilary could in his *Commentary on Matthew* find a world-week typology in the fact that Christ revealed himself in transfigured glory

---

44. Hagopian, *Genesis Debate*, 100.
45. M. Durst, "Hilary of Poitiers," *DECL*, 284.
46. See the section on ANE literature in chapter 1.
47. *Myst.* 2.10. Text from Hilary of Poitiers, *Opera. Part IV: Tractatus Mysteriorum, etc.*, ed. Alfred Feder, CSEL 65 (Vienna: Tempsky, 1916), 35. On all of Hilary's works relating to the world-week theme, see Wikenhauser, "Weltwoche und Tausendjähriges Reich," 404–6.

to select disciples "after six days" in Matthew 17:1–2.[48] Hilary's typology of the Parable of the Workers in the Vineyard (Matt. 20:1–16) is fuller and represents his distinctive new contribution to this genre.[49] He understands the twelve hours into which the work day is divided as a typology of sacred history made up of covenantal eras.[50] The workers recruited in the early morning, understood as the first hour of the day, are those people involved in the covenant with Noah; the third hour relates to the Abrahamic covenant; the sixth, the Mosaic; and the ninth, the Davidic covenant. Finally, in the eleventh hour, the special recruit is the Son of God incarnate. This suits taking Jesus's advent at the traditional 5500 mark in a six-thousand-year world history and makes this an essentially a nonmil-lenniallist scheme, since it leaves no room for a seventh unit of historical time.[51] It also establishes a real correlation between the leading figures and covenants of redemptive history and the world-week scheme, whereas the six millennia of earlier versions of the world-week were only nominal and without distinguished content or subdivision into distinct periods.

So, while Hilary's seventh day was (normally) a reference to the glorified, eternal future, the preceding six millennia begin to correlate with redemptive history in its phases. Notice, however, that Hilary's scheme is not as historical as it might look. While a Davidic covenant at the ninth hour would place a Davidic regime one thousand years in the past tolerably well, going on a millennium for every two "hours," working backward at five hundred years per hour would yield a Mosaic covenant at about 2500 BCE (the sixth hour), an Abrahamic covenant at 4000 BCE (the third hour), and place Noah at 5000 BCE! This is clearly not what Hilary is claiming. Luneau and Schwarte rightly note that Hilary is thinking symbolically rather than historically.[52] However, Hilary was among the known influences on Augustine's thought and so this world-week scheme represents a potential precedent for Augustine's periodizing efforts.[53]

48. PL 9:1013–14; Luneau, *Âges du monde*, 235.

49. Schwarte, *Vorgeschichte*, 151 nn. 119 and 227–28.

50. PL 9:1029–30.

51. Luneau, *Âges du monde*, 237–39; Wikenhauser, "Weltwoche und Tausendjähriges Reich," 405; Schwarte, *Vorgeschichte*, 226–32, 270–71; Daley, *Hope of the Early Church*, 94–96.

52. Luneau, *Âges du monde*, 238; Schwarte, *Vorgeschichte*, 230–32.

53. Richard A. Norris Jr., "Augustine and the Close of the Ancient Period of Interpretation," *AHBI* 1:386; Luneau, *Âges du monde*, 245.

Tyconius

One further link needs to be put in place before we reach Augustine's world-week, and that is another of the major influences on Augustine's hermeneutical procedure, the thought of the North African Tyconius (ca. 330–390). Though only mentioned among our debaters by Young and Stearley once again,[54] Tyconius, in his *Book of Rules*, "set down the first Christian hermeneutics, that is, the first unified systematic theory of scriptural exegesis in an independent work."[55]

In the fifth book of his *Book of Rules*, Tyconius articulates the place of world-week belief in the context of Christian typology while considering the role of numbers in biblical interpretation. He states as a principle, apparently hardly needing supporting argument, "The world's age is six days, i.e., six thousand years." He adds that the sixth "world day" (i.e., the current millennium) is known to Christians as "the thousand years of the first resurrection," so named not only because Christ rose from the dead, but also because it is the era in "which the church rose from the dead" in a spiritual sense.[56] He returns to world-week interpretation more directly a little later, explaining that Jesus is able to say, "My Father is working even until now" (John 5:17) because it is only the sixth day of the world and the Father does not rest until the seventh day arrives. When he says here that "the first seven days represent 7000 years," that would appear to allow for an earthly millennium, though Tyconius's general pattern is to avoid an apocalyptic brand of eschatology and seek meanings related to present spiritual realities in the Bible.[57] Tyconius also gives consideration to the distance between key biblical figures in numbers of generations (e.g., finding seven between Adam and Enoch, ten between Adam and Noah, and ten between Noah and Abraham). Both in world-week belief and in this attention to measuring out redemptive his-

54. Young and Stearley, *Bible, Rocks and Time*, 36.

55. Karla Pollmann, "Tyconius," *DECL*, 587.

56. William S. Babcock, ed., *Tyconius: The Book of Rules* (Atlanta: Scholars Press, 1989), 90–91.

57. Babcock, *Book of Rules*, 100–101; Pamela Bright, *The Book of Rules of Tyconius: Its Purpose and Inner Logic* (Notre Dame: University of Notre Dame Press, 1988), 9–11; Richard Allen Landes, "Lest the Millennium Be Fulfilled: Apocalyptic Expectations and the Pattern of Western Chronography 100–800 CE," in *Use and Abuse of Eschatology in the Middle Ages*, ed. Werner Verbeke, Daniel Verhelst, and Andries Welkenhuysen (Leuven: Leuven University Press, 1988), 156.

tory in spans of generations, Tyconius, whose *Book of Rules* is well known to have influenced Augustine and inspired his hermeneutical work *On Christian Doctrine*, may well have helped also to inspire Augustine's unique world-week scheme.[58]

Augustine's Synthesis of the World-Week Scheme

Augustine (354–430), as in so many other areas of Christian theology, bequeathed to the Middle Ages "the summit and the synthesis of patristic [thought]" on the six ages of the world.[59] Augustine "combined the diverse currents of ancient culture and the Christian tradition into an impressive synthesis and . . . created the foundations for further theological development in the West."[60] His world-week scheme echoed down through the ages, dominating medieval historical discussions and influencing thinkers as late as James Ussher in the sixteenth century (for whom creation was exactly four millennia before Christ's birth)[61] and the founder of modern, seven-phase dispensational theology, John Nelson Darby, in the nineteenth.[62] Moreover, by filling out this basic framework with an ongoing argument about the nature of the spiritual commonwealth of God's people in the world in his famous *City of God*, he left to Western Christianity the first "global philosophy of history."[63] "Theology of history" would be just as accurate.[64] Augustine set the paradigm for this creation-based typology going forward. Its impact and the need to distinguish it from a *prehistoric* day-age interpretation is why Augustine's "six ages of the world" scheme requires our attention here.

58. Landes, "Apocalyptic Expectations," 155–57; Gerald Bray, *Biblical Interpretation: Past and Present* (Downers Grove, IL: InterVarsity Press, 1996), 107–10; Paula Fredriksen, "Apocalypse and Redemption in Early Christianity: From John of Patmos to Augustine of Hippo," *VC* 45.2 (1991): 151, 157; Norris, "Augustine," 399–403.

59. Luneau, *Âges du monde*, 284. My translation.

60. *HBI* 2:76.

61. James Ussher, *The Annals of the Old Testament: From the Beginning of the World.* (London: Tyler, 1658); see the unpaginated "Epistle to the Reader."

62. Glenn W. Shuck, "Christian Dispensationalism," in *The Oxford Handbook of Millennialism*, ed. Catherine Wessinger (Oxford: Oxford University Press, 2016), 517–19.

63. Charles Kannengiesser, "Augustine of Hippo," *HHMBI*, 25.

64. O. Rousseau, "La typologie augustinienne de l'Hexaemeron et la théologie du temps," *Maison-Dieu* 65 (1961): 94–95.

The World-Week in Augustine's Writings

The correspondence between the six days of creation and six periods of redemptive history fired Augustine's imagination. It features in a wide range of his writings spanning his ministry career. His fullest explanation of this model of history appears in his first Genesis commentary, *On Genesis against the Manicheans* 1.23.35–41. This work was written within a year or so of Augustine's return to Africa in late 388 CE, in a period when much of Augustine's energy was devoted to resisting the dualistic, quasi-gnostic Manichean sect of which he had himself been a listener or low-level adherent through most of the 370s and early 380s.[65] The Manicheans enjoyed mocking those parts of the Old Testament where God was described in anthropomorphic terms; for example, God's "rest" in Genesis 2:1–3 after the work of creation inspired their mockery, as they highlighted a contradiction with John 5:17 where Jesus says, "My Father is always at his work to this very day."[66] Augustine's full presentation of the world-week interpretation of Genesis 1:1–2:3 here formed part of his strategy of turning aside their hyperliteral interpretation.[67] Yet even after this motivation ceased to matter, Augustine would remain both intrigued with the early chapters of Genesis and committed to enunciating a theology of history. Leaving *On Genesis against the Manicheans* for a moment, we turn first to perhaps Augustine's much later *City of God* for a handy, compact expression of the world-week scheme itself.

The world-week concept of history exercises a subtle structuring role through the second major part of Augustine's *City of God*. Books 1–10 contain Augustine's polemic against pagan idolatry or polytheism and its philosophical advocates. Books 11–22 follow with a historical overview of the twin careers of the "city of God," the community of God's people persisting through history as aliens in the world, and its counterpart, the human city. Books 11–14 tell of their origins, treating creation closely in the process, books 15–18 tell of their historical progress,

---

65. W. Geerlings, "Augustine," *DECL*, 62.

66. *Gen. Man.* 1.22.33. Augustine, *On Genesis*, ed. John E. Rotelle, trans. Edmund Hill, The Works of Saint Augustine I/13 (Hyde Park, NY: New City, 2002), 60–61. See also Augustine, *The Literal Meaning of Genesis*, ed. John Hammond Taylor, ACW 41 (New York: Newman, 1982), 1:1–2.

67. Augustine, *On Genesis: Two Books on Genesis against the Manichees and On the Literal Interpretation of Genesis; An Unfinished Book*, trans. Roland J. Teske, FC 84 (Washington, DC: Catholic University of America Press, 1991), 19–24.

and books 19–22 describe their eternal destinies, equating to heaven and hell, respectively.[68] Occasionally Augustine will indicate where his treatment is up to in relation to the six ages of the world, indicating that it is subtly helping to shape his presentation.[69] Then in the final lines of his conclusion in *City of God* 22.30 we read a final summary of his world-week scheme. Speaking of the blissful eternal destiny of the citizens of the city of God, Augustine promises, "Restored by him and perfected by greater grace we shall rest for ever, and see always that he is God, and we shall be filled with him when he himself shall be all in all," before continuing:

> The very number of ages also, like the number of days in Creation, if reckoned according to the divisions of time which seem to be indicated in the Scriptures, throws more light on that Sabbath rest, for it comes out as the seventh age. The first age, corresponding to the first day, is from Adam to the flood, the second, from then on till Abraham. These are equal, not in years, but in the number of generations, for each age is found to have ten. From this point, as the evangelist Matthew marks off the periods, three ages follow, reaching to the coming of Christ, each of which is completed in fourteen generations: one from Abraham to David, the second from then till the deportation to Babylon, the third from then until the birth of Christ in the flesh. Thus there are five ages in all. The sixth is now in progress, and is not to be measured by any fixed number of generations, for the Scripture says: "It is not for you to know the times which the Father has fixed by his own power." After this age God will rest, as on the seventh day, when he will cause the seventh day, that is, us, to rest in God himself. ... But this seventh will be our Sabbath, and its end will not be an evening, but the Lord's Day, an eighth eternal day ... the eternal rest of both spirit and body. There we shall be still and see, shall see and love, shall love and praise. Behold what shall be in the end without end! For what else is our end, except to reach the kingdom which has no end? (*Civ.* 22.30)[70]

68. See the summary of the book's structure in Augustine, *City of God. Volume III: Books 8–11*, trans. David S. Wiesen, LCL (Cambridge: Harvard University Press, 1968), ix–x.

69. E.g., *Civ.* 16.43. See Augustine, *City of God. Volume V: Books 16–18.35*, trans. Eva M. Samford and William M. Green, LCL (Cambridge: Harvard University Press, 1965), 200–205.

70. Translation from Augustine, *City of God. Volume VII: Books 21–22*, trans. William M. Green, LCL (Cambridge: Harvard University Press, 1972), 380–85.

This passage is sufficiently detailed to introduce us to the way in which Augustine combined a number of hitherto separate ideas about divinely structured world-time into the best-known and most influential "ages of the world" scheme to emerge from the patristic period. To a world-week typology that was already double-layered, comparing the seven days of creation and redemptive history, Augustine will add further correspondences! Let's try to distinguish traditional from innovative elements in Augustine's presentation of the creation week as a prophetic anticipation of redemptive history.

A World-Week without an Earthly Millennium?

Augustine toned down his presentation of a future, earthly millennial kingdom over time. He admits earlier in the *City of God* 20.7 that he had once himself believed in a literal, terrestrial reign of the resurrected saints with the returned Christ prior to the eternal future. This is most clearly seen in Sermon 259, "For the Octave of Easter," in the context of explanation of the world-week with the millennium as the seventh age, as well as in a few of his other writings that separate from the world-week idea.[71] But Augustine felt put-off by the kind of indulgent and materialistic image some Christians had of the kind of lifestyle the saints would enjoy during that period. Explaining his more mature position later in *City of God* 20.7, Augustine considered that the thousand years of Revelation 20:1–6 might signify either the victorious life of God's people in all ages, or else the remaining part of the present age, the sixth "day" of the world.[72]

71. For detail on Sermon 259 and as indicative of the literature on this topic, including which of Augustine's other works are or are not millenarian, see Mary Sarah Muldowney, ed., *Sermons on the Liturgical Seasons*, FC 38 (Washington, DC: Catholic University of America Press, 2010), 368–70; Georges Folliet, "La typologie du sabbat chez saint Augustin. Son interprétation millénariste entre 389 et 400," *Revue d'Etudes Augustiniennes et Patristiques* 2.3–4 (1956): 388; Schwarte, *Vorgeschichte*, 278–79; Martine Dulaey, "A quelle date Augustin a-t-il pris ses distances vis-à-vis du millénarisme?," *Revue des Études Augustiniennes* 46 (2000): 36–39; McGinn, "Augustine's Attack on Apocalypticism," 784; Gerald Bonner, "Augustine and Millenarianism," in *The Making of Orthodoxy: Essays in Honour of Henry Chadwick* (Cambridge: Cambridge University Press, 1989), 237–38; Daley, *Hope of the Early Church*, 150.

72. *Civ.* 20.7. Augustine, *City of God. Volume VI: Books 18.36–20*, trans. William Chase Greene, LCL (Cambridge: Harvard University Press, 1960), 282–91. His admission of his past belief in a literal millennium appears on 284–85.

This leaves the seventh day of the scheme not as a thousand-year kingdom but as a symbol of a spiritual mode of life, which was how Hilary of Poitiers and, before him, Origen thought of the seventh day.[73] Yet his seven-day scheme (e.g., at the end of *City of God*) still leaves the door open for an earthly seventh "day," while the eighth day (*ogdoad*) to follow, associated with Christ's resurrection, offers the better symbol for the eternal future.[74] Several scholars have noted that Augustine the (eventual) amillennialist, by providing such a time scheme, inadvertently cemented the foundation for numerous future schemes that featured a prominent, future earthly millennium.[75] Yet as we see in the passage quoted above, and in keeping with his pastoral responsibilities, Augustine actively discouraged date-setting concerning the end of the present age and the return of Christ, a recurring temptation for the church, thus damping down Christian anticipations of an earthly millennium.[76]

A World-Week without a Six-Thousand-Year Timer or Equal-Length Days

One way that Augustine takes the apocalyptic heat out of the world-week model is that he denies that the sixth, present age is definable in years or even in a total number of generations. Carefully refuting any date-setting tendency, he denies that the world is destined to last six thousand years, dispensing with a tradition that had lasted since Barnabas and the watershed system proposed by Irenaeus. Very important to Augustine was the statement of Jesus to his apostles in Acts 1:7 (NIV), "It is not for you to know the times or dates the Father has set by his own authority," in his answer to their question whether the era of the kingdom of God had arrived. This is effectively the motto of Augustine's carefully worked-out letter to Hesychius (*Epistle* 199), wherein his skepticism about a six-thousand-year scheme, one that sounds as though it is built on the Parable of the Workers in the Vineyard (Matthew 20) already expounded in world-period terms in Hilary of Poitiers, is palpable.[77] He says there that the world of apostolic times was far younger than 5,500 years old; he probably has in mind a Eusebian chronology

73. Daniélou, *Jewish Christianity*, 400.
74. Luneau, *Âges du monde*, 325.
75. Landes, "Apocalyptic Expectations," 159.
76. Typical is Hill's acknowledgment of "the authoritative and enormously influential rejection of chiliasm by Augustine." Hill, *Regnum Caelorum*, 3.
77. *Ep.* 199.17–18. For a translation see Augustine, *Saint Augustine. Letters. Vol. IV*

where there are about 5,200 world-years prior to Christ's first advent. Elsewhere, now thinking of a longer scheme that includes an earthly millennium, he objects that if we know that the world is destined to last precisely seven thousand years, then we have a better idea of the time of the end than the Son himself (Mark 13:32)! This would be "unspeakable presumption."[78]

In the same vein, question 58 out of what are known as his *Eighty-Three Different Questions* warns "that old age alone can be as long as all the other earlier ages," precisely in reference to the sixth age of the world.[79] Importantly, his Genesis-based ages of the world are not equal in length to each other. One of Augustine's original contributions to a Genesis-based world-week is to utilize the structure offered in the genealogy of Matthew 1:1–17, where fourteen generations separate Abraham from David, David from the Jewish exile to Babylon, and the exile from Christ's birth.[80] Then Augustine, on the basis of the genealogies in Genesis 5 and 11:10–26, finds that the first two ages are each measured off by ten generations, yielding five ages prior to Christ's first advent rather than four.[81] A certain symmetry remains, but the idea that because a thousand years is like a day to God each day of the creation week must correspond to a thousand-year period is absent.

A World-Week of Millennial Age-Days?

Some scholars have implied that Augustine abandoned the idea of six successive millennium-long ages corresponding to the six days or was exceptional in not taking that idea up.[82] Certainly, his ages are not one thousand years long, since they

---

(165–203), trans. Sister Wilfrid Parsons, FC 30 (New York: Fathers of the Church, 1955), 368–70. On Acts 1:7, see 199.1–4 (356–60).

78. *Enarrat. Ps.* 6.1. Translation from Augustine, *Psalms*, trans. Scholastica Hebgin and Felicitas Corrigan (London: Longmans, Green, 1960), 61–62.

79. *Div. quaest. LXXXIII* 58.2. Translation from Augustine, *Eighty-Three Different Questions*, trans. David Mosher, FC 70 (Washington, DC: Catholic University of America Press, 1977), 107.

80. Green, *City of God V*, x n. 1. Schwarte succeeds in showing a substantial precedent for this move in the *Quaestiones veteris et novi testamenti* penned by the elusive patristic figure Ambrosiaster in the time of Pope Damasus (366–384 CE): Schwarte, *Vorgeschichte*, 248, 254–56.

81. Genesis 5 lists ten generations including Adam and Noah at either end. Genesis 11:10–26 amounts to ten generations including Shem and Noah at either end.

82. R. A. Markus, *Saeculum: History and Society in the Theology of St. Augustine* (Cam-

are clearly inequal to each other and the sixth is of indefinite duration and might be as long as all the others combined. The surprise is that we cannot prove that *anyone* prior to Augustine developed a scheme of arranging history in six or seven individual millennia. McGinn's description manifests the misconception:

> Like Augustine and many other early Christians, Lactantius adhered to the "world week" schema, according to which the course of history, mirroring the Genesis creation account, would consist of six ages of a thousand years each, to be followed by the millennium of the reign of the returned Christ and the saints on earth, as predicted in Apocalypse [Revelation] 20.[83]

This is a great summary of a fully developed world-week idea, except that no patristic figure offers such an explicit scheme of six or seven millennia, one after the other, spanning redemptive history. Georges Folliet chided Daniélou precisely for indicating that it was "the concept of a total world history as composed of seven millennia, of which the latter corresponds to the reign of Christ" from which Augustine sought to distance himself.[84] Augustine could not do so because the precise concept did not exist, as Schwarte carefully establishes.[85] There are some apparent exceptions:

1. The early argument that if days are a millennium long, Adam indeed dies in the "day" he eats the fruit (e.g., Justin and Irenaeus).
2. Julius Africanus's placement of Peleg at the precise three-thousand-year point in his *Chronography*.
3. The 5,500-year incarnation in the same class of Septuagint-based biblical chronology, in Julius Africanus's *Chronography*, Hippolytus's *Chronicon* and subsequently, as if to neatly divide a sixth millennium.
4. Talk of a literal seventh millennium by those who thought of it as earthly.

Taken together, these factors seem conclusive. Yet realistic biblical chronologies and world-week typological schemata excluded each other like oil and water.

---

bridge: Cambridge University Press, 1970), 19–20; Trompf, *Historical Recurrence*, 209; Luneau, *Âges du monde*, 411.

83. McGinn, "Augustine's Attack on Apocalypticism," 781–82.
84. Folliet, "La typologie du sabbat," 387; Daniélou, "La typologie millénariste," 1.
85. Schwarte, *Vorgeschichte*, 275–77.

Hippolytus used both, but entirely separately except for the 5,500-year incarnation.[86] Lactantius did both tasks within the same work in his *Divine Institutes*, but apart from limited cross-pollination argued by Nicholson, where the exodus from Egypt and Solomon's temple construction seem attracted to millennial intervals in his chronology, they remain unintegrated.[87] Biblical chronologies could not locate figures like Noah or Moses, not to mention the exile, at millennial intervals, as we saw concerning Hilary and the Parable of the Workers in the Vineyard. If the "ages" were to be distinct eras defining phases in the redemptive story known from the biblical narratives, strict millennia were not going to work.

A World-Week with Real Subdivisions of the Pre-Christian Era

This is the most surprising part. Not only did Augustine have no prior model for *millennial* age-days of redemptive history, there was no prior world-week model that subdivided pre-Christ history *at all*. As Schwarte argues, despite exceptions like Africanus's odd Peleg situation, the 5,500 years often seen as having elapsed prior to Christ was essentially a single, undifferentiated block of time in world-week schemes. Biblical chronologies had subdivisions, certainly. The genealogy of Matthew 1 provided an explicit model of demarcation for Augustine and helps to explain why such a key figure as Moses does not appear in Augustine's scheme.[88] The figurative interpretation of the Parable of the Workers in the Vineyard (Matt. 20:1–16), seen above in Hilary of Poitiers and before him in Origen's Matthew commentary, also divided redemptive history into periods defined by pivotal individuals through whom God worked as it were in covenantal dispensations.[89] Yet the actual use of these hitherto independent schemes for subdividing redemptive history in conjunction with the world-week typological interpretation of Genesis 1:1–2:3 was purely Augustine's innovation. It had not been done before.

In this way Augustine emerges as a synthesizer and systematist of a series of separate threads of patristic theology and biblical interpretation. He took the idea of boundary figures from sources such as Matthew and the sense of covenantal

---

86. Schwarte, *Vorgeschichte*, 276.

87. Schwarte, *Vorgeschichte*, 226; Trompf, *Historical Recurrence*, 210–11.

88. Rousseau, "La typologie augustinienne," 92.

89. Roderich Schmidt, "Aetates Mundi: Die Weltalter als Gliederungsprinzip der Geschichte," *Zeitschrift für Kirchengeschichte* 67.3 (1955): 301–3. Origen, *Comm. Matt.* 15.32–34 (PG 13:1347–54).

phases from OT history as mediated through the Vineyard Parable typology and married them with the hitherto largely historically vacant and undivided world-week framework. He even utilized the evening-and-morning idea from Genesis 1 to express the decline of each era through human sin and the subsequent punishment by God, as at the flood, and then the dawn of new hope with a fresh act of divine mercy, as when God raised up Noah at the dawn of the second age, or Abraham at the dawn of the third. This created the possibility of real texture (and a degree of cyclicity) in such a presentation of redemptive history and was truly unique.[90] As Schwarte emphasizes, "Augustine's world-age doctrine *as a hexaemeron typology* represents a concept that is without precedent."[91] He had created a definitive model that could survive the passing of the kinds of would-be parousias that the strict, six-thousand-year version might lead Christians to expect.[92]

The Additional Layers of Typological Correspondence

We might feel here that Augustine innovated a little too much, but another of his contributions to the world-week model would combine it with a literary tradition from outside the church (in Seneca, Florus, and Ammianus Marcellinus) that saw the entire human race or civilized world (i.e., Rome) as having a life cycle of its own.[93] (This would yield in Augustine's time and much later the idea that the world was "growing old" and due to perish or else be renewed in God's new age.) For Augustine's world-week it supplied a way to characterize the six ages of the world as its infancy, childhood, adolescence, young adulthood, middle age (Augustine's addition), and old age (e.g., *Gen. Man.* 1.23). This human life cycle typology constitutes an additional layer that runs throughout Augustine's coverage of the world's ages in *On Genesis against the Manichaeans* 1.23.35–41 and is neatly summarized in *City of God* 16.43 and *Eighty-Three Different Questions* 58.2.

The next section of *On Genesis against the Manichaeans* adds one further layer of typology for good measure. In 1.24.42, Augustine explains the potential awkwardness of inequal typological age-days by taking a numerological route. It

---

90. Schwarte, *Vorgeschichte*, 40–43.

91. Schwarte, *Vorgeschichte*, 276–77, my translation.

92. Smith, "Ages of the World," 130; Trompf, *Historical Recurrence*, 212; Schmidt, "Aetates Mundi," 292, 310, 315–16; Rousseau, "La typologie augustinienne," 83.

93. Schwarte, *Vorgeschichte*, 43–45; Luneau, *Âges du monde*, 51–52, 290–95.

is the numbers involved that matter, not the actual chronological periods. This kind of interpretation might struggle to convince us today, but is a regular fixture in the biblical interpretation of Augustine, as seen for example in his *Eighty-Three Different Questions* 57 and the explanation of the Genesis days in *City of God* 11.30. It also dominates Victorinus's handling of the creation week, showing that it carried real conviction for the audiences of his day. World history moved in six stages because creation had six stages. And creation had six stages because six was the number that best expressed perfection or completion, being the sum of its parts. This numerology is for Augustine *the* essential explanation for why six was the right number of creation days and thus of world ages.[94]

Augustine had created something new: a double-barreled creation week typology, punctuated by heroes of the faith, that paved the way for his ambitious theology of history as especially revealed in the *City of God*. He explained history as God's long-term, step-by-step rescue mission to restore fallen humanity to his presence.

THE LEGACY AND IMPORTANCE OF AUGUSTINE'S WORLD-WEEK INTERPRETATION

Augustine's Genesis-based ages of the world framework for understanding history remained highly influential through the millennium following his death, like so many other aspects of his thought.[95] Some of Augustine's contemporaries completely forgot his cautious lead and used the world-week periodization and biblical chronology to announce the end times, especially in the light of the Vandal invasions that Augustine lived to see.[96] Later thinkers would mix and match aspects of Augustine's pattern with elements of alternative models from Origen and Hippolytus through Eusebius, Jerome, Gregory the Great, and onward.[97] Christian thinkers on the cusp of the medieval period mediated the world-week model to the coming era, notably John of Damascus (b. ca. 650) in the East and especially Isidore of Seville (ca. 560–636) in Visigothic Spain in the West.[98] Augustine had already stocked the world-week typological framework with the con-

---

94. Luneau, *Âges du monde*, 333–56, esp. 355. This was a strong feature of Victorinus's world-week offering.

95. Trompf, *Historical Recurrence*, 212.

96. Fredriksen, "Apocalypse and Redemption," 166–67.

97. Schmidt, "Aetates Mundi," 314–16.

98. See John of Damascus, *Orthodox Faith* 2.1. For a translation, see John of Damascus,

tent of biblical redemptive history. Utilizing Augustine's six-ages model, Isidore, while explicitly denouncing date-setting, strengthened it further by fusing Augustine's meaty world-week periodization with a detailed biblical chronology, still using the particular Septuagint-based dating scheme that stemmed back through Jerome to Eusebius.[99] The present came out at AM 5814, so despite the fact that Isidore's previous ages of the world were still not exact millennia, and that he closed by warning against calculating the end, we can imagine that the looming six thousand figure might have stirred some imaginations.[100]

Like Isidore, English churchman "the Venerable" Bede (ca. 673–735), really a medieval figure, was the standout Christian scholar of his generation. Like Isidore, he adopted Augustine's world-week as his framework for explaining history in his own chronicle, *On Times*, though with a couple of interesting twists. At a time when, according to Isidore's chronology, six thousand years of world history were nearly up, Bede stripped the dates out of Isidore's text as he revised it and carried through the logical implications of Jerome's Vulgate translation—made from the Hebrew text of the OT centuries before—by switching to a shorter chronology based on the dates in the Hebrew text. Thus, Bede identifies the year of Christ's birth as AM 3952, much sooner after creation than in any prior proposal, dampening any imminent apocalyptic expectations that existed.[101] Yet the model retained a powerful grip on the Western imagination and its echoes were still recognizable in early modern biblical chronologies such as those of Ussher (1658) and French churchman Bossuet (1686).[102] Naturalistic seven-part echoes survived in early "deep time" models of earth history, such as those of Thomas

---

Writings, trans. F. H. Chase, FC 37 (Washington, DC: Catholic University of America Press, 1958), 204. Mentioned, e.g., in Young and Stearley, *Bible, Rocks and Time*, 36–37.

99. Bede, *On the Nature of Things and On Times*, ed. Calvin B. Kendall and Faith Wallis (Liverpool: Liverpool University Press, 2010), 29; Landes, "Apocalyptic Expectations," 165–66. Note that Eusebius's version gave more room to move than did those of Theophilus or Julius Africanus, since he placed Christ's advent at around AM 5200.

100. For the text of Isidore of Seville, *Chronica*, see PL 83:1017–58. Translation can be found in Isidore of Seville, "Chronicon. English Translation," trans. Kenneth B. Wolf, 2004, http://www.ccel.org/ccel/pearse/morefathers/files/isidore_chronicon_01_trans .htm; Landes, "Apocalyptic Expectations," 165–74.

101. Kendall and Wallis, *On the Nature of Things*, 28–30; Landes, "Apocalyptic Expectations," 174–76.

102. Paul Archambault, "The Ages of Man and the Ages of the World. A Study of Two Traditions," *Revue des Études Augustiniennes* 12 (1966): 210.

Burnet, *Sacred Theory of the Earth* (first in Latin, 1681), and Louis Buffon, *Les époques de la nature* (1780), to sow the seed of subsequent geological hexaemeral schemes or day-age ideas.

EVALUATION OF THE WORLD-WEEK TRADITION

World-week belief based on the creation week of Genesis 1:1–2:3 proved to be a powerful way to theologically integrate creation with history and thus see the hand of God not only in the origin of things but in the grand narrative of redemptive history.[103] It sprouted in an intellectual climate where people had a keen eye for correspondences and expected that a divinely inspired text like Genesis would be replete with spiritual meaning, notably forward-referring prophetic significance that could be unlocked using interpretive keys taken from elsewhere in Scripture (e.g., Ps. 90:4).

This was its vulnerability in the longer term. There is no solid reason why the six days of creation should find a direct correspondence in the same number of eras of history or of God's working in the world. Schmidt, Luneau, and others have shown that it was possible to divide redemptive history, based on key figures and modes of God's working, into anything from three to eight or more phases. Like a potential storm cloud that develops promisingly in good conditions but then begins to evaporate from the base upward as atmospheric pressure begins to rise, the world-week idea left superstructural elements that survived as late as the seven phases of the dispensational view of history, long after the conditions that gave it birth disappeared.

Yet much of value survives in Augustine's theology of history and the kind of grand vision embodied in his *City of God*.[104] Augustine's version of the world-week was the most durable example of the genre, tied neither to actual millennia nor to a specific, biblical chronology. It recognized the different modes of God's relationship with people from one period to the next of redemptive history as portrayed in the biblical narrative. Turning it into a deterministic, box-like structure for compartmentalizing history dooms it to redundancy, but its intention to retain a theological view of history that can separate visible nations and institutions from God's spiritual kingdom without utterly secularizing history remains

103. Schwarte, *Vorgeschichte*, 58–61, 273 n. 1, 289–90.
104. Markus, *Saeculum*, 9–11, 157–61, 166–67.

a Christian worldview ideal today. The God who created the world and made history possible through the deliberate creation of will-possessing creatures remains capable still of steering that history to his desired outcome for it—not in order to evacuate and discard creation, but in order to renew it.

But what can clarifying the history of Genesis-based world-week beliefs contribute to modern creation debates? Certain conservative writers such as Sarfati and Mook have offered reliable descriptions of the typological interpretive method undergirding this idea. World-week typology was compatible with a literal understanding of the creation week narrative and could presume it.[105] Figurative and literal readings of Genesis were rarely mutually exclusive; "Both views could be maintained alongside one another."[106] Young and Stearley are right: "The striking feature of this patristic view . . . is that the equation of days to millennia was applied not to the length of the creation week but rather to the length of human history. There is no evidence that the fathers of the church believed that the work of creation had taken six millennia to complete."[107] World-week belief was always a periodization of human, rather than prehuman, history. Prehuman history remained largely outside the Christian imagination.[108]

105. Mook, "Church Fathers," 38–48; Sarfati, *Refuting Compromise*, 114–17.

106. Walter Hilbrands, "Die Länge der Schöpfungstage. Eine exegetische und rezeptionsgeschichtliche Untersuchung von Yom („Tag") in Gen 1,1–2,3," *Biblische Notizen* 149 (2011): 3.

107. Young and Stearley, *Bible, Rocks and Time*, 34.

108. One exception was Origen's belief, expressed clearly in *Princ.* 3.5.3, that our world is just one in an infinite series of worlds in time. For a hint of prehuman ages in Augustine, see later in chapter 6.

Chapter Four

THREE PATRISTIC LITERAL INTERPRETATIONS
OF THE CREATION WEEK

It might seem strange that it is not until now that we turn to the literal interpretation of the Genesis creation week. This is meant to reflect that, at least as far as the surviving literature on Genesis goes, figurative modes dominated Christian interpretation of Genesis 1:1–2:3 during the earliest centuries of the church.[1] Literal interpretation that read the passage as describing God's creation of the physical world, especially with any defense of literal creation days, only slowly came to prominence. Philo's interpretation in *On the Creation*, we recall, understood day one of creation (i.e., all of Gen. 1:1–5) to describe creation in the world of pure forms, of invisible realities. Days two through six concerned the physical realm, but the creative process did not occupy any time. Clement and Origen were more interested in the invisible, noetic world than the world perceived by the senses, and their creation references are no more physically oriented than Philo's. Typological interpretation of the creation week as corresponding to a week of world history certainly did not *exclude* reference in Genesis 1 to physical origins, but reading the primary documents as a collection leaves the impression that this biblical text was seen to be full of symbolic significance and that there was greater interest in exploring such deeper meanings than in thinking about the direct references to the works of creation. That significance might be christological, indicating that the preexistent Son of God was intimately involved in creation as the Father's Word or Wisdom. It might be redemptive-historical,

---

1. Including christological and historical typology and allegory.

implying the stages of biblical history across six or seven millennia. It might be moral, suggesting the qualities of soul that would bring the believer nearer to God. It could easily be all of these and more at the same time, because an inspired text was not limited to a single meaning.

But although finding higher spiritual meanings was a strong attraction, especially for those of a Platonic cast of mind such as our Alexandrians, there was also a kind of commonsense countercurrent in early Christian thought that wondered about the physical origin of God's world and valued physical existence. It sometimes perceived interpretive gymnastics in allegorical interpretations. Literal interpretation of Genesis 1, after a tenuous beginning, found a foothold in early Christian thought, arguably driven by the need to counter the power of alternate gnostic theologies that often paid close attention to the creation narratives in Genesis but could not endorse the goodness and rightness of physical creation and divorced this world's creator "god" from the true, High God.[2] Since these more literal efforts were driven by strong theological motivations, they were still strongly inclined to prioritize hints of the roles of Christ and the Spirit in creation and they still shifted into figurative mode for moral applications through the perceived symbolic value of textual details. Literal interpretation could also be so highly geared philosophically that it does not look literal to us, though it is still directed at understanding creation.

Terms like "literal," "allegorical," and "typological" and their cognates are the subject of constant debate. That is why Craig Allert's recent book, *Early Christian Readings of Genesis One* (2019), has a whole chapter entitled "What Does 'Literal' Mean?" Allert is a patristics specialist and is well equipped to speak to this issue.[3] His major point, framed as a critique of James Mook's essay, "The Church Fathers on Genesis,"[4] is announced early in the chapter:

2. G. May, *Creatio Ex Nihilo: The Doctrine of Creation out of Nothing in Early Christian Thought* (Edinburgh: T&T Clark, 1995), 26–27, 53, 117.

3. Craig D. Allert, *Revelation, Truth, Canon and Interpretation: Studies in Justin Martyr's Dialogue with Trypho*, VCSup 64 (Leiden: Brill, 2002) represents the revised form of his PhD thesis on the topic.

4. James R. Mook, "The Church Fathers on Genesis, the Flood, and the Age of the Earth," in *Coming to Grips with Genesis: Biblical Authority and the Age of the Earth*, ed. Terry Mortenson and Thane H. Ury (Green Forest, AR: Master Books, 2008), 23–51.

The claim of a tension in the early church is an issue that has received much attention in patristic studies. It is commonly addressed as the difference between the Alexandrian (spiritual/allegorical) and the Antiochene (literal) approach to biblical interpretation. Unfortunately, it is also the source of much confusion. The simple delineation of the church fathers into allegorists or literalists not only oversimplifies the context but also glosses over some very important issues that have bearing on mustering support for a literal . . . reading of Genesis.[5]

To conclude the chapter, he reiterates the point: "To assume that the Fathers read 'literally' in the same way we mean 'literal' is a misrepresentation of their context. It needs to be corrected if we are to move forward and speak meaningfully about how the Fathers understood Genesis 1."[6]

This is true. Even when the church fathers use the terms familiar to us, they often understand them differently, manifest different concerns than ours, and seek answers to different questions. Allert's sensitivity to patristic hermeneutics and the relationship of literal to allegorical interpretation reflects the influence of Frances Young's classic treatment of the issue in *Biblical Exegesis and the Formation of Christian Culture.*[7] Around the mid-twentieth century, it was popular to draw a strong distinction between allegory, perceived as an abuse of the text or interpretive overreach by figures such as Origen, and typology, a form of figurative interpretation that retained a positive historical grounding by remaining within the stream of salvation history, looking forward from OT persons and events to the NT realities they foreshadowed.[8] The Alexandrian fathers were understood to indulge quite fully in allegorical interpretation, while a group of fathers associated

5. Craig D. Allert, *Early Christian Readings of Genesis One: Patristic Exegesis and Literal Interpretation* (Downers Grove, IL: InterVarsity, 2018), 96.

6. Allert, *Early Christian Readings,* 158.

7. Frances M. Young, *Biblical Exegesis and the Formation of Christian Culture* (Cambridge: Cambridge University Press, 1997), 161–85 and 186–213 (chapters 8 and 9). The first concerns the infamous Antiochene vs. Alexandrian issue, and the second returns to understand allegorical, typological, and "plain sense" interpretation in the patristic period.

8. Classically associated with G. W. H. Lampe and K. J. Woollcombe, eds., *Essays on Typology* (London: SCM, 1957); J. Daniélou, *From Shadow to Reality: Studies in the Biblical Typology of the Fathers,* trans. W. Hubbard (London: Burns and Oates, 1960);

with the city of Antioch, including Diodore of Tarsus and Theodore of Mopsuestia, limited their figurative readings to typology as they sought to understand the unfolding of the sacred economy.

This position has since broken down to a considerable degree, troubled by (1) the lack of equivalent distinctions of terms by the fathers themselves in practice; (2) overlap in the actual practice of figurative interpretation between the two "schools" of Alexandria and Antioch; and (3) the difficulty of proving that Antiochene figurative interpretation always retained a defining historical element.[9] Like so many things, it was not as simple as allegory being bad, typology being okay, and literal being even better; these categories reflect modern prejudices too much. Keep in mind, though, Antiochene figures such as Diodore did protest *something* in Alexandrian allegory. I recommend to you some of the most recent writings on this issue.[10] It does affect our discussion of creation because Ephrem the Syrian (below) and Basil the Great (chapter 5) will warn against the dangers of allegorizing the hexaemeral narrative, as we will see. They were nervous about endangering the theology of both creation and eschaton, the beginning and the end of the Christian "grand narrative" of salvation, by inferring dramatic transfers of meaning in textual statements.[11]

In the meantime, we return to an earlier point in the patristic period to a thinker who certainly predates fourth-century debates over biblical interpreta-

R. P. C. Hanson, *Allegory and Event: A Study of the Sources and Significance of Origen's Interpretation of Scripture* (London: SCM, 1959).

9. M. Simonetti, "Allegory-Typology," in *Encyclopedia of Ancient Christianity*, ed. A. di Berardino, trans. Adrian Walford (Cambridge: Institutum Patristicum Augustinianum, 2014), 86–87; Frances Young, *Exegesis and Theology in Early Christianity* (Farnham: Ashgate, 2012), esp. chapter 6 "Allegory and the Ethics of Reading"; Young, "Alexandrian and Antiochene Exegesis," *AHBI* 1:334–54.

10. Two of the best introductions to the issues are: Donald Fairbairn, "Patristic Exegesis and Theology: The Cart and the Horse," *WTJ* 69.1 (2007): 1–19; Peter W. Martens, "Revisiting the Allegory/Typology Distinction: The Case of Origen," *JECS* 16.3 (2008): 283–317.

11. Frances Young, "The Fourth Century Reaction against Allegory," in *Exegesis and Theology in Early Christianity* (London: Routledge, 2018), 120–25, a reprint of a 1997 article in the series Studia Patristica. Bradley Nassif, "Antiochene Θεωρία in John Chrysostom's Exegesis," in *Ancient & Postmodern Christianity: Paleo-Orthodoxy in the 21st Century: Essays in Honor of Thomas C. Oden* (Downers Grove, IL: InterVarsity Press, 2002), 55.

tion, and who at least pauses for a certain sort of literal interpretation of Genesis 1 before moving on to its symbolic significance.[12] When we come to Ephrem the Syrian and John Chrysostom as well as Basil in the following chapter, we will encounter fourth-century figures making conscious choices about whether to imitate or avoid the interpretive models of Origen and his successors.

THEOPHILUS'S TWIN TRACKS

Theophilus of Antioch was one of the second-century Christian apologists. These were still pioneering days for Christian scholarship. We cannot be more specific about his lifespan other than noting that the pioneering world chronology he offers in book 3 of his *To Autolycus* records the death of Roman emperor Marcus Aurelius (180 CE). Two further clues to his biography survive. In his *Ecclesiastical History*, Eusebius of Caesarea identifies Theophilus as the sixth postapostolic bishop of Antioch (*Hist. eccl.* 4.20.1) and the author of "three elementary treatises . . . addressed to Autolycus" together with a few other works now lost (*Hist. eccl.* 4.24.1). Later, Jerome updates this report by listing Theophilus in his *Lives of Illustrious Men*, locating his writings "in the reign of the emperor Marcus Antoninus Verus" (i.e., Marcus Aurelius, r. 161–180), and sounding complimentary.[13] In another biographical clue, Theophilus refers his own conversion to Christianity to the discovery of fulfilled prophecy in Scripture in *To Autolycus* 1.14.

The work now known as *To Autolycus* represents the combination of these three original treatises referred to by Eusebius.[14] In the context of present-day creation debates, despite our relative lack of external clues to help us understand it, *To Autolycus* attracts interest for these reasons: (1) It contains the nearest thing to a sequential explanation of the early chapters of Genesis seen to this point in Christian history; (2) this treatment has a literal aspect; (3) Theophilus articulates a clear "creation out of nothing" (*creatio ex nihilo*) stance; and (4) he ends this set of writings with

---

12. Although included in a discussion of this interpretive issue in Sten Hidal, "Exegesis of the Old Testament in the Antiochene School with Its Prevalent Literal and Historical Method," *HB/OT* 1.1:544.

13. For these details and a clear biographical background, see Rick Rogers, "Theophilus of Antioch," *The Expository Times* 120.5 (2009): 214–17.

14. Rogers, "Theophilus of Antioch," 216; Stuart Parsons, "Coherence, Rhetoric, and Scripture in Theophilus of Antioch's Ad Autolycum," *The Greek Orthodox Theological Review* 53.1–4 (2008): 163.

a pioneering biblical chronology that comes close to a 5,500-year age for the world at the advent of Christ, in keeping with Septuagint (Greek) rather than Masoretic Text (Hebrew) OT dates and with the chronological works of Hippolytus and Julius Africanus soon to follow.[15] As writers with patristic expertise such as Bouteneff, Louth, Presley, and Allert have entered the conversation, portrayal of Theophilus's contributions on creation has matured in a positive direction, generally in keeping with a recent trend in patristic scholarship to avoid making premature judgments about Theophilus's theological shortcomings in favor of seeking a deeper understanding of his rhetorical methods and purpose in *To Autolycus*.[16]

I mentioned earlier that early Christianity had to define itself in terms of three other social and intellectual contexts: Judaism, sectarian quasi-Christianity (notably Gnosticism), and pagan polytheism. The last of these is Theophilus's primary target as the thing that appeals to his correspondent. *To Autolycus* was evidently addressed to an educated non-Christian much as Luke-Acts was.[17] It seeks to demonstrate that Greco-Roman ideas and their best-known writings about creation and about God are inferior to biblical teaching, mutually contradictory, and morally compromised. The goal seems to be Autolycus's conversion to a Christian worldview and lifestyle, though we are perhaps dealing with an "open letter" persuasive genre crafted with a wider, secondary audience in mind too.

15. Interested in one or more of these aspects in relation to current creation discussions are: Jack P. Lewis, "The Days of Creation: An Historical Survey of Interpretation," *JETS* 32 (1989): 437; Stanley Jaki, *Genesis 1 through the Ages*, 2nd ed. (Royal Oak, MI: Real View, 1998), 65–66; Peter C. Bouteneff, *Beginnings: Ancient Christian Readings of the Biblical Creation Narratives* (Grand Rapids: Baker Academic, 2008), 68–73; Andrew Louth, "The Six Days of Creation according to the Greek Fathers," in *Reading Genesis after Darwin*, ed. Stephen C. Barton and David Wilkinson (Oxford: Oxford University Press, 2009), 40–44; Louth, "The Fathers on Genesis," in *The Book of Genesis: Composition, Reception, and Interpretation*, ed. David L. Petersen, Craig A. Evans, and Joel N. Lohr, VTSup 152 (Leiden: Brill, 2012), 562–69; William Dembski, *The End of Christianity* (Nashville: B&H, 2009), 52; Stephen O. Presley, "Interpretations of Genesis 1–2 among the Ante-Nicene Fathers," in *Since the Beginning: Interpreting Genesis 1 and 2 through the Ages*, ed. Kyle R. Greenwood (Grand Rapids: Baker Academic, 2018), 99–110; Allert, *Early Christian Readings*, 214–220, 229–33, and often elsewhere.

16. Rogers, "Theophilus of Antioch," 214; Parsons, "Coherence, Rhetoric, and Scripture," 155, 209; Stuart E. Parsons, *Ancient Apologetic Exegesis: Introducing and Recovering Theophilus's World* (Cambridge: Clarke & Co, 2015), 13–20.

17. Luke 1:1–4; Acts 1:1, where the addressee is coincidentally also called Theophilus.

At the center of *To Autolycus*, in the middle of book 2, appears an exposition of the early chapters of Genesis with a focus on Genesis 1–3. Having spent *To Autolycus* 2.1–8 lambasting the convoluted polytheist while salvaging glimmers of truth about God's providence from a few classical sources, chapter 9 of book 2 seeks to establish the prophetic authority of the Hebrew Scriptures (and the Greek Sibyl!) before chapter 10 establishes a doctrine and metaphysic of the Logos as the mediating agency of creation.[18] This is the deepest part of his creation treatment, requiring our careful attention.

Theophilus here uses John 1:1–3 as his interpretive key to find that the "word" of divine command that does all of the creative work in Genesis 1 is actually the *Logos*, an intermediate entity self-generated by God to be his instrument of creation production and, later, creation interaction. He also introduces alongside the *Logos*, the *Sophia* (Gk. wisdom) of God, which he derives from another vital text: Proverbs 8:27–29. This pair reminds us of Irenaeus's soon-to-appear "two hands" doctrine of creation, wherein God creates via the twin agents of Son and Spirit.[19] Both *logos* and *sophia* were freighted terms both in Greek philosophy and in gnostic belief.[20] As in John's Gospel, the choice to use such terms required a Christian commentator to take and mold their inevitable semantic baggage.[21] The *Logos* already under discussion is equated with the Spirit of God in *To Autolycus* 2.10.[22] However, it is difficult to tell how "hypostatized" the *Logos* and *Sophia* are in Theophilus's explanation (i.e., whether Theophilus wants to present them as separate manifestations or even personal agents of God).[23]

18. Translation from Theophilus of Antioch, *Ad Autolycum*, trans. Robert M. Grant (Oxford: Clarendon, 1970), 34–41.

19. E.g., Bouteneff, *Beginnings*, 71.

20. Their entries occupy multiple columns in G. W. H. Lampe, *Patristic Greek Lexicon* (Oxford: Clarendon, 1961), 807–11, 1244–46.

21. Kathleen McVey, "The Use of Stoic Cosmogony in Theophilus of Antioch's Hexaemeron," in *Biblical Hermeneutics in Historical Perspective: Studies in Honor of Karlfried Froehlich on His Sixtieth Birthday*, ed. Mark S. Burrows and Paul Rorem (Grand Rapids: Eerdmans, 1991), 35, 41–42, 49–51; Louth, "Fathers on Genesis," 566, 568.

22. For the text, see also Tatian and Theophilus of Antioch, *Tatiani Oratio ad Graecos / Theophili Antiocheni Ad Autolycum*, ed. Miroslav Marcovich, Patristische Texte und Studien 43 (Berlin: de Gruyter, 1995), 53. This is the newest critical edition.

23. Therefore, where the traditional translation of one line in *Autol.* 2.10 by Marcus Dods in *ANF* 2 reads, "For the divine wisdom foreknew," treating *sophia* merely as a qual-

This presentation of the *Logos* is the closest Theophilus comes to naming Jesus Christ or offering a Christology in his work. Stuart Parsons reads this as his apologetic tactic toward Autolycus, as Theophilus sought to establish a basic groundwork for Christian belief and held back aspects of theology for which Autolycus was not ready.[24] Moreover, Bouteneff, like Rogers, countenances the possibility of "a conversion from Judaism that was not fully realized in Theophilus's thought."[25] Yet the implicit Christology arguably embodied in Theophilus's Logos teaching would help set the tone for later Christian explanations of Christ's agency in creation.

Also in *To Autolycus* 2.10, Theophilus frames his Logos presentation with his teaching of *creatio ex nihilo*. Having spent the preceding section (2.9) establishing the authority of the Hebrew prophets (and therefore Moses) to speak of God, he lays out the premier truth that they have communicated in the Christian Scriptures in these framing statements:

> In the first place, in complete harmony they taught us that he made everything out of the non-existent. For there was nothing coeval with God; he was his own locus; he lacked nothing; he *existed before the ages* [Ps. 55:20 MT]. He wished to make man so that he might be known by him; for him, then, he prepared the world. . . .
>
> These are the first teachings which the divine scripture gives. It indicates that the matter from which God made and fashioned the world was in a way created, having been made by God. (*Autol.* 2.10 [Grant])

Although creation out of nothing would soon become well embedded in orthodox Christian teaching about creation, it was not the original position, as best exemplified in Justin Martyr (*1 Apol.* 1.10).[26] The classic study of Gerhard May on the topic concludes, "We have to see in Theophilus and Irenaeus the specific founders of the church doctrine of *creatio ex nihilo*."[27] Of the two, Theophilus is

---

ity of God, Grant, on the other hand, has the more adventurous, "For the divine Sophia knew," assuming a hypostasis (i.e., a separate being).

24. Rogers, "Theophilus of Antioch," 218–23; Parsons, *Ancient Apologetic Exegesis*, 13–20, finds Rogers too quick to conclude that Theophilus is not orthodox.

25. Bouteneff, *Beginnings*, 70–71, also 73. Oskar Skarsaune, "The Development of Scriptural Interpretation in the Second and Third Centuries—Except Clement and Origen," *HB/OT* 1.1:414–17.

26. Louth, "Fathers on Genesis," 566; Louth, "Six Days of Creation," 42.

27. May, *Creatio Ex Nihilo*, 178, and see 148, 156–63.

probably earlier, providing a precedent for Irenaeus and grounding an important point of Christian doctrine.[28]

To Autolycus 2.11–19 then features the earliest-surviving, sustained exposition of Genesis 1:1–2:3. Theophilus's exposition also explicitly uses the term *hexaemeron* in 2.12 for the first time in surviving Christian exposition. He is generally regarded as the fountainhead of ensuing Christian commentary on the creation week narrative in Genesis, including self-consciously hexaemeral literature.[29] Still in 2.12, after complaining that rival cosmogonies by other writers pale by comparison, Theophilus begins to contrast Genesis 1 with Hesiod's *Theogony*, a classical early Greek creation account heavily populated with deities (*Autol.* 2.12–13). He portrays God's superior power in creation, saying that unlike a human builder God is able to create the cosmic structure not just in its form but in its very material and then build it from the roof (heaven) downward. Carefully defining the initial terms of the passage, he describes the result of the initial creation of Genesis 1:1–2: "Like a vaulted ceiling . . . the heaven surrounded matter, which was like a lump. . . . Therefore the Command of God, [that is] his Logos, shining like a lamp in a closed room, illuminated the region under the heaven" (*Autol.* 2.13 [Grant]). The water was then separated into upper and lower collections on day two, then the lower water was gathered, and the ground was thus adorned with vegetation of all kinds.

So far, so literal, although since the narrative describes events so clearly and simply, a direct explanation can feel like a paraphrase. But just at this point, Theophilus begins to find deeper spiritual truths embedded in the text through a figurative reading. For example, just as the inflow from rivers keeps the sea from becoming brackish, so the inflow of the law of God and inspired prophecy keeps the world from growing corrupt with moral evil (*Autol.* 2.14). Theophilus returns briefly to a literal exposition of day four before adding, "And these things contain

28. E.g., U. Hamm, "Irenaeus of Lyons," *DECL*, 302.

29. Winden, "Hexaemeron," *RAC* 14:1251, 1260; F. Robbins, *The Hexaemeral Literature: A Study of the Greek and Latin Commentaries in Genesis* (Chicago: University of Chicago Press, 1912), 36–39; Louth, "Fathers on Genesis," 562; Louth, "Six Days of Creation," 40; E. ten Napel, "Some Remarks on the Hexaemeral Literature in Syriac," in *IV Symposium Syriacum 1984: Literary Genres in Syriac Literature (Groningen – Oosterhesselen 10–12 September 1984)*, ed. H. W. J. Drijvers et al., Orientalia Christiana Analecta 229 (Rome: Pontificium Institutum Studiorum Orientalium, 1987), 59; S. Zincone, "Hexaemeron," in *Encyclopedia of the Early Church*, ed. A. di Berardino, trans. Adrian Walford (Cambridge: Clarke, 1993), 1:380.

a pattern and type of a great mystery," and proceeds to find the sun and moon to be types of God and humanity, respectively. "Similarly the three days prior to the luminaries are types of the triad of God and his Logos and his Sophia."[30] Then the fixed stars typify the faithful righteous, while the stars that wander irregularly around the sky (i.e., our planets) "are a type of the men who depart from God, abandoning his law and ordinances" (*Autol.* 2.15 [Grant]). The explanations of days five and six continue in this manner, offering a literal interpretation followed by an allegorical one until the creation of humanity (through Gen. 2:7) and the "rest" of God on the seventh day are explained in a literal manner (*Autol.* 2.16–19).

So, does Theophilus treat the days of creation literally or not? Given the way his exposition begins and ends rather literally, with a leaning toward typology in relation to Genesis 1:11–25, or we might say creation days 3b through 6a, I find a balance between literal and allegorical or typological readings regarding the *content* of the creation days.[31] Forster and Marston feel that "By our standards today it is actually highly allegorical," which I see as a function of the fact that (1) we are much more sensitive to the unfamiliar than the familiar; and (2) Forster and Marston are trying to deny that early church interpretation of the creation narratives was universally literal.[32] Yet such a counterpoint is necessary for any assumption that Theophilus represents a baldly literal approach. Theophilus departs a literal for a figurative reading and back again without reluctance or resistance, instinctively perceiving the two as complementary understandings.[33]

For Theophilus's time figurative readings of Genesis 1 were apparently the rule rather than the exception; Barnabas 15, Clement of Alexandria, Origen, and the various gnostic readings all belong to that era. The literal approach of Theophilus stands out as more distinctive. The realism of his literal reading justifies Paul Seely's claim that Theophilus's argument that the stars cannot be responsible for producing vegetation if they appeared after the emergence of vegetation pre-

---

30. This might be the kind of statement that prompts Edwards to call Theophilus "the earliest writer to speak of the Godhead as a Trinity." But it is not the Trinity as modern Christian orthodoxy knows it. M. Edwards, "Christianity, A.D. 70–192," *CAH* 12:576; Stuart E. Parsons, "Very Early Trinitarian Expressions," *Tyndale Bulletin* 65.1 (2014): 141–44, 148–52.

31. This is about where we find Jaki, *Genesis 1*, 66.

32. Roger Forster and Paul Marston, *Reason, Science and Faith* (Crowborough: Monarch, 1999), 202.

33. Presley, "Interpretations of Genesis 1–2," 102, 105–6; Bouteneff, *Beginnings*, 69–70.

sumes a genuine temporal progression in the creation week.[34] It is equally justified to conclude from Theophilus's roughly AM 5500-year chronology at the end of the work (*Autol.* 3.29) that the creation week read literally referred to a normal, temporal week.[35] To classify Theophilus as a young-earth creationist, though, is simply too simplistic and anachronistic.[36] He thinks too differently from that position to fit the label.

Ephrem the Syrian and the Syrian Church

Ephrem the Syrian (d. 373) had a foot in more than one cultural camp. Ephrem was a speaker and writer of Syriac, a branch of Aramaic, the language of chapters 2–7 of the biblical book of Daniel. Syriac had become another major language of the church alongside Latin and Greek and was the medium of the eastern, Syrian fringe of Roman Empire. Ephrem lived his life within the bounds of the Roman Empire, serving the church for most of his life in the Roman frontier fortress of Nisibis, slightly west of the Tigris River, now near the eastern end of the Turkish border with Syria. Once the Sassanid Persian ruler Shapur II seized Nisibis from the Romans in 363, the Christian population of Nisibis was allowed to migrate westward to Roman territory, and with them went Ephrem to Edessa.[37] So Ephrem remained a lifelong Roman citizen, but spoke and wrote a non-Roman language, reminding us that early Christianity extended beyond the Greek and Latin sphere. He became the best known and respected of the Syrian fathers, his influential writings and hymns being "translated into virtually every language known to Christianity."[38]

---

34. Paul H. Seely, "The First Four Days of Genesis in Concordist Theory and in Biblical Context," *PSCF* 49 (1997): 95 n. 57.

35. Davis A. Young and Ralph Stearley, *The Bible, Rocks and Time: Geological Evidence for the Age of the Earth* (Downers Grove, IL: InterVarsity Press, 2008), 37; Andrew Kulikovsky, *Creation, Fall, Restoration: A Biblical Theology of Creation* (Fearn: Mentor, 2009), 61.

36. Dembski, *End of Christianity*, 52.

37. See for instance the two historical introductions to Ephrem in Edward G. Mathews Jr. and Joseph P. Amar, trans., *St. Ephrem the Syrian: Selected Prose Works*, ed. Kathleen E. McVey, FC 91 (Washington, DC: Catholic University of America Press, 1994), 25–37; McVey, ed., *Hymns* (Mahwah, NJ: Paulist, 1989), 8–28.

38. Matthew, Amar, and McVey, *Hymns*, 4; *ODCC*, "Syriac," 1333–34; ten Napel, "Hexaemeral Literature in Syriac," 65.

Ephrem is the only representative of Syrian Christianity who enters modern creation discussions, though in fact other Syrian writers from Aphrahat (ca. 280–ca. 345) to Narsai of Nisibis (399–502) and Jacob of Sarug (ca. 451–521) talked about creation and used Genesis 1 in their writings and songs.[39] Ephrem's reputation and influence affected the entire fourth-century church, not just the Syrian Monophysite or Nestorian churches. It is surprising that writers looking for precedents for a stricter literal cosmological employment of Genesis 1 do not utilize Ephrem more. Jack Lewis notes Ephrem's cosmologically straightforward and yet poetic and symbolic treatment.[40] Jaki lambasts him (as he does many others) for a perceived concordist literalism.[41] Craig Allert devotes large sections of *Early Christian Readings* to Ephrem's advocacy for creation out of nothing and Ephrem's literal creation week expressed in lyrical doxology.[42] The general lack of polemical heat here need not detract from the value of giving attention to Ephrem's important legacy.

Ephrem provides the longest exposition of creation in Genesis in realistic, physical terms up to his time in his *Commentary on Genesis*, probably written during his Edessa period (363–373).[43] His rendition of the days of creation is plainly literal and opens with a firm programmatic opposition to allegorical interpretation of this narrative (after an introduction and outline of the content of Genesis):

> So let no one think that there is anything allegorical in the works of the six days. No one can rightly say that the things that pertain to these days were symbolic, nor . . . that other things were symbolized for us by their names. Rather, let us know in just what manner heaven and earth were created in the beginning. (*Comm. Gen.* 1.1 [Mathews, Amar, and McVey])

Ephrem's wording reminds us of the way Philo and Origen interpreted the details of the creation week narrative, and Kronholm sees an anti-Alexandrian theme in his work.[44] But Ephrem's more immediate point of departure (or opposition)

---

39. E.g., Narsai of Nisibis, "On the Expression, 'In the Beginning,' and Concerning the Existence of God," in *Biblical Interpretation*, ed. J. W. Trigg, Message of the Fathers of the Church 9 (Wilmington, DE: Michael Glazier, 1988), 216–17.
40. Lewis, "Days of Creation," 444–45.
41. Jaki, *Genesis 1*, 77–79.
42. Allert, *Early Christian Readings*, 220–25, 233–41.
43. Mathews, Amar, and McVey, *Prose Works*, 36, 60.
44. T. Kronholm, *Motifs from Genesis I–XI in the Genuine Hymns of Ephrem the Syr-*

was probably the speculative, quasi-gnostic views of the earlier, eclectic Syrian intellectual Bardesanes (Bardaisan), who conceived of air, water, fire, light, and darkness as preexistent and ultimately self-existent entities.[45] This move toward the literal sense must reflect a broader *Zeitgeist* too; among hexaemeral works soon to follow prioritization of the literal sense is prominent first in Basil's *Homilies on the Hexaemeron* (ca. 378) and then in Augustine's *The Literal Meaning of Genesis*, begun in 401 CE.[46]

Literal explanation of the creation week is certainly a feature of Ephrem's commentary, as several of our debaters note.[47] While he is never compelled to say something as graphic as "Each of these days lasted twenty-four hours," he clearly has a temporal succession in mind when he says of day three, for example, "The grass that would be required as food for the animals who were created two days later was [thus] made ready. And the new corn that would be food for Adam and his descendants, who would be thrown out of Paradise four days later, was [thus] prepared" (*Comm. Gen.* 23.2 [Mathews, Amar, and McVey]). And in fact the individual entities created appeared instantaneously: "Just as the trees, the vegetation, the animals, the birds, and even mankind were old, so also were they young. They were old according to the appearance of their limbs and their substances, yet they were young because of the hour and moment of their creation" (*Comm. Gen.* 25.1 [Mathews, Amar, and McVey]).

This is the challenging but inevitable consequence of any special creation teaching. If God creates any part of the world directly and not through mediating causes, instantly complete, it will inevitably have the dreaded "appearance of

---

ian with Particular Reference to the Influence of Jewish Exegetical Tradition, Coniectanea Biblica: Old Testament Series 11 (Lund: Gleerup, 1978), 26.

45. Mathews, Amar, and McVey, *Prose Works*, 60–62; Paul Féghali, "Les premiers jours de la création: commentaire de GN 1,1–2,4 par Saint Ephrem," *Parole de l'Orient* 13 (1986): 3–30; Lucas Van Rompay, "Antiochene Biblical Interpretation: Greek and Syriac," in *The Book of Genesis in Jewish and Oriental Christian Interpretation: A Collection of Essays*, ed. Judith Frishman and Lucas Van Rompay (Leuven: Peeters, 1997), 113. Kronholm says that this is true of his creation-related hymns also, e.g., the *Hymn on Faith* 6.13: Kronholm, *Motifs from Genesis I–XI*, 35, 40.

46. For Basil in particular, see chapter 5.

47. Mook, "Church Fathers," 30; Jud Davis, "Unresolved Major Questions: Evangelicals and Genesis 1–2," in *Reading Genesis 1–2: An Evangelical Conversation*, ed. J. Daryl Charles (Peabody, MA: Hendrickson, 2013), 216–17; Jaki, *Genesis 1*, 77–78; Allert, *Early Christian Readings*, 239–40.

age" that Ephrem teaches here. On the other hand, appearance of age, carried to its logical extreme, can nullify all fossil and even archaeological evidence of the past, and extend to our family ancestry or even our own memories. The past risks becoming pure illusion. Nonetheless, between Ephrem's initial, programmatic statement and this kind of evidence for its implementation in relation to Genesis 1, we must admit with Allert that "we cannot doubt that Ephrem assumes the days of Genesis being twenty-four-hours long,"[48] though we will see that to call him a thoroughgoing literalist would be to misunderstand him.

Returning to Ephrem, though, we note that his concept of the physical world is realistic and much less abstract than the speculative ontologies of the Alexandrians and particularly the various gnostic cosmogonies. In fact, it verges on the simplistic. There must have been clouds created on day one too, thinks Ephrem, though they are not mentioned, because something must shade the earth from the inherent brightness of the celestial realm to create the darkness of the first evening. "The firmament was created on the second evening and henceforth its shadow rendered service for all subsequent nights" (*Comm. Gen.* 5.2 [Mathews, Amar, and McVey]). Something like an upturned bowl, one wonders? But before we scoff or shudder like Jaki at "Ephrem's literalist interpretation" or misguided concordism, we really ought to let Ephrem be a man of his time.[49] His cosmology is naïve, an ancestor of the flat earth cosmology of sixth-century globetrotter Cosmas Indicopleustes.[50] Yet a physical interpretation of the creation narrative in Genesis 1 seems more natural than the abstract ontology of Origen's *On First Principles* or the complex speculations of the gnostics.

But as Jack Lewis observes in his survey article of the hexaemeral literature and Allert has emphasized more recently, Ephrem did not write primarily in prose or in the commentary form. He preferred to express himself in poems and hymns and was famous for his gift of expressing profound Christian theology and worship in Syriac poetry.[51] In his poetic or musical corpus, says Lewis, Ephrem

48. Allert, *Early Christian Readings*, 239.

49. Jaki, *Genesis 1*, 78.

50. Cosmas (Indicopleustes), *Christianikē Topographia: The Christian Topography of Cosmas, an Egyptian Monk*, ed. J. W. McCrindle (London: Franklin, 1897). This work is accessible online through the Tertullian Project: http://www.tertullian.org/fathers/index .htm#Cosmas_Indicopleustes. See also Jeffrey B. Russell, *Inventing the Flat Earth* (New York: Praeger, 1991), 21–24, 33–35.

51. Rosa Maria Hunt, "The Self-Enclosing God: John Chrysostom and Ephrem Syrus on Divine Self-Limitation as Gift of Love in Genesis 1–3" (PhD diss., Vrije Universiteit

"is allegorical and mystical."[52] Where Ephrem treats creation in his hymns or "teaching songs"—the latter being Griffith's preferred translation of the Syriac *madrashē*[53]—it is harder to pin down his attitude to the meaning of the creation days in relation to time, but he "thoroughly explores the mythopoeic character of the opening narratives of Genesis" in a way that transcends what we might think of as literal interpretation.[54] In his *Hymns on Paradise*, Ephrem expresses a two-tier hermeneutic that pervades his entire body of work, although it is more obvious in his teaching songs: as he approaches the Eden narrative, he says, "I cross over and enter; my eye remains outside, but my mind enters within. I begin to wander amid things unwritten."[55] For Ephrem, there is a level of meaning in Scripture beyond the letter that is accessible to the trained and reverent heart.

If we are to grasp Ephrem's mind at all, we need to reckon with this side of his biblical interpretation. A suitable example is Hymn 26 in his *Hymns on the Nativity*. Each day of the week, along with an eighth day—familiar by this point as the day of the resurrection and symbol of eternity—and even a tenth, is called to bring praise to the newborn Savior Christ. Take for example the fourth day:

> Let the fourth day confess fourfold
> the birth of Him Who created on the fourth day
> the pair of luminaries that fools worship

Amsterdam, 2015), 54–59; Joseph P. Amar, "Christianity at the Crossroads: The Legacy of Ephrem the Syrian," *Religion & Literature* 43.2 (2011): 2, 8; Sten Hidal, *Interpretatio Syriaca: Die Kommentare des heiligen Ephräm des Syrers zu Genesis und Exodus mit besonderer Berücksichtigung ihrer auslegungsgeschichtlichen Stellung*, trans. Christiane Boehncke Sjoberg, Coniectanea Biblica: Old Testament Series 6 (Lund: Gleerup, 1974), 7; C. Rebecca Rine, "Interpretations of Genesis 1–2 among the Nicene and Post-Nicene Fathers," in *Since the Beginning: Interpreting Genesis 1 and 2 through the Ages*, ed. Kyle R. Greenwood (Grand Rapids: Baker Academic, 2018), 125.

52. Lewis, "Days of Creation," 444.

53. Sidney Griffith, "Syriac/Antiochene Exegesis in Saint Ephrem's Teaching Songs *De Paradiso*: The 'Types of Paradise' in the 'Treasury of Revelations,'" in *Syriac and Antiochian Exegesis and Biblical Theology for the 3rd Millennium*, ed. Robert D. Miller (Piscataway, NJ: Gorgias, 2008), 27 and throughout.

54. Paul M. Blowers, *Drama of the Divine Economy: Creator and Creation in Early Christian Theology and Piety*, OECS (Oxford: Oxford University Press, 2012), 108; Allert, *Early Christian Readings*, 222–24.

55. *Hymn. Parad.* 5.4–5, quoted in Griffith, "Ephrem's Teaching Songs," 33; Hunt, "Self-Enclosing God," 103.

and they are blind and unseeing.

He, the Lord of the luminaries, came down,

and like the sun He shone on us from the womb.

His radiances have opened [the eyes of] the blind;

His rays have enlightened the straying.

(*Hymn. Nativ.* 26.7 [McVey])[56]

The correspondence Ephrem celebrates here is akin to Paul's use of the first creation command of Genesis 1:3 in 2 Corinthians 4:6, illustrating how other positive uses can be made of the Genesis creation texts beyond a literal reading related to the physical origin of the world. Such correspondences, not really definable according to traditional categories such as literal versus allegorical, animate Ephrem's poetry and even his Genesis commentary and provide access to deeper meaning.[57] Like Basil after him, Ephrem encourages us to allow the hexaemeron to act as a motivation and means for the praise of the Creator and the work of the Savior.

Ephrem's resistance to allegorical interpretation of the hexaemeral narrative, then, does not prevent him from seeking deeper spiritual truths in biblical texts. He seizes the literal sense of the text but finds numerous typological connections to other things with a rich use of imagery, for example, *Hymn. Nativ.* 26. Why is there less nervousness about figurative understanding here than in his Genesis commentary? Beside the inherent genre differences, there is a risk of undercutting a robust creation doctrine if the elements of Genesis 1 are treated as ciphers for other ideas, that is, if they do not really relate to creation.[58] Ephrem defends the creation of everything other than God out of nothing, just as we saw Theophilus do. Rival theologies, notably those of Bardaisan and followers of Marcion, held to the preexistence of other entities besides God, such as material elements or even space itself.[59] The Bible's meristic opening statement in Genesis 1:1, "In the beginning, God created the heavens and the earth," was best read, claimed Ephrem,

56. For fuller examples, see Rine, "Interpretations of Genesis 1–2," 140–41; Allert, *Early Christian Readings*, 233–36.

57. Hidal, *Interpretatio Syriaca*, 23–25; Jeffrey Wickes, "Ephrem's Interpretation of Genesis," *St. Vladimir's Theological Quarterly* 52.1 (2008): 63.

58. Hinted at in Allert, *Early Christian Readings*, 223.

59. Regarding material elements, see Kronholm, *Motifs from Genesis I–XI*, 28–32; Allert, *Early Christian Readings*, 220–21. Regarding space itself, see Hunt, "Self-Enclosing God," 71–75.

as covering the known cosmos and its occupants rather than excluding certain foundational principles or entities from their scope.[60] Wickes therefore sees the basic concern here as theological, in that not taking the literal meaning of Genesis seriously risks chiseling away the scriptural support for creation belief.[61]

Ephrem's *Commentary on Genesis*, unlike many of its antique counterparts, has survived in full and in its original language, headed by clear and practical exposition of Genesis 1. His literal stance is clearly articulated, emphasizing the importance of allowing Genesis 1–2 to speak of creation without being subverted into ciphers or dissolved into presumptuous metaphysics—but not without finding frequent adumbrations of the person and work of the Son of God.[62] Ephrem's reputation within the Syrian church and beyond[63]—despite his limited influence on the Latin church—and the simple concreteness of his cosmology mean that we ought to give serious regard to his theological presentation and what is probably the clearest literal explanation of Genesis 1 that we see among the church fathers.[64]

JOHN CHRYSOSTOM AND THE ANTIOCHENE SCHOOL

The rush of sermons and commentaries expounding the creation week in Genesis would continue with Basil the Great, Gregory of Nyssa, Ambrose, and Augustine, but also involved the most famous representative of the Antiochene school of interpretation: John Chrysostom. The modern scholarly reaction against the simplistic contrast of allegorical versus literal approaches to Scripture has prompted uncertainty over the very reference to distinct Alexandrian and Antiochene schools. The terminology has been generally retained in recent discussion, with the qualification that Alexandria had a formal catechetical school whereas Antiochene thinking about biblical interpretation did not occur in a formal setting.[65] As the East Syrian

---

60. This term "meristic" refers to the deliberate literary device where two opposite poles are named to implicitly include everything in between them or all of their contents. Thus "Heavens and earth" becomes shorthand for "everything."

61. Wickes, "Ephrem's Interpretation of Genesis," 48 n. 10.

62. Hunt, "Self-Enclosing God," 97–106 (i.e., section 2.2.3–2.3.1); Griffith, "Ephrem's Teaching Songs," 27–38.

63. McVey, *Hymns*, 3–5, 27–28; Lucas Van Rompay, "The Christian Syriac Tradition of Interpretation," *HB/OT* 1.1:622; ten Napel, "Hexaemeral Literature in Syriac," 65.

64. Mathews, Amar, and McVey, *Prose Works*, 75.

65. R. B. ter Haar Romeny, "Eusebius of Emesa's Commentary on Genesis and the

Ephrem in the previous section represented the range of Christian fathers writing in Syriac, the West Syrian John Chrysostom will represent his colleagues writing in Greek in this Antiochene "school."[66] These Antiochene theologians are not prominent in modern creation debates, although their creation-related comments are becoming increasingly accessible in English translations.[67]

"Chrysostom" is really a nickname (Gk. golden-mouth) earned by virtue of John's winsome preaching. As a Greek father linguistically, like the Cappadocians, John Chrysostom had an ecclesiastical career that was, at least temporarily, very successful. John established his giftedness as a preacher in Antioch, a Syrian city of cultural and administrative importance that hosted an already ancient and prominent yet fractured Christian community.[68] He rose to become the influential bishop of the eastern Roman capital Constantinople in 397, though political battles, both ecclesiastical and secular, got the better of him, and he died on his way into exile in 407.[69] His reputation soon bounced back after his death, and

Origins of the Antiochene School," in *The Book of Genesis in Jewish and Oriental Christian Interpretation: A Collection of Essays*, ed. Judith Frishman and Lucas Van Rompay (Leuven: Peeters, 1997), 127. Regarding the persistence of this terminological distinction, see Bradley Nassif, "Introduction," in *The School of Antioch: Biblical Theology and the Church in Syria*, ed. Vahan S. Hovhanessian (New York: Lang, 2016), 2–3.

66. Justified and summarized in Hidal, "Antiochene School," 557–62. Shared concern for preserving the literal sense and historical element of Old Testament texts has raised the question of the relationship between Ephrem and the Antiochene school. Van Rompay concludes "that the distance between Ephrem's Commentary [on Genesis] and the works of the Antiochenes is quite considerable." Van Rompay, "Antiochene Biblical Interpretation," 122.

67. E.g., Severian of Gabala, "Homilies on Creation and Fall," in *Commentaries on Genesis 1–3*, ed. Robert C. Hill, Michael Glerup, and Gerald L. Bray, Ancient Christian Texts (Downers Grove, IL: InterVarsity Press, 2010), 1–94; Theodoret of Cyrrhus, *Questions on the Octateuch*, trans. R. C. Hill, Library of Early Christianity (Washington, DC: Catholic University Press of America, 2006). Others who commented on Genesis in a generally Antiochene mode include Eusebius of Emesa, Theodore of Mopsuestia, and Acacius of Caesarea. See *DOC*, 35–38. In modern creation-related presentations, Jack Lewis briefly mentions this group; see Lewis, "Days of Creation," 446.

68. J. N. D. Kelly, *Golden Mouth: The Story of John Chrysostom – Ascetic, Preacher, Bishop* (Ithaca, NY: Cornell University Press, 1998), 1–57; Pauline Allen and Wendy Mayer, *John Chrysostom* (London: Routledge, 2002), 3–22, 26–33.

69. R. Kaczynksi, "John Chrysostom," *DECL*, 330–31; J. Quasten, *Patrology*, vol. 3 of *The Golden Age of Greek Patristic Literature* (Westminster: Newman, 1960), 424–29.

thanks to his freedom from any suspicion of Nestorianism, which led to the destruction of the works of many of his fellow Antiochenes, his literary output survived virtually in its entirety. His literary legacy, mostly composed of texts of his sermon series but also including letters and treatises, runs to more than nine hundred individual pieces, the greatest store of any Greek father.[70]

Genesis occupies a significant place in his expository output, since his major Genesis series runs to sixty-seven homilies, itself replacing a set of eight homilies on Genesis 1–3 that were among John's very first sermons following his ordination as priest, which were delivered during the Lent of 386. Lent was already an established site in the liturgical calendar for Genesis exposition.[71] These early sermons and his *Homilies on the Statutes* 7–9 both take a "common places" approach, addressing particular theological questions rather than offering continuous exposition of the Genesis text. Thus, they both skip directly from the issue of absolute beginnings in relation to Genesis 1:1–3 to later theological questions relating to Genesis without dwelling on the events of the creation days.[72]

Therefore it is the longer set of Genesis sermons that elicits most modern commentary, often via R. C. Hill's 1985 translation, so this series will be our focus. The dating of these sermons is quite uncertain, with firmer proposals by Hill (as early as 385), Quasten (388), and Kelly (389) disputed by Sandwell, who explains that we cannot even be sure the series belongs to Chrysostom's time at Antioch.[73] That the fuller series probably utilizes the earlier Lenten efforts and likely also had to await John's ordination before being preached means that it probably follows the 386 and 387 series.[74] So we are surer of the liturgical and cultural setting of

---

70. Kaczynksi, "John Chrysostom," 332; Quasten, *Patrology*, 429–30, 433–34; John Chrysostom, *Homilies on Genesis 1–17*, trans. R. C. Hill, FC 74 (Washington, DC: Catholic University of America Press, 1985), 3–4. A ready way to grasp the scale of this output is to see that the entire first series of *Nicene and Post-Nicene Fathers* is occupied by the works of Augustine (eight volumes) and Chrysostom (six volumes) alone.

71. Kaczynksi, "John Chrysostom," 332; Monique Alexandre, *Le commencement du livre Genèse I–V: La version grecque de la Septente et sa réception*, Christianisme Antique 3 (Paris: Beauchesne, 1988), 48; Kelly, *Golden Mouth*, 58.

72. Kelly, *Golden Mouth*, 58–60. Text of the *Sermones in Genesim* in PG 54:581–92 (for Genesis 1); for the *Homilies on the Statutes*, see *NPNF*[1] 9:315–489.

73. Quasten, *Patrology*, 434; Hill, *Homilies on Genesis 1–17*, 4–6; Kelly, *Golden Mouth*, 89; Isabella Sandwell, "How to Teach Genesis 1:1–19: John Chrysostom and Basil of Caesarea on the Creation of the World," *JECS* 19.4 (2011): 590 and n. 4.

74. Kelly, *Golden Mouth*, 39.

this longer series than its specific dating. It consists of continuous exposition of the Genesis text and follows Chrysostom's habit of exegeting details of the text before moving on to moral exhortation connected to the passage cited.[75] Despite suspicions that not all of John's surviving homily series represent live sermons, there is wide agreement that this particular series frequently reflects John's live engagement with a listening audience, seen for example in references back to the previous day's sermon content (*Hom. Gen.* 3.3) or urgent calls for close attention (*Hom. Gen.* 4.9).[76] John, like many other church fathers, had enjoyed a full rhetorical education, and employed all he had learned about effective oral communication in his sermon delivery.[77] John deliberately spoke for audience impact and life change; his Genesis sermons, like his other homilies, are directed at the full realization of spiritual renewal in daily life, and so they are dominated by a moral-spiritual focus with correct doctrine as second priority in the face of threatening heresies. "Patristic teachings on Gen. 1–2 are always more than explanations of what these opening chapters of the Bible might mean. They are also attempts to lead listeners into a life of faith."[78]

Chrysostom is a little hard to pin down for an opinion on the nature of the creation days. In chapter 5, Basil will prove cautious about falling into unreliable speculation about the nature and origin of the cosmos as he explains Genesis 1, but Chrysostom in these sermons seems positively jaundiced by the possibility of learning anything supplementary to the Genesis account through other avenues of knowledge and stoutly avoids offering any physical description of creation based on Genesis 1.[79] His sermons are relatively accessible for the modern Christian reader because of their practicality and pastoral sensitivity, but they are frustrating for the potential "recruiter" because they downplay the physical history of the cosmos. As Forster and Marston put it, Chrysostom "appears to take the days 'literally' but in truth is totally unconcerned with scientific issues."[80] The most

---

75. Allen and Mayer, *John Chrysostom*, 30; Young, *Biblical Exegesis*, 249.

76. Kelly, *Golden Mouth*, 93.

77. Kaczynksi, "John Chrysostom," 330; Allen and Mayer, *John Chrysostom*, 27–29; Young, *Biblical Exegesis*, 97, 115, 170–76.

78. Rine, "Interpretations of Genesis 1–2," 129.

79. Sandwell, "How to Teach Genesis 1," 549, 562.

80. Forster and Marston, *Reason, Science and Faith*, 207. One exception is arguably his insistence on creation *ex nihilo* (*Hom. Gen.* 2.6, 11; 3.5).

Chrysostom gives away concerning the relationship of the creation days to time comes in the passage most often cited in recent debates:

> Then, when he had assigned to each its own name [i.e., "day" to light and "night" to darkness], he linked the two together in the words, "Evening came, and morning came: one day." He made a point of speaking of the end of the day and the end of the night as one, so as to grasp a certain order and sequence in visible things and avoid any impression of confusion.
>
> Now, we are in a position to learn from the Holy Spirit, through the tongue of this blessed author, what things were created on the first day and what things on the other days. This itself is a mark of the considerateness of the loving God. I mean, his all-powerful hand and boundless wisdom were not at a loss even to create everything in one day. Why say "one day"? even in a brief moment. Yet it was not because of its utility to him that he produced anything that exists, since being self-sufficient he is in need of nothing. It was rather out of his loving kindness and goodness that he created everything; accordingly he created things in sequence and provided us with a clear instruction about created things through the tongue of the blessed author, so that we might learn about them precisely and not fall into the error of those led by purely human reasoning. (*Hom. Gen.* 3.11–12 [Hill])

Andrew Louth summarizes Chrysostom's point this way: "The concept of a 'day' cannot be reduced to an instant but implies a process."[81] That temporal succession is in view becomes clearer in Chrysostom's ensuing discussion of creation events, where the appearance of light or vegetation prior to the heavenly bodies is theologically significant and directs false honor away from the sun and moon in themselves (*Hom. Gen.* 5.11–13; 6.12–14).[82] His three days before the sun are very real! Yet the individual acts of creation are displayed as instantaneous; no sooner was the command to the earth to produce vegetation uttered than "In an instant you could see the earth, which just before had been shapeless and unkempt, take on such beauty as almost to defy comparison with heaven" (*Hom. Gen.* 5.13

---

81. Andrew Louth, ed., *Genesis 1–11*, Ancient Christian Commentary on Scripture (Downers Grove, IL: InterVarsity Press, 2001), 43, 45.

82. For recognition of this in the "recruitment" literature see Lewis, "Days of Creation," 447–48; Jaki, *Genesis 1*, 80; Kulikovsky, *Creation, Fall, Restoration*, 63–64.

[Hill]). Rine notes the attraction of an instantaneous creation for Chrysostom, who consequently attributes the staggered nature of creation acts to the needs of human comprehension that creation has God as its author.[83]

John's creation presentation is conservative, believing, and exclusively biblical. Recruitment of his stance in creation debates is usually faithful, aside from the pitfalls of offering of quotations from an ancient author such as Chrysostom as if they are unambiguous and self-explanatory. Given the sheer cognitive and historical distance between the ancient setting and ours, modern writers really need to tell their readers what they understand such ancient figures to have meant by their words. Worse is the practice of antique name-dropping, such as mentioning Chrysostom in lists of authorities supporting young-earth creation without even the inclusion of a citation or reference or urging audiences to "read John Chrysostom and the Eastern Fathers," with a vague hint that they do not support theistic evolution.[84] The encouragement to read these figures I support; the inclusion of their names in lists of "heroes of the faith who are on our side" without additional evidence is not very meaningful.

Does Chrysostom, then, acknowledge the temporal reality of the creation week? Evidently so. The quoted passage expounds the idea that though the power of God makes an instantaneous creation very feasible, the "sequence"[85] of created things is for human benefit, "so that we might learn about them precisely[86] and not fall into the error of those led by purely human reasoning" (*Hom. Gen.* 3.12

83. Rine, "Interpretations of Genesis 1–2," 130.

84. Quotation from Paul Nelson and John Mark Reynolds, "Young Earth Creationism," in *Three Views on Creation and Evolution*, ed. J. P. Moreland and J. M. Reynolds (Grand Rapids: Zondervan, 1999), 74 with quotation. See also the responses of Duncan and Hall in "Part One: The 24-Hour View," in *The Genesis Debate: Three Views on the Days of Creation*, ed. David Hagopian (Mission Viejo, CA: Crux, 2001), 102, 111; David W. Hall, "The Evolution of Mythology: Classic Creation Survives as the Fittest among Its Critics," in *Did God Create in Six Days?*, ed. J. A. Pipa Jr. and D. W. Hall (White Hall, WV: Tolle Lege, 2005), 301.

85. "Sequence" in Hill's translation of our quoted passage from 3.11 represents a favorite word of Chrysostom and other Antiochene interpreters: ἀκολουθία (*akolouthia*). The second time "sequence" appears in the passage it represents a phrase that means "in stages" or "step by step": κατὰ μέρος (*kata meros*).

86. This is another of John's technical terms derived from his rhetorical background and related to his understanding of biblical inspiration: ἀκριβῶς (*akribōs*). See PG 53.35d (fourth to the last line).

[Hill]). He does not appear to mean that creation is timeless but requires a sequential presentation in the text as an accommodation to human weakness, even though Chrysostom repeatedly emphasizes that God accommodates the words of Scripture to limited human cognitive capacity. His term for God's motivation to communicate simply for the sake of human understanding is *synkatabasis*, traditionally translated "condescension" but rendered "considerateness" by R. C. Hill in the passage quoted above to avoid any unintended negative connotation.[87]

So Genesis 1 is characterized by "considerateness." To speak of God as evaluating his own work as good, or creating man by breathing into soil, is all language accommodated to weak minds not ready for fuller spiritual truths.[88] That Genesis 1 is so focused on physical creation and hardly expounds spiritual mysteries found in the more impressive prologue to John's Gospel or in Colossians 1 is a potential embarrassment that Chrysostom strives to resolve by recourse to the limitations of the original audience (*Hom. Gen.* 2.7–8; 3.7). Yet Chrysostom does not therefore dissolve the creation sequence of Genesis 1 into a didactic literary device. No, as for Calvin later it is God's creative *action* that is accommodated to human weakness here, and not just his narrative *expression*. This is very much in keeping with the Antiochenes' consciousness of history, and although Chrysostom never comes out and says that the creation week is 168 hours long, which would really violate his disinterest in natural cosmic origins for their own sake, he does retain a sequential, "before-and-after" understanding of the narrative of Genesis 1, where each creation day's events build upon those of the day before.

Isabella Sandwell offers a fascinating comparison between the approaches to Genesis 1 of Chrysostom and of Basil the Great.[89] Finding that Basil engaged in explanation of what the creation narrative had to say about the physical cosmos, whereas Chrysostom studiously avoided such explanation, she weighs up the pros and cons of these choices. Avoidance of physical explanation avoids the risk of redundancy as cosmological conceptions change, making Chrysostom's tactic seem judicious. On the other hand, it fails to address the believer's need to reconcile

---

87. Paul Nadim Tarazi, "Exegesis for John Chrysostom: Preaching and Teaching the Bible," in *The School of Antioch: Biblical Theology and the Church in Syria*, ed. Vahan S. Hovhanessian (New York: Lang, 2016), 14; Stephen Westerholm and Martin Westerholm, *Reading Sacred Scripture: Voices from the History of Biblical Interpretation* (Grand Rapids: Eerdmans, 2016), 116 and n. 32.

88. See, e.g., *Hom. Gen.* 3.9–10; 4.11; 12.15 .

89. Sandwell, "How to Teach Genesis 1," esp. 555–62.

biblical teaching with real data about nature that do exist beneath the obscuring cloud of changeable theories and carry conviction for the well-educated outsider to Christianity, as Augustine will famously recognize.[90] There will be something to admire about Basil's more sincere interest in the concreteness of creation as a praiseworthy object of spiritual contemplation. This interest required Basil to offer at least some help to his audience to understand how the narrative's depiction related to the outside world they saw daily, and so it is to Basil's *Hexaemeron* that we now turn.

90. *Gen. litt.* 1.19.39. See chapter 6 and again the critique of Chrysostom in Sandwell, "How to Teach Genesis 1," 555, 564.

Chapter Five

BASIL'S BORDERLANDS CREATION AND
HIS HEXAEMERAL DISCIPLES

Basil of Caesarea (or Basil the Great) (ca. 330–378) was one of the Cappadocian Fathers along with his younger brother Gregory of Nyssa (ca. 335–396)[1] and close friend Gregory of Nazianzus (ca. 326–ca. 390). All three became bishops within the same province, Cappadocia, in central Asia Minor.[2] Through their spiritual example, sophisticated theology, and ecclesiastical influence, the Cappadocian Fathers came to have disproportionate importance in the Eastern, Greek-speaking patristic church. Basil's location at Caesarea placed him at an influential crossroads between the capital of the eastern Empire, Constantinople, and the eastern frontiers of the Empire in Mesopotamia and Armenia, and Basil met imperial officials all the way up to the emperor Valens.[3]

Basil and the two Gregorys were frequently involved in church politics and doctrinal controversies with other leaders, amounting most of the time to "virtual civil war" and often with the strategic nearby Christian city of Antioch.[4]

---

1. Relying here for Gregory's life span on George Karamanolis, "Gregory of Nyssa," in *Brill Encyclopedia of Early Christianity Online* (Leiden: Brill, 2018), http://dx.doi.org /10.1163/2589-7993_EECO_SIM_00001480.

2. The administrative division of Cappadocia during Basil's time challenged his ecclesiastical control and helped prompt the appointment of his brother Gregory to the See of Nyssa: Philip Rousseau, *Basil of Caesarea*, Transformation of the Classical Heritage 20 (Berkeley: University of California Press, 1994), 235.

3. Rousseau, *Basil of Caesarea*, 133–34, 283.

4. Rousseau, *Basil of Caesarea*, 87.

All three fathers were highly educated: Basil and Gregory of Nazianzus were student colleagues in Athens, the Oxford of their time, while Gregory of Nyssa, initially tutored by Basil, seems ultimately to have at least equaled him in contemporary philosophical learning, judging by a comparison of their two hexaemeral works.[5] Basil was left with significant reservations about the value of such "secular" learning.[6] Whenever human philosophy and spiritual priorities seem to compete, he prefers to "let the simplicity of faith be stronger than the deductions of reason."[7] But he nevertheless brings to his preaching and writing both a robust and thoughtful use of contemporary philosophy. Basil also had a pioneering role in the church's definition of its doctrine of the Trinity.[8]

In *Homilies on the Hexaemeron*, Basil offers one of the highest-profile expositions of biblical creation among the church fathers, second only to Augustine's, and the first surviving hexaemeron in the stricter sense of a work devoted solely to the exposition of the creation week of Genesis 1.[9] His *Hexaemeron* predates and inspires the other stand-alone hexaemera that survive from this period and utilizes the Genesis writings of predecessors such as Philo, Origen, (probably)

5. Rousseau, *Basil of Caesarea*, 27–60, 62.

6. Adam Rasmussen, *Genesis and Cosmos: Basil and Origen on Genesis 1 and Cosmology*, BAC 14 (Leiden: Brill, 2019), 29–33.

7. *Hex.* 1.10. Translation from Basil of Caesarea, "On the Hexaemeron," in *Exegetic Homilies*, ed. Agnes Clare Way, FC 46 (Washington, DC: Catholic University of America Press, 1963), 17,; Rousseau, *Basil of Caesarea*, 40, 48. See also *NPNF²* 8:51–107. For the Greek text I am chiefly using Basil of Caesarea, *Homélies sur l'Hexaéméron*, trans. Stanislas Giet, 2nd ed., SC 26 (Paris: Cerf, 1968). However see the recent Basil of Caesarea, *Homilien zum Hexaemeron*, ed. Emmanuel Amand de Mendieta and Stig Y. Rudberg, GCSNF 2 (Berlin: Akademie, 1997).

8. Stephen M. Hildebrand, *The Trinitarian Theology of Basil of Caesarea: A Synthesis of Greek Thought and Biblical Truth* (Washington, DC: Catholic University of America Press, 2007), 28–31, 188–91.

9. E.g., J. C. M. van Winden, "Hexaemeron," *RAC* 14:1260–62; F. Robbins, *The Hexaemeral Literature: A Study of the Greek and Latin Commentaries in Genesis* (Chicago: University of Chicago Press, 1912), 42; Otto Zöckler, *Geschichte der Beziehungen zwischen Theologie und Naturwissenschaft: Mit besonderer Rücksicht auf Schöpfungsgeschichte*, 2 vols. (Gütersloh: Bertelsmann, 1877), 1:186, 197; Paul M. Blowers, *Drama of the Divine Economy: Creator and Creation in Early Christian Theology and Piety*, OECS (Oxford: Oxford University Press, 2012), 107–38; Andrew Brown, "Hexaemeron," in *Brill Encyclopedia of Early Christianity Online* (Leiden: Brill, 2021), https://doi.org/10.1163/2589-7993_EECO_SIM_00001554.

Hippolytus, and Theophilus of Antioch, as well as creation themes from Plato's *Timaeus* or Aristotle's theory of the four elements.[10]

Basil's *Hexaemeron* did not start life as a biblical commentary but rather as a set of homilies or sermons. The nine sermons, whose attribution to Basil is widely accepted, were preached over five days (Monday through Friday) during the celebration of Lent, meaning that Basil's audience faced the challenge of attending sermons either side of the working day and often on an empty stomach! (We see Basil pulling his audience into line at times when their attention was wandering or their stomachs were growling.)[11] Basil was cleverly leading his congregation through the creation week in parallel with the passing week of their present time in a walk-through-the-creation exercise. We have already seen with John Chrysostom that these chapters of Genesis had become part of Christian Lenten liturgy and the pattern will continue with Ambrose, as we will observe later in this chapter.[12]

The *Hexaemeron*, probably Basil's culminating work, is thought to date to the year he died (378 CE).[13] The fact that it appeared first in preached form suits Basil's first calling as a bishop overseeing and exhorting the faithful to seek God and to live faithfully in the world. Because his audience was quite mixed, representing a range of classes, occupations, and educational levels, Basil could not unleash the full might of his impressive education. What seems at points a philosophically technical treatment of creation is in fact quite restrained, since Basil is very mindful that his sermon series is much more a pastoral than an intellectual exercise. He is willing to consider philosophical (physical and metaphysical) questions, but

10. Charlotte Köckert, *Christliche Kosmologie und kaiserzeitliche Philosophie: Die Auslegung des Schöpfungsberichtes bei Origenes, Basilius und Gregor von Nyssa vor dem Hintergrund kaiserzeitlicher Timaeus-Interpretation*, STAC 56 (Tübingen: Mohr Siebeck, 2009), 313, 322–24.

11. See, e.g., *Hex.* 8.8 .

12. Andrew Louth, "The Fathers on Genesis," in *The Book of Genesis: Composition, Reception, and Interpretation*, ed. David L. Petersen, Craig A. Evans, and Joel N. Lohr, VTSup 152 (Leiden: Brill, 2012), 44–47; Monique Alexandre, *Le commencement du livre Genèse I–V: La version grecque de la Septente et sa réception*, Christianisme Antique 3 (Paris: Beauchesne, 1988), 48; Yves M.-J. Congar, "Le thème de Dieu-créateur et les explications de l'Hexaméron dans la tradition chrétienne," in *L'Homme devant Dieu: Mélanges offerts au père Henri de Lubac*, 3 vols. (Paris: Aubier, 1963), 1:192–93.

13. J. Pauli, "Basil of Caesarea," *DECL*, 95, 97; Rousseau, *Basil of Caesarea*, 318–19, 346; Christopher Hall, *Reading Scripture with the Church Fathers* (Downers Grove, IL: InterVarsity Press, 1998), 85.

he never forgets to prioritize his hearers' spiritual benefit. As soon as he feels that questions of natural philosophy, such as whether the earth is spherical or lies at the center of the cosmos, are offering diminishing spiritual returns, he lets them drop and returns to his core business of building up the souls of the believers (e.g., *Hex.* 1.10; 9.1). That Basil had to trim his intellectual sails for an everyday audience makes his *Hexaemeron* relatively accessible and edifying for the present-day Christian reader in a way that the more philosophical offerings from Gregory of Nyssa or John Philoponus (d. ca. 570) are not.[14]

Basil receives considerable commentary in our modern creation-related literature, although he comes at a rather distant second to Augustine. Debate over who can claim Basil as an interpretive ancestor warms debate between young-earth creation and day-age advocates.[15] Basil's explicit literalism in this work makes him a hero for strict creationists, who like his definition of the first creation day in terms of twenty-four hours.[16] Even commentators without a literalist agenda often admit that Basil is among the most obviously literal ancient interpreters of the creation week in Genesis.[17] On the other hand, he is recognized as making statements early in the homilies that seem to espouse an instantaneous creation, using the terms "day" and "age" in close proximity, though the significance of the association may be left unstated and unclear.[18] Forster and Marston want to deny

14. Zöckler, *Geschichte*, 1:187.

15. Ross and Archer, "The Day-Age Response," in *The Genesis Debate: Three Views on the Days of Creation*, ed. David Hagopian (Mission Viejo, CA: Crux, 2001), 69; Duncan and Hall, "The 24-Hour Response," in Hagopian, *Genesis Debate*, 170; Jonathan D. Sarfati, *Refuting Compromise* (Green Forest, AR: Master Books, 2004), 113; Roger Forster and Paul Marston, *Reason, Science and Faith* (Crowborough: Monarch, 1999), 210.

16. James R. Mook, "The Church Fathers on Genesis, the Flood, and the Age of the Earth," in *Coming to Grips with Genesis: Biblical Authority and the Age of the Earth*, ed. Terry Mortenson and Thane H. Ury (Green Forest, AR: Master Books, 2008), 30–31; Jud Davis, "Unresolved Major Questions: Evangelicals and Genesis 1–2," in *Reading Genesis 1–2: An Evangelical Conversation*, ed. J. Daryl Charles (Peabody, MA: Hendrickson, 2013), 217; Don Batten, "Genesis Means What It Says: Basil (AD 329–379)," Answers in Genesis, September 1, 1994, https://answersingenesis.org/genesis/genesis-means-what-it-says-basil-ad-329-379/; Sarfati, *Refuting Compromise*, 112–13. Oddly, the first paragraphs concerning Basil in the Sarfati and Batten creationist pieces are identical, though neither credits the other for the content.

17. See the comments of Irons and Kline in Hagopian, *Genesis Debate*, 90; Davis A. Young and Ralph Stearley, *The Bible, Rocks and Time: Geological Evidence for the Age of the Earth* (Downers Grove, IL: InterVarsity Press, 2008), 40.

18. Hugh Ross, *Creation and Time* (Colorado Springs, CO: Navpress, 1994), 21–22;

Basil to the literalist camp.[19] The surveys of Robert Letham and Jack Lewis reveal a measure of confusion as they try to reconcile Basil's statements about instantaneous creation with his more realistic treatment of elements in the account such as light before the sun.[20]

Basil's creation interpretation in the *Hexaemeron*, then, is one of the key interpretations of the creation week in the patristic era and follows this structure: Homily 1 covers Genesis 1:1 alone, with all the theological and philosophical questions it raises. Homily 2 sees Basil with his hands equally full explaining all the issues raised in Genesis 1:2. Homily 3 is concerned with the "firmament" (Heb. *rāqîaʿ*) of the second day of creation (Gen. 1:6–8), which for Origen and Gregory of Nyssa forms the boundary between the physical and time-bound world we know and the timeless and eternal realm of God above, yet Basil treats instead as a physical barrier within the cosmos.[21] This homily also hosts the first of Basil's position statements regarding allegorical interpretation of early Genesis.

Homily 4 concerns the first part of day three of creation, the separation of land and sea, requiring further explanation of the two Aristotelian elements of earth and water. Homily 5 turns to the appearance of vegetation in the second part of day three, noting that a causal role for the sun in the production of vegetation is ruled out, since the sun is yet to come in the creative sequence (*Hex.* 5.1). Here Basil begins to find evidence for God's provision for human life in the properties of various plant species and edges toward the kind of moral (or "tropological") object lessons seen earlier in Theophilus of Antioch, *To Autolycus* 2.14–19.

Homily 6 concerns the luminaries of day four and strives to debunk the religious error that leads to their worship or to astrology. The sea creatures of day five

Ross, *A Matter of Days: Resolving a Creation Controversy* (Colorado Springs, CO: Navpress, 2004), 46–47; Hagopian, *Genesis Debate*, 69, 205; Peter C. Bouteneff, *Beginnings: Ancient Christian Readings of the Biblical Creation Narratives* (Grand Rapids: Baker Academic, 2008), 134.

19. Forster and Marston, *Reason, Science and Faith*, 206–7.

20. Robert Letham, "'In the Space of Six Days': The Days of Creation from Origen to the Westminster Assembly," *WTJ* 61.2 (1999): 152–53; Jack P. Lewis, "The Days of Creation: An Historical Survey of Interpretation," *JETS* 32 (1989): 446–47.

21. This is contra I. P. Sheldon-Williams, "The Greek Christian Platonist Tradition from the Cappadocians to Maximus and Eriugena," *CHLGEMP*, 435–37. The logic of Basil's fine-yet-real waters above the firmament in *Hex.* 3.8–11 precludes this. See Alenka Arko, "Between Literal and Allegorical Exegesis: The Cappadocian Fathers on *Hexaemeron*," *Lateranum* 79.2 (2013): 498; David C. DeMarco, "The Presentation and Reception of Basil's *Homiliae in Hexaemeron* in Gregory's *In Hexaemeron*," *ZAC* 17.2 (2013): 346.

provide fodder for a range of tropological lessons about human life in Homily 7. Thinking he has taken care of day five, Basil turns to the appearance of land animals, belonging to day six of the creation week, in Homily 8. But the nods and winks of his audience alert him to the fact that he has forgotten to expound the moral lessons found in the characteristics of birds (8.2), and he hastily backtracks (unless this was preplanned, complete with mock surprise). Thus, the lessons to be drawn from land animals is postponed until Homily 9. This leaves little time in that homily for treating the significance of human creation, which is touched on briefly before Basil admits that the sun has long set and he had better let everyone go. He expresses the hope that "we shall later add a more perfect examination of the facts lying before us" (*Hex.* 9.6 [Way]). Basil thus becomes the patron saint of every rushed sermon ending or fast-forwarded lecture. His fuller treatment evidently never appeared, or if it did, the transmission of the final two homilies (10 and 11) was more complicated and uncertain than that of the first nine. The perceived deficit in the finished work (if such it was) would be addressed by his brother Gregory with his *On the Making of Humankind* (*De opificio hominis*).[22]

BASIL'S LITERAL APPROACH TO INTERPRETATION OF THE CREATION WEEK

We have to read almost to the end of Basil's *Hexaemeron* to find his famous statement on his choice of literal over allegorical interpretation in relation to the hexaemeral narrative, one often noted by contributors to modern creation debates along with patristics scholars:[23]

22. Louth, "Fathers on Genesis," 569; Bouteneff, *Beginnings*, 136–37; Arko, "Between Literal and Allegorical Exegesis," 486 and n. 4; Philip Rousseau, "Human Nature and Its Material Setting in Basil of Caesarea's Sermons on the Creation," *Heythrop Journal* 49.2 (2008): 222–23; Craig D. Allert, *Early Christian Readings of Genesis One: Patristic Exegesis and Literal Interpretation* (Downers Grove, IL: InterVarsity Press, 2018), 306–15, who accepts and expounds the two further homilies as Basil's work. The primary edition of the Greek text is Basil of Caesarea, *Sur l'origine de l'homme: (Hom. 10. et 11. de l'Hexaéméron)*, ed. Alexis Smets and Michel van Esbroeck, SC 160 (Paris: Cerf, 1970); in translation, see Nonna Verna Harrison, ed., *St. Basil the Great on the Human Condition*, Popular Patristics 30 (Crestwood, NY: St. Vladimir's Seminary Press, 2005).

23. Lewis, "Days of Creation," 446; Letham, "Space of Six Days," 152; Mook, "Church Fathers," 30; Andrew Kulikovsky, *Creation, Fall, Restoration: A Biblical Theology of Creation* (Fearn: Mentor, 2009), 62–63; Batten, "Genesis Means What It Says"; Sujin Pak,

> I know the laws of allegory, although I did not invent them of myself, but
> have met them in the works of others. Those who do not admit the common
> meaning of the Scriptures say that water is not water, but some other nature,
> and they explain a plant and a fish according to their opinion. They describe
> also the production of reptiles and wild animals, changing it according to their
> own notions, just like the dream interpreters, who interpret for their own ends
> the appearances seen in their dreams. When I hear "grass," I think of grass, and
> in the same manner I understand everything as it is said, a plant, a fish, a wild
> animal, and an ox. "Indeed, I am not ashamed of the gospel." (*Hex.* 9.1 [Way])

This seems a funny place to quote Romans 1:16, but Basil means that he is not
ashamed of the natural meaning of Scripture and does not feel compelled to make
interpretive somersaults to make it more palatable to the educated mind. What
was the possible objection of the educated mind to Genesis 1? Basil goes on to
mention ideas of the shape of the earth, its potential circumference, and how its
shadow might cause eclipses of the moon. These are the things that the natural
philosopher wants explained about the cosmos but finds no mention of them in
Genesis 1. Evidently some took offense at Scripture over this, and Basil implies
that some allegorical treatments of Genesis 1 strove to insert these important
topics cryptically into the text of Genesis. Greek philosophers had been doing
this with their own treasured literature, such as Homer's writings, for centuries.[24]
What is Basil's explanation in defense of Genesis?

> Since he left unsaid, as useless for us, things in no way pertaining to us, shall
> we for this reason believe that the words of the Spirit are of less value than
> their foolish wisdom? Or shall I rather give glory to Him who has not kept
> our mind occupied with vanities but has ordained that all things be written
> for the edification and guidance of our souls? This is a thing of which they
> seem to me to have been unaware, who have attempted by false arguments
> and allegorical interpretations to bestow on the Scripture a dignity of their
> own imagining. But, theirs is the attitude of one who considers himself wiser

---

"Pre-Modern Readings of Genesis 1, Part 1," BioLogos, October 9, 2012, https://biologos
.org/articles/pre-modern-readings-of-genesis-1.

24. E.g., *HBI* 1:33–40. We will shortly see Augustine do something similar when he
finds that angels inexplicably do not feature in the creation account.

than the revelations of the Spirit and introduces his own ideas in pretense of an explanation (Gk. *exēgēsis*). Therefore, let it be understood as it has been written. (*Hex.* 9.1 [Way])

Therefore, a possible motivation for treating a text like Genesis 1 allegorically is to protect the reputation of Scripture where its literal sense seems, using modern terminology, scientifically absurd, incomplete, or morally offensive. Perhaps better than saying "scientifically absurd" would be to say "philosophically implausible." Even a moderately educated listener in Basil's day might ask why, given the well-known "gravity" of water that made it fall lower than the air, Genesis 1 spoke of an upper level of waters higher than the atmosphere. Or a Neoplatonist with a rather emanationist view of reality whereby creation emerges from the being of God from the top down, starting with the most important, purest, and most powerful spiritual beings or entities, might be troubled as to why no created personalities or powers higher than humans are mentioned in Genesis 1. Basil is eager to defend the intellectual credibility of Scripture in these sermons, but views allegory as an undignified and high-handed cutting of the interpretive knot.

Basil doesn't name his target(s) here, and scholars debate whether he is trying to distance himself from Origen or from sectarian use of allegory to support unorthodox positions. We recall Origen's amusement at the idea of imagining days before the sun, which for Origen was Scripture's clue that its words were not referring to historical realities (*Princ.* 4.3.1). Another interpretation that Basil refutes is evidently Origen's view that the upper waters demarcated on day two of creation must refer to angelic or purely spiritual beings.[25] Yet Basil was influenced by Origen too, especially through the third-century bishop Gregory Thaumaturgus.[26] Shortly after their student days, Basil and Gregory of Nazianzus had jointly distilled Origen's thought into their *Philocalia* in a gesture of admiration combined with a subtle sanitization of his legacy (although this historical

25. Paget, "Alexandrian Tradition," *HB/OT* 1.1:539; Richard Lim, "The Politics of Interpretation in Basil of Caesarea's Hexaemeron," *VC* 44 (1990): 355; Blowers, *Drama of the Divine Economy*, 127; Alexander H. Pierce, "Reconsidering Ambrose's Reception of Basil's Homiliae in Hexaemeron: The Lasting Legacy of Origen," *ZAC* 23.3 (2019): 430–31; Rasmussen, *Genesis and Cosmos*, 140–42. Lim is the voice of dissent in this group.
26. Rousseau, *Basil of Caesarea*, 11–14; H. Scheider, "Gregory the Wonderworker," *DECL*, 269.

claim has recently come into question).[27] Some writers have suggested that Basil had moved away from Origen's approach over time, perhaps through the more literalist influence of figures such as Diodore of Tarsus, or in the anti-Origenist climate engendered by Epiphanius's inclusion of Origenism in his catalogue of heresies in the *Panarion*.[28] Others think that the hyper-allegorism of heretical sects like the Manicheans, by which the meaning of a text such as Genesis 1 could be thoroughly distorted to suit their teachings, is the true target of Basil's ire.[29] Yet Basil's cautionary statements about allegory seem broad enough to include much of Origen's interpretation of Genesis 1–3, to the extent that we can still discover it, even while his cosmology remains partly Origenist.[30]

While some see Basil's renunciation of allegory here as quite far-reaching, many commentators ask whether it might apply to this sermon series in a more limited way.[31] Some believe that Basil's audience is the key, being a relatively unsophisticated group unprepared for the delicate art of allegorical interpretation, a suggestion supported by some opening comments from Basil's brother Gregory of Nyssa in his own *Apologia in hexaemeron* soon to come.[32] Hildebrand counters that the audience of Basil's *Homilies on the Psalms* were no less of a motley crew; yet there we find Basil freely using allegory alongside literal interpretation to draw spiritual lessons or extract truths about Christ.[33] He suggests that what we see in the *Hexaemeron* is not a blanket rejection of allegory but an increased sensitivity

27. Rousseau, *Basil of Caesarea*, 82–84. Robbins, *Hexaemeral Literature*, 39, 42–44; Köckert, *Christliche Kosmologie*, 323–24. For doubts about their editing of the *Philocalia* see: Paget, "Alexandrian Tradition," 538–39; Rasmussen, *Genesis and Cosmos*, 39, 66.

28. Mostly in rejection of these (older) suggestions, see Lim, "Basil of Caesarea's Hexaemeron," 352–55; Bouteneff, *Beginnings*, 128–29; Paget, "Alexandrian Tradition," 540.

29. Lim, "Basil of Caesarea's Hexaemeron," 359–60; William Horbury, "Old Testament Interpretation in the Writings of the Church Fathers," in *Mikra: Text, Translation, Reading and Interpretation of the Hebrew Bible in Ancient Judaism and Early Christianity*, ed. Martin Jan Mulder (Assen: Van Gorcum, 1990), 768; Hall, *Reading Scripture*, 87; Bouteneff, *Beginnings*, 129.

30. Carl O'Brien, "St Basil's Explanation of Creation," in *The Actuality of St. Basil the Great*, ed. G. Hällström (Turku: Åbo Akademi University Press, 2011), 194–224.

31. Paget, "Alexandrian Tradition," 540.

32. Lim, "Basil of Caesarea's Hexaemeron," 352, 357, 361–64; O'Brien, "St Basil's Explanation of Creation," 6; Bouteneff, *Beginnings*, 130–31.

33. Stephen M. Hildebrand, *Basil of Caesarea*, Foundations of Theological Exegesis and Christian Spirituality (Grand Rapids: Baker Academic, 2014), 48–52.

"to the abuses of the allegorical method" on Basil's part.[34] This point also makes it less likely that the homily form was regarded by Basil as an unsuitable vehicle for the use of allegory. I would suggest that the key factor in Basil's literal interpretation of Genesis 1 might have been his sense that as *the* biblical cosmogony, it warranted a real-world interpretive approach focused on worship of the Creator that would retain the value of physical nature within a Christian cosmogony.[35] Andrew Louth puts it well: "Basil's point is that the account of the six days of creation is about the origin of the created order.... Allegorizing the account ... draws attention away from the point of the creation narrative: to proclaim the Creator and the goodness of his creation."[36]

Given that Basil in this passage confronts his hearers and readers with "one of the most vigorous criticisms of allegorical exegesis to come from any orthodox Christian theologian" in this period,[37] how does Basil himself interpret Genesis 1 in these sermons? Even here in his *Hexaemeron*, Basil clearly finds moral symbols in the various kinds of plants and animals of days three and five of creation, so that what starts out as an admiring discussion of the abundance and providential purposes revealed in the various elements of nature often shifts into the drawing of moral and spiritual lessons for believers' conduct in the world. The phases of the moon make Basil think of human fickleness and vulnerability to changing circumstances (*Hex.* 6.10). Considering sexual reproduction in trees and the crossbreeding techniques of cultivators, Basil finds an application where virtue observed in people who are outside the orthodox Christian community may inspire those within to greater virtue (*Hex.* 5.8). The ant, classically, is an example of hardworking character, but so too is the hedgehog, both of whom are included among the living beings brought forth by the land on day six (*Hex.* 9.3).

What should we call this hermeneutical practice on Basil's part? Is it allegory or something else? Numerous books and articles seek to define what allegory is.

34. Hildebrand, *Basil of Caesarea*, 55; Hildebrand, *Trinitarian Theology*, 136–39.

35. Darren Sarisky, "Who Can Listen to Sermons on Genesis: Theological Exegesis and Theological Anthropology in Basil of Caesarea's Hexaemeron Homilies," Studia Patristica 67 (2013): 14 n. 1; Rasmussen, *Genesis and Cosmos*, 43, 77–78.

36. Andrew Louth, "The Six Days of Creation according to the Greek Fathers," in *Reading Genesis after Darwin*, ed. Stephen C. Barton and David Wilkinson (Oxford: Oxford University Press, 2009), 47; Horbury, "Old Testament Interpretation," 768; Paget, "Alexandrian Tradition," 540.

37. Jaroslav Pelikan, quoted in Hall, *Reading Scripture*, 86.

Such works traditionally refer to the fourfold senses of Scripture as articulated by the monk John Cassian (ca. 360–ca. 435), who lived a generation after Basil. These four senses are the literal, the moral or "tropological," the allegorical, and the anagogical, the latter signifying the spiritual destiny of the believer or the church as a whole.[38] The latter three are varieties of spiritual or figurative interpretation according to this model, which although simplistic is probably sufficient for our purposes here. Put simply, when Basil draws spiritual lessons from the characteristics and behaviors of plants and animals and other elements of nature, this is what is normally called moral or tropological interpretation, the second of Cassian's categories.[39] But is such moral interpretation any different from allegory, for instance when Basil uses the octopus as an example of the person who changes his views of right and wrong conduct to suit his current company (*Hex.* 7.3)? Is this taking "fish" literally as fish and "grass" as grass?

Now this moral interpretation occupies only a portion of the *Hexaemeron.* There is a real natural-philosophical focus to this work, so that for large tracts Basil is listing, in a tone of wonder and reverent celebration, the variety of living species and their precise tailoring (the contemporary word is "adaptation") to their environments. Where it is not the wonderful design of living species that inspires praise, it is their providential value for human life, and Basil also seems to have a naturalist's appreciation for the sheer interestingness of things in and of themselves. His excursions into moral interpretation are quite restrained. He dials down moral interpretation of the sun and moon to a minimum compared to the example of Theophilus of Antioch before him.[40] Ambrose's follow-up to Basil's *Hexaemeron* is much more liberal with its moral passages.

Basil seems most confident to pursue such a moralizing interpretation when he has a New Testament precedent for doing so. The illustrative use of the same natural entity in one of the parables of Jesus provides such a warrant or model. The Parable of the Wheat and the Weeds (Matt. 13:24–30, 36–42) gives Basil the confidence to declare that the darnel or false wheat in the parable "may be com-

38. See for example Reventlow, *HBI* 2:73; Gerald Bray, *Biblical Interpretation: Past and Present* (Downers Grove, IL: InterVarsity Press, 1996), 133, 147; Manlio Simonetti, *Biblical Interpretation in the Early Church: An Historical Introduction to Patristic Exegesis*, trans. J. A. Hughes (Edinburgh: T&T Clark, 1994), 119.

39. Peter Harrison, *The Bible, Protestantism, and the Rise of Natural Science* (Cambridge: Cambridge University Press, 1998), 21.

40. Compare Theophilus, *Autol.* 2.15 with Basil, *Hex.* 6.10.

pared with [lit. "fulfils the image of"] those who pervert the teachings of the Lord and . . . join themselves to the sound body of the Church in order that they may secretly inflict their harm on the more guileless."[41] Next, Christ's use of the vine imagery in John 15:1–8 allows fuller exploration of how this pictures Christ and the church (*Hex.* 5.6). This example of the vine animates Craig Allert's argument against Mook's "simplistic" characterization of Basil as a "literalist."[42] Mook's lining up of patristic Genesis interpreters into opposing lines of allegorists and literalists is indeed simplistic, but when Allert finds Basil "wringing meaning out of Genesis 1:11 based on its suggestion of the vine,"[43] he does not realize that the only detail available for use in Genesis was the general category of vegetation. Basil makes the connection to various types that fall within that class and then explores these elsewhere in Scripture (e.g., Isa. 5:1; Matt. 21:33; Luke 13:8), finding figurative meanings in texts whose intention is already metaphorical or figurative. This is not so much a figurative interpretation of the details of Genesis 1 as it is a scriptural association exercise quite common in Jewish and patristic Christian interpretation.

This moralizing is barely allegory if at all. It is not far from what we might think of as illustrative application of a biblical passage today. Basil is treating nature as symbolic of spiritual truths rather than the Genesis text. To borrow Peter Harrison's description of medieval allegory, this is "a way of reading things, not words."[44] By broad acknowledgment it follows the example of an early and anonymous Christian text called the *Physiologus*, which features forty-eight short stories, basically fables, that largely draw moral lessons from different animals (e.g., the dying-and-rising phoenix).[45] So, for Basil, references to fish categories are interpreted in terms of actual, natural fish, and then individual fish species are interpreted a second time as symbols of spiritual truths. This is figurative in the sense that it is no longer about literal fish or literal vines, but it is not based on de-

41. *Hex.* 5.5 (Way). See the Greek reflected in my insertion in PG 29:104b. Way's translation makes Basil sound more tentative than he really is here.

42. Allert, *Early Christian Readings*, 166–68; Mook, "Church Fathers," 30–31.

43. Allert, *Early Christian Readings*, 180–82.

44. Harrison, *Bible, Protestantism*, 28. See also 18–23.

45. U. Treu, "Physiologus," *DECL*, 489; Beryl Rowland, "The Relationship of St. Basil's Hexaemeron to the Physiologus," in *Epopée animale, fable, fabliau: Actes du IVe. Colloque de la Société Internationale Renardienne (Evreux, 7–11 Septembre 1981)*, ed. G. Bianciotto and Michel Salvat, Cahiers d'études Médiévales (Paris: Publications de L'Université de Rouen, 1984), 489–98.

tails in the Genesis text. Basil is interpreting the elements of nature in this way, not the text, and in any case the spiritual meaning is not substituted for the physical reality but complements it. Indeed, Paul Blowers classifies this as a literal interpretation, while broadening our sense of what "literal" or "theologically literal" could constitute in Basil's usage in a way that Allert would in fact approve.[46]

A stronger candidate for allegorical interpretation is Allert's preceding two-fold example, where first the voice of God's creative commands must be the "Word," since God has no need of audible speech to execute his will, and then the one who in Genesis 1:15 executes the command of 1:14, "Let there be lights"; both reveal the presence of Christ as Second Person of the Trinity and executor of the divine command (*Hex.* 3.2). The second instance is supported by the pregnant statement, "Everywhere in history the teachings of theology are mystically interspersed" (*Hex.* 6.2).[47] Even these two instances, however, do not allegorize details that are present in the text, but read between the lines, as it were, drawing theologically significant implications that are not obvious or explicit in the words themselves. Perhaps we might call this christological allegory applied to the inferred gaps in Genesis 1, prompted in the first case by an apparently impossible anthropomorphism applied to God.

Therefore, Basil seems eager to safeguard the real-world referentiality of the Genesis text, interpreting its categories in relation to the origin of the real world in which his hearers live prior to exploring the network of scriptural associations that the members of those categories might evoke.[48] That realism is important if Genesis 1 is to fulfil the function of undergirding Christian theology more broadly with a strong creation aspect. Perhaps it was the same impulse, or the influence of Basil's work, that led Augustine, after some rather abortive early efforts, to finally interpret the early chapters of Genesis literally.

THE CREATION WEEK AND TIME IN BASIL'S INTERPRETATION

Many who try to explain Basil's view of creation struggle to reconcile his different statements, some emphasizing instantaneous creation, some expounding a tem-

---

46. Blowers, *Drama of the Divine Economy*, 127–28.

47. Allert, *Early Christian Readings*, 177–78.

48. Andrew Brown, "Basil: Philosophical Literacy Meets Biblical Literalism?," *ZAC* 26.1 (2022): 95–106.

poral sequence. Similarly Letham: "It appears that Basil's more literal method of exegesis would lead him to consider the days of creation as solar days. However, he also affirms that creation took place in less than an instant."[49] "It is hard to see how far Basil takes the 'days' literally," mull Forster and Marston, and old conflict thesis guru A. D. White detected an inherent contradiction.[50] In her extremely thorough study, Charlotte Köckert also feels that the emphasis on the instantaneous fulfilment of God's creative will in this work results in an inherent tension in Basil's goals: the sequential nature of the creation account is a device for teaching the faithful that God is the true source and originator of created things, and yet Basil retains a natural-philosophical approach that takes the temporal element of the creation week seriously.[51]

This is a significant issue: if Basil's creation conception is truly instantaneous, it could represent an important precedent for a nonliteral interpretation of the chronological framework of the Genesis 1 creation account out of philosophical or even scientific considerations, and this from the putative flag-bearer of patristic literalism over the creation week. I will try to break down Basil's teaching according to the parts of these homilies that are most often cited in modern discussions, taking into account that his habit of considering more than one interpretive option before making a choice (if any) warns us against taking premature excerpts.

The Scope of the Instantaneous Creation of Genesis 1:1

The first of the two passages that is commonly cited (*Hex.* 1.6) sounds as if Basil is indeed following in Origen's footsteps and believes in instantaneous or timeless creation. One version quoted is Blomfield's older translation from the *Nicene and Post-Nicene Fathers* second series: "Thus then, if it is said, 'In the beginning God created,' it is to teach us that at the will of God the world arose in less than an instant, and it is to convey this meaning more clearly that other interpreters have

---

49. Letham, "Space of Six Days," 153. In a short article, Köckert lists Basil as a literal interpreter of creation, but hints that *Hex.* 1.6 might be taken as counter-evidence: Charlotte Köckert, "Hexaemeron," *EBR* 5:998.

50. Forster and Marston, *Reason, Science and Faith*, 206; Andrew Dickson White, *A History of the Warfare of Science with Theology in Christendom* (New York: Appleton, 1896), 6.

51. Köckert, *Christliche Kosmologie*, 335, 361, 365.

said: 'God made summarily' that is to say all at once and in a moment."[52] Forster and Marston quote a somewhat earlier statement from Way's 1963 translation: "[Or,] perhaps, the words 'In the beginning he created,' were used because of the instantaneous and timeless act of creation, since the beginning is something immeasurable and indivisible."

Genesis 1:1 begins in the Greek with *en archē*. While "in the beginning" is still a workable English translation of that Greek phrase, *archē* is one of those words that carried an awful lot of semantic freight in Greco-Roman thought. Explaining its various meanings occupies more than four columns of Lampe's *Patristic Greek Lexicon*.[53] In patristic thought it might refer to a beginning in time or, more subtly, a nonchronological beginning outside of time; the beginning point in spatial movement; an element or basic constituent; a principle; a cause, including God the Father or God the Son as creative cause; or an authority. Basil's task as he begins to exegete Genesis 1 is to establish which meaning applies in this case. Agnes Way points out that his guide is a list of such meanings found in Aristotle's *Metaphysics*, the kind of educational resource familiar to the classically trained Basil.[54] In *Hexaemeron* 1.5 he fields all of Aristotle's possibilities: a beginning point, a cause, the defining part of something, an initiation of action, and a creative art. In *Hexaemeron* 1.6, Basil wants to claim all five as viable meanings, showing how each can make sense in Genesis 1:1. It can refer to "the first day of the generation of the world," and "the first movement in time," and the material "foundation" of the world order, referring to "heaven and earth," and the rationale of creation, and finally the place of training for "rational souls."

With so many options, where does Basil emerge? He prefers to understand "in the beginning" as a reference to an absolute beginning, not so much in time as of time, an indivisible, dimensionless point from which the cosmos's temporal career begins. "As the beginning of the road is not yet the road, . . . so also, the beginning of time is not yet time . . . not even the least part of it" (*Hex.* 1.6 [Way]). Allert importantly points out that theological meanings such as the "beginning" signifying Christ, and then metaphysical or ontological meanings normally suggested themselves to patristic interpreters before physical, temporal, and historical

---

52. *NPNF*[2] 8:55. This is quoted by Letham, "Space of Six Days," 152; Batten, "Genesis Means What It Says."

53. G. W. H. Lampe, *Patristic Greek Lexicon* (Oxford: Clarendon, 1961), 234–36.

54. Way, "On the Hexaemeron," 10 n. 18.

meanings.[55] We will learn that interpreting the "beginning" of Genesis 1:1 as a reference to Christ was a distinctive contribution of Ambrose's *Hexameron* in contrast to that of Basil, who does not take this step. This leaves Basil investigating the *metaphysical* significance of the beginning, that is, the second sense, and prioritizing it over temporal aspects while still retaining the third sense of a beginning of real-world time alongside the second.[56]

Charlotte Köckert explains that for Basil time is an inevitable coefficient of the physical cosmos, while the spiritual realm exists timeless beyond it. The creative action of Genesis 1:1 is the impulse of God's will that the world should exist, and because God's will must inevitably and instantly be done, the realization of that will is in the immediate existence of the cosmos.[57] The eternal God wishes that there be a world in time, and so there is, without delay. The realm of time is born.[58] Yet Basil's statements about the instantaneous creation of heaven and earth relate specifically to Genesis 1:1. Here in 1.6, Basil calls heaven and earth the "foundations and footings" of creation only, implying that the rest is to come.[59] We are not safe to extrapolate their instantaneous production in a primordial moment to cover the works of the whole creation week. We will need to check Basil's continuing treatment.

The Archetypal First Day

The most quoted passage of Basil's *Hexaemeron* in modern creation discussions comes from 2.8, as Basil explains the meaning of "And there was evening and morning, one day" in Genesis 1:5. The section is long, and the way it is excerpted differs depending on the sympathies of the modern writer. Young-earth creationists love the section that speaks of twenty-four-hour days. Introducing an already long-standing exegetical hot spot, Basil wonders aloud:

'And there was evening and morning, one day.' Why did he say 'one' and not 'first'?[60] And yet, it is more consistent for him who intends to introduce a second and a third and a fourth day, to call the one which begins the series

55. Allert, *Early Christian Readings*, 63.
56. Allert, *Early Christian Readings*, 64.
57. Köckert, *Christliche Kosmologie*, 331–35.
58. See also Louth, "Six Days of Creation," 49.
59. θεμέλιοί . . . καὶ κρηπῖδες: *Hex.* 1.6.
60. Blomfield's translation of this clause, "Why does Scripture say 'one day the first

'first.' But, he said 'one' because he was defining the measure of day and night and combining the time of a night and day, since the twenty-four hours fill up the interval of one day.... It is as if one would say that the measure of twenty-four hours is the length of one day; so that, as often as through the revolution of the sun evening and morning traverse the world, the circle is completed ... in the space of one day. (*Hex.*2.8 [Way]) [61]

Basil is worried about two possible linguistic/philosophical inconsistencies: first, that a numbered list might begin with the cardinal "one" and then continue with ordinals (i.e., second, third, etc.); and second, the double use of the term "day" to represent both the daylight hours and a twenty-four-hour period. Perhaps Genesis 1:5 reads this way, says Basil, to tell us that the term "day" can embrace both dark and light parts of the diurnal cycle. As so often, he is trying to answer questions that are different from what his twenty-first century readers are often asking. Nevertheless, Basil is talking about the first day of the creation week as if it is defined by, or better is itself the very definition of, a twenty-four-hour period.

Somewhat less popular to quote and less transparent to the modern reader is the second possible explanation that Basil can offer for the phrasing "one day." This explanation is the one "handed down as one of the *hidden meanings* of Scripture,"[62] here interpreting the key Greek term *aporrētos* as a reference to a traditional Christian spiritual or allegorical meaning for this text.[63]

God, having prepared the nature of time, set as measures and limits for it the intervals of the days, and measuring it out for a week, He orders the week, in counting the change of time, always to return again in a circle to itself?

---

day'?" (*NPNF*[2] 8:64) looks like a mistranslation of the Greek, Τίνος ἕνεκεν οὐκ εἶπε πρῶτον, ἀλλὰ μίαν.

61. Citing this part of the passage, with varying beginning points and endpoints, are: Mook, "Church Fathers," 31; Sarfati, *Refuting Compromise*, 112–13; Davis, "Unresolved Major Questions," 217; Batten, "Genesis Means What It Says"; Kulikovsky, *Creation, Fall, Restoration*, 63; Duncan and Hall in Hagopian, *Genesis Debate*, 101–2.

62. My translation. Blomfield's translation, "But must we believe in a mysterious reason for this?" is idiosyncratic (*NPNF*[2] 8:64). Way's translation, "is the reason handed down in the mysteries more authoritative," is slightly better. The Greek is available at Giet, *Homélies*, 180; PG 29:49c.

63. Lampe, *Patristic Greek Lexicon*, 206; H. G. Liddell and Robert Scott, eds., *An Intermediate Greek-English Lexicon* (Oxford: Clarendon, 1889), 106.

> Again, He orders that one day by recurring seven times complete a week. . . .
> In fact, it is also characteristic of eternity to turn back upon itself and never to
> be brought to an end. Therefore, He called the beginning of time not a 'first
> day,' but 'one day,' in order that from the name it might have kinship with
> eternity. (*Hex.* 2.8 [Way])

Basil strongly affirms a definite, chronological beginning for the cosmos throughout this work, but aside from that he draws a quite cyclical view of time from
Platonist and Pythagorean precedents.[64] The wording "one day" is his clue that
the first day of creation stands alone as an archetypal unit of time, fundamental in
that it will measure one of the basic chronological cycles for as long as time (i.e.,
the cosmos) will last. Then, based on the archetype of the day, the creation week
is another archetype of another basic cycle of time.[65] Both because it comes right
at "the beginning" of creation, and because it cycles indefinitely, the archetypal
"one day" is a window on eternity for Basil.

Finally, we come to a third element in this passage, sometimes quoted for different reasons.

> If, however, the Scripture presents to us many ages, saying in various places 'age of
> age,' and 'ages of ages' [i.e., "forever and ever" in English translation], still in those
> places neither the first, nor the second, nor the third age is enumerated for us, so
> that, by this, differences of conditions and of various circumstances are shown
> to us but not limits and boundaries and successions of ages. (*Hex* 2.8 [Way])

Basil goes on to speak about a very dark "day," the "day of the Lord" as announced
by Amos (Amos 5:18–20) and about a bright "day," the final or, in Christian tradition, "eighth" day that was understood as a term for the glorious eternal future.
These suit his point because neither use of the word "day" has definite boundaries.
Basil continues: "Therefore, whether you say 'day' or 'age' you will express the same
idea. . . . In order, therefore, to lead our thoughts to a future life, he called that
day 'one,' which is an image of eternity." Writers seeking precedents for a modern
day-age interpretation of the creation week sometimes cite this ending portion of

---

64. Köckert, *Christliche Kosmologie*, 322, 326–28, 335, 339; Auguste Luneau, *L'histoire
du salut chez les pères de l'église: La doctrine des âges du monde* (Paris: Editions Beauchesne,
1964), 140, 143; Sheldon-Williams, "Greek Christian Platonist Tradition," 436.

65. Alexandre, *Le commencement du livre Genèse*, 99, 101.

Hexaemeron 2.8 for its mention of "days" and "ages" in close proximity.[66] Hugh Ross accuses his opponents of deliberately leaving this part out of their citations.[67] Bouteneff, a competent scholar and no superficial "recruiter," still finds this passage confusing: Basil "appears to take for granted that the days of creation were twenty-four-hour periods, yet he follows with a discussion of ages and eras."[68]

The tension within Basil's view of creation between the temporal and the atemporal is a function of a difficult philosophical conundrum for the classical mind. It has two sides, one related to time and the other to matter.[69] The latter puzzle is how an immaterial God could produce a material world so utterly unlike himself. More important right now is the corresponding puzzle over time, well expressed by Paul Blowers: "How could the timeless Creator produce a time-bound world without compromising his transcendence? How could eternity and time conceivably overlap in the 'moment God created'?"[70] This philosophical challenge energized Christian exposition both of the term "beginning" in Genesis 1:1 and of the term "day" throughout the chapter but especially in 1:5. The creation hermeneutic of the Cappadocian Fathers, Ambrose, and Augustine hovered on the boundary of the physical and the metaphysical, the historical and the ontological, what becomes and what is, because that is how they saw the very nature of the first day. It was a one-way portal from eternity into time. That is why, in both *Hexaemeron* 1.6 and 2.8, Basil wants to expound it carefully, combining temporal and atemporal senses, and is comfortable with accepting multiple meanings for the same biblical text.

Instant Creation Productions on the Remaining Days

One of these meanings is that when Basil imagines the creative actions of the later creation days out loud, he describes them in terms of instantaneous appearance. These examples are conveniently assembled by creationist Don Batten:

66. Ross, *Matter of Days*, 46–47; Ross, *Creation and Time*, 21; Ross and Archer in Hagopian, *Genesis Debate*, 205; Forster and Marston, *Reason, Science and Faith*, 206; Bouteneff, *Beginnings*, 134.

67. Hagopian, *Genesis Debate*, 69.

68. Bouteneff, *Beginnings*, 134.

69. Anna Marmodoro, "Gregory of Nyssa on the Creation of the World," in *Creation and Causation in Late Antiquity*, ed. Anna Marmodoto and Brian D. Prince (Cambridge: Cambrdge University Press, 2015), 94–110.

70. Blowers, *Drama of the Divine Economy*, 144; also carefully discussed in Allert, *Early Christian Readings*, 64, 241–44.

"Let the earth", the Creator adds, "bring forth the fruit tree yielding fruit after his kind, whose seed is in itself." At this command every copse was thickly planted; all the trees, fir, cedar, cypress, pine, rose to their greatest height, the shrubs were straightway clothed with thick foliage. [*Hex.* 5.6] . . . "Let the earth bring forth." This short command was in a moment a vast nature, an elaborate system. Swifter than thought it produced the countless qualities of plants. [*Hex.* 5.10]

"And God said, Let the waters bring forth abundantly the moving creature that hath life" after their kind, "and fowl that may fly above the earth" after their kind." . . . The command was given, and immediately the rivers and lakes becoming fruitful brought forth their natural broods; the sea travailed with all kinds of swimming creatures; not even in mud and marshes did the water remain idle; it took its part in creation. . . . Thus everywhere the water hastened to obey the Creator's command. [*Hex.* 7.1][71]

Do we have here a series of instantaneous creations at the first minute after midnight across the series of the creation days? Basil clearly imagines the different creative works as occurring instantaneously, and this is what we would expect given his concept of God's power to command, where for God even to wish something is instantly to have it.[72] Does this mean that the creation days all collapse into a set of instantaneous actions? No, because Basil clearly treats the days' events as a logical and temporal sequence. For instance, as for Theophilus of Antioch, vegetation appears on the day before the appearance of the sun to ram home the lesson that we should not overestimate the sun's role in creation; God was able to produce vegetation without its help (*Hex.* 5.1). And Basil affirms that there is such a thing as light before the sun, which was made after the fact on day four to be the bearer and mediating source of that light.[73] So Basil takes the sequence of the creative acts seriously; "the 'six days' are clearly understood literally."[74]

71. Batten, "Genesis Means What It Says." Translation used by Batten found in *NPNF*[2] 8:78, 81, 89–90.

72. See *Hex.* 2.7; 7.1; Köckert, *Christliche Kosmologie*, 335–36, 365.

73. See *Hex.* 2.8; 6.2–3; Letham, "Space of Six Days," 153; Lewis, "Days of Creation," 446.

74. Winden, "Hexaemeron," 1261; Zöckler, *Geschichte*, 1:188; E. Mangenot, "Hexaméron," *DTC* 6:2336; Johannes Zahlten, *Creatio Mundi: Darstellungen der sechs Schöpfungstage und naturwissenschaftliches Weltbild im Mittelalter*, Geschichte und Politik 13 (Stuttgart: Klett-Cotta, 1979), 91.

A Young-Earth Creationist Ahead of His Time?

On the other hand, is Basil the ideal young-earth creation recruit? Several young-earth advocates clearly think so, and some of their opponents seem happy to grant it. "Most of the church fathers plainly regarded the six days as ordinary days. Basil, for example, explicitly spoke of the day as a twenty-four-hour period," say Young and Stearley, and Deborah and Loren Haarsma add, "Before the development of modern geology these alternative interpretations [such as Augustine's less literal one] were rare. Most Christians held a young-earth interpretation of Genesis and believed that the earth was created in six twenty-four-hour days just a few thousand years ago."[75]

There is a degree of truth to this. Basil regards the Genesis text as divinely inspired and highly authoritative as a young-earth creationist would today. He explains that the first day of creation defines our twenty-four-hour time period and interprets the creative acts as occurring in narrated sequence so that earlier ones, like the appearance of light, occur prior to later ones, like the establishment of the luminaries. He describes these creations realistically by offering physical explanations, the classic example being the behavior of light before the sun. He never remotely hints at *expanding* the time required by creation and would inevitably subscribe to a short biblical chronology like his fellows, though avoiding any kind of world-week style scheduling of redemptive history.[76]

But let me reiterate Andrew Louth's comment: "[I]t is . . . a foreign country that we enter when we read the fathers; they do things differently there."[77] Though Basil's explanation of Genesis 1 has shifted the philosophical balance in this work toward physical rather than metaphysical concerns, or toward "becoming," the present temporal world with its changes rather than "being," the early sermons are still quite abstract and metaphysical, discussing the constitution of the Aristotelian elements and the reality of a noetic world behind and before our material world. How can historical, earthly time begin in the context of eternity? How can an eternal God act in time? What does a "day" mean when there has never been any time? Questions that seemed important to Basil and his audience might no

---

75. Young and Stearley, *Bible, Rocks and Time*, 40; Deborah B. Haarsma and Loren D. Haarsma, *Origins: Christian Perspectives on Creation, Evolution, and Intelligent Design*, 2nd ed. (Grand Rapids: Faith Alive, 2011), 104.

76. Luneau, *Âges du monde*, 142.

77. Louth, "Six Days of Creation," 39.

longer keep us awake at night. The historical aspect of the creation week narrative is still a little translucent until Basil's plant and animal illustrations make the *Hexaemeron* feel more grounded.[78] Basil seems to want to retain the theological virtues of Origen's instantaneous creation while maintaining the real-world connection that a temporal description of the creation week offers.

Though not without internal tensions, Basil's creation exposition pointed out the path for the church's future interpretation of creation in Genesis. He was a key driver of the trend identified by Paul Blowers: a reaction against the background of the highly ontological orientation of Origen. "Especially from the fourth century on . . . Christian thinkers placed an increasing emphasis on the *temporal* beginning of the whole of creation."[79]

A FORGOTTEN VOICE: GREGORY OF NYSSA

While Basil's friend from student days, Gregory of Nazianzus, showed "no particular interest in the Hexaemeron,"[80] Basil's younger brother Gregory of Nyssa wrote two works relating to Genesis 1 that tied in closely to Basil's sermon series. Gregory of Nyssa is one of the "forgotten voices" of Genesis 1 interpretation and is rarely mentioned in modern creation debates. He wrote two weighty works on creation that were better recognized in the Eastern than the Western church. The first, *On the Making of Humankind*, was intended to make up for the fact that Basil's *Hexaemeron* concluded just as the treatment of human creation on day six began.[81] The other, *Apologia in Hexaemeron*, was meant to complement Basil's *Hexaemeron* with a more robust treatment of creation in Genesis 1 for the philosophically astute reader.[82] The former work, in the absence of an undisputed equivalent treatment of human creation from Basil, had greater influence than the latter.[83] Both remained important in the Greek tradition through the Byzantine period and were rediscovered in the West during the quest for ancient

78. Köckert, *Christliche Kosmologie*, 365, 426–27.
79. Blowers, *Drama of the Divine Economy*, 143.
80. Bouteneff, *Beginnings*, 167.
81. We saw in discussing Basil that two further homilies possibly attributable to him might have supplied this lack, but that this remains disputed.
82. Bouteneff, *Beginnings*, 154; Louth, "Six Days of Creation," 44; Robbins, *Hexaemeral Literature*, 53–54.
83. Robbins, *Hexaemeral Literature*, 55.

sources in the Renaissance.[84] In the intervening period Gregory's *Apologia in Hexaemeron*, never translated into Latin, fell out of Western consciousness. The possibility that Augustine, whose command of Greek was poor early in his career but gradually improved, might have drawn some of his ideas about creation from Gregory's *Hexaemeron* is difficult to confidently prove but has been considered.[85] The present-day profile of his creation contributions is limited by the lack of an English translation, despite the appearance of fresh critical editions.[86]

Although Gregory's hexaemeral interpretation is philosophically more profound and systematic than Basil's, and thus much discussed by patristics scholars and historians of philosophy,[87] his low profile in present-day creation debates means that a nutshell synopsis will have to do here.[88] "Gregory of Nyssa's theory of creation is hard to interpret," says Sorabji, especially when we must decipher dense patristic Greek to do so.[89] Gregory's synthesis of the temporal and atemporal aspects of creation is similar to Basil's, but it is independently and more systematically explained in an apologetic for the way Genesis 1 describes cos-

84. F. Dünzl, "Gregory of Nyssa," *DECL*, 266.

85. One example would be that they both held to a teaching of "seminal reasons," too complex to explain here. See Richard Sorabji, *Time, Creation, and the Continuum: Theories in Antiquity and the Early Middle Ages* (London: Duckworth, 1983), 94–95, 235, 290; Gerald Bonner, "Augustine as Biblical Scholar," in *From the Beginnings to Jerome*, vol. 1 of *Cambridge History of the Bible*, ed. P. R. Ackroyd and C. F. Evans (Cambridge: Cambridge University Press, 1970), 550; Bonner, *St Augustine of Hippo: Life and Controversies* (London: SCM, 1963), 395.

86. Gregory of Nyssa, *Über das Sechstagewerk*, ed. Franz Xavier, Peter Wirth, and Wilhelm Gessel Risch (Stuttgart: Hiersemann, 1999); Gregory of Nyssa, *In Hexaemeron*, vol. 1 of *Opera Exegetica in Genesim*, ed. Hubertus R. Drobner, Gregorii Nysseni Opera 4.1 (Leiden: Brill, 2009). German and Italian translations exist; see F. Dünzl, "Gregory of Nyssa," 266.

87. Just to illustrate recent examples: Bouteneff, *Beginnings*, 152–66; Lucas Francisco Mateo-Seco and Giulio Maspero, eds., *The Brill Dictionary of Gregory of Nyssa* (Leiden: Brill, 2010); Charlotte Köckert, "Hexaemeron," *EBR* 5:400–517; Doru Costache, "Approaching an Apology for the Hexaemeron," *Phronema* 27.2 (2012): 53–81; Doru Costache, "Making Sense of the World: Theology and Science in St Gregory of Nyssa's An Apology for the Hexaemeron," *Phronema* 28.1 (2013): 1; Blowers, *Drama of the Divine Economy*, 65, 112, 120, 146–53, 184; Marmodoro, "Creation of the World," 94–110.

88. See, however, in typically comprehensive-yet-condescending fashion, Stanley Jaki, *Genesis 1 through the Ages*, 2nd ed. (Royal Oak, MI: Real View, 1998), 75–76.

89. Sorabji, *Time, Creation, and the Continuum*, 287.

mic origins. Gregory too conceives of an instantaneous founding of the cosmos (Gen. 1:1) but thinks of temporal development in relation to the events of the creation days.[90] For example, Basil's physical suggestion about the working of light before the sun is retained by Gregory, still temporally, and explained in terms of the Aristotelian element fire.[91] He essentially argues that the order of events in the Genesis narrative rightly represents the characteristic behaviors of the four elements, which is a metaphysical literal approach rather than an allegorical one. He is asserting that the thinking person in his society can take seriously the Mosaic account (as it was seen by the fathers) as a philosophically credible account of creation. Ironically, the stronger intellectual credentials of Gregory's *Hexaemeron* left it less durable as the philosophical wind changed and so less useful than Basil's for the present-day reader.

Creative Imitation in Classical, Biblical, and Patristic Literature

Gregory's *Apologia in Hexaemeron* is at times quite close to the model of Basil's *Hexaemeron*, raising a point about ancient genres as we prepare to look at Ambrose's *Hexameron* below.[92] There is a concept in classical studies called *imitatio* or "creative imitation," which acknowledges that it was accepted (although contested) practice in the Greco-Roman world to take a worthy piece of literature and improve and republish it. This creative imitation often went unacknowledged but might be distinguished from the plagiarism that troubles educators today in that it was "open borrowing" and "relie[d] on [the] readers noticing the appropriation and appreciating [the writer's] craft." "Only when the shadow of the original text is recognizable will the talent of the thieving-poet be fully appreciated by his readers." Borrowing that sought to conceal the source could be despised then as now.[93]

John Van Seters brought this creative imitation idea from classical scholarship to bear on the field of biblical studies, noting (in his rather cynical style) how

90. Köckert, *Christliche Kosmologie*, 365, 395, 406–10, 425–26, 436.

91. See PG 44:77a–b; 116c; 120a.

92. DeMarco, "Reception of Basil's *Homiliae*," 342.

93. Gian Biagio Conte, *Stealing the Club from Hercules: On Imitation in Latin Poetry* (Berlin: de Gruyter, 2017). A defining work in the field is David West, Tony Woodman, and Anthony John Woodman, eds., *Creative Imitation and Latin Literature* (Cambridge: Cambridge University Press, 1979) and esp. the opening essay by Russell, "De Imitatione."

much creative imitation occurs in biblical texts. This simple concept explains the relationship between the Synoptic Gospels, for instance, as both Matthew and Luke clearly utilize Mark's Gospel but with their own distinctive and comprehensive reordering and expansion work. The writer of Chronicles does the same with Samuel-Kings, and biblical examples could be multiplied greatly.[94] For our purposes, this quite commonsense category and its implied expectation of reader recognition of prior literary models will be important for our appreciation of what Ambrose is trying to do as he (extensively!) utilizes Basil's sermon series on the creation week to create his own. In the hexaemeral literature and works touching on Genesis and biblical creation, as in so many other genres, such literary remixing will often come to the alert reader's attention right down through the tradition to our final example, John Wesley's *Survey of the Wisdom of God in Creation* (1763), which (explicitly) begins life as a rewrite of J. F. Budde's *Elementa Philosophiae Theoretica* (1706).[95]

AMBROSE AS MEDIATOR OF BASIL'S HEXAEMERON TO THE WEST

The well-known Latin church father Ambrose of Milan (339–397) was bishop of Milan in northern Italy in the closing years of the fourth century. Well educated as were Basil and Chrysostom and with above-average Greek fluency for his time, he rose quickly through political ranks until about 370 when he became governor of a double province of northern Italy based in Milan, which was by then the administrative capital of the western Roman Empire, having eclipsed Rome.[96] In the stressed climate of the Nicene controversies over the definition of the relation of Christ to the Godhead, the powerful anti-Nicene (Homoian) bishop of Milan, Auxentius, died in 373. In the doctrinally divided climate, the church's

---

94. John Van Seters, "Creative Imitation in the Hebrew Bible," *Studies in Religion/ Sciences Religieuses* 29.4 (2000): 395–409; since reprinted as chapter 22 in John Van Seters, *Studies in the History, Literature and Religion of Biblical Israel*, vol. 1 of *Changing Perspectives* (New York: Routledge, 2014).

95. Wesley writes in his preface, "The Text is in great Measure translated from the *Latin* Work of *John Francis Buddaeus*, the late celebrated Professor of Philosophy. . . . But I have found occasion to retrench, inlarge or alter every Chapter, and almost every Section." That is creative imitation to a tee. John Wesley, *A Survey of the Wisdom of God in the Creation: Or a Compendium of Natural Philosophy* (Bristol: Pine, 1763), 1.iv.

96. *HBI* 2:46; C. Markschies, "Ambrose of Milan," *DECL*, 12–13.

choice of a successor required the oversight of the governor, and Ambrose soon found himself not just chairing the process but being elected bishop himself in 374.[97] Ambrose was not yet a priest at the time and had not even been baptized as a Christian, since baptism functioned at the time as a step of high spiritual commitment implying a strict and holy lifestyle. He was duly baptized and had to rapidly up-skill in Christian theology and church oversight while already in office.[98] His theological and exegetical formation came principally through Greek patristic models: Origen, Athanasius, Basil, and Didymus the Blind, as well as the Jew Philo, the unwitting pioneer of Christian allegory.[99] Ambrose's subsequent status as one of the leading Latin fathers is testimony to the success and ultimate authenticity of this career crossover. He does not write as though his Christian spirituality is a cover of convenience.

Ambrose appears in our story because he, too, produced a hexaemeron in the form of a sermon series. There is not just a resemblance of form to Basil's undertaking; Ambrose in fact consciously and heavily depended on Basil's *Hexaemeron* in crafting his own sermon series for a similar, Lenten setting (probably Holy Week in 387) despite not acknowledging Basil by name.[100] L. J. Swift explains the connection: "Scarcely a page of Ambrose's *[H]exameron* is without a borrowed thought, a reworked passage or a translated excerpt from the Cappadocian's work.... [I]t is clear that he had Basil in front of him as he wrote."[101] This led older scholarship to assessments like Robbins's: "The importance of the *Hexameron* of Ambrose lies in the fact that it, even more than the [Latin] translation by Eustathius, introduced the ideas of Basil to the western church. As an independent work the *Hexaemeron*

97. *HBI* 2:46; Markschies, "Ambrose of Milan," 13; Henry Chadwick, "Orthodoxy and Heresy from the Death of Constantine to the Eve of the First Council of Ephesus," *CAH* 13:578–80; Paul Elliott, *Creation and Literary Re-Creation: Ambrose's Use of Philo in the Hexaemeral Letters*, Gorgias Studies in Early Christianity and Patristics 72 (Piscataway, NJ: Gorgias, 2019), 4–6.

98. Markschies, "Ambrose of Milan," *DECL*, 13; *HBI* 2:45–47.

99. *HBI* 2:49–51; Luneau, *Âges du monde*, 247, 250; Elliott, *Creation and Literary Re-Creation*, 1–2, 33–37.

100. Ambrose, *Hexameron, Paradise, and Cain and Abel*, trans. John J. Savage, FC 42 (Washington, DC: Catholic University of America Press, 1961), vi; Alexandre, *Le commencement du livre Genèse*, 48; Rainer Henke, *Basilius und Ambrosius über das Sechstagewerk: Eine vergleiche Studie* (Basel: Schwabe, 2000), 15–16.

101. Louis J. Swift, "Basil and Ambrose on the Six Days of Creation," *Augustinianum* 21.2 (1981): 317–18.

has little value."[102] Ambrose's *Hexameron* was seen as derivative and unimaginative, if not plagiaristic, and therefore of little inherent merit.

Yet recent years have seen a dramatic reappraisal of the value of Ambrose's works that is now "attentive to the ways that Ambrose transforms his sources by adapting them to his time and needs."[103] The result is a change in tone concerning his *Hexameron*, such as Trigg's comment that Ambrose "elegantly adapted for Latin readers Basil's *On the Hexaemeron.*"[104] Swift's article has been followed by increasingly careful attempts to explain what makes Ambrose's sermon content distinctive and original in the context of a better understanding of the classical literary habit of "creative imitation" (*aemulatio* or *imitatio*) treated above. Jerome made a snide remark about Ambrose's degree of dependence on Basil for this work (*Ep.* 84.7), but considering that Ambrose expected his readers to be aware of Basil's work, which was quickly becoming renowned, he was implicitly inviting comparison between the two while giving it his own theological coloring and rhetorical improvements as he made it available to his congregation and his wider Latin Christian readership.[105] The coherent and distinctive final product offers "a sophisticated biblical cosmogony to rival the notion of uncreated matter."[106]

With Hilary of Poitiers, Ambrose is considered one of the two Latin theologians who properly grasped and utilized an Origenist interpretation of Scripture.[107] He thus helped to propagate allegorical biblical interpretation in the Latin sphere as an exegete and preacher of great status. "It was through Ambrose that Augustine became Origen's unwitting disciple," says Van Fleteren, since Ambrose was Augustine's first guide and teacher in the orthodox Christian faith.[108] But

102. Robbins, *Hexaemeral Literature*, 58.

103. A. Fitzgerald, "Ambrose," *EBR* 1:958; Christoph Jacob, "The Reception of the Origenist Tradition in Latin Exegesis," *HB/OT* 1.1:690–91.

104. Joseph Wilson Trigg, *Biblical Interpretation*, Message of the Fathers of the Church 9 (Wilmington, DE: Glazier, 1988), 42.

105. Elliott, *Creation and Literary Re-Creation*, 16–22; Pierce, "Reconsidering Ambrose's Reception," 414–18, 443–44; Henke, *Basilius und Ambrosius*, 28–36, the most important treatments of the topic.

106. Pierce, "Reconsidering Ambrose's Reception," 444.

107. Jacob, "Origenist Tradition," 682–83.

108. Frederick Van Fleteren, "Principles of Augustine's Hermeneutic: An Overview," in *Augustine: Biblical Exegete*, ed. Frederick Van Fleteren and Joseph C. Schnaubelt (New York: Lang, 2001), 4, and see Roland J. Teske, "Origen and St Augustine's First Commentary on Genesis," in *Origeniana Quinta* (Leuven: Leuven University Press, 1992), 183;

unless "allegory" is defined very broadly,[109] Ambrose consciously avoids utilizing in the *Hexameron* the allegory he freely utilizes in his other writings.[110] Reventlow finds in an exposition of Ambrose on Psalm 36 a handy presentation of his threefold hermeneutic as it applies to the Pentateuch:

> All Scripture is either natural or mystical or moral: nature in Genesis, which expresses how heaven, seas, lands were made; mystical in Leviticus, in which the mystery of the priesthood is conceived; moral in Deuteronomy, in which human life is formed according to the instruction of the law.[111]

So, Ambrose firmly limits allegory in treating the creation narratives, because a realist, natural, or literal reading is better suited to their cosmogonic subject matter. But the moral or tropological reading of natural things mentioned in the Genesis text as symbols suggestive of principles of spiritual living, already seen in Basil's *Hexaemeron*, is alive and thriving in Ambrose's. Comparing the two, we find that Ambrose follows Basil's general outline quite closely while rearranging, paraphrasing, and altering Basil's text at the detail level. Ambrose has less faith than Basil in the possibility of spiritual benefit from philosophical inquiry, seeing it as a dead-end road for believers, but shares with Basil the priority on refuting false teachings while building up the faithful in true belief and right living.[112] By the end of the two sermon series, the two speakers have diverged considerably in focus; Ambrose does not carry over Basil's apparent disillusionment with allegory and employs it in a restrained way at times, as when he allows that the "beginning" in Genesis 1:1 may refer mystically to Christ, something Basil does not do in his *Hexaemeron*.[113]

Henry Chadwick, "Augustine," in *Dictionary of Biblical Interpretation*, ed. John H. Hayes (Nashville: Abingdon, 1999), 68.

109. As when Farrar in the late nineteenth century described Ambrose as following Origen in "the allegoristic interpretation of ... the days of Creation," F. W. Farrar, *History of Interpretation* (London: Macmillan, 1886), 205.

110. K.-H. Schwarte, *Die Vorgeschichte der augustinischen Weltalterlehre* (Bonn: Habelt, 1966), 234.

111. *HBI* 2:59.

112. Swift, "Basil and Ambrose," 318–21.

113. Swift, "Basil and Ambrose," 323–26. Compare Basil, *Hex.* 9.1 and Ambrose, *Hex.* 6.2.6 . For the Christ reference, see Ambrose, *Hex.* 1.4.15 and also Robbins, *Hexae-*

Ambrose's interpretation of the "days" of creation in his *Hexameron* has generated a fair amount of heat in modern creation debates, serving as a sort of warm-up prior to the next major Genesis interpreter, Augustine, over whose legacy the greatest conflict erupts. We find much the same kind of discussion of Ambrose as of Basil, including the challenge of reconciling comments about a twenty-four-hour day with tracts that seem to speak of instantaneous creation.[114] In evaluating the claims made about Ambrose, we can be briefer than we were about Basil, because the resemblance in the arguments over the two figures reflects that Ambrose keeps close to his source on these points.

Ambrose does celebrate instantaneous creation early in his sermons: "He who in a momentary exercise of His will completed such a majestic work employed no art or skill so that those things which were not were so quickly brought into existence; the will did not outrun the creation, not the creation, the will" (*Hex.* 1.3.8 [Savage]). Ambrose indeed seems eager to advertise this principle and preempts its position in Basil's sermons, where he mentions it again.[115] As with Basil, the principle sounds applicable to all of creation theologically, and his citation of Psalm 148:5 in its biblical context would cover not just the creation of the heavens but the celestial bodies, too (*Hex.* 1.3.8).

Yet the connection of these statements with Genesis 1:1 warns us against their extrapolation to the "forming and filling" of creation that follows in the Genesis narrative. Furthermore, Ambrose, like Basil and Theophilus of Antioch, celebrates the fact that the vegetation of day three predates the creation of the sun on day four: "The sun [is] younger than the green shoot, younger than the green plant!" (*Hex.* 3.6.27 [Savage]). Andrew Louth draws our attention to Ambrose's clearest statements on the matter and, adjusting his quotation parameters a little, we find this preclusion of a strictly instantaneous creation:

> And perhaps they may say: Why did not God, in accordance with the words, 'He spoke and they were made,' grant to the elements at the same time as they

---

meral Literature, 59; Winden, "Hexaemeron," 1263; Alex Fogleman, "'Since Those Days All Things Have Progressed for the Better': Tradition, Progress, and Creation in Ambrose of Milan," *HTR* 113.4 (October 2020): 440–59.

114. John Baptist Ku, "Interpreting Genesis 1 with the Fathers of the Church," Thomistic Evolution (blog), https://www.thomisticevolution.org/wp-content/uploads/sites/182 /2020/05/Thomistic-Evolution-16.pdf /.

115. *Hex.* 1.4.16 and also 1.2.5. Compare Basil, *Hex.* 1.6.

arose their appropriate adornments, as if He, at the moment of creation, were unable to cause the heavens immediately to gleam with studded stars and the earth to be clothed with flowers and fruit? That could very well have happened. Yet Scripture points out that things were first created and afterwards put in order, lest it be supposed that they were not actually created and that they had no beginning. (*Hex.* 1.7.27 [Savage])[116]

This vindicates the opinion that Ambrose joins Basil in advocating the instantaneous creation of the basic fabric of heaven and earth based on Genesis 1:1 and then the construction of habitable creation and its furnishing over the creation week.[117] This is important because this becomes the standard Christian view of biblical creation as the patristic era moves toward its close, while Augustine's genuinely instantaneous creation position will stand alongside it as the one clear alternative view. Medieval and Renaissance Christian scholars were all familiar with these two options, along with Aristotle's eternal cosmos, as they considered their own interpretations of the Genesis text.

Therefore, we can be fairly confident that Ambrose's discussion about "one day" was phrased this way because its paradigmatic importance is consistent with an overall literal view of the creation days. This leads us to the passage that is most often quoted from Ambrose's *Hexameron* in creation debates:

In notable fashion has Scripture spoken of a 'day,' not the 'first day.' Because a second, then a third, and finally the remaining days were to follow, a 'first day' could have been mentioned. . . . But Scripture established a law that twenty-four hours, including both day and night, should be given the name of day only, as if one were to say the length of one day is twenty-four hours in extent. . . . Therefore, just as there is a single revolution of time, so there is but one day. (*Hex.* 1.10.37 [Savage])

116. See also Andrew Louth, ed., *Genesis 1–11*, Ancient Christian Commentary on Scripture (Downers Grove, IL: InterVarsity Press, 2001), 5.
117. *Hex.* 1.7.25. See also Mangenot, "Hexaméron," 2338; Zahlten, *Creatio Mundi*, 92; Thomas Aquinas, *Summa Theologiae: Latin Text and English Translation*, vol. 10, *Cosmogony (1a. 65–74)*, ed. William A. Wallace (London: Blackfriars, 1967), 208; Schwarte, *Vorgeschichte*, 234, thinks Ambrose "denies any temporal extension of divine creative activity"; Zöckler, *Geschichte*, 1:228, 230, finds Ambrose unclear or inconsistent here but ultimately supports the majority on this question, acknowledging that the "forming and filling" stage of creation is temporal.

David Hall blesses the two phrases "twenty-four hours" with bold font, lest the point be missed, and this quote appears in a number of other conservative treatments in discussion closely aligned with that concerning Basil.[118] You will recall from our Basil discussion a point that also applies here: the problem being addressed is a perceived linguistic ambiguity in the creation account, where "day" is used to mean both the daylight period and the diurnal cycle. That this is not an issue for us should not make it invisible in our reading of the primary documents. Ambrose, like Basil, has no need to emphasize twenty-four-hour creation days in contrast to the vastly longer creation "days" when nothing like a day-age view has yet been contemplated.

Ambrose moves next, as did Basil, to a discussion of the cyclical aspect of days and weeks, and then to "ages." Ross's complaint that strict creationists deliberately avoid these texts covers Ambrose as well as Basil, but our thinkers are glancing from one unique "day" of Scripture to another, such as the eschatological "day of the Lord," without equating them or implying that creation days are ages.[119] Ambrose, like Basil, is transfixed by the prospect of a future, eternal "day" of glory for the righteous and has to "snap out of it" to conclude the point about the definition of a "day" as including night. Does Ambrose "vacillate" on whether the days are twenty-four hours long or not, as Ross says at one point?[120] No: he leaves us in no doubt that daylight alone doesn't exhaust the definition of "day," whether or not that is our burning question.

Is Ambrose's interpretation of the creation week, on the other hand, a "quite literal scheme"?[121] It is apparently literal about the prototypical "day one" and about the sequential nature of the creation week. But it is not quite a version of premodern young-earth creationism. Ambrose is interested in the constitution of physical creation. His treatment of the sun and moon in *Hexameron* 4.1.1–4.2.7, for example, reveals a genuine interest in the way the sun and moon function, though he is most inclined to explore them (admittedly allegorically) as symbols for Christ and spiritual realities. What he lacks is any real sense of a *history* of physical creation. The creation process is notionally spread across seven days, but

118. Hall, "Evolution of Mythology," 275; Douglas F. Kelly, *Creation and Change: Genesis 1.1–2.4 in the Light of Changing Scientific Paradigms* (Fearn: Mentor, 1997), 112; Van Bebber and Taylor, *Creation and Time*, 93–94; Mook, "Church Fathers," 35; Davis, "Unresolved Major Questions," 217; Hagopian, *Genesis Debate*, 47.

119. Ross, *Creation and Time*, 22–23; Ross, *A Matter of Days*, 47.

120. Hagopian, *Genesis Debate*, 126, 170.

121. Duncan and Hall in Hagopian, *Genesis Debate*, 102.

its description here feels, while sequential, nonhistorical from our perspective. "History" for Ambrose applies to human society, not to the origin of the cosmos. The chronological framework of the week is never questioned, and it is effectively confirmed by the twenty-four-hour definition of "day one." But it feels chronologically flat in the reading, like a hand of seven playing cards rather than a stack of seven boxes. Each day's content is explicitly instantaneous, as it was with Basil, lacking any chronological depth. The result is a creation whose causation in God is fundamentally important for Ambrose and Basil, against belief in a self-existent, eternal world. But their perspective, especially Ambrose's, is dominated by being rather than becoming. Perhaps it is the retention of a being-dominated or essentially static cosmos that is one key to how modern young-earth creationism is so different to a scientific culture where becoming, that is, a sense of "things in development," predominates.

Chapter Six

AUGUSTINE'S INSTANTANEOUS CREATION

In modern creation debates, Augustine is the patristic equivalent of that athletic schoolmate who was always picked first for any sports team. No giant of the faith is more eagerly recruited to authorize modern positions. No Christian thinker's legacy for the interpretation of creation themes in Genesis 1 is more hotly contested. Francis Collins is probably correct to claim that "theistic evolution is the dominant position of serious biologists who are also serious believers," but to add, "I believe that this is also the view that . . . Saint Augustine would espouse today if . . . presented with the scientific evidence for evolution" is simple recruitment with no evidential value, notwithstanding Collins's peerless scientific credentials.[1] On the other side of the evolutionary fence, David Hall complains, "Augustine must be one of the most misunderstood men of ancient history on this subject," but shows a gift for drawing the boundaries of the debate in order to include Augustine in a vast list of other church authorities in opposition to the novelty of the day-age theory.[2] This claim is not so much wrong as it is superficial and illustrative of the dubious enterprise of claiming Augustine's quite unique and somewhat alien position as support for any modern stance on creation. What

1. Francis Collins, *The Language of God: A Scientist Presents Evidence for Belief* (New York: Free Press, 2006), 199–200.

2. David W. Hall, "The Evolution of Mythology: Classic Creation Survives as the Fittest Among Its Critics," in *Did God Create in Six Days?*, ed. J. A. Pipa Jr. and D. W. Hall (White Hall, WV: Tolle Lege, 2005), 275, 301.

Karla Pollmann says about past use of Augustine's hermeneutic is also true of his recruitment in contemporary debates: "In most cases it is characteristic that, rather than the whole theory of Augustine's hermeneutics, parts of it are quoted out of context to support one's own intention."[3]

Why does Augustine, more than any other ancient Christian thinker, receive such determined reharnessing? He certainly was a giant of church history, combining evidence of a genuinely changed life through the intervention of God with theological profundity and the rhetorical skills to express it. The tag sometimes given to him, "second founder of the faith," gives some sense of his importance for defining Christian theology as we now know it.[4] He could see the big picture and express it in viable models that had apologetic weight and resilience in the marketplace of ideas, penning many of the defining statements of patristic Christian thought. He showed an unusual degree of interpretive self-awareness throughout his writings, opening up the workings of his mind to admit his reader into his interpretive logic at many points.

Augustine's Genesis writings are no exception to this. The early chapters of Genesis fascinated him, eliciting five different treatments of Genesis 1 in the course of his writing career.[5] Edmund Hill notes that Augustine's synthesizing legacy applies here as well: "The currents of tradition in both western and eastern theology flowed together in Augustine's several commentaries on Genesis to form a new whole marked by a marvellous richness and intellectual depth."[6] Augustine's thought was hugely influential on the church's attitude to creation, as in many other areas, for the next millennium and beyond. Nor was he narrowly theological. His classical education gave him an appreciation for the worthy and unworthy elements of pagan learned traditions, and he was famously aware that the Christian attitude to knowledge acquired by the direct study of nature had implications for Christian outreach to the well-educated. He was no cosseted churchman. As a giant figure in the systematization of

3. Karla Pollmann, "Hermeneutical Presuppositions," *ATTA*, 429.

4. E.g., Frederick Van Fleteren and Joseph C. Schnaubelt, eds., *Augustine: "Second Founder of the Faith,"* Collectanea Augustiniana (New York: Lang, 1990).

5. E.g., Karlfried Froehlich, "'Take Up and Read': Basics of Augustine's Biblical Interpretation," *Interpretation* 58.1 (2004): 6.

6. For Hill's quote, see *On Genesis*, ed. John E. Rotelle, trans. Edmund Hill, The Works of Saint Augustine I/13 (Hyde Park, NY: New City, 2002), 19. See also J. C. M. van Winden, "Hexaemeron," *RAC* 14:1266.

the Christian view of God and the world in the mature phase of the patristic period, Augustine is the most cited and most recruited church father on Genesis 1 for good reason.

AUGUSTINE'S CAREER OF INVOLVEMENT WITH GENESIS

Augustine's focus on Genesis 1–3 is not simply a function of this text's paradigmatic importance in the biblical revelation. Second only perhaps to the writings of Paul, which were so formative for Augustine's theology of God, humanity, and the drama of salvation, Genesis 1–3 was the biblical text most involved in Augustine's initial skepticism about Christianity, his later change of heart about its credibility, and his subsequent defense of its credibility.

Augustine was born in 354 in Thagaste in the countryside of the Roman province of Numidia, now in eastern Algeria. Ethnically, then, he was probably native North African (i.e., Berber), but linguistically and culturally he was Latin and Roman. As a result, in terms of church influence Augustine was always linked to the special, distinct identity of the North African church, as earlier personified by Tertullian (ca. 160–220) and Cyprian of Carthage (ca. 200–258).[7] Educated as well as his parents of limited means could manage, he was already teaching grammar back in his home town by 374, and later returned to teach rhetoric in the provincial capital Carthage with "great expectations" for a notable career as an intellectual with the wealth that might attend it.[8]

Despite the strong Christian example of his mother, Monica, for the bulk of the period between 374 and his departure for Rome in 383 Augustine was scandalized by the failure of Christian Scriptures to live up to his educated expectations and lived as an adherent of the Manichean sect. This movement combined elements of gnostic quasi-Christian mysticism with Persian religious dualism and a Marcionite derision for the OT into an odd mixture of skepticism, superstitious credulity, and asceticism that thrived in fourth-century Greco-Roman

7. G. Bonner, "Augustine as Biblical Scholar," in *From the Beginnings to Jerome*, vol. 1 of *Cambridge History of the Bible*, ed. P. R. Ackroyd and C. F. Evans (Cambridge: Cambridge University Press, 1970), 36–38; R. A. Markus, *Saeculum: History and Society in the Theology of St. Augustine* (Cambridge: Cambridge University Press, 1970), 105–31.

8. Augustine's biography is related in too many sources to list here, plus his autobiography in his *Confessions*. For one brief introduction, see W. Geerlings, "Augustine," *DECL*, 61–62.

society. The Manicheans read OT Scripture literalistically and found ideas like God's rest following the creation week or God's formation of the first human from mud laughable.[9] In books 5 through 7 of his famous *Confessions*, Augustine relates how he became dissatisfied with Manichean teaching, and how a career move to Milan brought him under the influence both of Neoplatonist thought and of the local bishop, Ambrose. It was Ambrose's expository preaching in an allegorical style that began to restore Augustine's confidence in the credibility of the OT writings. This probably included hearing some of Ambrose's Holy Week sermon series on the hexaemeron in 386.[10] If Augustine did hear them, Ambrose's handling of the hexaemeron in those homilies would be a clear and direct precedent for Augustine and would locate him in an exegetical tradition reaching back to Basil's antecedents such as Origen, Hippolytus, Theophilos of Antioch, and perhaps Diodore of Tarsus. This was perhaps the very same period of time that saw Augustine's conversion when he was compelled to "take up and read" the Bible and, upon reading Romans 13:13, was confronted by the need to put away his undisciplined life and fully commit to Christ (*Confessions* book 8).[11] Following his conversion, Augustine was baptized by Ambrose and took up a calling to celibacy and Christian service.

9. See *Gen. Man.* 1.22.33; 2.7.8. Translation by Edmund Hill in Augustine, "On Genesis: A Refutation of the Manichees," in Rotelle, *Saint Augustine on Genesis*.

10. For Augustine's general comments about experiencing Ambrose's preaching, without specifying the topics involved, see *Conf.* 5.13.23–14.24. Translation from Augustine, *Confessions*, trans. Henry Chadwick (Oxford: Oxford University Press, 1991), 87–89. Support for Augustine's presence for these sermons includes Alexander H. Pierce, "Reconsidering Ambrose's Reception of Basil's Homiliae in Hexaemeron: The Lasting Legacy of Origen," *ZAC* 23.3 (2019): 444; Pierre Courcelle, *Recherches sur les Confessions de saint Augustin* (Paris: Boccard, 1968), 101–2. Cf. Alex Fogleman, "'Since Those Days All Things Have Progressed for the Better': Tradition, Progress, and Creation in Ambrose of Milan," *HTR* 113.4 (2020): 442 n. 6, who indicates that uncertainty remains on the point.

11. Bertrand de Margerie, *An Introduction to the History of Exegesis*, vol. 3, *Augustine* (Petersham, MA: Saint Bede's, 1991), 12–13; Roland J. Teske, "Origen and St Augustine's First Commentary on Genesis," in *Origeniana Quinta* (Leuven: Leuven University Press, 1992), 183; Ambrose, *Hexameron, Paradise, and Cain and Abel*, trans. John J. Savage, FC 42 (Washington, DC: Catholic University of America Press, 1961), vi; Frederick Van Fleteren, "Principles of Augustine's Hermeneutic: An Overview," in *Augustine: Biblical Exegete*, ed. Frederick Van Fleteren and Joseph C. Schnaubelt (New York: Lang, 2001), 4–5; Froehlich, "Augustine's Biblical Interpretation," 7; Carol Harrison, Andreas Bücker, and Diane Apostolos-Cappadona, "Augustine of Hippo," *EBR* 3:98.

His life thus profoundly changed, Augustine soon returned to North Africa determined to combat the Manicheans. He did this in a series of writings composed primarily in the period leading up to 400 CE. As Geerlings observes, "[t]he controversy with the Manichees was largely over the exegesis of Genesis."[12] As such, the opening polemical salvo from Augustine came in the form of his *On Genesis against the Manicheans* (388/389).[13] There his strategy was to interpret in a spiritual sense aspects of the creation narratives that seemed problematic when taken literally. It seems clear that both God's rest on the seventh day and the whole weekly creation framework were targets for Manichean mockery, the latter involving three days, complete with mornings and evenings, before the sun's creation (*Gen. Man.* 1.14.20). In rebuttal, Augustine suggests that humans can sense the passing of days even without access to the sun. But he feels compelled by the language of the text, where evening and morning are said to be "made," to understand "morning" and "evening" as the starting and end points of the respective works of God on the analogy of human workdays. That is, steps of creation that are notionally distinct are given a chronological dress to aid human comprehension.

This might already look like allegorical interpretation of the creation week, yet in the twofold hermeneutical distinction that Augustine provides in this work, *historia* and *prophetia*, this explanation of the days still falls into the *historia* section. Augustine explains the difference like this:

> So then, this whole text must first be discussed in terms of history [*historia*], and then in terms of prophecy [*prophetia*]. In terms of history deeds and events are being related, in terms of prophecy future events are being foretold.... Anyone who wants to take everything that is said here absolutely literally, and who can avoid blasphemy in so doing, and present everything as in accordance with Catholic faith ... one should hold up as ... outstanding.... If, however, no other way is available of reaching an understanding of what is written that is religious and worthy of God, except by supposing that it has all been set before us in a figurative sense and in riddles, we have the authority of the apostles for doing this.... Let us then ... unravel all these figurative

12. Geerlings, "Augustine," 67.

13. Kevin J. Coyle, "Genesi Adversus Manicheos, De," *ATTA*, 378–79; Roland J. Teske, "The Genesis Accounts of Creation," *ATTA*, 379–80.

statements in accordance with Catholic faith, whether they are statements
of history or of prophecy, without prejudice to any better and more diligent
commentary. (*Gen. Man.* 2.2.3 [Hill])

This is a vital passage for understanding how Augustine interprets Genesis. While
we may at first be tempted to understand *historia* to mean a text one should interpret literally and *prophetia* as roughly equivalent to allegory, Augustine's comment late in this passage indicates that figurative statements might fall into either
category—history or prophecy—and forces us to rethink that conclusion.

A helpful clue comes from another paragraph on hermeneutics presented in
Augustine's *Unfinished Literal Commentary on Genesis* (393) to be treated further
below. This time he offers four categories of writing in Scripture: history, allegory,
analogy, and aetiology. Here Augustine clarifies, "History is when things done
by God or man are recounted" (*Gen. imp.* 2.5).[14] And things done by God often
require a special form of narrative thanks to God's transcendence. Back in the
passage from *On Genesis against the Manicheans* that concerns days before the
sun Augustine explains, "The transference, you see, of words from human matters to express things divine is common form with the divine scriptures" (*Gen.
Man.* 1.14.20 [Hill]). Workdays with mornings and evenings are narrated "from
their similarity with human work," that is, they are an anthropomorphism.

So, historical narrative can be figurative, says Augustine (at this stage of his
interpretive career), particularly where God is the agent involved. That said, Augustine in this Genesis commentary prefers to explain the hexaemeral form of the
first narrative about creation (Gen. 1:1–2:3) as demanded by its second, prophetic
function. After Genesis 1:1 announces the creation of "heaven and earth" (i.e., creation as a whole), "he expounded God's works one by one consecutively through
the sequence of days, in a way required by their prophetic significance" (*Gen.
Man.* 2.3.4 [Hill]). What was that prophetic significance? It was its analogous relationship to the seven ages of world history (1.23.35–41), already discussed in depth
in chapter 3, and the following analogy with the seven stages of a believer's spiritual
development (1.25.43). So in *On Genesis against the Manicheans*, the days of creation are both figurative *and* typological or prophetic, but these are two different
functions, and the figurative function is an aspect of their *historical* meaning.

14. Translation by Edmund Hill in Augustine, "Unfinished Literal Commentary on
Genesis," in Rotelle, *Saint Augustine on Genesis.*

Thus, Augustine countered the hyper-literalism of the Manicheans, an interpretive choice so tempting to those who *want* Scripture to look scandalous, with an interpretation that emphasized the figurative, whether it was functioning historically (relating to the narrator's past) or prophetically (relating to the narrator's future). However, following his appointment as a priest at Hippo on the Numidian (now Tunisian) coast in 391, Augustine became dissatisfied with his earlier interpretation of Genesis, as if he had too easily defaulted to figurative meanings. In his last great Genesis commentary, he confesses, "Now at that time it had not yet dawned on me how everything . . . could be taken in its proper literal sense. . . . So . . . I explained with what brevity and clarity I could muster what those things, for which I was not able to find a suitable literal meaning, stood for in a figurative sense" (*Gen. litt.* 8.2.5).[15] It was actually the content of the paradise story or the Eden narrative (Gen. 2:4–3:24) that had given Augustine the most trouble to interpret literally, although he had trouble with the hexaemeron as well.

Now more confident, in about 393 he returned to the task and began dictating a Genesis commentary to show "how what is said there can be taken as strictly historical," but later admits that "I soon collapsed under the weight of such a burden" (*Retract.* 1.18).[16] The commentary remained unfinished from the mention of Genesis 1:26, as if literal explanation of the image of God in humans, a delicate point around Manicheans, was the heart of the problem. The preceding exposition, presented mostly as a series of brief thought experiments, is thoughtful and valuable on its own terms, but need not delay us long here. Suffice it to say that at a couple of points concerning the creation days, Augustine anticipates his thinking to come in his fuller Genesis commentary. There are no literal days prior to the sun's creation, and the sheer power of God forbids us to imagine that any creative work of his should occupy any period of time (*Gen. imp.* 7.27; 11.34). The creative commands of each day represent the noetic or intellectual creation, "first effected in the thoughts of the intelligent creation," that is, the angelic mind, with physical creation following, as indicated by "and it was so" and similar statements (*Gen. imp.* 10.32). This stems from the separation of form, or the ideal plan of a thing, and its physical manifestation as an object in Platonic thought. To lay out the logic of

15. Translation by Edmund Hill in Augustine, "The Literal Meaning of Genesis," in Rotelle, *Saint Augustine on Genesis*.

16. As cited by Hill in Rotelle, *Saint Augustine on Genesis*, 112.

the creative process as a chronological series of days is a concession to weaker intellects, which cannot directly comprehend the divine plan (*Gen. imp.* 3.8; 7.28).

Augustine's other main consideration of the creation narratives in Genesis prior to his major Genesis commentary appears in chapters 11–13 of the *Confessions*, written after becoming bishop of Hippo in 396. Chapters 11 and 12 function like a prolegomenon to a commentary on Genesis; in the prayer-like mode that characterizes the *Confessions*, Augustine treats the background philosophical issues that need resolution prior to undertaking direct interpretation of the Genesis text. Chapter 11 wrestles with the philosophical problem of the sudden intrusion of a creation "in time" into the eternal calm of God's existence. Chapter 12 considers the meaning of a biblical text, concluding that God's abundant wisdom might incorporate into a biblical text more meanings than its human author could have consciously intended, thus explaining why faithful Christian interpreters can find more than one meaning in the same text all the while doing honor to the faith. Chapter 13 embarks on the kind of allegorical interpretation of the hexaemeron that, oddly enough, does not appear in *On Genesis against the Manicheans*, where true allegory was restricted to Augustine's treatment of the Eden narrative (Gen. 2:4–3:24) in book 2. The problem of time and eternity is not an allegorical concern but an ontological one and so belongs to the literal interpretation of the Genesis text, but other than this there is no true, sequential and literal Genesis commentary to be found here, though chapter 12 helps us understand Augustine's biblical hermeneutics.

The *Confessions* is a very personal, devotional, and self-reflective work. That origins questions appear so prominently and occupy the last three of its thirteen chapters reflects how central creation, and thus Genesis 1–3, was to Augustine's spiritual identity and Christian worldview. This supports the probability that Ambrose's hexaemeral sermons in 386 and his creation teaching more generally were indeed a timely and prominent part of Augustine's conversion experience in Milan.[17] The connection was formed for life: Augustine understood his conversion in terms of a personal re-creation and creation as a kind of conversion to God.[18] The twin theological poles of creation and redemption were intimately connected for him. This can help us to make sense of his otherwise quite alien

---

17. See biographical discussion and references earlier in this section.

18. M. A. Vannier, "Le rôle de l'hexaéméron dans l'interprétation augustinienne de la création," *Revue des Sciences philosophiques et theologiques* 71.4 (1987): 537–47; Hill, ed., Augustine, *On Genesis*, 14–15.

theory of the creation days as phases of angelic knowledge, as we will see below. The truest light is the light that fills the mind turned to God in direct contemplation, and this is the light of the mornings of the creation days for Augustine.

THE MEANING OF THE LITERAL MEANING OF GENESIS

This brings us to Augustine's culminating writing on Genesis 1–3. *The Literal Meaning of Genesis* was composed between 401 and 414, mostly at the front end of that period, about the same time *Confessions* was completed. Scholars seem to agree that his coverage of the same ground in chapter 11 of his epic *City of God* (412–426) followed the completion of *Literal Meaning*, and in fact it presents a rather handy summary of Augustine's meaning in the larger work.[19]

In Augustine's mature Genesis interpretation, an instantaneous creation week found a defender of undisputed authority and orthodoxy, unlike Origen, whose undoubted genius could not save him from a reputation in swift decline by this time, more than a century after his death, under suspicion or outright accusation of unorthodoxy. Jerome's (d. 420) about-face from being a sympathizer of Origen to a critic in the late 390s through the controversy stirred up by Epiphanius of Salamis (d. 403) is indicative of the changing mood.[20] Yet Origen's influence on Christian theology and biblical hermeneutics was already pervasive in both Western and Eastern churches, and though it became less politic to admit any debt to Origen, the Origenist flavor of interpretations like Augustine's is not hard to see upon comparison of their writings on Genesis.

Roland Teske is perhaps right that Augustine most likely imbibed his Origenist ideas (many of them Philo's ideas also) indirectly through Ambrose, since they pervaded Ambrose's preaching when Augustine was in Milan.[21] Direct influence from Gregory of Nyssa is considered unlikely, as Augustine was not a strong

---

19. *Retract.* 2.24; Andrew Louth, "The Fathers on Genesis," in *The Book of Genesis: Composition, Reception, and Interpretation*, ed. David L. Petersen, Craig A. Evans, and Joel N. Lohr, VTSup 152 (Leiden: Brill, 2012), 571–72; Teske, "Genesis Accounts," 183; Augustine, *De Civitate Dei: The City of God. Books 1 and 2*, ed. P. G. Walsh (Oxford: Oxbow, 2005), 5; Augustine, *The Literal Meaning of Genesis*, ed. John Hammond Taylor, ACW 41 (New York: Newman, 1982), 1:1–4.

20. E. M. Harding, "Origenist Crises," in *The SCM Press A-Z of Origen*, ed. John Anthony McGuckin (London: SCM, 2006), 164; *HBI* 2:43.

21. Teske, "First Commentary on Genesis," 179, 183–85; Van Fleteren, "Augustine's Hermeneutic," 4.

reader of Greek and lacked an available Latin translation of Gregory's work, but Augustine seems to allude to Basil's ideas about creation in a way that suggests he was familiar with Basil's *Hexaemeron* via Eustathius's Latin translation.[22] He certainly shares the key idea of "generative principles" (*rationes seminales*, from Gk. *logoi spermatikoi*) with the Cappadocians, though he may have obtained this idea (to be explained below) directly from his Neoplatonic sources. Augustine's growing attraction to the merits of a literal understanding of Genesis 1–3 represents a partial distancing from Origen's approach, but he was never able to settle with Basil's more physical and (apparently) temporal creation week, despite flirting briefly with Basil's idea of an oscillating physical light, provided by God, producing the first three days of the creation week prior to the sun's creation.[23] Augustine's whole thought structure made Basil's explanation seem contrived, implausible, and just too physical.

Several factors played a part in Augustine's thought structure, all of them deserving of far deeper consideration than these pages can accommodate. They include:

- A Christian, Neoplatonic cast of mind focused on eternal, spiritual realities, particularly the nature of God, in preference to the changeable physical world, notwithstanding the historical sensibility Augustine displays in works like the *City of God*.
- Similarly, a conviction that not only could angels not be left out of the creation account, as we might at first conclude, but that as a vital part of ultimate reality, inferior only to God himself, they must be incorporated in Genesis 1 in some enigmatic way.
- A theology that emphasized the transcendence of God, such as might be shared by many Christian readers of the present day, so that a series of literal twenty-four-hour periods seemed redundant. How could the all-powerful God experience any time delay at all between wanting something done and having it done?[24]

22. Teske, "First Commentary on Genesis," 184; Richard Sorabji, *Time, Creation, and the Continuum: Theories in Antiquity and the Early Middle Ages* (London: Duckworth, 1983), 235; Taylor, *Literal Meaning*, 1:6.

23. *Gen. litt.* 1.11.23, 16.31; 4.22.39; *Civ.* 11.7.2. For the connection with Basil, see Taylor, *Literal Meaning*, 1:32, 37, 129.

24. *Gen. litt.* 1.10.19. This conviction is clearest in e.g., *Gen. imp.* 7.28; 11.34.

- Apparent confirmation from other biblical passages. Some implied the absolute author and ease of God's creative commands: "For he spoke, and it came to be; he commanded, and it stood firm" (Ps. 33:9 NIV, quoted in *Gen. litt.* 4.33.51) and "He commanded, and they were created" (Ps. 148:5b, quoted in *Gen. litt.* 4.8.15).

More explicit and, for Augustine, still scriptural was Sirach 18:1: "He who lives for ever has created the sum of all things" (NJB). First cited in a critical passage (*Gen. litt.* 4.33.52) not long after Psalm 33:9, it is a clear statement that Augustine holds as true and authoritative for establishing a true picture of creation. Thus, he cites it repeatedly, although noting at one point (5.3.6) that it is not indispensable to his argument.[25] The catch is that the relevant word in the Septuagint (*koinē*, i.e., en masse) was rendered *simul* in the Old Latin Bible read by Augustine. The Greek text of this verse could best be understood, as it appears in Metzger's edition of the Apocrypha, "He who lives forever created the whole universe [*ta panta koinē*]," while the Latin *omnia simul* can bear the same sense of "everything *in toto*," but lends itself more easily to a temporal understanding, "everything at once."[26] We will discover that another biblical text much closer at hand suggested the same idea to Augustine, but first let us gain some sense of Augustine's explanation of an instantaneous creation framed in a timeless creation week:

> But if the angelic mind is able to grasp all the things simultaneously, which the text puts one after the other in an ordered chain of causes, does that mean that the things which were being made were all made simultaneously . . . and not made one after the other at intervals according to the predetermined days?
>
> The creator . . . about whom scripture told this story of how he completed and finished his works in six days, is the same as the one about whom it is written elsewhere . . . without . . . any contradiction, that *he created all things simultaneously together* (Sir. 18:1). And consequently, the one who made all things simultaneously together also made simultaneously these six or seven days, or rather this one day six or seven times repeated. So then, what need was there for the six days to be recounted so distinctly and methodically? It

---

25. Further citations may be found at *Gen. litt.* 5.17.35; 6.3.4, 6.11, 9.16; 7.28.41; 8.20.39.

26. B. M. Metzger, ed., *The Oxford Annotated Apocrypha*, exp. ed. (Oxford: Oxford University Press, 1977), 150.

was for the sake of those who cannot arrive at an understanding of the text
[from Sirach] unless scripture accompanies them more slowly, step by step.

Just as the whole created universe, after all, was made simultaneously, so
the angelic light [i.e., mind] could simultaneously both account for day by
contemplating it all in the original and unchangeable ideas according to which
it was fashioned, and account for evening by knowing it all in its own proper
nature, and account for morning by rising to praise the creator from that
inferior knowledge too. (*Gen. litt.* 4.33.51–34.53 [Hill])

Although there was a precedent for understanding either the "heaven" of Genesis 1:1 or the upper waters of 1:7 as an oblique reference to the angelic population,
Augustine preferred to understand the "day" of Genesis 1:5 as an allusion to angels.
He saw angels as retaining the kind of direct, intuitive knowledge of God and of
the things of God that humans had forsaken when they sinned in the garden:

The first day created knew the whole array of creatures arranged in hierarchical
order. Through this knowledge creation was revealed to it as if in six steps
called days, and thus was unfolded all that was created; but in reality there
was only one day. That day knew creation first in the Creator and then in the
creatures themselves. (*Gen. litt.* 5.5.15 [Taylor])[27]

Convinced that the creation week framework was an instance of figurative,
rather than literal, historical narrative, Augustine found here the necessary, figurative meanings of "day," "evening," and "morning" needed to make sense of a
figurative creation week (*Civ.* 11.7.2–4). To know what God was creating intui-
tively, in the Platonic sense of ideal forms in the mind of God, represented the
"day." To know things by observation upon their physical production, as it were
by empirical observation, an inferior knowledge still available to fallen human
beings, was "evening." Finally, to direct the resultant knowledge of created things
back to God in praise was "morning."

If that is what the creation narrative is trying to say, why apportion the creative
works out through six creative days specifically? There are two parts to Augustine's
answer to this question. We could call them an internal logic of revelation and an
external logic of revelation. The internal logic of revelation involves the innate,

27. See also *Gen. litt.* 5.2.4.

direct knowledge that angels have of the things of God. Their mental grasp of the creative work of God in its original, eternal plan would naturally, thinks Augustine, fall into six parts, since six is the perfect number, the lowest number to be the sum of its factors: one, two, and three (*Gen. litt.* 7.13–14).[28] And those three factors effectively subdivide the six creation days. To day one belongs the spiritual creation, the angelic population indicated by "light." Two days (two and three) are devoted to the formation of the visible cosmos, including vegetation that does not move, while three days (four through six) belong to the animate creation (*Gen. litt.* 2.13.27). This is not far from the logic of the modern framework hypothesis: the week is a logical rather than a temporal order.[29]

If this explanation of the internal logic of the six days as revelation to the angels is numerological, his explanation of their external logic as revelation to humans is heuristic. It boils down to accommodation to limited human capacity.

> The scriptural style comes down to the level of the little ones and adjusts itself to their capacity by putting before them each single kind of creature one by one. (*Gen. litt.* 2.6.13 [Hill])

> So now you should understand that this day was repeated seven times . . . and also grasp if you can . . . that this sixfold or sevenfold repetition happened without any intervals or periods of time. And if you are not yet able to grasp this, leave the contemplation of it to those who have the capacity, while you yourself go on making progress by walking more slowly with the scripture at your side. (*Gen. litt.* 3.5.6 [Hill])

> We have seen, after all, how by mentioning that day . . . he signified that one day was made by God, and that it was when the day was made that God then made heaven and earth, so that we should ponder as best we could God making all things simultaneously at once, even though the count of six days earlier on seemed to show intervals of time between his works. (*Gen. litt.* 5.6.19 [Hill])

---

28. See Robert Letham, "'In the Space of Six Days': The Days of Creation from Origen to the Westminster Assembly," *WTJ* 61.2 (1999): 155.

29. Also the opinion of Gavin Ortlund, *Retrieving Augustine's Doctrine of Creation: Ancient Wisdom for Current Controversy* (Downers Grove, IL: InterVarsity Press, 2020); see chapter 3, esp. the section "Augustine's View in Historical Context."

This sounds patronizing, and perhaps it is, though Augustine seems genuine in feeling that Scripture is designed by God to cater to the deep thinker with profound concepts and to the simpler thinker with more approachable and perhaps anthropomorphic ideas.

This esoteric-sounding interpretation of the creation week solved another exegetical problem for Augustine, and this one too was partly generated by his limitation to the Old Latin Bible and the Septuagint upon which it was based. In the NIV, Genesis 2:4–5a reads, "This is the account of the heavens and the earth when they were created, when the Lord God made the earth and the heavens. Now no shrub had yet appeared on the earth and no plant had yet sprung up, for the Lord God had not sent rain on the earth." The punctuation here reflects the Hebrew of the Masoretic Text, where the *waw*-conjunction that begins verse 5 (*wəkōl śiaḥ* "and every shrub") is best understood as joining discrete clauses. The Septuagint translator, however, appears to have taken the *waw* as a conjunction between nouns in a series that extends into verse 5. Thus, Augustine reports his Latin text as equating to, "This is the book of the creation of heaven and earth. When day was made, God made heaven and earth and every green thing of the field."[30] Combined with this was a characteristically literal translation of the Hebrew *bəyôm* in verse 4 as "in the day" (Gk. *hē hēmera*) and likewise in the Latin, whereas "when" would have been a more faithful translation of the intended meaning.

This left an interpreter like Augustine with the apparent challenge of explaining how the earth and heavens were created in a single day. Now this could be explained as an initial act on day one of creation, if Genesis 1:1–2 were included in the first day's events. But with verse 5's appearance of vegetation now included in the same sentence through the Septuagint's punctuation, Augustine also had to explain how vegetation was created on the *same day* as the earth and heavens, and even while that vegetation had not yet appeared visibly on the earth! A problem caused by accidents of translation, we might think, but it confirmed to Augustine the principle already apparent to him from Sirach 18:1, that everything had been created simultaneously.

Augustine's philosophical explanation for how this could be, as I flagged above, was his "generative principles" idea.[31] Derived originally from Stoic phi-

---

30. *Gen. litt.* 5.3.5 (Taylor). For a critical edition of the Greek text, see John W. Wevers, ed., *Genesis*, Septuaginta Vetus Testamentum Graecum 1 (Göttingen: Vandenhoeck & Ruprecht, 1974), 83.

31. "Generative principles" is one offering in G. W. H. Lampe, *Patristic Greek Lexicon*

losophy and filtered through Neoplatonist thinkers nearer to Augustine, this idea goes under a range of names, both in Augustine's own Latin usage and also in modern discussions, where it takes names like "seminal causes" or "seminal reasons."[32] This sophisticated idea is something like that of DNA in the realm of biology or, taking a technological analogy, the computer code that defines the design for an object destined to be 3D-printed. While it is a design only, prior to production, you can't point to its physical form or location. It is nowhere at all, physically, but it is not nothing. It exists virtually. Thus Augustine's "virtual seeds" (nearer the intended metaphor) describe the "ideas," codes or designs of things, sourced in the mind of God, that are implanted in the cosmos, ready to be realized in physical form within historical time. Like DNA, they encode the instructions for their own development. They act as a logical step between eternal ideas existing in the mind of God and things found existing in physical form in the world (*Gen. litt.* 5.11.27).

On top of all these factors that go to form this interpretation of Augustine, we must add one more. Augustine noticed a degree of duplication between Genesis 1:3–2:3 and 2:6–25, while 2:4–5 exercised a transitional role, about which I will comment below. The duplication is seen in that humans are created in Genesis 1:26–27, both male and female, and then a man or Adam is created in 2:7, while his wife, Eve, is created in 2:21–22 from his rib. Vegetation appears on day three (1:11–12), and then God plants a garden (2:8–9). And whereas animals are the product of day six (1:24–25), they are clearly made as a response to the isolation of the newly created man (2:19). These are differing sequences, complicating the

---

(Oxford: Clarendon, 1961), 1248. This is a difficult term to translate in a way that conveys its sense effectively.

32. The discussion of this concept may be found in sources such as: Taylor, *Literal Meaning*, 1:252–54; Frederick Copleston, SJ, *A History of Philosophy*, vol. 2, *Augustine to Scotus* (New York: Doubleday, 1950), 75–77; R. A. Markus, "Marius Victorinus and Augustine," *CHLGEMP*, 398–400; Rowan Williams, "Creation," *ATTA*, 252; Kenneth J. Howell, "Natural Knowledge and Textual Meaning in Augustine's Interpretation of Genesis: The Three Functions of Natural Philosophy," in *Nature and Scripture in the Abrahamic Religions: Up to 1700*, ed. Jitse M. van der Meer and Scott Mandelbrote, 2 vols. (Leiden: Brill, 2008), 1:136–39; W. A. Christian, "Augustine on the Creation of the World," *HTR* 46 (1953): 16–17; Matthew Drever, "Image, Identity, and Embodiment: Augustine's Interpretation of the Human Person in Genesis 1–2," in *Genesis and Christian Theology*, ed. Nathan MacDonald, Mark W. Elliott, and Grant Macaskill (Grand Rapids: Eerdmans, 2012), 119–20.

attempt to cast the events of 2:6–25 as a recapitulation of aspects of the creation week, a hypothesis Augustine tries out first.[33] He is most concerned to maintain that nothing new is created following the creation week, since it was finished and very good (*Gen. litt.* 5.23.36). Meanwhile, as far as he understands, spontaneous generation is a reality; creatures can emerge from rotten material such as animal corpses (*Gen. litt.* 3.14.22).

Thus Augustine's "generative principles" idea takes careful note of the apparent single day of Genesis 2:4, the apparent inclusion of vegetation in that single day in Genesis 2:5, and the need to reconcile rather different-sounding accounts of the production of plants, animals, and humans in the two creation narratives on either side of this transition. (The generative principles idea does *not* apply to the heavenly bodies of day four, the firmament, land or sea; see *Gen. litt.* 6.1.2.) Having argued quite carefully for the inclusion of humans within this explanation in *Literal Meaning of Genesis* 6.1.1–6.4.6, he recapitulates:

> In accordance, therefore, with the original work of creation, in which God made all things together, He created potentially and in their causes works from which He rested on the seventh day. But He works in a different manner now, as we see in those beings which He creates in the course of time, working even yet. Consequently, it was in days as we know them with their corporeal light caused by the sun . . . that Eve was made from the side of her husband. For it was then that God again formed the beasts and birds from the earth, and since among them no helper was found for Adam similar to him, Eve was formed. It was, therefore, in such days as these that God also formed Adam from the slime of the earth.
>
> First they were created in potency through the word of God and inserted seminally into the worlds when He created all things together. . . . [I]n time Adam would be made from the slime of the earth and the woman from the side of her husband. (*Gen. litt.* 6.5.7–8 [Taylor])

Hence Kim's conclusion: "In this commentary, the concept of causal formulae mediates exegetically the two accounts of creation. . . . The first account narrates

---

33. *Gen. litt.* 6.2.3–4.6, also 5.4.11. See Yoon Kyung Kim, *Augustine's Changing Interpretations of Genesis 1–3: From De Genesi contra Manichaeos to De Genesi ad Litteram* (Lewiston, NY: Mellen, 2006), 153, 155.

the simultaneous creation. The second deals with the temporal development of the non-temporal simultaneous creation."[34] This is quite correct, but it is not the same thing as saying that Genesis 1:1–2:3 narrates an ideal or spiritual creation while Genesis 2:6–25 describes a real, this-worldly creation, as van Winden says.[35] For as we have said, *Literal Meaning of Genesis* 6.1.2 portrays a *physical* world of land, sea, and firmament, including stars, as created instantaneously in the (notional) creation week. The ideal creation, the spiritual or angelic world, belongs to the first day of creation alone, and in fact is signified by the term "day" in Genesis 1:5 (*Gen. litt.* 4.28.45; 5.4.9; 5.5.15). This is essentially Philo's position, which was nearly four centuries old by this time.

Genesis 2:4–5, then, does not mark the transition from the invisible world to the visible, but from the timeless to the temporal: "With the motion of creatures, time began to run its course" (*Gen. litt.* 5.5.12 [Taylor]). "So then between those works of God from which he rested on the seventh day, and these which he is working on until now, scripture inserted a kind of joint in her narrative, advising us that she had finished unrolling those and was beginning now to weave these on the loom" (*Gen. litt.* 5.11.27 [Hill]).[36] There are "two moments of creation," one timeless and one temporal. In fact, temporal creation ultimately permeates all historical time, so that the tree that springs from the shoot and the baby born today, "the things that he produces from those [former] works even now," can still be called the creations of God despite the cessation of his creation work after the sixth "day."[37]

The Viability and Value of Augustine's Creation Stance

The difference is profound when we compare *Literal Meaning* with *On Genesis against the Manicheans* book 2. Now he is treating the six days of creation as logical steps in angelic comprehension of the creative plan of God in potential, performance, and praise, respectively? How is that literal? Augustine anticipates

---

34. Kim, *Interpretations of Genesis 1–3*, 151.

35. Winden, "Hexaemeron," 1267–68.

36. Hill's translation style is more free and lyrical than Taylor's.

37. *Gen. litt.* 5.11.27; 5.12.28 (Taylor). See also Craig D. Allert, *Early Christian Readings of Genesis One: Patristic Exegesis and Literal Interpretation* (Downers Grove, IL: InterVarsity Press, 2018), 287–90; Paul M. Blowers, *Drama of the Divine Economy: Creator and Creation in Early Christian Theology and Piety*, OECS (Oxford: Oxford University Press, 2012), 11, 153–59, 184, who refers to this as a double creation concept.

the challenge but insists: "Please let nobody assume that what I have said . . . all belongs to a kind of figurative and allegorical understanding of day and evening and morning" (*Gen. litt.* 4.28.45 [Hill]). True contemplation of the creator is a truer light than the light of our world, he pleads. This perhaps sounds interpretively strained to us, but there is a logical consistency to Augustine's claim. If *historia* may consist of the acts of God as well as of people, and if the acts of God often require metaphorical or figurative language to communicate, then it would not be surprising if the works of God in creation required figurative expression in Genesis.

Again, how can Augustine claim that this is the literal meaning? Notice that he is not learning from the text of Genesis about the relationship of Christ and the church, or the ascent of the redeemed soul by stages to the Father, or the progress of the ages of the world. These are recognizable topics of allegorical or typological interpretation. Once when Augustine begins to take "evening" "to signify the sin of rational creatures," and morning as "their restoration," he catches himself: "But this is an interpretation on the lines of prophetic allegory, which is not what we have undertaken in this work" (*Gen. litt.* 1.17.33–34). Allegorical interpretation involves a transfer of reference from the apparent topic of discussion, in this case the world's creation, to some other topic of spiritual importance. That would be *prophetia* in the categories employed in the *Unfinished Literal Commentary on Genesis*.

Augustine wants to avoid doing that here. He attempts to expound the Genesis text as *historia* only, the history of creation.[38] But when the creative work of God is involved and much of that work of creation transcends the visible, *historia* involves figurative language but not allegory. Moreover, the involvement of the members of the Trinity is fundamental to this "history": God is mentioned immediately in Genesis 1:1, the Spirit in 1:2, and Christ is enigmatically indicated by the "beginning" in 1:1 (*Gen. litt.* 1.6.12). Likewise, even in the creation of "light" or "day" (the spiritual beings) on day one, the Father is the commander, the Son is the commanding Word, and the Spirit offers the approval "good," so that the threefold "let there be," "and there was," and "it was good" structure of each day is another Trinitarian marker. Several commentators point out that the discovery of

---

38. Thomas Williams, "Biblical Interpretation," in *The Cambridge Companion to Augustine*, ed. David Vincent Meconi and Eleonore Stump (Cambridge: Cambridge University Press, 2001), 62. Among many who think Augustine was presenting an allegorical treatment of the creation week here are: F. Robbins, *The Hexaemeral Literature: A Study of the Greek and Latin Commentaries in Genesis* (Chicago: University of Chicago Press, 1912), 64; Jack P. Lewis, "The Days of Creation: An Historical Survey of Interpretation," *JETS* 32 (1989): 443; Winden, "Hexaemeron," 1266.

such Trinitarian and christological content within the literal meaning of Genesis demonstrates that the literal meaning remains theological and "sacramental" for Augustine and all the church fathers, fulfilling the spiritual perception required in the Christian interpreter of Scripture (*theoria*).[39]

What about the continuing viability of his interpretation of the creation week? Does it survive intact as a real option for the present-day Christian reading Genesis? Protestant Christians at least feel uncompelled to admit the testimony of the book of Sirach as indisputable. In any case, when translated properly, Sirach 18:1 does not require instantaneous creation. Nor does the phrasing of Genesis 2:4–5 in the Hebrew place any such demands on the reader, as it did for Augustine, who was convinced of the inspiration of the Septuagint and linguistically cut off from the Hebrew.

The philosophical climate has changed greatly too since Augustine's day. Like soluble stitches closing a wound, the philosophical framework that gave Augustine's position its strength and structure has dissolved for most modern people, though intellectual history has witnessed repeated resurgences of Platonism and will probably continue to do so.[40] When Platonism was strong, Augustine's scheme did well; the latter weakened when the former did. The theory of angelic cognition in particular loses its viability without this philosophical substructure. The idea of seminal reasons, even without the support of Stoicism or Neoplatonism, is easier to imagine reappearing in some form in the philosophy of nature and continues to evoke scholarly discussion, partly because it offers possibilities for reconciling cosmic or biological novelty with creation "in the beginning."[41]

39. Hans Boersma, *Scripture as Real Presence: Sacramental Exegesis in the Early Church* (Grand Rapids: Baker Academic, 2017), 47–54; Paul M. Blowers, "Entering 'This Sublime and Blessed Amphitheatre': Contemplation of Nature and Interpretation of the Bible in the Patristic Period," in *Nature and Scripture in the Abrahamic Religions: Up to 1700*, ed. Jitse M. van der Meer and Scott Mandelbrote (Leiden: Brill, 2008), 1:168–72; Blowers, *Drama of the Divine Economy*, 105–7, 121–22; Cameron Schweitzer, "Finding the Typical in the Literal: Augustine's Typological Exegesis in His Literal Commentary on Genesis," *Puritan Reformed Journal* 13.2 (2021): 43–53, although I believe that Schweitzer at times confuses "literal" with "intended by the author."

40. For a nineteenth-century Christian example, see Tayler Lewis, *The Six Days of Creation; or, The Scriptural Cosmology, with the Ancient Idea of Time-Worlds, in Distinction from Worlds in Space* (Schenectady, NY: Van Debogert, 1855). For a twentieth-century example, I see Meredith Kline's "upper-register cosmogony" as rather Platonist: Meredith G. Kline, "Space and Time in the Genesis Cosmogony," *PSCF* 48.1 (1996): 2–15.

41. E.g., Blowers, *Drama of the Divine Economy*, 157.

The strongest of Augustine's supports is the theological one: that an almighty God requires no time to create, but that the communication of his creative work might justify or even require the imposition of a chronological framework on the analogy of a human working week. Biblically, this would place Genesis 1 and Exodus 20:11 in a kind of feedback loop of meaning. God is described as working over six days because we do, Israel works six days and rests the seventh because God does. If that seems purely circular, it need not be; the more graphic expression in Exodus 31:17 that God "rested and was refreshed" on the seventh day reminds us to expect anthropomorphisms when the action of God in the world is being described to human minds. Otherwise, the Manicheans were right to mock Christian belief as crudely anthropomorphist.

I am saying, then, that Augustine's creation interpretation as a whole system is not *viable*, but it is still *valuable* in certain respects. It is a model of a thoroughly worked out interpretation, exegetically attentive and philosophically astute. Blowers calls it "a classic model for observing how natural-philosophical issues and considerations are drawn into . . . a contemplative reading of scriptural creation texts."[42] It retains a concern for real-world referentiality as well as theological profundity. It is genuinely integrative. How can any explanation of human or world origins expect to command attention in an apologetic environment, outside the "Christian bubble," if it is ignorant or negligent of the stronger points of contemporary philosophy or the historical sciences? Christian exegetes of Scripture otherwise risk simply preaching to the choir. I am full of admiration for the seriousness and weightiness and internal coherence of Augustine's proposal, although in the contemporary environment it is not convincing as a complete system. That it was taken seriously for more than a thousand years is testimony to its substance. But the Protestant John Calvin and Jesuit Francisco Suarez shared one telling criticism of it: it was ultimately just too clever.[43] Having outrun its philosophical matrix it sounded abstract and obscure. An interpretation that did not convince the average "person in the pew" would not last forever. Yet Augustine's diligence in interpretation, his pastoral concern, and his tentativeness and

42. Blowers, "Sublime and Blessed Amphitheatre," 168.

43. John Calvin, *Genesis*, ed. J. King, The Geneva Series of Commentaries (London: Banner of Truth, 1965), 78 on Gen. 1:5; Francisco Suarez, "Tractatus de opere sex dierum," in *Francisci Suarez opera omnia*, ed. D. M. André (Paris: Vivès, 1856), 3:81a.

humility in presenting his exegesis are to be admired.[44] Aspects of his position still provoke serious thought, as we are about to see.

KEEPING AUGUSTINE'S RECRUITERS HONEST

It escapes me how anyone can claim that Augustine's interpretation of the creation days is literal if that means that they were days of *time*. It is either naïve or disingenuous to say, "Augustine and others never repudiated Ambrose's quite literal scheme. That attempt would not come until the twentieth century,"[45] when readers might easily envisage a scheme of creation days that involve the passing of time. Augustine's instantaneous creation was inherently different from Basil's more literal scheme and at the least explicitly formalized an emphasis on instantaneous creation that remained rather enigmatic and elusive in Ambrose's *Hexameron*. Having marked out the route, Augustine had prominent equally nonliteral followers prior to the twentieth century, including Peter Abelard, John Colet, and Cardinal Cajetan.[46] While not truly an allegorical interpretation, Augustine's approach was rather figurative for a literal one in that neither the works of the different days nor even the days themselves involve any span of time.[47]

Young-earth creation supporters counter that day-age sympathizers can take no comfort from Augustine's position, since his creation is infinitely quicker than one week rather than vastly slower.[48] I agree that he teaches nothing like a day-age view of Genesis 1. Suggestions along such lines seem to conflate his world-week teaching and his figurative hermeneutic at this point. It is still possible sometimes

44. See the conclusion to Ortlund, *Retrieving Augustine's Doctrine of Creation*.

45. See the responses of Duncan and Hall in David Hagopian, ed., *The Genesis Debate: Three Views on the Days of Creation* (Mission Viejo, CA: Crux, 2001), 102.

46. Mentioned in chapters 7, 9, and 8, respectively, although I list them here in chronological order.

47. Forster and Marston are not far off the mark at this point: Roger Forster and Paul Marston, *Reason, Science and Faith* (Crowborough: Monarch, 1999), 211.

48. Jonathan D. Sarfati, *Refuting Compromise* (Green Forest, AR: Master Books, 2004), 118; Hall, "Evolution of Mythology," 276–77; James R. Mook, "The Church Fathers on Genesis, the Flood, and the Age of the Earth," in *Coming to Grips with Genesis: Biblical Authority and the Age of the Earth*, ed. Terry Mortenson and Thane H. Ury (Green Forest, AR: Master Books, 2008), 36.

to encounter opinions like this, for instance, from otherwise insightful Australian historian John Dickson:

> Perhaps history's most influential theologian, Saint Augustine, famously championed a quite sophisticated, non-literalistic reading of the text. Augustine understood the 'days' in Genesis 1 as successive epochs in which the substance of matter, which God had created in an instant in the distant past, was fashioned into the various forms we now recognise.[49]

This is not accurate. Augustine's creation days are utterly timeless, unless we are thinking of his "ages of the world," which are not concerned with creation. Augustine cannot be recruited for a day-age style concordist position.[50] On the other hand, I wonder whether some who would celebrate this last statement fully appreciate the implications of Augustine's generative principles teaching. Augustine draws such a profound distinction between the original, instantaneous creation of the angelic world, physical cosmos, and "seeds" of living things in pure potentiality that there is no implicit measure in his philosophy for the proximity between that first creation and when those "virtual seeds" actually come to fruition in creation. The first human creation in Genesis 2:7 is no more necessarily chronologically contiguous to the creation week than the appearance of a mushroom in my front yard tomorrow. Both are simply the realization in historical time of a potentiality put into creation originally by God, although a special (i.e., direct) creation element is cautiously retained. The physical formations of Adam and Eve are not events of the sixth day of the creation week in Augustine's scheme.[51] Sarfati misses this when he says, "Since he believed creation was in an instant, then in Augustine's thinking, the time from Adam to the present was also the time from the beginning of creation to the present, which was less than six thousand years."[52]

Perhaps the error has crept in through a critical mistranslation in the English version of Augustine's *City of God* that many readers access: Marcus Dods's trans-

---

49. John P. Dickson, "The Genesis of Everything: An Historical Account of the Bible's Opening Chapter," *ISCAST Online Journal* 4 (2008): 5.

50. For general comments, see B. Ramm, *The Christian View of Science and Scripture* (Exeter: Paternoster, 1955), 146–47; C. John Collins, "How Old Is the Earth? Anthropomorphic Days in Genesis 1:1–2:3," *Presbyterion* 20 (Fall 1994): 114.

51. See the balanced explanation in Ortlund, *Retrieving Augustine's Doctrine of Creation*, chapter 5, "Can We Evolve on Evolution without Falling from the Fall?"

52. Sarfati, *Refuting Compromise*, 119.

lation belonging to the *Nicene and Post-Nicene Fathers*, which is readily available online in the Christian Classics Ethereal Library. The much-used quote from the *City of God* in Dods's version reads, "They are deceived, too, by those highly mendacious documents which profess to give the history of many thousand years, though, reckoning by the sacred writings, we find that not 6000 years have yet passed."[53] Many writers on both sides of the age of the earth debate in conservative Christian circles have felt that the case on Augustine's view of the earth's age is closed with this apparently definitive statement.[54]

But as William Christian points out, three words in the Latin original are un-represented in Dods's translation.[55] Every Latin edition I have been able to check reads the same way with no indication of manuscript variants: "*cum ex litteris sacris ab institutione hominis nondum complete annorum sex milia computemus.*"[56] That untranslated phrase means "from the creation of humankind," which changes the impression considerably; it is no longer a statement about the age of the world, but insists on a young humanity against Egyptian and Babylonian claims to far deeper ancestries. Other places where Augustine mocks deep ancestries carry the same qualifier (*Civ.* 12.13.1–2; 18.40). It is always about recent *human* creation. That is as far back as a biblical chronology could take us. On Augustine's logic, the creation week is not the first step of that chronology; Adam's creation is that first step.

What about time before human creation? Augustine continues in *City of God*, "I confess that I do not know what ages elapsed before the human race was established, but I have no doubt that no creature whatever is coeternal with the Creator" (12.17.1 [Walsh]). This leaves the door open for an old earth, but perhaps inadvertently. My sense from reading *City of God* is that Augustine is considering the possibility of an angelic history that predates human creation,

53. *Civ.* 12.10 in Dods's edition, but 12.11.1 in the others mentioned below: *NPNF¹* 2:232.

54. E.g. Mook, "Church Fathers," 37; William Dembski, *The End of Christianity* (Nashville: B&H Publishing, 2009), 52; Sarfati, *Refuting Compromise*, 119; Benno Zuiddam, "Does Genesis Allow Any Scientific Theory of Origin?—A Response to JP Dickson," *Journal of Creation* 26.1 (2012): 109; Davis A. Young and Ralph Stearley, *The Bible, Rocks and Time: Geological Evidence for the Age of the Earth* (Downers Grove, IL: InterVarsity Press, 2008), 38, though with an apt sense of caution.

55. Christian, "Augustine on the Creation," 17 n. 39.

56. Other than the spelling variation milia/millia, this clause is identical in PL 41:358; Walsh, *De Civitate Dei*, 128; Augustine, *City of God. Volume IV: Books 12–15*, trans. Philip Levine, LCL (Cambridge: Harvard University Press, 1966), 48; Augustine, *Sancti Aurelii Augustini episcopi. De civitate Dei libri XXII. Vol. I. Lib. I—XIII*, ed. Bernhard Dombart and Alfonsus Kalb, 3rd ed. (Leipzig: Teubner, 1921), 527.

a belief evidenced in certain other church fathers such as Gregory of Nazianzus (*Or.* 38.9–10).[57] But that the *planet* itself might have a long prehuman story would probably have seemed too close to Epicurean naturalism to a thinker such as Augustine. Nor does he assert a young earth, bound by the limits of biblical chronology. He simply does not close that issue.

One position that I think can claim a real, though partial, precedent in Augustine's scheme is the framework hypothesis, which regards the creation week as a kind of heuristic or logical framework, a chronological dress that does not represent an actual week-long chronological process. In spirit, this is not so far from the way Augustine treats the creation week, as its advocates claim.[58] Opponents are indignant: "Augustine advocated a quicker span for creation than most, . . . but whatever figurative hermeneutic he employed never suggested anything as urbane as the framework triads."[59] But we saw above, Augustine offers just such a rationale for the creation week framework (*Gen. litt.* 2.13.27). After trying out a menorah-like symmetry around the fourth day and not finding it viable, he turns to and is satisfied with a 1-2-3 breakdown that is not far from the forming/filling logic of the usual framework parallelism of days one through three and days four through six. It restricts the "forming" to days two and three and leaves day one as a unique "day" concerned with a transcendent, noetic creation, the angels. Both schemas are cognitive. The framework hypothesis, however, understands the reader's mind to house this cognition, while for Augustine it represents the cognition of the best equipped mind for understanding divine truths, the angelic mind.

There are plenty of reasons to cite Augustine in more general science and religion discussions, and he is cited abundantly, for example, in Howard Van Til's quest to appropriate Augustine's indications concerning divine action, for

57. Translation from Gregory of Nazianzus, *Gregory of Nazianzus*, ed. and trans. Brian E. Daley, Early Christian Fathers (London: Routledge, 2006), 121; Peter C. Bouteneff, *Beginnings: Ancient Christian Readings of the Biblical Creation Narratives* (Grand Rapids: Baker Academic, 2008), 147.

58. See the comments by Irons and Kline in Hagopian, *Genesis Debate*, 224, 291; Ortlund, *Retrieving Augustine's Doctrine of Creation*, esp. chapter 3, "Augustine on the Literal Meaning of Genesis 1."

59. See the comments of Duncan and Hall in Hagopian, *Genesis Debate*, 111. See also 266–67 where the accusation, "the framework essay kidnaps Augustine from his context," seems unfair to me.

example.[60] But I leave you with a favorite Augustine quote for numerous Christian participants in science and religion discussion, because it is worth heeding:

> Usually, even a non-Christian knows something about the earth, the heavens, and the other elements of this world, about the motion and orbit of the stars . . . about the kinds of animals, shrubs, stones, and so forth, and this knowledge he holds to as being certain from reason and experience. Now, it is a disgraceful and dangerous thing for an infidel to hear a Christian, presumably giving the meaning of Holy Scripture, talking nonsense on these topics, and we should take all means to prevent such an embarrassing situation, in which people show up vast ignorance in a Christian and laugh it to scorn. The shame is not so much that an ignorant individual is derided, but that people outside the household of the faith think our sacred writers held such opinion, and, to the great loss of those for whose salvation we toil, the writers of our Scripture are criticized and rejected as unlearned men. (*Gen. litt.* 1.19.39 [Taylor])[61]

The reason for its popularity is obvious. There are plenty of feet where that shoe still fits. Augustine, like Calvin a millennium later, does not conclude that just because the study of nature falls outside of his personal strengths or calling it can have no contribution to the discovery of genuine truth.

60. H. J. Van Til, "Basil, Augustine and the Doctrine of Creation's Functional Integrity," *Science & Christian Belief* 8 (1996): 21–38.

61. See, as one example among many, Denis Alexander, *Creation or Evolution: Do We Have to Choose?*, 2nd ed. (Oxford: Monarch, 2014), 462.

Chapter Seven

THE MIDDLE AGES FROM BEDE TO AQUINAS

Whether they knew it or not, Augustine and his immediate predecessors, especially Basil, had synthesized the biblical creation narratives into a Christian cosmogony informed to varying degrees by Neoplatonism and also elements of Aristotelian, Pythagorean, and Stoic thought. Augustine's creation *tour de force*, *The Literal Meaning of Genesis*, took contemporary philosophy seriously, although its true basis was Christian theology. Its sophistication complicated its reception in the church, and Basil's restriction of instantaneous creation to the fundamental matter of creation alone (i.e., Gen. 1:1), mediated via the notable early pope Gregory the Great (ca. 540–604), was a solution that appealed to most.[1] It acknowledged the claim of Sirach 18:1 while honoring the plain sense of Genesis 1, which sounded to the ordinary person like a chronological description of a temporal creation process. Yet Augustine's unequaled stature meant that every medieval commentator or theologian touching on creation would have to reckon with his stance, albeit critically, given the existence of an alternative.

The dominating question of medieval exposition of the creation week of Genesis 1 was therefore how much scope to give to instantaneous creation in the face of Augustine's powerful but, for many, difficult to assimilate interpretation. This debate clearly operates on a different axis to modern creation debates, which of-

---

1. *Moral.* 32.12.16; See Gregory the Great, *Moralia in Iob libri XXIII–XXXV*, ed. M. Adriaen, CCSL 143B (Turnhout: Brepols, 1985), 1640–41. On the vital role of Gregory as a mediator of patristic learning, see Stephen Ch. Kessler, "Gregory the Great: A Figure of Tradition and Transition in Church Exegesis," *HB/OT* 1.2:136.

ten concern either the age and physical origin of the earth in its current form, or the evolutionary versus special creation explanations of life on earth. Why then should we be concerned here with this question of an instantaneous creation?

Its relevance does not spring from the natural appeal of an instantaneous creation belief per se, but from the enduring importance of the question, "Are the days of Genesis 1 to be taken as a literal and historical seven-day series?" The reasons for and against this question today will inevitably differ today from what they were in the thirteenth century, except that participants in these debates continue to share the high view of biblical authority that belonged to the medieval discussion. But the essential choice whether to take the creation week as literal or as a kind of figurative, literary framework remains much the same.

One risk to genuine understanding of medieval thinkers' positions calls for our attention throughout the following survey. It is striking how often writers can come to opposing conclusions about what a medieval (or patristic) thinker was really saying about creation. A contributing factor may be the sheer difficulty of doing the necessary work to read these thinkers' writing directly and at length. Many of the relevant works are not or have only recently become available in English. Furthermore, many medieval discourses on creation do not lend themselves to ready-to-order soundbites that clearly indicate their position. The Scholastic method involved setting out the pros and cons for a certain claim and letting them "duke it out" in the intellectual arena prior to deciding for one over the other. A hasty sample taken in support of a favorite position may be misleading if it is extracted from a written discourse that is only halfway through this process of argument and counterargument. Particularly when we deal with Thomas Aquinas, it will be important to look for the ultimate outcome of his thought processes about creation if we really want to know what he thought at that time instead of simply finding confirmation for our own presuppositions.

Traditional Western neglect of medieval history has produced a corresponding disregard of the medieval ideas that is only recently being remedied. There was, of course, plenty of both intellectual and general development during the millennium 500–1500 CE. James Hannam reminds us that the Middle Ages saw the European invention of the mechanical clock, the windmill, the blast furnace, and movable metal type to accompany Europe's acquisition of paper, gunpowder, and the compass from the East.[2] European sailors had reached India and discov-

---

2. James Hannam, *God's Philosophers: How the Medieval World Laid the Foundations of Modern Science* (London: Icon, 2009), 1–5, 209.

ered the Americas (more than once) by 1500. Medieval scholars understood that the earth was a globe, which was a concept central to the prevailing Aristotelian cosmology.[3] Later medieval Christian Scholasticism was, famously, a marriage of traditional Christian theology and much of the classical Aristotelian heritage, freshly discovered via translation after its incubation in the Islamic world. Perhaps through a combination of Enlightenment prejudice and Protestant dismissal of a Catholic past, the sense that nothing important took place between 500 and 1500 CE seems to be reflected in some of the more argumentative creation dispute literature, which often does not mention any medieval figures or only mentions them superficially.

BEDE: AN ENGLISH MONK ON THE CUSP OF THE MIDDLE AGES

The important Anglo-Saxon scholar and monk Bede "the Venerable" (672–735) is a case in point. His occasional mention in young-earth literature comes on account of his "round-earth" belief, which is an accurate representation despite the prooftexting.[4] Forster and Marston are vague on his significance, while the too-brief mentions by Jack Lewis and John Dickson offer contrasting assessments, the former identifying Bede as a supporter of six literal creation days, and the latter as an advocate of Augustine's instantaneous creation.[5]

Early medieval writers can appear to be mere collectors of patristic opinions, but Bede's work on Genesis, though it made heavy use of patristic sources, was thoughtful, integrative, and influential in the early medieval European church.[6]

3. Jeffrey B. Russell, *Inventing the Flat Earth* (New York: Praeger, 1991).

4. See the comments of Duncan and Hall in *The Genesis Debate: Three Views on the Days of Creation*, ed. David Hagopian (Mission Viejo, CA: Crux, 2001), 116. For a very recruitment-minded web example, see Bede's mention in http://creation.com/creation-scientists#medieval. On his spherical earth belief, see for example Bede, *On Genesis*, trans. Calvin Kendall (Liverpool: Liverpool University Press, 2008), 30 and n. 153.

5. Roger Forster and Paul Marston, *Reason, Science and Faith* (Crowborough: Monarch, 1999), 212–13; Jack P. Lewis, "The Days of Creation: An Historical Survey of Interpretation," *JETS* 32 (1989): 451; John P. Dickson, "The Genesis of Everything: An Historical Account of the Bible's Opening Chapter," *ISCAST Online Journal* 4 (2008): 5.

6. E.g., Gerald Bray, *Biblical Interpretation: Past and Present* (Downers Grove, IL: InterVarsity Press, 1996), 135. Hauser and Watson, "Introduction and Overview," *AHBI* 2:2; Claudio Leonardi, "Aspects of Old Testament Interpretation in the Church from the Seventh to the Tenth Century," *HB/OT* 1.2:191–93.

(We have already seen his innovations in relation to the prevailing understanding of biblical chronology in chapter 3.) With a commentary on Genesis and a briefer hexaemeron to his name, he has a greater claim to the attention of modern interpreters of creation than does Anselm of Canterbury (ca. 1033–1109), treated below, whose lone passing comment on instantaneous creation seems to generate as much discussion as Bede's entire commentary on creation in Genesis.

The best way to understand Bede's stance on the days of creation is to see him as the first medieval representative of a common position on the temporal reality of the creation days, one that took notice of Augustine's Genesis commentary yet restricted the concept of instantaneous creation to the entities named in Genesis 1:1, heaven and earth. This was essentially Basil's position and, despite Augustine's status, the dominant final position of the patristic church.[7] Now Bede certainly emphasizes the omnipotence of God, which means that created things spring into being at the very moment of God's willing it so. They arrive instantaneously. Yet the "forming" and "adorning" of the world, though achieved instantly as far as each creature goes, is still accomplished over the course of a familiar week of time. Bede's early discussion of day four of creation will demonstrate the distinction:

> For after God created heaven, earth, and water before any day whatever of this age, that is, that higher and spiritual world with its inhabitants and the unformed matter of all this world, according to that which has been written, *He that lives forever created all things together*, on the first day of this age he made light to render other created things capable of receiving form. On the second day he solidified the firmament of heaven. . . . On the third day in the lower parts he separated the sea and the lands into their places. . . . Therefore it was proper that the elements should receive the benefit of fuller adornment in the same order in which they were created, that is, that on the fourth day, heaven should be adorned with lights; and that on the fifth day the air and the sea and on the sixth day the earth should be filled with their living creatures. (*In Gen.* 1.15 [Kendall])

---

7. Timothy J. Furry, *Allegorizing History: The Venerable Bede, Figural Exegesis and Historical Theory* (Cambridge: Clarke, 2014), 76–77; Timothy Bellamah, "Medieval Christian Interpretations of Genesis 1–2," in *Since the Beginning: Interpreting Genesis 1 and 2 through the Ages*, ed. Kyle R. Greenwood (Grand Rapids: Baker Academic, 2018), 176 and esp. n. 24.

So, the symmetry between three days of forming and three days of adorning (or "filling" in recent treatments), fondly held by modern framework hypothesis advocates, is already firmly in place. Yet this does not serve a nonconcordist or atemporal scheme. Instantaneous creation, capable in Augustine's scheme of covering the entire creation week, is restricted to a grand, initial act of creation prior to the events of day one. This is confirmed by the quite physical description of how the primordial light orbited the earth to produce the first three days and nights prior to the arrival of the sun. Bede, although aware of Basil's thinking about a light given out and withdrawn in turn by God as producing these days, offers his own independent suggestion, whereby "the lower heaven, half light and half dark, revolves around the stationary earth."[8] So even the first three days of the creation week are produced in real time by a physical cause. This realism is confirmed by statements such as the one concerning the conclusion of the first day by the agency of the orbiting of this primordial light, where Bede adds that it was "without doubt a day of twenty-four hours" (*In Gen.* 9).[9]

Thus, as Frank Robbins noted a century ago in his famous study, Bede established the dominant medieval position on creation.[10] Timothy Furry laments that Bede left Augustine's atemporal creation for an empirical reading that meant, in age of the earth terms, that "he painted himself into a corner."[11] He feels that Augustine had articulated a fine balance between instantaneous original creation and the ongoing appearance of new things in the world via what we have called his generative principles idea, so that creation would not be divorced from providence and Christian theology would be well prepared to deal with modern challenges.[12] By taking a more concrete, literal interpretive tack in Genesis 1 under the influence of Isidore of Seville, Furry feels that Bede missed a trick and left the

8. Kendall, *On Genesis*, 30; Otto Zöckler, *Geschichte der Beziehungen zwischen Theologie und Naturwissenschaft: Mit besonderer Rücksicht auf Schöpfungsgeschichte* (Gütersloh: Bertelsmann, 1877), 1.247–248.

9. Bede says this concerning Gen. 1:5.

10. F. Robbins, *The Hexaemeral Literature: A Study of the Greek and Latin Commentaries in Genesis* (Chicago: University of Chicago Press, 1912), 78–79; E. Mangenot, "Hexaméron," *DTC* 6:2339.

11. Timothy J. Furry, "Time, Text, & Creation: The Venerable Bede on Genesis 1," Henry Center for Theological Understanding (blog), May 24, 2017, http://henrycenter .tiu.edu/2017/05/time-text-creation-the-venerable-bede-on-genesis-1/.

12. Furry, *Allegorizing History*, 79–82, 89–90.

church less equipped in its creation theology going forward.[13] But was not the inability of Augustine's interpretation to retain a broad popular following indicative of the difficulty such an idealistic reading of Genesis had gaining traction in the everyday believer's mind? The age of the earth did later become a pressing issue for the church, but Christian believers ancient and modern have often concluded that an interpretation of Genesis that involves the level of abstraction contemplated by Augustine takes liberties with the biblical text.

Wrangling Creation and Time toward the Middle of the Middle Ages

The ongoing neglect of the Middle Ages in modern Protestant creation discussions, along with a tendency of early medieval commentary to be derivative of patristic sources, means that few medieval figures following Bede feature in the debate until we reach Thomas Aquinas in the mid-thirteenth century. But in the face of a general dominance of Bede's position on the temporality of creation, which was essentially that of Basil, Ambrose (somewhat ambiguously), and Gregory the Great, there continued to be a stream of thought that stood more resolutely with Augustine's instantaneous creation, particularly prior to Aquinas. Anselm of Canterbury (ca. 1033–1109) is the earliest and best known medieval representative noticed more out of respect for his reputation as a theologian than for the extensiveness of his creation treatment, which features briefly within his famous *Why God Became Man* (*Cur Deus Homo*) amid a classically medieval discourse on whether and how the number of fallen angels might be replaced:

> But if the whole creation was produced at once, and the "days" of Moses' account, where he seems to say that the world was not made all at once, are not to be equated with the days in which we live, I cannot understand how the angels were made in that complete number.[14]

---

13. Furry, *Allegorizing History*, 64, 67, 78, 86–87, 89, 91. This is essentially the theme of this chapter of his book.

14. *Cur Deus Homo* 1.18. Translation from Anselm, "Why God Became Man," in *A Scholastic Miscellany: Anselm to Ockham*, ed. Eugene R. Fairweather, trans. E. Prout, The Library of Christian Classics (Philadelphia: Westminster, 1982), 127.

Despite some exposure in the modern debates, modern commentators fail to get much blood out of this exegetical stone.[15] Marcia Colish points out a clearer statement in a paragraph of Anselm's theological sentences where he addresses the topic. But although Colish understands him as renouncing both Bede's and Augustine's positions, to my eye he follows closely in Augustine's train, interpreting the days as a figure signifying phases of angelic knowledge.[16] This aligns with the support for Augustine's instantaneous creation of figures like Peter Abelard (1079–1142), Honorius of Autun (or Augustodunensis, ca. 1090–ca. 1156), Arnold of Bonneval (d. ca. 1160), Peter Cantor (d. 1197), and finally Aquinas's mentor, Albert the Great (ca. 1170–1245), whose creation stance was woven into his synthesis of Christian theology with the Aristotelian viewpoints that had by then percolated through medieval Europe.[17] But Augustine's brand of timeless creation was hedged with caution in the *Sentences* of Peter Lombard and respectfully declined in the *Summa theologiae* of Thomas Aquinas, these works representing the two most prominent handbooks of medieval Scholasticism.

15. C. John Collins, "How Old Is the Earth? Anthropomorphic Days in Genesis 1:1–2:3," *Presbyterion* 20 (1994): 113, 124–25; David W. Hall, "The Evolution of Mythology: Classic Creation Survives as the Fittest Among Its Critics," in *Did God Create in Six Days?*, ed. J. A. Pipa Jr. and D. W. Hall (White Hall, WV: Tolle Lege, 2005), 277–78; Robert Letham, "'In the Space of Six Days': The Days of Creation from Origen to the Westminster Assembly," *WTJ* 61.2 (1999): 159–60; Hagopian, *Genesis Debate*, 47, 90.

16. Anselm von Laon, *Systematische Sentenzen*, ed. Franz Johannes Plazidus Bliemetzrieder, Beiträge zur Geschichte der Philosophie des Mittelalters 18 (Münster: Aschendorffschen Verlagsbuchhandlung, 1919), 12–14; Marcia L. Colish, *Peter Lombard*, 2 vols. (Leiden: Brill, 1994), 1:329. It is Augustine, not Bede, who urges a figurative (*propter figuram*) reading of Genesis 1 according to Anselm here. He favors Augustine by giving him the last word on p. 12 and takes up his angelic interpretation on p. 13.

17. Peter Abelard, "Expositio in hexameron," PL 178:745c–d; Honorius of Autun, "Hexaemeron," PL 172:255–62; Arnold of Bonneval, "De Operibus Sex Dierum," PL 189:1515–20; Petrus Cantor, *Glossae super Genesim. Prologus et capitula 1–3*, trans. Agneta Sylwan, Studia Graeca et Latina Gothoburgensia 55 (Göteborg: Acta Universitatis Gothoburgensis, 1992), prologue; Albert the Great, *B. Alberti Magni opera omnia*, vol. 32, *Summa theologiae pars secunda*, ed. A. Borgnet (Paris: Vivès, 1895), 518–19, 530–32. There is some debate about this interpretation of some of these figures, especially Albert. See my more detailed discussion in *DOC*, 71–75, 85–87.

PETER LOMBARD

From an apparently humble birth in Lombardy (now in northern Italy), Peter Lombard (ca. 1095–1169) made his way to Paris and rose through the ecclesiastical ranks while teaching at the cathedral school at Notre Dame, finally becoming bishop of Paris in 1159.[18] If we regard Thomas Aquinas's *Summa theologiae* as the most famous theological treatise of the Middle Ages, second in line is probably Lombard's *Sentences*, whose first edition appeared in 1154, followed by a second, expanded edition in 1158.[19] Particularly after its endorsement as orthodox by the Fourth Lateran Council of 1215, Lombard's *Sentences* took its place as the essential theological textbook of the later Middle Ages to the point that writing a commentary on the *Sentences* became an educational rite of passage for trainee theologians.[20] Lombard's profound influence was due to his erudition, competence, comprehensiveness, and even-handedness in his coverage of theological issues, making him genuinely indicative of the state of theology in his day.[21] Because Lombard wields the same kind of vague authority in the modern Christian mind as Anselm, his is one of the few medieval names to penetrate modern creation debates, but often without enough context to permit the reader to make any kind of informed assessment of his position. Before evaluating the scant detail of the claims made on Lombard's behalf, let me first comment on what the *Sentences* set out to do.

The standard study Bible of the Middle Ages, first edited around the mid-twelfth century, was the *Glossa ordinaria*. Most of its content comprises explanatory notes drawn from patristic and more recent authorities. It is available in a facsimile edition that reveals its page structure: a small portion of biblical (Vulgate) text in the center interleaved with a brief interlinear gloss, all surrounded by the much more extensive marginal gloss.[22] In this tradition of "glossing" or commenting on the biblical text,

---

18. Philipp W. Rosemann, *Peter Lombard* (Oxford: Oxford University Press, 2004), 34–37.

19. Rosemann, *Peter Lombard*, 55.

20. Ulrich Köpf, "The Institutional Framework of Christian Exegesis in the Middle Ages," *HB/OT* 1.2:175–76; *ODCC*, "Peter Lombard (*c.* 1100–60)," 1073.

21. Jacques-Guy Bougerol, "The Church Fathers and the Sentences of Peter Lombard," in *The Reception of the Church Fathers in the West*, vol. 1, *From the Carolingians to the Maurists*, ed. Irena Backus (Leiden: Brill, 1997), 160; Rosemann, *Peter Lombard*, 5–7; Colish, *Peter Lombard*, 1:30–33.

22. Karlfried Froehlich and Margaret T. Gibson, eds., *Biblia Latina cum Glossa Ordi-*

key theological cruxes in the text elicited longer "questions" (*quaestiones*), like excurses in a modern commentary. "Soon," explains Marie Mayeski, "the *quaestiones*, with their extended explanations, were extracted from the commentary and circulated as texts in themselves."[23] These compilations of theological questions would in time be rearranged on a topical plan, Lombard's *Sentences* being the textbook example. The *Sentences* represents a distillation of excurses once attached to biblical texts but now reordered topically and written as a coherent theological treatise. Thus, Lombard is credited as the inventor of a new medieval literary genre.[24]

Through his *Sentences*, Lombard offered the medieval church a balanced creation position that mediated between two sets of voices. The first set was the patristic tradition and especially the voice of Augustine, copiously cited in the work, so that we may say "that the *Book of Sentences* belongs squarely in the Augustinian tradition."[25] "Peter Lombard thought of his work as a repository of patristic material arranged under topic headings."[26] The second set of voices was the discussion surrounding the biblical creation texts generated by the revival of Neoplatonism in the twelfth century led by the scholars of the cathedral school at Chartres, including Thierry of Chartres and William of Conches.[27] This movement generated responses ranging from mildly to strongly opposed to these Platonist ideas, coming from Scholastic theologians such as Peter Abelard, Lombard's one-time teacher, and Hugh of St. Victor, author of the influential theological handbook *On the Sacraments of the Christian Faith*.[28] Though Abelard's *Yes and No* (*Sic et non*) had clearly

---

naria: *Facsimile Reprint of the Editio Princeps Adolph Rusch of Strassburg 1480/81* (Turnhout: Brepols 1992).

23. Mary A. Mayeski, "Early Medieval Exegesis: Gregory I to the Twelfth Century," *AHBI* 2:102.

24. For the content of this paragraph, see for example: Beryl Smalley, *The Study of the Bible in the Middle Ages* (Oxford: Blackwell, 1952), 64; Gillian R. Evans, *The Language and Logic of the Bible: The Earlier Middle Ages* (Cambridge: Cambridge University Press, 1984), 135; Evans, *The Language and Logic of the Bible: The Road to Reformation* (Cambridge: Cambridge University Press, 1985), 102–3; Mayeski, "Early Medieval Exegesis," 100–103; Hannam, *God's Philosophers*, 75.

25. Rosemann, *Peter Lombard*, 56; Bougerol, "Church Fathers," 115.

26. Evans, *Road to Reformation*, 103.

27. Marcia Colish has offered the authoritative explanation of this context for Lombard's handling of creation in book 2 of the *Sentences*: Colish, *Peter Lombard*, 1:303–336. See esp. 309–15 on the two figures mentioned.

28. Evans, *Earlier Middle Ages*, 166.

influenced Lombard's overall plan for the *Sentences*, it was the thought of Hugh of St. Victor that mostly set the tone for Lombard's thinking on creation along with the older Bede and Alcuin of York.[29] The recent English translation of Lombard's *Sentences* by Giulio Silano has now made his thinking much more accessible.

Some references to Lombard in creation debate literature constitute glaring examples of superficial recruiting tactics or else of summary rejection. Catholic scientist Stanley Jaki, although far from ignorant about medieval Christian thought, nevertheless belittles Lombard as a mindless follower of patristic ancestors into the trap of concordism, "clearly overwhelmed by the weight of tradition."[30] This lack of any real effort to understand Lombard sympathetically in his historical context despite good familiarity with the primary texts is typical of Jaki's approach. Then there is Lombard's inclusion in lists of "long-dead church leaders who think like us" in Protestant creation debates. In such cases, no exploration into Lombard's thought is offered in any form, other than to deny him to the other team or claim him for one's own.[31] Jack Lewis meanwhile sounds perplexed: "Peter Lombard and Hugh of St. Victor give support to the idea that creation was instantaneous but still was in six days."[32] Forster and Marston admit Lombard's literalism and young-earth supporter Joel Beeke finds Lombard's creation days clearly defined as twenty-four-hour ones even though "the allegorical approach to the Bible prevailed in the Middle Ages."[33]

Historians speaking outside the confines of evangelical creation debates usually arrive at the same conclusion. Philipp Rosemann says of the relevant passage, *Sentences* book 2, distinction 12, "Lombard's own preferences are quite clear

29. Regarding the latter see Mangenot, "Hexaméron," 2339; Zöckler, *Geschichte*, 413–14. Regarding the influence of Hugh of St. Victor, see Colish, *Peter Lombard*, 1:325–27, 334, 336–40; Zöckler, *Geschichte*, 413. Hugh himself is occasionally mentioned among the figures cited in modern discussions of creation issues: Davis A. Young and Ralph Stearley, *The Bible, Rocks and Time: Geological Evidence for the Age of the Earth* (Downers Grove, IL: InterVarsity Press, 2008), 43; Stanley Jaki, *Genesis 1 through the Ages*, 2nd ed. (Royal Oak, MI: Real View, 1998), 114–15; Lewis, "Days of Creation," 449, 451.

30. Jaki, *Genesis 1*, 115.

31. Hall, "Evolution of Mythology," 277, 301; Hagopian, *Genesis Debate*, 47, 90, 109–11, 219, 266–67.

32. Lewis, "Days of Creation," 449.

33. Forster and Marston, *Reason, Science and Faith*, 213; Joel R. Beeke, "What Did the Reformers Believe about the Age of the Earth?," in *The New Answers Book 4*, ed. Ken Ham (Green Forest, AR: Master Books, 2013), 101.

from this passage: he leans to the more literal interpretation which he deems to be doing greater justice to the scriptural texts."[34] William Wallace, editor of the creation-related part of a famous edition of Thomas Aquinas's *Summa theologiae* (see below), is slightly more cautious: "Without explicitly rejecting St Augustine, the author indicates his preference for the second interpretation as being more consonant with the literal sense of *Genesis*."[35] Yet a minority view exists that sees Lombard as favoring Augustine's view; an early passage in book 2 leads historian of science Edward Grant to cautiously claim so (*Sent.* 2.2.5).[36] A glimpse at Lombard's more direct, later statements may help us to isolate his position concerning the relationship of creation to time.

Book 2 of the four books of Lombard's *Sentences* is devoted to creation. Following a lengthy treatment of the place of angels in creation and the cosmos (*Sent.* 2.2–11), Lombard takes distinctions 12–15 to treat the creative works of creation days one through six, only with human creation and biblical anthropology to follow in distinction 16. Very soon in distinction 12, Lombard appears to make his position very clear: God "did not form" the individual entities of creation "simultaneously, as it pleased some of the Fathers [to hold], but at intervals of time and in the course of six days, as it has seemed to others" (*Sent.* 2.12.1.2).[37] That there is such a polarity of opinions on this question is something of a problem for a medieval Christian thinker, for whom both Scripture and patristic testimony have great authority: "Indeed, some of the holy Fathers . . . appear to have written almost opposite things regarding this.—For some taught that all things were created simultaneously in matter and form; this appears to have been Augustine's opinion." Yet the more widespread tradition represented "by Gregory [the Great], Jerome, Bede, and many others," holding to the formation of creatures "at intervals over six days . . . seems more congruent with the Scripture of Genesis" (2.12.2). Lombard continues, "And so let us examine the order and mode of creation according to this latter tradition" (2.12.13).

34. Rosemann, *Peter Lombard*, 104; Cf. Mangenot, "Hexaméron," 2339.

35. William A. Wallace, ed., *Summa Theologiae: Latin Text and English Translation*, vol. 10, *Cosmogony (1a. 65–74)*, (London: Blackfriars, 1964), 214.

36. Edward Grant, *Planets, Stars, and Orbs: The Medieval Cosmos, 1200–1687* (Cambridge: Cambridge University Press, 1996), 85–86.

37. Unless otherwise noted, translation from Peter Lombard, *The Sentences. Book 2: On Creation*, trans. Giulio Silano, Mediaeval Sources in Translation 43 (Toronto: Pontifical Institute of Mediaeval Studies, 2007).

This decisive point is reinforced by later statements, for example, "As the Scripture of Genesis teaches, in six days God distinguished and reduced to their proper forms all that he had made materially and simultaneously" (2.12.5.4).[38] Even the first day of creation is defined as "one day of twenty-four hours, namely a natural day," and the light that differentiated day from night as a natural, physical light (2.13.4–5). As he finishes treating prehuman creation, Lombard affirms once more:

> Some say that things were created and distinguished according to their kinds at intervals in the course of six days. Because their view seems to be better supported by the literal meaning of Genesis, and the Church favours it, we have thus far studiously taught that common and formless matter was made first, and afterwards the various classes of corporeal things were formed distinctly from it over the course of six days. (*Sent.* 2.15.5.2 [Silano])

Just as we are putting all doubt to rest, however, Lombard takes distinction 15.6 to once again present Augustine's position that treats the days of Genesis 1 as a "manner of speech" on Moses's part meant for the comprehension of uneducated listeners, "speaking of God by analogy with man, who completes his works over periods of time." Those who think this way "term those six days which Scripture recalls the six classes of things, or distinctions, which were made simultaneously" (2.15.6.2). And thus ends the discussion of the point. After such emphatic statements in favor of a realistic, that is, temporal reading of the creation narrative, Lombard surprisingly chooses to give the Augustinian minority position the last word.

Now the apparent dominance of those earlier statements is enough to convince expert readers past and present that Lombard rejects the instantaneous creation of Augustine and his immediate predecessor Hugh of St. Victor to submit to the majority interpretation.[39] But there are other medieval works that consciously operate on two levels, first on a "plain sense" level for more popular Christian consumption, and second using a more sophisticated, philosophical

---

38. See also 2.12.5.2, 12.6.

39. For an older assessment, see Zöckler, *Geschichte*, 413. The best recent example is Colish, *Peter Lombard*, 1:339. Colish says that Lombard is guided here by an existing Scholastic work, the *Sententiae divinitatis*.

and figurative reading of the text for the learned reader capable of handling it. Lombard's contemporary Honorius of Autun in his *Hexaemeron* expounds the creation week as if it was a real time period, yet frames this exposition with clear instantaneous-creation statements, especially this at the end:

> [Scripture] narrates to the wise that God created all things together in one day on the one hand, but relates to those who are slower that God completed his works in six days: since indeed the more competent can hardly grasp that God in one day, even in a blink of an eye, is said to have created everything at once.[40]

This is why I hesitate to simply deem Lombard an advocate of a more familiar, "real-time" creation week. Like the author of 2 Samuel, who on the surface could write an apparent celebration of David's kingship and yet could imply serious questions about his reign, our medieval writers were capable of writing on different levels for different audiences, and perhaps implying that their students should do so in ministry settings.

Nevertheless, on a plain reading, Lombard offers an irenic, practical synthesis of medieval creation theology, engaging with Augustine and implicitly conversing with more recent voices on creation topics. The obvious level of his creation synthesis would become increasingly influential as coming generations sought to better comprehend the physical cosmos. For our purposes, Lombard represents an excellent, "objective witness of the theological knowledge of his age."[41] He gave the Middle Ages permission to disagree with Augustine and formalized the consensus drawn from predecessors like Bede and Hugh of St. Victor that Genesis 1:1–2 describes a stage of creation that precedes the formal creation week. Days one through three thus describe the arrangement of physical creation (*dispositio*), and days four through six describe its adornment (*ornatio*).[42]

---

40. My translation from PL 172:262d. His *Hexaemeron* occupies 253–62. Colish comments on Honorius's treatment of creation in his *Elucidarium*, but not his *Hexaemeron*: Colish, *Peter Lombard*, 1:321–22. For a more detailed treatment, see *DOC*, 74–75. Gillian Evans also finds him holding to instantaneous creation in his better known *Elucidarium*: Gillian R. Evans, "Masters and Disciples: Aspects of Christian Interpretation of the Old Testament in the Eleventh and Twelfth Centuries," *HB/OT* 1.2:252.

41. Bougerol, "Church Fathers," 160.

42. *Sent.* 2.14.9.2. This appears as distinction 14.6 in some other editions of the *Sentences*.

Thomas Aquinas

Thomas's Setting in Medieval History and Current Debates

The textbook exception to the bypassing of the medieval period in modern Protestant creation debates is usually Thomas Aquinas, commonly regarded as the foremost Christian philosopher and theologian of the medieval church.[43] His fame does not relate to his exegetical powers, yet he produced noteworthy biblical commentary and was operating in a rather exegetical mode when he dealt with creation in theological works like his *Summa theologiae*.[44] The hexaemeron had become a hot topic thanks to the revived prominence of Aristotle's eternal cosmos concept, yielding a rush of commentary on Genesis 1.[45] Nonetheless, in contrast with Basil's hexaemeral sermons or Augustine's Genesis commentaries, we are now examining a different genre of Christian writing: systematic theology in the dialectical mode prized by medieval Scholasticism.

Opening one of the sixty-one volumes of Gilby's edition of Aquinas's *Summa* at random and reading a passage might persuade the reader that Aquinas speaks a different language from us. Yet his apparent suitability for recruitment in modern debates revolves around how literally he understands the days of Genesis 1. Aquinas faces the choice that Lombard did, whether or not to side with ancient heavyweight Augustine when he interprets the creation week as an ontological (i.e., about essential being) and noetic (about angelic knowledge) structure rather than a historical sequence. Simply put, will he decide with Augustine that creation in Genesis 1 is instantaneous or instead that it took a literal week? While instantaneous creation is not a common belief for Christians today, a literal reading of the creation week by Aquinas could provide an important precedent for a literal,

---

43. For an approachable introduction with a feel for traditional Evangelical attitudes toward Aquinas, see Norman Geisler, *Thomas Aquinas: An Evangelical Appraisal* (Eugene, OR: Wipf and Stock, 2003).

44. Thomas Aquinas, *Summa Theologiae: Latin Text and English Translation*. vol. 1, *Christian Theology (1a. 1)*, ed. Thomas Gilby (London: Blackfriars, 1964), 43; K. Froehlich, "Thomas Aquinas (1224/25–1274)," *DMBI*, 984.

45. Karlfried Froehlich, "Christian Interpretation of the Old Testament in the High Middle Ages," *HB/OT* 1.2:525–27; Johannes Zahlten, *Creatio Mundi: Darstellungen der sechs Schöpfungstage und naturwissenschaftliches Weltbild im Mittelalter*, Geschichte und Politik 13 (Stuttgart: Klett-Cotta, 1979), 86–101, 217–20.

creationist understanding of Genesis today.[46] Any decision by Aquinas to understand the creation week as a conceptual schema might on the other hand offer a precedent for nonliteral contemporary readings.

This is how the alternatives are received in creation debates of recent decades. One anachronistic claim can be quickly dismissed: that Aquinas interprets "the creation days of Genesis 1 as long periods of time," as if to anticipate the periodic day or "day-age" interpretation of more recent times. This was the inaccurate claim of Hugh Ross in *The Fingerprint of God*, which was not only scorned by young-earth opponents, as expected, but rightly disowned by C. John Collins.[47] But some commentators feel that Aquinas's review of Augustine's timeless view of the creation days amounts to an endorsement[48]—or at least an openness[49]— to Augustine's position, and find warrant here for something like the modern framework hypothesis.[50] William Dembski's investigation of the matter leads him to the opposite conclusion: "Aquinas was therefore a six-day, six-thousand-year young-earth creationist!"[51] Robert Letham reluctantly admits that Aquinas "appears to come down on the side of an order and sequence in creation," meaning a temporal sequence, while hinting at the difficulty of clearly ascertaining Aquinas's position.[52] Can we hope to do any better?

46. I have encountered one Christian believer who preferred an instantaneous creation position.

47. Hugh Ross, *The Fingerprint of God: Recent Scientific Discoveries Reveal the Unmistakable Identity of the Creator* (Orange, CA: Promise, 1989), 141; Collins, "How Old Is the Earth?," 126; Duncan and Hall in Hagopian, *Genesis Debate*, 48 and n. 63; Hall, "Evolution of Mythology," 273–78.

48. Dickson, "Genesis of Everything," 5. See the detailed rebuttal regarding Aquinas undertaken by Benno Zuiddam, "Does Genesis Allow Any Scientific Theory of Origin?—A Response to JP Dickson," *Journal of Creation* 26.1 (2012): 109.

49. Karl W. Giberson and Francis S. Collins, *The Language of Science and Faith* (Downers Grove, IL: InterVarsity Press, 2011), 75, 101; Forster and Marston, *Reason, Science and Faith*, 214.

50. In addition to just-cited references, see Henri Blocher, *In the Beginning*, ed. David G. Preston (Downers Grove, IL: InterVarsity Press, 1984), 50, following Ceuppens; Irons and Kline, in Hagopian, *Genesis Debate*, 90; C. John Collins, "Reading Genesis 1:1–2:3 as an Act of Communication: Discourse Analysis and Literal Interpretation," in *Did God Create in Six Days?*, ed. J. A. Pipa Jr. and D. W. Hall (White Hall, WV: Tolle Lege, 1999), 145; Letham, "Space of Six Days," 163.

51. William Dembski, *The End of Christianity* (Nashville: B&H, 2009), 53.

52. Letham, "Space of Six Days," 163. For a treatment rich in quotations and lean on explanation, see Lewis, "Days of Creation," 451–52.

On the way to seeking greater clarity on Thomas's thinking, let us boil down a complex variety of background influences on that thinking to three factors. The first factor important to note is the rapid rise of universities in Europe, beginning about 1200 with the founding of the University of Paris.[53] When Thomas was still only fourteen or fifteen, he was sent to the newly established University of Naples in 1239 where he encountered both the Aristotelian philosophy and literature that so influenced his thinking and the Dominican order that would have his lifelong allegiance.[54] University theological study prized the study of texts via "reading" (*lectio*), first of all the biblical text and then, as a second stage in the student's development, Peter Lombard's *Sentences*, explaining why one of Aquinas's early literary products was a commentary on Lombard's work. University-based learning also involved the pedagogical use of debate (*disputatio*), which provided the inspiration for the pro-and-con style of works like Aquinas's *Summa*.[55]

A second important factor is that the century preceding Aquinas's arrival in Naples had witnessed an unprecedented surge of Aristotle's writings into the Latin scholarship of Europe through earnest translation work in regions where European and Islamic intellectual and cultural worlds met, such as Spain and Sicily.[56] The more adventurous philosophical interpretations of creation in Genesis in the preceding, twelfth century experimented with Neoplatonism or the speculative writings of Pseudo-Dionysius.[57] This resurgence of Aristotle in the West set the tone for thirteenth-century intellectual debate: "The central intellectual feature of Thomas's time is precisely the question of the relation between Aristotle and Christianity."[58] Aquinas's German mentor Albert the Great broke much ground in mastering this new corpus of literature and processing its implications for Christian theology, but Aquinas would be responsible for the most thorough, critical synthesis of Latin Christianity and Aristotelian philosophy.

---

53. Ralph McInerny, ed., *Thomas Aquinas: Selected Writings* (London: Penguin, 1998), xxi. See also Köpf, "Institutional Framework," 148–49, 161–78.

54. Jan A. Aertsen, "Aquinas's Philosophy in Its Historical Setting," in *The Cambridge Companion to Aquinas*, ed. Norman Kretzmann and Eleonore Stump (Cambridge: Cambridge University Press, 1993), 12–15.

55. Froehlich, "Thomas Aquinas," 979–82; *HBI* 2:186, 189.

56. Aertsen, "Aquinas's Philosophy," 20–22.

57. For an example of the former (in Latin only), see Thierry of Chartres, "Tractatus de sex dierum operibus," in *Commentaries on Boethius by Thierry of Chartres and His School*, ed. N. M. Häring (Toronto: Pontifical Institute of Medieval Studies, 1971), 553–75.

58. McInerny, *Selected Writings*, xii–xiii.

William Carroll, explaining the relevance of Aquinas's thought for modern understanding of science and religion issues, draws our attention to a third factor: a then-recent conciliar statement from the Catholic church bearing on creation doctrine. The Fourth Lateran Council, hosted at the papal property in 1215, represents the most significant of the seven acknowledged general councils of the medieval era.[59] The seventy canons of its final text are hardly oriented around the doctrine of creation, but note what is said in the opening creedal definition:

> We firmly believe and openly confess that there is only one true God, eternal and immense, omnipotent, unchangeable, incomprehensible, and ineffable, Father, Son, and Holy Ghost; three Persons indeed but one essence,[60] substance, or nature absolutely simple; the Father (proceeding) from no one, but the Son from the Father only, and the Holy Ghost equally from both, always without beginning and end. The Father begetting, the Son begotten, and the Holy Ghost proceeding; consubstantial and coequal, co-omnipotent and coeternal, the one principle of the universe, Creator of all things invisible and visible, spiritual and corporeal, who from the beginning of time and by His omnipotent power made from nothing creatures both spiritual and corporeal, angelic, namely, and mundane, and then human, as it were, common, composed of spirit and body.[61]

This compact, carefully worded creedal statement notably preserves the importance of creation "from nothing" (*de nihilo*), a concept truly fundamental to Aquinas's explanation of creation, and another feature unfortunately concealed in this translation: the claim that both spiritual and physical domains of creation were brought forth "together from the beginning of time" (*simul ab initio tem-*

---

59. William E. Carroll, "Aquinas and the Big Bang," *First Things* 97 (1999): 18–20; Christopher M. Bellitto, *The General Councils: A History of the Twenty-One General Councils from Nicaea to Vatican II* (Mahwah, NJ: Paulist, 2002), 53–56; Reinhold Rieger, "Lateran Councils," in *Religion Past and Present*, ed. Hans Dieter Betz et al., 4th ed. (Leiden: Brill, 2010), 7:337–38.

60. I have corrected 'essense' to 'essence' here.

61. Paul Halsall, "Medieval Sourcebook: Twelfth Ecumenical Council: Lateran IV 1215," Internet History Sourcebooks Project, 1996, https://sourcebooks.fordham.edu/halsall/basis/lateran4.asp.

poris).[62] Notwithstanding the prefacing of human creation with "then" (*deinde*), I would see this statement as aligned rather closely with an Augustinian instantaneous creation, though its brevity allowed supporters of a creation over six actual days to find room for their position, doubtless by limiting "simul" creation to the initial substance of the things to be formed.[63] This alignment makes sense given the defenses of instantaneous creation in Augustine's mold by Abelard, Honorius, and the other figures mentioned above.[64]

This brings us to Thomas Aquinas's own handling of creation in relation to time and to the framework of the creation week in Genesis 1. Thomas too appears to begin sympathetic to Augustinian instantaneous creation, but then shifts in a realistic, temporal direction in his later works, perhaps as part of a broader shift in the thirteenth-century theological mood as it concerned biblical creation. But before we study three of Aquinas's most significant writings on creation in Genesis 1, it is important that we understand the dialectical debate structure built into each of these writings. Thomas's discourse will ricochet between for and against cases on a topic before eventually arriving at a solution. Understanding this will warn us to properly contextualize any statement we might read in Aquinas's works, checking whether that statement represents Aquinas's own position or one that he intends eventually to refute. I will revisit this issue of structure as we reach the third writing, the *Summa*.

Early Indications in the Commentary on the Sentences

While in his early twenties studying at the University of Paris, Aquinas completed his commentary on Lombard's *Sentences*, a standard second stage for the scholar-in-training following his biblical studies and a prerequisite for his subsequent qualification as a master of theology. Qualifying as master in 1256, he occupied one of two chairs at the University.[65] So his commentary on the *Sentences* was completed

62. Latin text from Johannes Dominicus Mansi, ed., *Sacrorum Conciliorum nova et amplissima Collectio* (Florence: Antonium Zatta, 1759), 22:981, accessible at http://patristica.net/mansi.
63. Compare the analysis in Grant, *Planets, Stars, and Orbs*, 83–85.
64. *DOC*, 72–75.
65. E.g., *HBI* 2:187; McInerny, *Selected Writings*, xi, 3–4; Froehlich, "High Middle Ages," 139, and for detail on the educational system, Köpf, "Institutional Framework," 170–78.

before 1256. We saw that Lombard made his fullest statements about instantaneous creation in *Sentences* 2.12 and, unsurprisingly, Aquinas's clearest response to the same issue appears at the corresponding point in his commentary on Lombard's work. Article two on *Sentences* 2.12 asks whether "all things [are] created simultaneously, distinct in their species" (*Comm. Sent.* 2.2.12.2). The alternative is the initial creation of basic matter—that is, the four elements of earth, water, air, and fire all blended together, to be differentiated over the six days of creation.

Responding in stage two of the argument structure to the question "Are all things created simultaneously?," the provisional answer follows: "It seems that they are."[66] The first supporting point cites the favorite prooftext, Sirach 18:1— "He who lives forever created all things together [Latin *simul*]"—long respected and understood in the church to support an instantaneous creation. Furthermore, continues Aquinas, Deuteronomy 32:4 says that the works of God are perfect, so why would not his created works be instantly perfect? This, after all, best reflects divine power. And if God's creative productions seem to appear instantly in the Genesis narrative, why create a day's worth of productions in a moment and then wait idle for twenty-four hours until the next day begins? For that matter, the parts of the universe are interdependent, so parts of it can hardly be made at chronologically separate times.

The following *sed contra* section (part three of the argument) uses Augustine against himself, quoting him to the effect that Scripture's authority trumps human reason so that if in Genesis "it is written that different creatures came to be over the course of six days," then "it seems necessary to maintain this." Moreover, nature witnesses many processes that proceed "from the imperfect to the perfect," so this should not seem foreign in creation.[67] Now, to this point we might expect that if Aquinas presents arguments for Augustine's instantaneous creation in his "objections" section (part two) and then presents opposing arguments here under *sed contra*, he must then be preparing to refute instantaneous creation. But we must go carefully. Aquinas is not always for the *sed contra* and against the objections of part two, and in fact he will finally rebut the *sed contra* arguments below.[68]

66. The English is the translation of McInerny, *Selected Writings*, 90. I have supplemented McInerny's wording from the Latin edition: Thomas Aquinas, *Scriptum super Libros Sententiarum* (Bologna: Edizioni Studio Domenicano, 2000), 3:586. This section is available at http://www.alim.dfll.univr.it/alim/letteratura.nsf/(testiID)/DAF08C12 C0F1C727C12570DA005ADFA2!opendocument.

67. McInerny, *Selected Writings*, 90.

68. A possibility noted for the structure by Gilby in Aquinas, *Summa Theologiae*, 1:46;

Aquinas pauses here to make a point that has struck some modern commentators as vitally important. Some of our beliefs, he says, are core beliefs, "of the substance of faith, such as that God is three and one." Such beliefs are indispensable to the integrity of the Christian gospel. "Other things are only incidental to faith" and subject to disagreement among "even the saints." "That the world began to be by creation," rather than being autonomous and eternal, as Aristotle thought, or perhaps an involuntary emanation from God, as Neoplatonism might say, is of the substance of faith. "But how and in what order this was done pertains to faith only incidentally [*per accidens*]" (*Comm. Sent.* 2.2.12.2).[69] I have often heard such caveats from contemporary Christians inclined to nonconcordist approaches to Genesis and have wondered whether they amount to an avoidance strategy concerning difficult questions of origins. But given Aquinas's authority in Christian tradition,[70] such a statement begs for our serious consideration.[71] If a creation model meets the requirements of the substance of faith by safeguarding God's identity and right relation to creation and finds biblical support, then it should not be the basis for judging its proponent heretical.

Then Aquinas comes to pit temporal and atemporal creation interpretations against one another. Augustine is reported as saying that certain things appeared fully developed at the first moment of creation, "such as the [four] elements, celestial bodies," which rolls days one and four together, "and spiritual substances," such as angels, while terrestrial life, animals, plants, and humans, are created only in a kind of "virtual seed" form to appear fully formed later, even after the creation week.[72] Just as a teacher explaining a geometrical figure must narrate a truth that actually has no chronology, "Moses . . . divides into parts what was done simultaneously."[73] On the other hand, the church father Ambrose (and his more impor-

---

Norman Kretzmann and Eleonore Stump, "Introduction," in *The Cambridge Companion to Aquinas*, ed. Norman Kretzmann and Eleonore Stump (Cambridge: Cambridge University Press, 1993), 6.

69. McInerny, *Selected Writings*, 91; Aquinas, *Scriptum super Libros Sententiarum*, 3:588.

70. Geisler, *Thomas Aquinas*, 11–23.

71. Joshua Lee Harris, "Terms of the Divine Art: Aquinas on Creation," Henry Center for Theological Understanding (blog), June 7, 2017, http://henrycenter.tiu.edu/2017/06/terms-of-the-divine-art-aquinas-on-creation/; William E. Carroll, "Aquinas and Contemporary Cosmology: Creation and Beginnings," *Science & Christian Belief* 24.1 (2012): 17.

72. The term "virtual seed" in Aquinas's text, already ancient by this time, is *rationes seminales*, the concept of Augustine discussed in the preceding chapter.

73. McInerny, *Selected Writings*, 91.

tant model, Basil, and many others) want to retain the chronological reality of the creation week. For Aquinas, "This is the more common opinion, and superficially seems more consonant with the text."[74] Augustine's stance "is more reasonable and better protects Sacred Scripture from the derision of infidels . . . and this opinion is more pleasing to me" (*Comm. Sent.* 2.2.12.2).[75]

Aquinas proceeds in the fifth part of the disputation of this article to rebut or qualify both the initial points made in part two *for* instantaneous creation, and those made in part three, the *sed contra*, against it. A reader could be forgiven for feeling confused at this point, but the preference Aquinas expressed in section four for an instantaneous creation is reinforced in article three to follow. Aquinas concludes that on the analogy of physical daylight, "the six kinds of [created] things can in a certain way be distinguished into six days without the distinction of time," without this becoming an interpretive abuse of the creation week framework (*Comm. Sent.* 2.2.12.3).[76] Aquinas believes this creation understanding is better equipped to stand up and contend for biblical credibility in the apologetic marketplace. But he hints at the difficulty of selling it to the Christian masses as a natural and straightforward reading of the Genesis narrative. This ancient tension, visible already in the patristic period, persists to this day as a problem for more sophisticated or abstract creation proposals.

The Philosophy of Instantaneous Creation in Summa contra Gentiles

The *Summa contra Gentiles*, whose early stages are dated by McInerny to the beginning of Aquinas's period in Italy (1259–65), is geared to the verification of the Christian gospel for the unconvinced outsider and thus largely avoids reliance on the authority of Scripture or Christian tradition.[77] Given the driving apologetic purpose of this work, then, we are not surprised to see that the few statements bearing on creation straightforwardly advocate an instantaneous creation, the position Aquinas thought most defensible to outsiders. Having stoutly defended creation from nothing—a countercultural idea for Aristotelians

74. This sounds like rather faint praise. The Latin is *haec quidem positio est communior, et magis consona videtur litterae quantum ad superficiem*: Aquinas, *Scriptum super Libros Sententiarum*, 3:590.
75. McInerny, *Selected Writings*, 92.
76. McInerny, *Selected Writings*, 95.
77. McInerny, *Selected Writings*, 241.

(*C. Gent.* 2.16)[78]—Aquinas emphasizes that skeptics of the idea of creation on the basis of the truism, "Nothing comes from nothing," had too small an idea of creation. Creation is not a movement representing the effect of a prior cause, nor a change in condition of a material entity, assuming a prior state of that entity. This radical change from nonexistence to existence is thus the only effect that requires no prior cause other than the ultimate First Cause, God, who alone can cause existence itself (*C. Gent.* 2.17–18). The only alternative to such a creation *ex nihilo* stance, says Aquinas, is "infinite regress" (2.18.4) or more mundanely, the world is "just turtles all the way down," with each effect requiring a prior cause. If creation is neither a change nor a movement, "It therefore remains that creation is instantaneous." Aquinas concludes, "And so it is that holy Scripture proclaims the creation of things to have been effected in an indivisible instant," permitting himself a rare scriptural citation (Gen. 1:1) and reference to Basil (*Hex.* 1.5) (*C. Gent.* 2.19).

Aquinas's argument through this part of the *Summa contra Gentiles* possesses impressive philosophical force and consistency, and instantaneous creation suddenly looks like the perfect antidote to a self-existent world. For Aquinas, the core idea of creation is the absolute dependence of the world on God for its existence, or what philosophers call "radical contingency." Carroll reads Aquinas correctly: "Creation is not essentially some distant event; rather, it is the on-going complete causation of the existence of all that is."[79] Because creation is not about time (becoming) so much as being, Aquinas believes that reason alone cannot determine whether the world is eternal or not; it could be eternally created, eternally derived from God. But Aquinas knows of revelation also, and it is thanks to divine revelation, a different way of knowing, that we learn that the world has a beginning.[80] Aristotle's eternal world, the primary intellectual threat to biblical creation in Aquinas's day, could only be refuted on theological and not purely philosophical grounds.[81]

78. Translation from Thomas Aquinas, *Summa contra Gentiles. Book Two: Creation*, trans. James F. Anderson (Notre Dame: University of Notre Dame Press, 1976).

79. Carroll, "Aquinas and Contemporary Cosmology," 16; Harris, "Terms of the Divine Art." See Carroll's entire explanation on 14–16, including 15 n. 28.

80. E. Gilson, *History of Christian Philosophy in the Middle Ages* (New York: Random House, 1955), 372–74.

81. "It was the genius of T. A. to distinguish between creation understood philosophically . . . and creation understood theologically, including the recognition that the

Thomas's Culminating Statement: The Summa Theologiae

Yet Aquinas seems less convinced of instantaneous creation by the time he treats creation in his most famous work, the *Summa theologiae*, which has been described as "the highest achievement of medieval scholarship."[82] Thomas wrote this great work over a protracted period, but much of it was completed during his time teaching in various Dominican houses in Italy from 1259 through 1268, and it is to the end of this period that Stephen Loughlin dates the completion of the first part of the *Summa*, including the part that concerns physical origins.[83]

In the *Summa*, a distinct topic for discussion is a "question" (*quaestio*), which might be divided up into several articles. Each article amounts to "a debate in miniature."[84] The argument process is usually executed in these stages:[85]

1. An article heading, cast as a choice between alternatives (e.g., "Whether God exists" in *ST* 1a.2.3).[86] As in this example, the reader often senses that the apologetic stakes are considerable.

2. A series of objections to the positive case for the question stated in the article heading. These are apparent and probably current objections to the position Aquinas intends to take, supported with biblical and/or philosophical reasoning and introduced with the term "it seems" (*videtur*).

3. The *sed contra*, "on the other hand," constituting "a gesture towards an alternative position recommended by approved authorities or by reason."[87] Peter Kreeft says that this is the point where "St. Thomas indicates his own position," and Aertsen says it "almost always prefigures Aquinas's reasoned reply."[88]

universe does have an absolute temporal beginning": Carroll, "Aquinas and Contemporary Cosmology," 17–18. See also Froehlich, "High Middle Ages," 526–27.

82. Hannam, *God's Philosophers*, 99.

83. McInerny, *Selected Writings*, xi–xii; Stephen J. Loughlin, *Aquinas' Summa Theologiae: A Reader's Guide* (London: T&T Clark, 2010), 4.

84. Gilby, *Summa Theologiae*, 1:46.

85. Gilby, *Summa Theologiae*, 1:43–46; Peter Kreeft, *Summa of the Summa: The Essential Philosophical Passages of the Summa Theologica* (San Francisco: Ignatius, 1990), 17–18; Kretzmann and Stump, "Introduction," 5–6; Aertsen, "Aquinas's Philosophy," 18–19.

86. This is the example presented in Aertsen, "Aquinas's Philosophy," 18.

87. Gilby, *Summa Theologiae*, 1:46.

88. Kreeft, *Summa of the Summa*, 17; Aertsen, "Aquinas's Philosophy," 19.

However, in his *Summa theologiae* 1a.74.1, bearing on creation in Genesis 1, neither part 2, the *videtur* objections, nor this part, the *sed contra*, represents Aquinas's own position. Point two offers reasons why seven days does not seem like enough days to cover creation (e.g., that birds and fish deserve different creation days), while the *sed contra* responds with reasons why they might be too many![89] The lesson is that we need to remain prepared for Aquinas to use this framework in a flexible way.

4.   The response, where having presented the major objections ahead of time, Aquinas states his own position and argues for it. This section naturally warrants our best attention as we seek Aquinas's own stance on theological issues.

5.   Point-by-point answers to the "objections" of part 2.

Step four, then, most deserves our scrutiny, keeping in mind Gilby's advice: "To appreciate where he stands the entire article must be read."[90]

The structuring principle of the *Summa* at the broadest level is the "emanation" of the universe of things visible and invisible from God.[91] This means that Thomas's treatment of theology begins with first principles and follows by treating God's essential being.[92] The next logical step is general discussion about the idea of God producing something other than himself, and so after treatise seven concerning the Trinity follows treatise eight on creation and evil.[93] Then, descending the "great chain of being,"[94] the first specific department of creation that warrants description, despite its surprising absence in Genesis 1, is the angelic population, the highest and holiest part of the created order.[95] This important topic occupies a large tract of fifteen questions (*ST* 1a.50–64).

---

89. Gilby, *Summa Theologiae*, 1:150–51.

90. Gilby, *Summa Theologiae*, 1:46; and in addition to the explanations by Kreeft and Aersten of this structure, see Kretzmann and Stump, "Introduction," 5–6.

91. This is an echo of patristic-era Neoplatonism rather than the Aristotelian influence for which Aquinas is more famous.

92. Kreeft, *Summa of the Summa*, 14–16.

93. The volume index appearing near the beginning of each volume in the edition by Thomas Gilby provides a ready reference for this general structure, and it is guiding this broad survey.

94. Famously explained in A. Lovejoy, *The Great Chain of Being* (Cambridge: Harvard University Press, 1936).

95. Many Christian thinkers, Augustine being the classic example, could not con-

The next topic is the birth or creation of the cosmos, occupying 1a.65–74, which comprises ten questions dealing with the content of Genesis 1:1–2:3, each containing multiple articles structured as mini-debates in the manner described above. (Human creation will follow in questions 75–83, with further exploration of Christian anthropology to follow.) As volume editor William Wallace notes, this section of the *Summa* is "primarily biblical and patristic" compared to the much more philosophical treatments on angels and humans on either side of it. He adds that this section of the *Summa* has fallen into disrepute and neglect among modern theologians on account of its obsolete cosmology, but urges rightly that Thomas be understood in the context of the "climate of opinion" of his own day rather than ours.[96]

This series of questions on creation, then, represents an ongoing conversation with both Scripture, especially Genesis 1, and the church fathers, especially Augustine. Early content covers material creation in principle (questions 65–66); the light of day one (67); the firmament of day two (68); the productions of days three through six (69–72); and finally day seven (73). Comments about Augustine's instantaneous creation are sprinkled right through questions 65–73 before Aquinas turns in question 74 to deal directly with the question of the legitimacy of Augustine's view of the creation week in relation to time.[97] It is risky to sample Aquinas's opinion only partway through this process as Forster and Marston do from his argument about the firmament, even though their detection of "a fairly clear acceptance of possible non-literality on the days" is a fair representation of Aquinas's argument at that point.[98] This is not yet Aquinas's final word on the matter.

Question 74 concerns "all seven days taken together," as its title proclaims. Article 1 asks whether the days are sufficient in number. We saw that the first position countenanced criticized the Genesis narrative for not featuring enough days to host all the works of creation, while the *sed contra* briefly presented the very opposite criticism that fewer than seven days are needed. Aquinas justifies the Genesis narrative, not on the basis that it narrates an actual history that took

template the actual omission of angels from any account of creation, and so found them referred to enigmatically as "light" or "day" or in some other cryptic form in Genesis 1.

96. Wallace, *Summa Theologiae*, 10:xx–xxiii.
97. Wallace, *Summa Theologiae*, 10:155 n. a.
98. Forster and Marston, *Reason, Science and Faith*, 214.

the six natural days the text reflects, but according to the inherent logic of distinction and ornamentation. The highest part of the cosmos, termed "heaven," is distinguished on day one and ornamented on day four with luminaries; The middle part, designated "water," is separated on day two and adorned on day five; while the lowest, "earth," is distinguished on day three and adorned with life on day six. This is the understanding of "some of the Fathers" rather than Augustine's numerical logic, which devotes one day to spiritual creation, then two to the formation of corporeal (physical) creatures, then the final three to ornamentation (*Summa* 1a.74.1). So far, continuity with Lombard's discussion (*Sent.* 2.14.9) as well as patristic and early medieval precedents is clear, and its logic is not bound to the question of whether the days are chronological or not.

More critical for our study is *Summa* 1a.74.2: "Are all these days really one day?" Aquinas now puts Augustine's creation scheme in the dock. Though the focus on Augustine's instantaneous creation is common to his *Commentary on the Sentences* 2.2.12.2, treated above, Aquinas's approach here in the *Summa* is more sophisticated. Both, however, put instantaneous creation first as the "contrary" case with its objections, suggesting at first blush that it is a position Aquinas means to debunk. "It seems [*videtur*] that all these days amount to only one," he begins, citing Genesis 2:4 as gathering all creation into "the day that the Lord made the heaven and the earth," notably including, according to the Latin Vulgate punctuation, "every green plant . . . before it sprung up" (*Summa* 1a.74.2). Sirach 18:1 with its *simul* soon follows, as does the concern that works instantaneously "done" leave all but a moment of each supposed twenty-four-hour period strangely vacant, an argument seen in his *Commentary on the Sentences.*

The *sed contra* simply presents the repeated language of the narrative: "The evening and the morning were the Xth day." The *responsio* follows by describing the gulf that exists between Augustine and "other commentators": Augustine sees in Genesis 1 a single (timeless) day "presented under a seven-fold aspect," while the rest hold the days to be distinct from one another. Aquinas explains that for Augustine "day" implies the enlightening of angelic minds with true knowledge of God's creative works. Contemplative values play out here, influenced by Philo and Origen, plus the strategy for finding angels in the creation narrative. "According to the other Fathers," however, "these days and the succession of time in them reflect successiveness in the actual production of things." At one level we can find common ground, says Aquinas, as both understandings retain the logical sequence portrayed in the creation week. But for those who hold to a temporal creation, time actually passes without visible land (until day three) and without a sun or moon (until day four).

Building toward his conclusion, Aquinas introduces the rebuttals or responses to his initial objections, which were sympathetic to instantaneous creation, by saying, "So as not to prejudice either view, we must deal with the reasons for both" (*Summa* 1a.74.2). That is, these final qualifications will keep both alternatives in view rather than resolve all objections to Aquinas's favored view, a procedure that Wallace finds "somewhat unusual" for the *Summa*, indicating perhaps the delicacy of making the final call, which Aquinas has normally done prior to this fifth part of the argument elsewhere. Unlike the corresponding conclusion to the *responsio* in *Comm. Sent.* 2.2.12.2, he has not yet declared his sympathy for one of the two. Searching the final five rejoinders offered against Augustinian kinds of claims about the creation narrative, we find point one concerning Genesis 2:4–5 leaning Augustine's way, and point two addressing the scope of the *simul* aspect of creation, leaning the other way: "But considering the finishing that was effected by differentiation and ornamentation, this was not done *at once* [*simul*]." We find another traditional statement in rejoinder four sympathetic to a temporal creation: God does not take time to create because he needs it, but to demonstrate creative order. The fifth rejoinder and conclusion to *Summa* 1a.74.2 simply says, "According to Augustine, this order of days should be referred to the natural ordering of the works assigned to the days" (i.e., not to a temporal progression).

Although the debate format of this literary genre can amplify the appearance of indecision, Aquinas seems caught on the horns of a double dilemma. In terms of tradition, it is simply Augustine against the rest, and the scales might seem to tip easily in favor of the rest. But Augustine is such a giant of Christian tradition for Aquinas that he nearly outweighs the rest of the fathers and early medieval authorities.[99] We have seen how Augustine's view of creation still had a considerable following in Aquinas's day. The other dilemma is the tension between a plain reading of Genesis 1 to which the ordinary Christian might be attracted and a philosophically sophisticated reading that would best preserve a "radically contingent" creation out of nothing against the philosophical challenges of the day.

Assessments differ on Aquinas's final position here. "Aquinas . . . appears to come down on the side of an order and sequence in creation," thinks Letham, and in his exhaustive survey of opinion from a century before Letham, Otto Zöckler

99. Leo J. Elders, "Thomas Aquinas and the Fathers of the Church," in *The Reception of the Church Fathers in the West*, ed. I. Backus (Leiden: Brill, 1997), 1:364.

finds Aquinas to "mainly" agree with the non-Augustinian position about "the reality of the six days." Thus the initial creation is indeed instantaneous, but the works of the creative days do occupy the stated time.[100] Edward Grant concludes that the fourth rejoinder about the need for time to represent order in the world represents Aquinas's final stance.[101] Wallace finds Aquinas more ambivalent than he was in the *Commentary on the Sentences*: "St Thomas does not indicate any preference between the two interpretations, but discusses them on an equal footing."[102] Ernan McMullin agrees: "This time, he does not endorse the Augustinian interpretation over its rival, but leaves it up to the reader to decide between them."[103] I wonder whether changed circumstances required a more subtle approach now than in his earlier declaration of his sympathy for Augustine's concept in the *Commentary on the Sentences*, but taking into account his ongoing dependence on an Augustinian explanation in *Summa theologiae* 1a.65–73 and his granting of the very last word to Augustine in the fifth rejoinder here, just as Lombard did, I conclude that Aquinas leaned toward the Augustinian side of the question.

Just before our concluding assessment of Aquinas and the trends we have observed in the Middle Ages, let me point out a phrase in *Summa* 1a.74.3 that has attracted young-earth creationist interest. This article faces the question, "Does Scripture employ apt language to describe the words of the six days?" One of the critical objections faced is that the phrase "one day" in Genesis 1:5 is not a good match for "second," "third," "fourth," and so on. Why would a numerical series start with a cardinal number and continue with ordinal numbers?[104] Addressing this ancient source of exegetical grief in his final rebuttal for this article, Aquinas explains, "The expression *one day* is used in connection with the first institution of day to show that a period of twenty-four hours makes up one day." The phrase "twenty-four hours" causes a little flutter of joy in some readers' hearts, but the main point is neither a literalist nor antiliteralist one.[105] Historically, it explains how the term "day" can cover a period of darkness as well as light, that is, why

100. Letham, "Space of Six Days," 163; Zöckler, *Geschichte*, 1:445; Lewis, "Days of Creation," 449, 452; Mangenot, "Hexaméron," 2340.

101. Grant, *Planets, Stars, and Orbs*, 85–87.

102. Wallace, *Summa Theologiae*, 10:223.

103. Ernan McMullin, "Darwin and the Other Christian Tradition," *Zygon: Journal of Religion & Science* 46.2 (2011): 301.

104. Wallace, *Summa Theologiae*, 10:160–63.

105. Hall, "Evolution of Mythology," 277; Duncan and Hall in Hagopian, *Genesis Debate*, 48.

we do not simply use "day" to describe the daylight period alone. Genesis 1:5 becomes the divine decree that "day" will cover both evening and morning. Yes, Aquinas is speaking of twenty-four-hour days here and sees the first day of creation as the model for our own, but he is not sure that creation actually involves any time at all.

Theistic evolutionists are attracted to Aquinas not just because he draws a clear distinction between philosophical and theological spheres, but because he retains Augustine's idea of what I have called "virtual seeds" (*rationes seminales*). McMullin concedes that this terminology has disappeared from the *Summa* in contrast to the *Commentary on the Sentences*.[106] However, Aquinas continues in *Summa theologiae* 1a.65–74 to expound Augustine's concept using the language of the "causal" or "potential" presence in the original (instantaneous) creation of the plants and animals that would subsequently appear.[107]

Otto Zöckler, an early commentator on the theological implications of Darwin's *Origin of Species*,[108] was sensitive to Aquinas's uptake of this concept: "In relation to the third day, he approves Augustine's stance on an only potential or causal, not actual, creation of the individual kinds of plants on this day, however without the serious extrapolation of any evolutionary consequences therefrom."[109] Giberson and Collins in *The Language of Science and Faith* say, "Aquinas, like Augustine eight centuries earlier, argues in favour of the view that God created all things with the *potential* to develop."[110] This is accurate, keeping in mind Aquinas's approval of classic biblical chronology elsewhere; no one was yet imagining vast tracts of prehuman *earth* history. But Aquinas's retention of the Augustinian possibility of the creation of certain parts of the living world in merely "potential" form leaves the door open to the delayed appearance of forms of life in creation.[111] Aquinas, like Augustine, is in some sense a young-earth developmentalist within a very unmodern philosophical framework.

106. McMullin, "Darwin," 301.
107. *ST* 1a.69.2; 71; 74.2.
108. Frederick Gregory, *Nature Lost? Natural Science and the German Theological Traditions of the Nineteenth Century* (Cambridge: Harvard University Press, 1992), 112–33.
109. My translation from Zöckler, *Geschichte*, 1.444.
110. Giberson and Collins, *The Language of Science and Faith*, 75.
111. For deeper analysis of Aquinas's theology and philosophy of creation based in a deep familiarity with his thought and writings, see Carroll, "Aquinas and Contemporary Cosmology," 16.

CONCLUSION: CREATION, TIME, AND GENESIS 1
IN THE MEDIEVAL PERIOD

Genesis commentaries and specifically hexaemera offering dedicated expositions of the six days of creation proliferated as the Middle Ages matured. We have examined only three medieval figures associated with such works, but Johannes Zahlten was able to list 192 such commentaries for the medieval period, demonstrating what exegetical riches remain to be explored.[112] Nor should we imagine that medieval works are without originality. After close replication of patristic models in the early centuries of the period, successive waves of theological and philosophical thought washed through medieval Europe, registering in original syntheses of biblical creation, some more traditional and conservative and some decidedly adventurous.

Interpretation of early Genesis in this period found two questions intertwined: first, whether to treat the creation week narrative literally or allegorically, and second, whether to regard it as an actual week of world time (temporal) or according to Augustine's instantaneous creation view (atemporal). The first question tended to yield the fruitful compromise that the Genesis text supports both literal and multiple allegorical senses, but that the allegorical senses rely on a well-handled literal sense. Some writers are clearly more interested in discovering truth about Christ or the stages of contemplative approach to God in the Genesis text via the allegorical route rather than asking questions about the physical origin of the cosmos, for example Bonaventure, *Collations on the Six Days* (left incomplete at his death in 1274) and *On the Holy Trinity and His Works* by Rupert of Deutz (ca. 1075–1129).[113] Yet Scholastic works such as Lombard's *Sentences* and Aquinas's *Summa theologiae* trade in the literal sense of Genesis in their quest to define theological truth.

The temporality of the creation week involved grave theological consequences on either hand relating to the interface between God's eternal mode of existence and the surprising phenomenon of a fundamentally temporal world housing hu-

---

112. Zahlten, *Creatio Mundi*, 86, and see Table 4 at the end of the book.

113. Bonaventure, *Collations on the Six Days*, trans. J. de Vinck (Paterson, NJ: St Anthony Guild, 1970); Rupert of Deutz, *De sancta Trinitate et operibus eius*, ed. Rhabanus Haacke, 4 vols., Corpus Christianorum Continuatio Mediaevalis 21–24 (Turnhout: Brepols, 1971–1972).

man life. How God could "touch" a temporal, material world at all was an almost insurmountable problem for some. Was this role delegated to a Platonic world soul, perhaps in the guise of the "Spirit of God" in Genesis 1:2? Would any action of God in the world be instantly perfect and complete, or would it be allowed to grow seed-like? Would that be automatic or require God's continued superintendence? Did a chronological creation week admit process or was it a sequence of instantaneous actions in any case?[114]

Augustine's model from *The Literal Meaning of Genesis* was the constant patristic touchstone for such questions. His model held greater sway early in the medieval period as a timeless creation week that seemingly safeguarded God's sovereign omnipotence, but a change in the intellectual and theological wind toward historical realism and interpretive literalism began to favor a temporal week. Peter Lombard and Thomas Aquinas seem reluctant to choose and sit atop the diplomatic fence while still leaning, I think, toward Augustine, despite the breeze beginning to blow the other way. Martin Luther will typify the further progress of this trend a couple of centuries later, seeing an analogy for the world's formation in that of the individual human being.[115]

114. For a sense of the options, see Charlotte Gross, "Twelfth-Century Concepts of Time: Three Reinterpretations of Augustine's Doctrine of Creation Simul," *Journal of the History of Philosophy* 23.3 (1985): 325–38, who compares three important and original thinkers: Thierry of Chartres, Hugh of St. Victor, and William of Conches. See *DOC*, 76–82 for a snapshot of their interpretations.

115. Martin Luther, *Über das erste Buch Mose* (WA 24:20); Mickey L. Mattox, "Faith in Creation: Martin Luther's Sermons on Genesis 1," *Trinity Journal* 39.2 (2018): 213.

Chapter Eight

MARTIN LUTHER'S STRAIGHTFORWARD CREATION

Martin Luther (1483–1546) is one of those weighty figures from church history; we won't always agree with him, yet we feel the power of his presence and thinking. Like his predecessor Augustine and his younger contemporary Calvin, his written legacy includes an opinion on nearly every conceivable point of Christian belief and practice, and he is often challenging and profound, notwithstanding his obvious flaws and overstepping of the bounds in his writings about peasants, Jews, and others who fell in the path of his flamethrower rhetoric. When he sinned, it seems he "sinned boldly,"[1] yet his faith was living and real and his theology mature and practical.

The present-day student of Luther faces an embarrassment of riches. Carl Meyer wrote, "His greatness can be gauged from the fact that during the four-hundred-plus years since his death, more books have been written about him than about any other figure in history, except Jesus of Nazareth."[2] Add to this the recent five-hundredth anniversary of the nailing of Luther's Ninety-Five Theses to the Wittenberg church door, and you have a recipe for truly copious reading in order to master recent Luther scholarship.

---

1. Mickey L Mattox, "Faith in Creation: Martin Luther's Sermons on Genesis 1," *Trinity Journal* 39.2 (2018): 209 n. 38.

2. Carl S. Meyer, "Luther, Martin (1483–1546)," *NIDCC*, 611.

Luther on Creation and on Genesis

Luther's thinking about creation attracts substantial scholarship of its own. Creation proves to be a vital part of his theological framework, maybe even its center.[3] Genesis represented a central interest in Luther's teaching and preaching.[4] We can imagine Luther's biblical teaching as a professor at the University of Wittenberg as bookended by two important Old Testament courses. He taught the Psalms as his first biblical course (1513–1515), while his vast lecture series on Genesis utilized the best of Luther's exegetical energies for the final years of his life (1535–1545), including his very last lecture, and amounted to one quarter of his entire exegetical output.[5] Though Luther valued his lectures on Galatians and his *Bondage of the Will* the most among his life works,[6] many scholars today would instead see his Genesis lectures as the capstone of his biblical study and theological reasoning.[7]

There exist whole books explaining Luther's teaching on creation, and it is no wonder; this is a rich and rewarding field of exploration, like a freshly discovered underwater cave system revealing still unseen chambers to a scuba diver. Nevertheless, let us attempt to touch on a few of the most striking aspects of his thought in this area prior to tackling his attitude to the timing of creation in Genesis 1.

Luther's role in unleashing the Reformation stemmed in part from his own personal reformation of heart centered on salvation by grace. Not surprisingly, then, his theology of creation was grounded in this life-changing understanding of how God retrieves people from their hopeless alienation from him. "Luther

---

3. Johannes Schwanke, "Martin Luther's Theology of Creation," *International Journal of Systematic Theology* 18.4 (2016): 413.

4. E.g., Mattox, "Faith in Creation," 206–9.

5. Mattox, "Faith in Creation," 206; Gerald Bray, *Biblical Interpretation: Past and Present* (Downers Grove, IL: InterVarsity Press, 1996), 173.

6. K. Hagen, "Luther, Martin (1482–1546)," *DMBI*, 688.

7. Martin Brecht, *Martin Luther: The Preservation of the Church, 1532–1546* (Minneapolis: Fortress, 1993), 141, also 134, 136; H. Bornkamm, *Luther and the Old Testament*, ed. Victor I. Gruhn, trans. Eric W. Gritsch and Ruth C. Gritsch (Philadelphia: Fortress, 1969), 7–8; Johannes Schwanke, "Luther on Creation," *Lutheran Quarterly* 16.4 (2002): 1; Preface by Timothy George in John Thompson, ed., *Genesis 1–11*, RCS 1 (Downers Grove, IL: InterVarsity Press, 2012), xxx; *HBI* 3:69, 87; Siegfried Raeder, "The Exegetical and Hermeneutical Work of Martin Luther," *HB/OT* 2:380.

depicts God's work of creation after the model of God's work of salvation."[8] Both are *ex nihilo* operations, dependent in no way on the merits or potential of what already existed, whether good inclinations in the human heart or a propensity for order in primordial matter.[9] Luther's focus on salvation appears clearly in this meditation on human creation in Genesis 1:27:

> [J]ust as at that time God rejoiced in the counsel and work by which man was created, so today, too, He takes pleasure in restoring this work of His through His Son and our Deliverer, Christ. It is useful to ponder these facts, namely, that God is most kindly inclined toward us and takes delight in His thought and plan of restoring all who have believed in Christ to spiritual life through the resurrection of the dead.[10]

So creation, like salvation, is a gift springing purely from the goodness of God and meant to permit human life to thrive.[11] What a surprise from a thinker with something of a hellfire and brimstone reputation! Indeed, Luther had a deep and dark sense of sin, both his own and that of all classes of humanity. Yet it would be accurate to characterize his theology with the saying, "Where sin runs deep, grace runs deeper." Prior to any human transgression in Luther's scheme of history is creation as the founding act of love of a good God, and his love is what preserves creation still.[12]

8. Niels Henrik Gregersen, "Grace in Nature and History: Luther's Doctrine of Creation Revisited," *Dialog: A Journal of Theology* 44.1 (2005): 20.

9. Paul Althaus, *The Theology of Martin Luther* (Philadelphia: Fortress, 1966), 119–20; Denis Kaiser, "'He Spake and It Was Done': Luther's Creation Theology and His 1535 Lectures on Genesis 1:1–2:4," *Journal of the Adventist Theological Society* 24.2 (2013): 118 and n. 13; Hans Schwarz, "Creation," in *Dictionary of Luther and the Lutheran Traditions*, ed. Mark A. Granquist et al. (Grand Rapids: Baker Academic, 2017), 176; Mattox, "Faith in Creation," 217–19; and esp. Schwanke, "Martin Luther's Theology of Creation," 402, 410–13.

10. Luther, *Lectures on Genesis Chapters 1–5* (LW 1:68); Luther, *Genesisvorlesung* (WA 42:51.27–32); Kaiser, "Luther's Creation Theology," 135.

11. *Lectures on Genesis Chapters 1–5* (LW 1:35). In response to Gen. 1:10–11. See also Kaiser, "Luther's Creation Theology," 125.

12. Gregersen, "Grace in Nature and History," 21; Kaiser, "Luther's Creation Theology" 127; Henry W. Reimann, "Luther on Creation: A Study in Theocentric Theology," *Concordia Theological Monthly* 24.1 (1953): 34–35.

Luther was not content to celebrate God's creation of the cosmos or of humanity in general. His teaching was always pastoral in spirit, and he makes the vital connection between creation doctrine and the life of the individual person by championing the creation of each individual by God. Have you ever tried to find a clear, direct statement of a theology of *personal* creation in a textbook of Christian theology? Sometimes Christian orthodoxy seems only to speak of the original creation of the human type, yet be "careless of the single life," that is, God's creation of you and me.[13] Biblical grounding for a theology of individual creation famously exists in Psalm 139's "fearfully and wonderfully made" and in further statements from the Old Testament Wisdom books (e.g., Job 10:8–12; 31:15; Prov. 14:31; 22:2).[14] But Luther leaves his growing flock confident of their status in his Small Catechism, designed for the most elementary level of Christian instruction, in the first article of the section concerning the Apostles' Creed:[15]

The First Article
I believe in God the Father Almighty, Maker of heaven and earth.

What does this mean?
I believe that God has made me and all creatures; that He has given me my body and soul, eyes, ears and all my members, my reason and all my senses, and still preserves them; that He richly and daily provides me with food and clothing, home and family, property and goods, and all that I need to support this body and life; that He protects me from all danger, guards and keeps me from all evil; and all this purely out of fatherly, divine goodness and mercy,

---

13. Quote from Alfred Tennyson, *In Memoriam* (Boston: Knight & Millet, 1901) 54.2.

14. We might add James 3:9 here, from a very wisdom-flavored New Testament book. Note the immediate ethical consequences of such a belief in God's creation of the individual in most of these texts.

15. The first three parts of his Small and Large Catechisms concern (1) the Ten Commandments; (2) the Apostles' Creed; and (3) the Lord's Prayer or Our Father. Friedmann Hebart explains in his introduction to the Larger Catechism that these three sections pertain to the three things Luther thought necessary for salvation, boiling down to (1) a knowledge of God's demands through the Law and our inability to keep them; (2) the solution to this dilemma in the gospel; and (3) the communication of the individual person with God to appropriate this solution; see *Luther's Large Catechism*, ed. Friedemann Hebart (Adelaide: Lutheran Publishing House, 1983), xix–xx.

without any merit or worthiness in me; for all which I am in duty bound to thank and praise, to serve and obey Him. This is most certainly true.[16]

We cannot blame Luther for expressing truth merely at the level of the abstract and generic! Creation truth is limited neither to broad categories such as humanity in general nor to the first moments of the world's existence. "God has made me and all creatures." The implications for one's view of self and one's relationship with God are immediate and tangible. Every asset of life is a gift of God, and your own existence in the world is utterly intentional on God's part. Your story begins in grace. Luther's ever present pastoral awareness emerges in his ability to directly apply theological truths, in this case creation, to the practical, daily lives of his hearers.[17]

Personalizing creation implies that God is not averse to creating through process. Christians sometimes imagine that any work of God must be immediately complete and perfect; how could God ever produce anything half-baked? The price of this seemingly logical assumption is to rule out not only the human individual but any feature of nature that evidences a history of formation out of the scope of God's creative work. This would be a high theological price to pay, and Luther for one is not willing to pay it. In one of his sermons (rather than lectures) on Genesis not yet translated into English, he responds to the idea that God could not require time to create by pointing to the everyday example of human creation, "since we ourselves are creatures of God and yet are not made complete in one moment."[18] For Luther, this justifies speaking of creation across six temporal days, although it has important implications for divine creation through process more generally. This incidentally dignifies human marriage and

16. http://els.org/beliefs/luthers-small-catechism/part-2-the-apostles-creed/.

17. Lester Meyer, "Luther in the Garden of Eden: His Commentary on Genesis 1–3," *Word & World* 4.4 (1984): 436; Bornkamm, *Luther and the Old Testament*, 101; Schwanke, "Luther on Creation," 2; Mickey Mattox, "Martin Luther: Student of the Creation," Henry Center for Theological Understanding (blog), June 14, 2017, http://henrycenter.tiu.edu/2017/06/martin-luther-student-of-the-creation/.

18. My translation from the Latin text of Luther, *Über das erste Buch Mose* (WA 24:20.5–6, 18–21). For the same idea in (or borrowed by) Luther's contemporary reformer, Oecolampadius, see Johann Oecolampadius, *An Exposition of Genesis*, ed. Mickey Leland Mattox, Reformation Texts with Translation 13 (Milwaukee: Marquette University Press, 2013), 46–47; Mattox, "Faith in Creation," 208 n. 36, 213, 216.

sexual reproduction, in which God condescends to allow the human couple to participate in his creative work.[19]

This truth of personal creation highlights the issue of mediating causal agency in creation. Luther's understanding of God's creation is very transcendent and direct, yet his inclusion of human gestation, the growth of grain, and other such things within the scope of God's creative work means that room is implied in his theological schema for "natural" processes (i.e., those subject to physical or scientific description) to find a place in the causal chain without excluding divine action.[20] This is despite the profound focus on God's sovereign power in creation in Luther's theology, or what we might call a strong emphasis on the First Cause versus secondary causation. The solution to this apparent paradox is that there is no such thing as a natural process in Luther's understanding; every new thing that appears in the world is a direct work of God.[21] It follows that not just the sudden and miraculous but also gradual and mediated action must be possible in God's creative method.

RECRUITMENT OF LUTHER IN CREATION DEBATES

We will return to this point about creation and process in a moment, since it is important to Luther's view of the creation week. In the meantime, why does Luther prove a popular figure when participants in modern creation debates recruit premodern supporters? He has a naturally high profile, of course. He is also popular among advocates of the young-earth position not only for his avowed literal approach to early Genesis but also because his statements in favor of a literal seven-day creation are some of the clearest among any of the figures featured in this book. He tops that off with scattered statements that presume an earth less than six thousand years old. These three features lead Jonathan Sarfati, for example, to conclude zealously that Luther "clearly reveals himself to be a staunch young-earth creationist."[22] That is a brutal anachronism; Luther can hardly take a

19. Schwarz, "Creation," 177; Meyer, "Garden of Eden," 432; Schwanke, "Luther on Creation," 5.

20. Schwarz, "Creation," 177.

21. Althaus, *Theology of Martin Luther*, 107–10. Typically unsympathetic is Stanley Jaki, *Genesis 1 through the Ages*, 2nd ed. (Royal Oak, MI: Real View, 1998), 143.

22. Jonathan D. Sarfati, *Refuting Compromise* (Green Forest, AR: Master Books, 2004), 123.

stance whose name implies a whole web of beliefs about the Bible and the world that include, for example, a flood-based model of the present arrangement of the earth's crust that simply did not exist when Luther lived.

Yet the truth in the label is that Luther believed in a young earth and a literal six-day creation, as is recognized by participants across the spectrum of the debate. Young-earth supporters often celebrate this.[23] Others concede it willingly or reluctantly.[24] Forster and Marston seek to minimize Luther's credibility on the basis of perceived arbitrariness, inconsistency, and "crass literalism" later in the commentary, failing to appreciate his historical importance and theological gravity.[25] Luther deserves more respect than that. His literal creation week is unsurprising for its time, yet represents a significant milestone in Reformation thought. Aside from esoteric engagements with Genesis 1 like that of Jacob Brocardus (ca. 1518–ca. 1594)[26] or the boldly Augustinian (but otherwise literal)

23. Don Batten, ed., *The Answers Book: Updated and Expanded* (Acacia Ridge: Answers in Genesis, 1999), 23, 28; David W. Hall, "A Brief Overview of the Exegesis of Genesis 1–11: Luther to Lyell," in *Coming to Grips with Genesis: Biblical Authority and the Age of the Earth*, ed. Terry Mortenson and Thane H. Ury (Green Forest, AR: Master Books, 2008), 55; Thane H. Ury, "Luther, Calvin, and Wesley on the Genesis of Natural Evil: Recovering Lost Rubrics for Defending a Very Good Creation," in Mortenson and Ury, *Coming to Grips with Genesis*, 403; Jud Davis, "Unresolved Major Questions: Evangelicals and Genesis 1–2," in *Reading Genesis 1–2: An Evangelical Conversation*, ed. J. Daryl Charles (Peabody, MA: Hendrickson, 2013), 218; Joel R. Beeke, "What Did the Reformers Believe about the Age of the Earth?," in *The New Answers Book 4*, ed. Ken Ham (Green Forest, AR: Master Books, 2013), 103–4.

24. Robert Letham, "'In the Space of Six Days': The Days of Creation from Origen to the Westminster Assembly," *WTJ* 61.2 (1999): 163–64; Davis A. Young and Ralph Stearley, *The Bible, Rocks and Time: Geological Evidence for the Age of the Earth* (Downers Grove, IL: InterVarsity Press, 2008), 44; John Lennox, *Seven Days That Divide the World: The Beginning according to Genesis and Science* (Grand Rapids: Zondervan, 2011), 40.

25. Roger Forster and Paul Marston, *Reason, Science and Faith* (Crowborough: Monarch, 1999), 215–17.

26. Arnold Ledgerwood Williams, *The Common Expositor: An Account of the Commentaries on Genesis 1527–1633* (Chapel Hill: University of North Carolina Press, 1948), 43 and n. 13; Jacobus Brocardus, *Mystica et prophetica libri Geneseos interpretatio* (Leyden: Batavorum, 1575). The work initially appears to consist of one long justification for interpretation of Genesis 1 purely as a typology of the ages of the world. See also Zöckler, *Geschichte*, 1:731; Rodney L. Petersen, "Reformed Worldviews and the Exegesis of the

Genesis interpretation (1531) of Cardinal Tommaso de Vio Cajetan (1469–1534)[27] Luther's literal creation week is consistent with a trend toward literal interpretation already established in Nicholas of Lyra's *Postilla*, Luther's classroom text for these Genesis lectures.[28]

LUTHER'S HANDLING OF CREATION IN GENESIS 1

The main primary source for Luther's opinions about creation remains his *Lectures on Genesis*. Earlier in the twentieth century, Luther scholar Peter Meinhold questioned whether the surviving editions of these lectures, notably the one that occupies volumes 42 through 44 of the recognized standard Weimar Edition, accurately represented the actual lectures or had instead been heavily redacted by students and admirers, compromising their value as a historical source. More recently, confidence in the reliability of their representation of Luther's lectures has been largely restored.[29] These lectures preserve, in close proximity, his stance on all three issues: literal versus allegorical interpretation of Genesis, a literal

---

Apocalypse," in *Aspects of Reforming: Theology and Practice in Sixteenth Century Europe*, ed. Michael Parsons (Milton Keynes: Authentic Media, 2014), 253–57.

27. Thomas de Vio Cajetan, *Opera omnia quotquot in Sacrae Scripturae expositionem reperiuntur*, vol. 1, *In Quinque Libros Mosis, iuxta sensum literalem, Commentarii: et primum in Genesim* (Rome, 1531; repr. Hildesheim: Olms, 2005), 6. Jared Wicks, "Catholic Old Testament Interpretation in the Reformation and Early Confessional Eras," *HB/OT* 2:617–23. Cardinal Cajetan was Luther's contemporary and sometimes opponent; see Eric Leland Saak, *Luther and the Reformation of the Later Middle Ages* (Cambridge: Cambridge University Press, 2017), 289–94.

28. Richard A. Muller, "Biblical Interpretation in the Era of the Reformation: The View from the Middle Ages," in *Biblical Interpretation in the Era of the Reformation*, ed. R. A. Muller and J. L. Thompson (Grand Rapids: Eerdmans, 1996), 8–13. Wicks, "Catholic Old Testament Interpretation," 645.

29. Peter Meinhold, *Die Genesisvorlesung Luthers und ihre Herausgeber*, Forschungen zur Kirchen- und Geistesgeschichte 8 (Stuttgart: Kohlhammer, 1936); Jaroslav Pelikan, "Introduction to Volume 1," in Luther, *Lectures on Genesis Chapters 1–5* (LW 1:ix–xii); Brecht, *Martin Luther*, 136, showing Meinhold's influence; John A. Maxfield, *Luther's Lectures on Genesis and the Formation of Evangelical Identity*, Sixteenth Century Essays & Studies 80 (Kirksville, MO: Truman State University Press, 2008), 41; Maxfield, "Martin Luther's Swan Song: Luther's Students, Melanchthon, and the Publication of the Lectures on Genesis (1544–1554)," *Lutherjahrbuch* 81 (2014): 224–25; Schwanke, "Luther on Creation," 1.

creation week, and a world only thousands of years old. Let us touch on each of these points in turn, noting other pertinent writings along the way.

Biblical Chronology

We encounter the last of these points already as we read Luther's preamble, concerning what we would call a "young world": "We know from Moses that the world was not in existence before 6,000 years ago."[30] Similarly, the opening article of his recommendation of a way to meditate on the Apostles' Creed (as we saw above in his Small Catechism) inspires the reader to ponder:

> You are God's creation, his handiwork, his workmanship. That is, of yourself and in yourself you are nothing, can do nothing, know nothing, are capable of nothing. What were you a thousand years ago? What were heaven and earth six thousand years ago? Nothing, just as that which will never be created is nothing. But what you are, know, can do, and can achieve is God's creation.... Therefore you have nothing to boast of before God.[31]

We notice again that pastoral and theological concerns outweigh chronological ones here and justly so. Yet Luther's chronological standpoint is clear, and it forms the backbone of Luther's contribution to the field of biblical chronology, *Computation of the Years of the World* (*Supputatio annorum mundi*) (1541). The traditional Christian calculation of a lapse of historical time of about four thousand years between creation and some part of Christ's life or work based on the Hebrew Old Testament chronology—having outcompeted the longer calculation of around 5,500 years known in patristic times thanks to Bede—was still alive and well in Luther's day.[32] Note, however, that whereas to the modern mind a span of earth time measured in thousands of years sounds brief, this was not the case for

---

30. *Lectures on Genesis Chapters 1–5* (LW 1:3; WA 42:3).

31. Luther, "A Simple Way to Pray, 1535" (LW 43:210).

32. See chapters 2 and 3 concerning world ages and biblical chronology in the church fathers, and for a general introduction to the biblical chronology tradition as it impacts the Reformation era, see James Barr, "Why the World Was Created in 4004 BC: Archbishop Ussher and Biblical Chronology," *Bulletin of the John Rylands Library* 67 (1985): 575–608; James Barr, "Pre-Scientific Chronology: The Bible and the Origin of the World," *Proceedings of the American Philosophical Society* 143 (1999): 379–87.

Luther and his contemporaries, who saw themselves as living in a "world grown old." He says elsewhere, "It would seem to me that we are approaching the end of the world. Christ is clearing His threshing floor with the Gospel, He is gathering the wheat into His granaries, and He will soon burn the chaff with unquenchable fire."[33] The disasters of his own day, such as the fact that the high tide of Ottoman Empire conquest of eastern Europe reached the gates of Vienna in 1529, only confirmed this sense of the impending end of the age.[34]

Luther's chronological scheme in the *Supputatio* leans on its nearest precedent, the *Chronicon Carionis* of 1532, as well as the seventy weeks of Daniel 9 (understood as 490 years), and the talmudic tradition whereby world history may be divided into three periods of two thousand years. The key elements of his scheme are a creation in 3960 BC, Christ's death and resurrection in 34 CE (the 3,994th year of the world), and the realization of the four thousandth year in 40 CE with the decree of the Jerusalem Council related in Acts 15.[35] The year in which Luther completed his calculations (1540) falls at exactly 5,500 years after creation, a traditional option for the coming of the Son of Man in the middle of the sixth millennial "day" (i.e., the day of the human). While Luther is too wise to predict Christ's return here, he does write in the column of his chronological table, "which is why the end of the world may be expected."[36] Thus Luther proves to be a man of his times in terms of the devotional and historical endeavor of biblical chronology, influenced by the world-week tradition long since linked typologically to Genesis 1, and yet a literal approach dominates in his exposition of that chapter.

Luther's overt literalism about Genesis is indisputable, though it is important to state what the alternatives might have been in his time. One alternative quickly

33. Luther, *Sermons on the Gospel of St. John* (LW 22:82–85).

34. *Lectures on Genesis Chapters 1–5* (LW 1:206, 208); Bornkamm, *Luther and the Old Testament*, 61; David M. Whitford, *Luther: A Guide for the Perplexed* (London: T&T Clark, 2011), 10–11; Eric Leland Saak, "The Reception of Augustine in the Later Middle Ages," in *The Reception of the Church Fathers in the West: From the Carolingians to the Maurists*, ed. I. Backus (Leiden: Brill, 1997), 1:26–33.

35. For the beginning and endpoints of this initial 4,000-year period, see Martin Luther, "Supputatio Annorum Mundi" (WA 53:28, 125).

36. Luther, *Quare sperandus est finis mundi* (WA 53:171); James Barr, "Luther and Biblical Chronology," *Bulletin of the John Rylands Library* 72 (1990): 52–53, 64–67; Brecht, *Martin Luther*, 138.

follows the six-thousand-year statement in the introduction to the *Lectures on Genesis*: "Aristotle . . . leans toward the opinion that [the world] *is* eternal," representing the philosophical position that creation from nothing falls outside of cause-and-effect reasoning, as per the rule of thumb, "Nothing comes from nothing." Christian orthodoxy had largely withstood the eternalism that always lurked within Aristotelianism, resurgent since the thirteenth century, though we saw that Aquinas had suggested quite powerfully that apart from biblical revelation, we might easily conclude that creation, while fully dependent on God for its being, might exist eternally in such dependence. Since a logical consequence would be either an infinite number of immortal souls, which seemed unphilosophical, or the mortality of the soul, which seemed heretical, Luther found no reliable guide here and questioned the purpose of "setting up a twofold knowledge," both philosophical and biblical, as he turned to the teachings of Moses.[37]

Within this same prefatory discussion, a more serious rival to a literal Genesis creation account resided at the other end of the spectrum:

> Hilary and Augustine, almost the two greatest lights of the church, hold that the world was created instantaneously, . . . not successively in the course of six days. Moreover, Augustine resorts to extraordinary trifling [*mirabiliter ludit*, "plays an astonishing kind of game"] in his treatment of the six days, which he makes out to be mystical days of knowledge among the angels, not natural ones.[38]

Luther advises any students who want to learn more about such theories to check their college textbook, Nicholas of Lyra's *Postilla*, but suggests that such theories will not help them to understand the Genesis account of creation:

> Nor does it serve any useful purpose to make Moses at the outset so mystical and allegorical. His purpose is to teach us, not about allegorical creatures and an allegorical world but about real creatures and a visible world apprehended

37. *Lectures on Genesis Chapters 1–5* (WA 42:3–4).

38. *Lectures on Genesis Chapters 1–5* (LW 1:4; WA 42:4). This comment could be one source of inspiration for Calvin's *violentum cavillum*, which I translate "[playing] a dangerous game." It arises in reference to the same point of interpretation and comes up for discussion in chapter 9 on Calvin, where we see that Calvin's access to Luther's Genesis lectures has been demonstrated by A. N. S. Lane.

by the senses. Therefore . . . he employs the terms "day" and "evening" without allegory, just as we customarily do.[39]

Literal Interpretation and a Realistic Creation Week

Luther here represents the pendulum swing, characteristic of his era of biblical interpretation, toward literal and commonsense interpretation of scriptures such as Genesis.[40] Bornkamm notes that especially in these *Lectures on Genesis* Luther resists allegory after showing some willingness to utilize it in other contexts.[41] In this regard he is similar to Basil, and like Basil, Luther is concerned for the integrity of creation teaching if allegorical interpretation of Genesis prevails; speaking of the Eden narrative (Gen. 2:4–3:24), Luther protests: "Origen makes heaven out of Paradise and angels out of the trees. If this is correct, what will be left of the doctrine of creation?"[42] Will Genesis still relate God's authorship of our familiar world in its physicality or temporality? That this commitment to literalism on Luther's part does not quite mean what we might think, however, I will address in a moment. For now, we come to its application to the days of the creation week.

> Therefore so far as this opinion of Augustine is concerned, we assert that Moses spoke in the literal sense, not allegorically or figuratively, i.e., that the world, with all its creatures, was created within six days, as the words read. If we do not comprehend the reason for this, let us remain pupils and leave the job of teacher to the Holy Spirit.[43]

The wording is so similar to the equivalent passage in Luther's 1524 sermon series on Genesis that it suggests that Luther might simply have revised his sermon series at this point. In an extract from that series cited in some creationist writings Luther admonishes, "But if you cannot understand how this could have been done in six days, then grant the Holy Spirit the honor of being more learned than

---

39. *Lectures on Genesis Chapters 1–5* (LW 1:5; WA 42:4–5).
40. Muller, "Biblical Interpretation," 10–12; Meyer, "Luther in the Garden of Eden," 436; Williams, *Common Expositor*, 20–21; Mattox, "Martin Luther."
41. Bornkamm, *Luther and the Old Testament*, 94–95 and see 87–96 generally.
42. *Lectures on Genesis Chapters 1–5* (LW 1:232).
43. *Lectures on Genesis Chapters 1–5* (LW 1:5; WA 42:5.15–18).

you."[44] Back in the *Lectures*, Luther's literal creation week is only confirmed by subsequent statements. Challenged to explain the nature of the primordial light that preceded the sun's creation on day four, he notes:

> This has given rise for some to look for an allegory . . . by saying that [light] is an angelic creature . . . [and] that He separated the good angels from the bad. But this is toying with ill-timed allegories (for Moses is relating history); it is not interpreting Scripture. Moreover, Moses wrote so that uneducated men might have clear accounts of the creation.[45]

Therefore, like Basil, Luther takes the primordial light as a physical reality: "I think that this light was in motion in such a way that it brought about a natural day, from its rising to its setting."[46] Such statements continue at intervals early in these lectures. Luther even includes Genesis 1:1–2 within the first day's events, defends a supernaturally quick but not instant appearance of vegetation on day three, and understands the events of Genesis 2:7–25 as occurring within day six of creation, including that "Eve was made sometime after Adam," confirming the passage of time within that day.[47]

There is no debate. Luther's stance on the creation days is plainly literal. Combine that with the understandable assumption that the patriarchs' lifespans, age at first parenting of a child, and other such chronological information from the OT narratives could be integrated into a continuous timeline and we have the reasonable outcome of a very compact human history. Assume furthermore that the *adam* referred to in Genesis 2–4 is the Adam who appears as the progenitor of a family line in Genesis 5, and that the same creation events are told from different points of view in Genesis 1 and 2, and a connection is made to the creation week. If the language of the creation week narrative is then understood literally, as Luther did, and especially if a further assumption is made that the "formless

---

44. Ewald M. Plass, ed., *What Luther Says: An Anthology* (St. Louis: Concordia, 1959), 93, 1523; Batten, *Answers Book*, 28; Sarfati, *Refuting Compromise*, 123. The German original of the *Sermons on Genesis* (WA 24:20.9–10) is: "Kanstu es aber nicht vernemen, wie es sechs tage sind gewesen, so thue dem heiligen geist die ehre, das er gelerter sey denn du" (antique spelling uncorrected).

45. *Lectures on Genesis Chapters 1–5* (LW 1:19; WA 42:15.29–35).

46. *Lectures on Genesis Chapters 1–5* (LW 1:19; WA 42:15.38–39).

47. *Lectures on Genesis Chapters 1–5* (LW 1:10, 37–38, 69, and see 122).

and empty" state of Genesis 1:2 does not persist for any significant length of time, then you have not just an earth but a cosmos only five days older than humanity. That involves a significant combination of assumptions, but they were assumptions that for most Christians of Luther's day were default ones, only questioned by avant-garde interpreters of the Bible. These did exist in Luther's century, for example the Epicureans about whom he complains in his *Sermons on the Gospel of John*, but they were still rare.[48]

Luther takes this literal stand, then, apart from any need to reckon with "deep time" in terms of earth history. We have referred to the eternalism of the Aristotelian tradition, which should not be mistaken for anything like an old earth view. An eternal world is a static world, not a world in development from simple to complex. A definite beginning a billion years ago would be no more amenable to this eternalist paradigm than one six thousand years ago. When "deep time" was contemplated at this point of Christian tradition, it was the surviving patristic idea that the angels might have had a history preceding that of humans, a teaching we noted in the Cappadocian Fathers and evidenced soon after Luther in the Dutch Remonstrant Simon Episcopius (1583–1643) and his theological heirs, including John Milton, whose *Paradise Lost* implies such a narrative sequence.[49]

No, the real challenge for Luther was that for the intellectual Christian, six days still risked looking far too long for creation. This problem forces Luther into some hedging about vegetation. Now it was the apparent inclusion of vegetation within the day on which heaven and earth was created in the wording of the Septuagint of Genesis 2:4–5 that helped create this dilemma.[50] This exegetical aspect of the problem does not arise in the Hebrew punctuation. But it is arguably a dilemma anyway: if God is going to make trees appear and already have fruit in time for Adam and Eve to be tempted by such on day six, that compresses what

48. See LW 22:75. On the rediscovery of classical skepticism, for example, Sextus Empiricus, see Richard H. Popkin, *History of Scepticism from Erasmus to Spinoza* (Berkeley: University of California Press, 1979), 18–35.

49. Simon Episcopius, *M. Simonis Episcopii institutiones theologicae, privatis lectionibus Amstelodami traditae*, ed. Étienne de Courcelles (Amsterdam: Blaeu, 1650), 4.3.1; Philipp van Limborch, *Theologia Christiana ad praxin pietatis ac promotionem pacis Christianae unice directa* (Amsterdam: Wetstenium, 1686), 2.10.4; Rosalie L. Colie, *Light and Enlightenment: A Study of the Cambridge Platonists and the Dutch Arminians* (Cambridge: Cambridge University Press, 1957), 1–30.

50. See chapter 6 on Augustine's confrontation with this textual-linguistic issue concerning vegetation in Gen. 2:4–5.

Luther admits is normally at least a six-month process into twenty-four hours. Why not simply envisage this act of creation as instantaneous? Or should we imagine the instantaneous production of each day's products, say, in the first minute after midnight, followed by an otherwise vacant creation day? In light of God's power to produce what he wills with a word, what need is there for any time at all? Luther identifies this logical challenge as the prompt for church father Hilary's resort to an instantaneous creation, but instead maintains his realistic presentation of the creation week by instead retaining a growth process that proceeded "more quickly than is customary today" and in time for Adam and Eve to find fruit on the sixth day. Yet it was not instantaneous, given the text's use of verbs for "sprouting" and "bearing fruit."[51]

Luther is consistent in this realism. While recognizing that to speak of God's repose on a royal, heavenly throne is an anthropomorphic figure of speech accommodated to human comprehension, Luther would not admit that the creation days represent such a concession.[52] His motivations—the protection of the clarity of the word of God and the authority of the Holy Spirit as its speaker, along with his vigorous defence of the right of access of ordinary, uneducated people to God through the plainness of Scripture—are thoroughly admirable.[53]

There was, however, a breadth to this literalism already seen in Augustine. Bray explains that for Luther, "Everything in Scripture pointed toward [Christ], and anything which was not read in the light of Christ was fundamentally misinterpreted."[54] In practice this meant that Luther's literal sense incorporated a christological sense; in a manner that might look to us allegorical at times, words spoken in and to an Old Testament setting could speak immediately of Christ and directly to the contemporary believer. Explaining that, working from John 1, Luther "found Christ clearly proven in Genesis 1," Bornkamm quotes a sermon on John 1:

> Who is so smart, who would contradict here? He must let the Word be something else than God, its speaker, and yet he must confess that it was there before all creatures and made the creatures through itself; so he must certainly let it be God also, for besides the creatures there is nothing but God.[55]

51. *Lectures on Genesis Chapters 1–5* (LW 1:38–39).
52. *Lectures on Genesis Chapters 1–5* (LW 1:15; WA 42:12.37–38).
53. Maxfield, *Luther's Lectures on Genesis*, 44–45.
54. Bray, *Biblical Interpretation*, 198.
55. Bornkamm, *Luther and the Old Testament*, 118.

This is very orthodox, traditional, and Christ-centred, and certainly illustrates Luther's principle of interpreting Scripture by Scripture with the New Testament, here the theologically pivotal prologue to John's Gospel, granted the determinative role. What it does not do is simply read the plain sense of the words of Genesis 1. We see that even Luther's straight-shooting hermeneutic cannot avoid containing a range of interpretive assumptions that exist to be unpacked and critiqued.

Strikingly naïve, then, is the interpretive principle once announced in quite a partisan Genesis commentary: "The only proper way to interpret Genesis 1 is not to 'interpret' it at all. That is, we accept the fact that it was meant to say exactly what it says."[56] Granted, some interpretations are more straightforward than others, and we can learn something from Luther's sixth sense for approaches that are just too philosophically clever to be confessionally faithful. Yet no one reads neutrally, mechanically, or without interpretation. Nonetheless, Luther's commonsense hermeneutic and constant awareness of its pastoral effects retain real value today. Keeping in mind that the patriarchal narratives loomed large in Luther's Genesis teaching priorities for their earthy realism, perhaps we should critically reconsider Mattox's summary statement: "If for Luther there is a how-to book for the Christian life, Genesis is it."[57]

56. Henry M. Morris, *The Genesis Record: A Scientific and Devotional Commentary on the Book of Beginnings* (Grand Rapids: Baker, 1976), 54.
57. Mattox, "Faith in Creation," 209.

Chapter Nine

JOHN CALVIN'S SPACE OF SIX DAYS

In dim memories of classes with my English literature professor in the southeastern United States decades ago, I recall her citing three figures of English literature that stood out above the rest: Chaucer, Shakespeare, and Milton. The last of these was mentioned at the end of the prior chapter for having adopted Dutch Arminian ideas about a primordial angelic fall. Milton was destined in turn to have a considerable influence on the Christian imagination of creation and the fall down to the present day through his epic poem *Paradise Lost*—though that is still a future element in our story.

Were we to nominate three figures most seminal for present-day Protestant Christianity, it would be hard to go past Augustine, Luther, and Calvin. When creation debates look to historic Christian thought for authoritative precedents, these three likewise continue to stand out, and in Reformed circles, Calvin most of all. In creation theology as in many other spheres, Calvin's theological legacy echoes powerfully through the generations of the Christian church to the present day. We will see, too, that Calvin had access to certain of Luther's works, the *Lectures on Genesis* included.[1]

John Calvin (1509–1564) is one of those historic Christian thinkers whose premier status is matched by the sheer breadth and volume of their theological

1. Randall C. Zachman, "Calvin as Commentator on Genesis," in *Calvin and the Bible*, ed. Donald K. McKim (Cambridge: Cambridge University Press, 2006), 19; R. Stauffer, "L'exégèse de Genèse 1/1–3 chez Luther et Calvin," in *Interprètes de la Bible: Études sur les réformateurs du XVIe siècle*, ed. R. Stauffer (Paris: Beauchesne, 1982), 84–85.

output. Gerald Bray lists his exegetical output in a table that distinguishes written commentaries from expository sermon series and teaching syllabi. Altogether these works cover most of the biblical corpus.[2] Alongside these consciously exegetical writings, the student of Calvin's thought on the Bible will inevitably turn also to his theological magnum opus, the *Institutes of the Christian Religion*, which went through numerous editions from 1536 to the final and definitive edition of 1559.[3]

The Profile of Genesis among Calvin's Works

We saw in the last chapter that the book of Genesis became a rather dominant feature of the teaching career of Luther as he lectured on Genesis for the last ten years of his life (1535–1545). While Genesis did not stand out to this extent above other interests for Calvin, its canonical and theological importance clearly attracted his energies. His important *Commentary on Genesis* was begun in 1550 and completed in 1554.[4] This text, crafted and collated by an editor (des Gallars) from lecture transcripts taken by several auditors of Calvin's teaching, will form our primary source for Calvin's thinking on creation.[5] We will notice that Calvin's positions taken here accord well with his statements about creation in the *Institutes* and in his *Sermons on Genesis*, which have recently appeared in a new critical edition and in English translation for the first time.[6] We will touch on the relevant passages from all three in the following treatment.

2. Gerald Bray, *Biblical Interpretation: Past and Present* (Downers Grove, IL: InterVarsity Press, 1996), 178–79. Note that citations for this chapter in particular are selective and representative. Information about, for example, Calvin's hermeneutical principles or his exegesis of Genesis could be cited from numerous secondary sources.

3. John Calvin, *Institutes of the Christian Religion*, ed. John T. McNeill, trans. Ford Lewis Battles, Library of Christian Classics (Louisville: Westminster John Knox, 1960), xxiii–xxiv.

4. Anthony N. S. Lane, *John Calvin: Student of the Church Fathers* (Edinburgh: T&T Clark, 1999), 205–6.

5. *HBI* 3:119, 127; Scott M. Manetsch, "Problems with the Patriarchs: John Calvin's Interpretation of Difficult Passages in Genesis," *WTJ* 67.1 (2005): 1–2.

6. John Calvin, *Sermons sur la Genèse, Chapitres 1.1–11.4*, ed. Max Engammare, Supplementa Calviniana 11.1 (Neukirchen-Vluyn: Neukirchener Verlag, 2000); John Calvin, *Sermons on Genesis, Chapters 1:1–11:4: Forty-Nine Sermons Delivered in Geneva, between*

RECRUITMENT OF CALVIN IN CREATION DEBATES

As a figure of great stature in Protestant theology, Calvin is a potential star recruit for modern advocates of creation-related ideological platforms. John Woodbridge, debating Jack Rogers and Donald McKim over biblical inerrancy back in the 1980s, wrote: "Christians from many backgrounds, in a spirit of triumphalism, have claimed Calvin as their own. They tend to elevate one aspect of Calvin's thought that coincides with their own theological preferences, while minimizing if not denying other teachings by the Reformer."[7] Randall Zachman adds that "Calvin is one of the very favourites of the anti-science Bible movements," while debate participants protest one another's appropriations of his authority.[8] Hall and his cowriters stand out for their enthusiastic recruitment of Calvin: "While we remain in the embrace of theologians such as Calvin, Luther, Lombard, Ambrose, and Basil, we suggest that our brethren who are influenced by modernism recognize the obscurity of their views and return to the ancient paths."[9] Jonathan Sarfati is more blunt: "It's interesting that on every point on which AiG [Answers in Genesis] disagrees with modern Christendom, Calvin took our side."[10] If this looks preferential, here's an equally incriminating example from the other end-zone: "Perhaps we ought to be on the same side as Augustine, Calvin and Wesley, these three giants."[11]

---

4 September 1559 and 23 January 1560, trans. Rob Roy McGregor (Edinburgh: Banner of Truth, 2009).

7. John D. Woodbridge, *Biblical Authority: A Critique of the Rogers/McKim Proposal* (Grand Rapids: Zondervan, 1982), 56.

8. Randall C. Zachman, *Reconsidering John Calvin* (Cambridge: Cambridge University Press, 2012), 23; and similarly, Ronald E. Osborn, *Death before the Fall: Biblical Literalism and the Problem of Animal Suffering* (Downers Grove, IL: IVP Academic, 2014), 100.

9. Duncan and Hall in *The Genesis Debate: Three Views on the Days of Creation*, ed. David Hagopian (Mission Viejo, CA: Crux, 2001), 109, also 24, 56, 102–4, 111, 113; David W. Hall, "The Evolution of Mythology: Classic Creation Survives as the Fittest among Its Critics," in *Did God Create in Six Days?*, ed. J. A. Pipa Jr. and D. W. Hall (White Hall, WV: Tolle Lege, 2005), 279–80, 301.

10. Jonathan D. Sarfati, *Refuting Compromise* (Green Forest, AR: Master Books, 2004), 124.

11. Darrel Falk, *Coming to Peace with Science: Bridging the Worlds between Faith and Biology* (Downers Grove, IL: InterVarsity Press, 2004), 36, 60. We will come to Wesley in the following chapter.

These are tier-one examples of what John Thompson calls "spectacularly bad ways . . . to read the past."[12] Mere citation of a voice of authority is not the problem; I just did that. The problem is selective, superficial, contextless, and tendentious cherry-picking of the history of interpretation. That is the rationale for returning to check claims about a figure like Calvin *in his context*, and we do so now.

CALVIN'S CREATION WEEK STANCE

Let us be frank. There is nothing obscure about whether Calvin interprets the creation days literally. He plainly does, and this is where conservatives like Hall mentioned above have the better side of the argument concerning his interpretive example, aside from the problem of artificially importing Calvin's view into the present day. The key passages, so often cited, are the following.

A Young and Old World

Early in Calvin's treatment of the doctrine of creation in the *Institutes*, we find confidence in the possibility of a biblical chronology. Given the risk of uncertainty in our creation theology,

> God wanted there to be a history of creation to support the faith of the church, so that it would not look for any other God besides the One presented by Moses as Creator and Founder of the world. Here the time is immediately noted, allowing the faithful to trace back via a continuous series of years to the origin of humanity and of everything else.[13]

So far Calvin explains the rationale that drove the ancient Christian scholarly enterprise of drafting a chronology of world history from creation forward, an exercise based on the implicit chain of genealogical data apparently supplied through the ancestral lines in Genesis, time spans accorded the Egyptian captivity, and so forth. This would explode into a full-blown Renaissance science beginning with

---

12. John Thompson, "Introduction to Genesis 1–11," in *Genesis 1–11*, ed. John Thompson, RCS 1 (Downers Grove, IL: InterVarsity Press, 2012), xlvi.
13. *Institutes* 1.14.1. These and following quotes are my translation from CO 2:117–118.

the pioneering *On Repairing the Calendar* (*De emendatione temporum*) (1583) of French Huguenot scholar Joseph Justus Scaliger.[14]

Calvin proceeds shortly afterward to cite again the ancient pagan mockery against the Christian idea of a recent creation:

> Nor should we be affected by that godless jibe that it's surprising that it didn't occur to God sooner to make heaven and earth, but idly allowed a vast period to drift by instead of producing [it all] thousands of ages ago, whereas the world has not yet reached six thousand years of age as it declines toward its final end.[15]

Calvin finishes a little weakly to our ears, "Why God delayed so long is not appropriate for us either to question or offer to resolve," when we think of Augustine's argument in his *Confessions* that outside of creation time has no meaning, making it illogical to ask what God was doing all that time. That would avoid the error of making God subject to his own creation in terms of time. The point of the jibe, of course, is not fundamentally affected by envisaging a world nearer six billion years old than six thousand; both are equally remote from eternity in practical terms, though not necessarily in terms of their mental impression. A created cosmos of any vintage is young by definition. Nonetheless, commentators across the spectrum acknowledge (young-earth supporters in particular with relish) that Calvin accepted what would now be called a very young world.[16] To Calvin and his contemporaries, though, it looked antiquated and ready to fail, a "world grown old."[17]

14. A. T. Grafton, "Joseph Scaliger and Historical Chronology: The Rise and Fall of a Discipline," *History and Theory* 14 (1975): 156–85.

15. *Institutes* 1.14.1.

16. E.g., advocating a young earth is Joel R. Beeke, "What Did the Reformers Believe about the Age of the Earth?," in *The New Answers Book 4*, ed. Ken Ham (Green Forest, AR: Master Books, 2013), 105; more generally, see William Dembski, *The End of Christianity* (Nashville: B&H, 2009), 53; Davis A. Young and Ralph Stearley, *The Bible, Rocks and Time: Geological Evidence for the Age of the Earth* (Downers Grove, IL: InterVarsity Press, 2008), 45.

17. The literature on this concept, traceable at least back to Augustine, can be found most effectively by searching reference databases for the Latin phrase *senectus mundi* (the old age of the world) or via James M. Dean, *The World Grown Old in Later Medieval Literature* (Cambridge: Medieval Academy of America, 1997). Eric Leland Saak, *Luther*

The little-cited closing sentences of this section on creation would suit the arguments of young-earth creationists better than those seeking support for unfettered inquiry. Protesting those who would speculate about a void or vacuum surrounding the cosmos and again mentioning the six-thousand-year span of history, Calvin refers to Augustine:

> Elsewhere the same man wisely warns that it is no less wrong to raise questions concerning immeasurable stretches of time than of space. . . . As if in the vast circle of heaven and earth enough things do not present themselves to engross all our senses with their incomprehensible brightness! As if within six thousand years God has not shown evidences enough on which to exercise our minds in earnest meditation! Therefore let us willingly remain enclosed within these bounds to which God has willed to confine us.[18]

While elsewhere Calvin does allow for legitimate research into nature and respects astronomical expertise, for instance, at this point he is rather cautious about the propensity of human reason for transgressing legitimate, God-given bounds. What young-earth supporter could not feel glad to see Calvin deem the six-thousand-year time span of biblical chronology to be a God-given boundary fence?

A Literal Creation Week

Calvin articulates a literal Genesis creation week in all three sources we have mentioned. Remaining first within the *Institutes*, the next section (1.14.2) opens like this:

> This is the very reason why Moses reports that God's work was completed not in a moment, but in six days, for by this feature[19] we are drawn away from all

---

and the Reformation of the Later Middle Ages (Cambridge: Cambridge University Press, 2017), 15–17, 21–23, 27–28, 32–33 sums up the zeitgeist. See also Susan E. Schreiner, *The Theater of His Glory: Nature and the Natural Order in the Thought of John Calvin* (Grand Rapids: Baker Academic, 2001), 97–98.

18. *Institutes* 1.14.1; translation by Battles.

19. Latin: *circumstantia*. It is difficult to know whether Calvin by this term refers to the six days as a feature of the text or as a feature of the world's real origin. The word itself

illusions to the one God, who distributed his work into six days so that we might have no problem spending our whole lives contemplating it.[20]

Shortly afterward he continues:

Here, too, human reason begins to shout objections that such a process is inconsistent with the power of God, until, submitting to faith, it learns to cultivate that quiet compliance to which the purification of the seventh day invites us. Yet we should diligently consider in the very order of things God's fatherly love toward humanity, because he did not create Adam until he had filled the world with all sorts of good things.[21]

So Calvin sees divine purpose in taking so long over creation as six days, despite the seeming insult to God's power, which was a true theological roadblock for some contemporary opponents as well as Origen, Augustine, and others centuries before. Calvin implies that their thinking was insufficiently submissive to God's scriptural givens.

Calvin's most famous statement on this topic arises from the phrase "the first day" in Genesis 1:5, which reads this way in King's translation of Calvin's *Commentary on Genesis*:[22]

Here the error of those is manifestly refuted, who maintain that the world was made in a moment. For it is too violent a cavil to contend that Moses distributes the work which God perfected at once into six days, for the mere

---

is rarely used, and the translation "feature" could be debated. Battles has "circumstance" and Beveridge offers "statement," the latter choosing the first of my suggested meanings.

20. Text from CO 2:118, my translation here and the next quotation below.

21. See also *Institutes* 1.14.22 for a parting reference to the six days that repeats this explanation.

22. It is surprising and deficient that there is no newer English translation of such a theologically and exegetically significant work than this one dating to 1847! Earnshaw finds nothing newer to use: Rebekah Earnshaw, *Creator and Creation according to Calvin on Genesis*, Reformed Historical Theology 64 (Göttingen: Vandenhoeck & Ruprecht, 2020), 9. Earnshaw explains on 11–16 that she seeks to make up a shortfall in scholarship by integrating discussion of Calvin's life story and his creation theology with careful examination of his exegesis of Genesis and what may be learned from his rather newly uncovered Genesis sermons.

purpose of conveying instruction. Let us rather conclude that God himself took the space of six days, for the purpose of accommodating his works to the capacity of men.[23]

The antiquated term "cavil" alone hints at the need for a new translation. The online Oxford Dictionary defines it as "a petty or unnecessary objection,"[24] so if the term has not fallen entirely out of use, its meaning at least seems to have diminished in strength since the Latin term *cavilla* connotes jeering or mockery.[25] "Violent" is no longer helpful, either; the pertinent sense of *violentus* is probably that of recklessness or impetuosity. I would suggest that Calvin means something like, "It is *playing a dangerous game* to contend" that it is a six-day format or schema, a purely literary device, by which Moses relates to us a creative work that was actually instantaneous.

After touching on the point of the six-day duration again briefly in connection with Genesis 1:26, Calvin is in more polemic mode regarding Genesis 2:1: "This epilogue . . . entirely refutes the error of those who imagine that the world was formed in a moment; for it declares that an end was only at length put to the work on the sixth day."[26]

Calvin's sermons on Genesis express similar sentiments at corresponding locations in his movement through the text. For example, concerning Genesis 1:5, Calvin preaches, "For it is necessary for us always to keep in mind . . . that God thus wanted to complete his works as it were by intervals, in order to seize us and induce us to better apply our attention to consider things that we might too lightly pass by."[27] In the same context, both here and in his Genesis commentary, Calvin defuses a biblical argument with which his opponents supported their instantaneous creation stance. In the Vulgate version of Sirach 18:1 Christian scholars had long read, "the One who lives in eternity created everything *simul*," interpreting the Latin *simul* to mean "all at once." Yet the original Septuagint

23. John Calvin, *Genesis*, ed. J. King, The Geneva Series of Commentaries (London: Banner of Truth, 1965), 78. All quotations of this work come from this translation. Compare the Latin text in CO 23:17–18.

24. https://en.oxforddictionaries.com/definition/cavil.

25. Charlton Thomas Lewis et al., eds., *A Latin Dictionary: Founded on Andrews' Edition of Freund's Latin Dictionary* (Oxford: Clarendon, 1879), 306.

26. King, *Genesis*, 103; see also 92, 105.

27. Engammare, *Sermons sur la Genèse*, 20; my translation. See also 9–10, 13, 21.

Greek term, *koinē*, is used adverbially to mean "universally," a description of scope rather than time, as Calvin rightly recognized. By means of his linguistic competence, Calvin was removing an interpretive false lead that had long troubled Genesis interpretation.

Looking in the Mirror of Calvin's Protests

Why was it still necessary to defend a literal creation week in this way? That it required four separate assertions in Calvin's commentary on Genesis 1:1–2:3 suggests the availability of a tempting alternative. The argument over Sirach 18:1 is a clue; this was an argument of Augustine's centuries before. Without naming Augustine, perhaps out of respect, Calvin was resisting, I believe, contemporaries who were appropriating Augustine's instantaneous creation for their own ends. Calvin was unlikely to accuse Augustine of playing a game with the Genesis text, but in rejecting modern adopters of his stance, he was effectively also rejecting Augustine's creation synthesis. Given Calvin's general distaste for allegorical interpretation and being thoroughly familiar with Luther's literal treatment of the creation week in his *Lectures on Genesis* as Lane has shown,[28] Calvin saw Augustine's timeless days as too divorced from the natural sense of the Genesis text at this point.[29]

Belief in instantaneous creation was still essentially an Augustinian position. It had proven rather too hardcore for most thinkers by the later Middle Ages, though it seemed always to have an advocate here and there right down to Cardinal Cajetan's 1531 Pentateuch commentary.[30] A slightly earlier English advocate of instantaneous creation was John Colet (ca. 1466–1519), whom Bray deems "the most outstanding English humanist of his time." This position appears in his *Letters to Radulphus on the Mosaic Account of Creation*.[31] Colet, interestingly,

---

28. Lane, *John Calvin*, 2, 193–94; Zachman, "Calvin as Commentator on Genesis," 19; Stauffer, "Luther et Calvin," 84–85.

29. Johannes Van Oort, "John Calvin and the Church Fathers," in *The Reception of the Church Fathers in the West: From the Carolingians to the Maurists*, ed. Irena Backus (Leiden: E. J. Brill, 1997), 2:277–78; K. E. Greene-McCreight, *Ad Litteram: How Augustine, Calvin, and Barth Read the "Plain Sense" of Genesis 1–3*, Issues in Systematic Theology 5 (Frankfurt am Main: Lang, 1999), 124, 132–33.

30. See chapter 8.

31. Bray, *Biblical Interpretation*, 171; John Colet, *Letters to Radulphus on the Mosaic Account of Creation: Together with Other Treatises* (London: Bell, 1876), 10, 27.

is hotly denied to modern day-age or framework view sympathizers by David Hall, who dismisses him as "follow[ing] Augustine at best, or . . . an eccentric Platonist at worst."[32] Yet he was an influential churchman, as Dean of St. Paul's Cathedral, and represents both an important surviving example of scholarship in pre-Reformation England (influenced in his case by contact with the Italian Renaissance)[33] and an example of Platonistic, nonliteral interpretation of the creation week to whose continued survival Sir Thomas Browne would attest a century later.[34] Belief in instantaneous creation survived Calvin's century and beyond as an intellectual alternative to a literal creation week, feeding off Scholastic and Renaissance-era Neoplatonism, on the one hand, and esoteric traditions (e.g., Paracelsianism) on the other. Its advocates relied on Augustine's rendering of the creation week, yet still typically citing Genesis, an unrivaled authority, to justify their positions.

A Creation That Took Time

As an interpreter well attuned to the historical texture of the Old Testament storyline, Calvin could not abide a timeless interpretation of a Genesis narrative that wore such time-structured form. For those who objected to the very idea of God taking time to create, as if by necessity, Calvin had both corroborating examples and a proposed rationale. His examples from his sermon on Genesis 1:3–5 draw on and augment those found in Luther's Genesis sermons relating to things created by God that take time to grow. Luther's example, apposite to his theology of individual creation, was the growth of the person to adulthood. If we include the living individual in the creative work of God, as in Luther's Small Catechism, then we must affirm that God does at least some of his creative work gradually.

Calvin, then, in his own equivalent Genesis sermon, adopts and endorses Luther's example while adding his own further examples. Nor, he says, does bread grow out of the ground ready to eat, nor do trees produce their flowers and fruit instantly. It is probably fair to say that Luther's original example remains the most

32. Hall, "Evolution of Mythology," 291, and see 277, 280–83, 290.
33. J. Arnold, "Colet, John (1467–1519)," *DMBI*, 320–24.
34. Thomas Browne, *Religio, Medici* (Leiden: Hackius, 1644), 143–44; English translation from Thomas Browne, *Religio Medici the Fourth Edition, Corrected and Amended* (London: Crook, 1656), 97. See chapter 10.

potent one in Calvin's sermon, demonstrating that although Deuteronomy 32:4 might proclaim that the works of God are perfect, this does not prohibit God from making things "by degree."[35]

This is a vital point of creation theology. The more orthodox exponents of instantaneous creation, like Augustine, were motivated in part by their inability to contemplate how God could need time to achieve anything. Instant perfection is what we might expect from the hand of God. An all-powerful God is expected to work "immediately" in both senses of the term: without the passage of time and without the need for means or instruments or creaturely cooperation—that is, without causal mediation. But to restrict divine action to the instant and direct is to insist that miracle is God's *only* way of working. Applied to creation teaching in a modern context, this strict theology of divine action underlies and energizes, I would propose, belief in a literal, six-day creation.[36] Calvin's (and Luther's) endorsement of creation "by degrees" warns us that limiting the work of God strictly to the timeless and miraculous risks excluding from the orbit of divine creation our own existence and formation, our ecosystems, and our physical landscape as just some examples. It is a barren world where anything revealing signs of development must be ruled out of the domain of God's creative work.

Having thus defended the theological possibility of creation by degrees, Calvin's rationale for taking a chronological week over creation appears multiple times in all three genres of his Genesis writings: theological treatise, commentary, and sermon. The logic is laid out most clearly in the *Institutes* 1.5–6, 14 and the surrounding context. Like many theologies, Calvin begins with epistemology, the question of how we know anything at all. By chapter 3, Calvin argues, "The human mind [is] naturally imbued with the knowledge of God." However, adds chapter 4, "This knowledge is stifled or corrupted" either deliberately or accidentally, a point Calvin argues, interestingly, without any reference to the story of the fall in Genesis 3.[37]

Chapter 5 returns to a positive argument, saying that God, in order to invite humans into the "blessed life," was glad "not only to deposit in our minds [a] seed of religion" (or awareness of God) but revealed himself and continues to daily "in

---

35. Engammare, *Sermons sur la Genèse*, 20; Stauffer, "Luther et Calvin," 79.

36. This was my conclusion in *DOC*, 297.

37. Translations of the *Institutes* in this section, unless otherwise noted, from John Calvin, *Institutes of the Christian Religion*, trans. Henry Beveridge (Grand Rapids: Eerdmans, 1989), 31.

the whole structure of the universe" (*Institutes* 1.5.1). Given the fundamental incomprehensibility of God to human intellect, Calvin adds that "God for the first time was arrayed in visible attire . . . in the creation of the world," or, in another much used image, creation became "a kind of mirror, in which we may behold God, though otherwise invisible," in particular, the trio of attributes, "his power, wisdom, and goodness" (*Institutes* 1.5.1–3). This trio had a remarkably steady career in Christian creation theology from patristic times. One could sooner count its absences from Genesis commentaries than its occurrences.

Yet human degeneracy and delusion mean that "in vain . . . does Creation exhibit so many bright lamps lighted up to show forth the glory of its Author. Though they beam upon us from every quarter, they are altogether insufficient of themselves to lead us into the right path" (*Institutes* 1.5.14). For this reason, chapter 6 begins to say, we need Scripture as our guide and teacher to lead us back to God as Creator (*Institutes* 1.6.1). "Therefore, as much as it is right for a person to focus the eyes to the works of God that deserve attention, since one has been put into this most majestic theatre to be a spectator of them, it is all the more important to attune the ears on the word for greater benefit" (*Institutes* 1.6.2).[38] Despite great tracts of intervening argument, the following statement from Calvin reveals the very next logical step: "Therefore, that we may apprehend with true faith what it profits us to know of God, it is important for us first to grasp first the history of the creation of the universe, as it has been set forth briefly by Moses, . . . and then has been more fully illustrated by saintly men, especially by Basil and Ambrose" (*Institutes* 1.14.20 [Battles]), church fathers whose hexaemera had the benefit of providing a solid, literal alternative to that of Augustine.

The key fact for our discussion is this: Calvin does not view the *literary form* of the creation narrative but the *actual process* of the creative work of God as the divine concession to limited human comprehension. As the famous quote from his Genesis commentary says, "God himself took the space of six days, for the purpose of accommodating his works to the capacity of men."[39] Human comprehension is compromised by sin, so the glories of God in creation, when displayed "by degrees" in the act and not just in the description, become more readily accessible to us.[40]

38. My translation of CO 2:54.
39. King, *Genesis*, 78, on Gen. 1:5.
40. King, *Genesis*, 78 on Gen. 1:5; cf. also *Institutes* 1.14.2, and Engammare, *Sermons*

Yet would not a figurative or literary week serve the "purpose of conveying instruction" just as well? After all, Calvin's much discussed and theologically important principle of "accommodation" or communicative condescension by God in order to make himself understood by lowly, sinful, and immature human audiences applies precisely to the literary form in which truths are expressed elsewhere in Genesis 1. When the narrative of day four of creation draws particular attention only to the sun and moon, embracing all other heavenly objects under the rubric "stars," this troubles Calvin because "astronomers prove, by conclusive reasons, that the star [*sidus*] of Saturn, which, on account of its great distance, appears the least of all, is greater than the moon (in size)."[41] Not only does Calvin take external (or scientific) data seriously as a knowledge source here, but his explanation relates to literary form: "Moses wrote in a popular style things which, without instruction, all ordinary persons, endued with common sense, are able to understand," while astronomers (*astrologi*) legitimately operate on a higher linguistic plane.[42]

This begins to explain why Calvin is not attracted to a framework-style explanation of a creation week that is a conceptual or heuristic tool alone. Divine accommodation is intended to make God's truth clearer to the "man in the street" in terms of the way things look to him or her. The heavenly lights are graded according to apparent magnitude to the naked eye, not absolute physical magnitude; the "waters above" in Genesis 1:6 are not some watery or crystalline sphere between the human cosmos and the divine realm as many thought, much less part of some angelic hierarchy, but are just clouds.[43] It is important to Calvin that God's self-revelation is not limited to the intellectual elite but is capable of reaching every ordinary person enlightened by the Spirit through Scripture.[44]

Therefore, a purely schematic creation week would not suit Calvin's deeply theological commitment to a plain-sense reading of Genesis, to use Greene-

---

sur la Genèse, 20. See e.g., Schreiner, *Theater of His Glory*, 15; Greene-McCreight, *Ad Litteram*, 133.

41. In antiquity the sun and moon were grouped together with the five known planets, Mercury, Venus, Mars, Jupiter, and Saturn, as the seven "planets" or "wanderers," making comparison between the moon and Saturn more natural.

42. King, *Genesis*, 86.

43. King, *Genesis*, 79–81.

44. See also Manetsch, "Problems with the Patriarchs," 1–16, which is largely occupied with these questions and Calvin's principle of accommodation.

McCreight's term. This is not what his accommodation principle means at this point. Some scholars get this significantly wrong. Kenton Sparks in *God's Word in Human Words* (2008) leans on Calvin's accommodation principle as one of his methodological anchors but does not demonstrate a clear understanding of how it works in relation to creation. Speaking initially of Calvin's handling of the "waters above the firmament" in Genesis 1:6, he writes:

> One should not, Calvin says, believe "by faith" that there are waters above the firmament when one knows good and well that this is not the case. Genesis merely accommodates itself to the ancient view that such waters existed. Calvin similarly argued that accommodation was at work in the chronological system used to enumerate the various creation days of Genesis 1. Because the text reflects accommodation to the ancient view of time, says Calvin, "It is useless to dispute whether this is the best and legitimate order or not."[45]

In a book that is often deep, relevant, and thought-provoking, Sparks here manages to compound three misreadings of Calvin's commentary into one short paragraph.[46] Calvin's point about the "waters above" is not that they do not exist, nor do qualifications about ancient Near Eastern cosmology enter his exegesis here. For Calvin, the expression is phenomenological; it is God's way of referring to the clouds observable by the average person, which means that read rightly the text expresses a natural truth.

Second, Sparks is a little disingenuous to write, "Calvin argued that accommodation was at work in the chronological system" of the creation week without acknowledging that Calvin clearly explained this as an accommodating *act* of God rather than an accommodated literary expression. We might feel differently, but we are talking about Calvin's opinion here. Third, and Poythress picks this point up too, Calvin's talk of "legitimate order" in context does *not* concern the

45. Kenton L. Sparks, *God's Word in Human Words: An Evangelical Appropriation of Critical Biblical Scholarship* (Grand Rapids: Baker, 2008), 235.

46. See also Vern S. Poythress, "A Misunderstanding of Calvin's Interpretation of Genesis 1:6–8 and 1:5 and Its Implications for Ideas of Accommodation," *WTJ* 76.1 (2014): 157–66. While I did not depend on this piece for my conclusions about Sparks, Poythress correctly identifies each of the three interpretive errors made here. See also Appendix C in Vern S. Poythress, *Interpreting Eden: A Guide to Faithfully Reading and Understanding Genesis 1–3* (Wheaton, IL: Crossway, 2019).

sequence of seven days, but the constitution of a twenty-four-hour day in evening-morning order in the expression that closes each day's events. This had run counter to the tastes of the Western reader since patristic times and generated pages of Genesis commentary that we might from our vantage point wish had been better spent; but Calvin knows it to be a nonissue and puts it quickly to bed. He does *not* think the sequence of the days to be trivial or meaningless.

Calvin has a further argument for why the sequence of creation days makes sense literally: it not only expedites the communication of God but demonstrates the care of God. How? By having a once-barren world prepared and ready when he introduced humanity. God "has so wonderfully adorned heaven and earth with ... unlimited abundance, variety, and beauty, ... quite like a spacious and splendid house, provided and filled with the most exquisite and at the same time most abundant furnishings." This should lead us "to recognize that God has destined all things for our good and salvation ... and so bestir ourselves to trust, invoke, praise, and love him" (*Institutes* 1.14.20, 22 [Battles]). God's care for humans is therefore revealed by the preparation of creation ahead of time to cater for all human needs, and this works most plainly if creation retains its chronological element.

THE VIRTUES AND VICES OF RECRUITING CALVIN

The Problem of Shifting Contexts

We have taken time to understand Calvin's stance on the creation week and the interpretive factors that justify it. We can confidently say that Calvin not only "favors" but openly advocates literal creation days, as most commentators recognize.[47] Those who are looking for a literal creation week from a figure of high authority of the church have yet another supporter in Calvin, and his great influence sowed the seed for numerous further examples, including those that feature in the following chapter. Given the clarity and solid theological rationale of his

47. Robert Letham, "'In the Space of Six Days': The Days of Creation from Origen to the Westminster Assembly," *WTJ* 61.2 (1999): 166–67, who even uses the term "favors" with reservations; compare Jack P. Lewis, "The Days of Creation: An Historical Survey of Interpretation," *JETS* 32 (1989): 452–53; R. Laird Harris, "The Length of the Creative Days in Genesis 1," in *Did God Create in Six Days?*, ed. J. A. Pipa Jr. and D. W. Hall (White Hall, WV: Tolle Lege, 2005), 106; C. John Collins, "How Old Is the Earth? Anthropomorphic Days in Genesis 1:1–2:3," *Presbyterion* 20 (1994): 126.

own position, is it not a straightforward matter simply to adopt his position on creation, wording and all, in a kind of "If it ain't broke, don't fix it" approach?

Perhaps an illustration might help here. Though brick-and-mortar bookstores have been on the wane in my home city as in many others, there is still one physical Christian bookstore on my side of the city that I occasionally visit, in the hope that some expensive biblical commentary will appear on the sale shelf for five or ten dollars. On such a visit I noticed for sale *The Timechart History of the World*, which is explicitly based on the historical and chronological scholarship of James Ussher, the Irish bishop of the mid-seventeenth century. The large, foldout chart is interesting, informative, and visually appealing. Yet at its core it seems to assume that historical scholarship more than three centuries old remains essentially viable, so long as it is anchored to biblical history. That "the compilers . . . of this Timechart had no difficulty in reconciling the results of nineteenth-century scientific, geological and natural history research with Ussher's timescale," as the product boasts, is no guarantee that we will not. It is a recent example of a centuries-old biblical chronology, a curious Renaissance museum piece supplemented with interesting contemporary details in a visually appealing format.[48]

If you can see the problem with trusting such a resource, you can probably see the corresponding problem with simply adopting Calvin's interpretive position. It is like taking an expert longbowman from the late Middle Ages and throwing him into a modern battle. The merit and general occupational relevance of his skills do not change the fact that he is being thrust into a radically new environment. It is not enough to say that if the longbow was good enough for Edward III at the Battle of Crécy (1346), it should be good enough for modern warfare. So we are not disputing the relevance of biblical creation; we are dealing with the new environment in which any biblical interpretation such as Calvin's must hold its own. As Davis Young observes:

> Calvin believed that Scripture taught that the Earth is only a few thousand years old and that the globe was covered by the flood of Noah. . . . Calvin's contemporaries believed the traditional views. Should he have been any different? Calvin also adopted a geocentric cosmological theory that has long since been completely repudiated by the scientific community. . . . Given the status

48. Edward Hull, *The Timechart History of the World*, ed. David Gibbons (Chippenham: Third Millennium, 2016).

of scientific endeavor in the sixteenth century, it is hardly surprising that he would adopt the views aforementioned. Given the absence of the mountains of physical evidence that support an old Earth and call into question a global deluge, Calvin did not have to deal with this powerful extra-biblical impetus to thorough re-examination of traditional views.[49]

You do not need to adhere to an old earth to recognize that the evidence for its age, always in the context of larger paradigms of knowledge, has persuaded the scientific community as a whole and so must be faced and dealt with today by those trying to understand the biblical accounts of origins. Rival views to a literal creation week up through the Reformation, such as Augustine's instantaneous creation, are quite different from the rival views competing with young-earth creationism now. What changed? Theologian Francis Watson explains that thanks to a mindset that the biblical text must contain *all* truth about origins, "the scriptural text entered into competition with modern science—and lost, conclusively and irrevocably."[50] Dembski describes the logical consequence for our quest for the truth about origins:

> For science to trump the most natural reading of Genesis and the overwhelming consensus of theologians up through the Reformation, either science has discovered momentous new truths or science has gone massively awry. In either case, science has raised a crucial challenge to young-earth creationism.[51]

While the dominance of a literal creation week through the history of interpretation is not as one-sided as this and there are arguable signals within the text of Genesis 1–3 and beyond hinting at less literal readings, there is nevertheless some truth to this analysis.[52] From the Renaissance forward, new data began to flood in about the natural world that increasingly strained Scripture's understood

---

49. Davis A. Young, *John Calvin and the Natural World* (Lanham, MD: University Press of America, 2007), 159.

50. Francis Watson, "Genesis before Darwin: Why Scripture Needed Liberating from Science," in *Reading Genesis after Darwin*, ed. Stephen C. Barton and David Wilkinson (Oxford: Oxford University Press, 2009), 24.

51. Dembski, *End of Christianity*, 54.

52. This is particularly true once we reach Genesis 2, although upon proper consideration the idea of performing a large task in a six-day working week sounds obviously

role and specifically Genesis 1's understood role in the Renaissance environment as the framework of all knowledge. Simply to harness Calvin's stance on creation as a dogmatic finality may claim the virtues of his robust theology and capable exegesis, but as far as dealing with the challenge of scientific evidence from nature, it ducks the question. It is bringing a longbow to a modern battle.

The Domains of Scripture and Science in Calvin's Thinking about Genesis

Yet this does not preclude us from benefiting from Calvin's profound exegetical work, and if we believe in the authority and durability of Christian Scripture, we may hope that Calvin might help us hear its enduring message on creation. Now it is not practical here to lay out a theology of the "two books" of God's revelation, that is, the idea that God offers us truth about himself in the "book of nature" as well as the "book of Scripture." To explain this properly would amount to a theology (and possibly a history) of science and Christianity. It has been well explained already.[53] The "two books" principle, which finds a strong base in Calvin's thought, holds that some truth reaches us from or at least resides in the natural world, that is, that Scripture is not the *exclusive* source of all truth. In one discourse, Jesus acknowledges the sense in the normal practice of predicting coming weather on the basis of past patterns (Luke 12:54–56), illustrating that we do draw valid conclusions from observation of nature. That there are limits on how much nature can tell of God or, as Calvin warns, real hindrances to our receptivity of truth from nature are important and enduring elements of the "two books" conversation through the centuries.

Does Calvin's handling of Genesis, then, offer any clues as to how evidence from nature can or should affect our reading of the Genesis text? Calvin's attitude toward the embryonic Copernican astronomy of his time is much discussed.[54] But as Davis Young points out, we can expect Calvin to be a man of his time.[55] Blam-

---

anthropomorphic to many readers; e.g., Collins, "How Old Is the Earth?" 109–30; Henri Blocher, *In the Beginning*, ed. David G. Preston (Leicester: InterVarsity, 1984), 50.

53. Peter Harrison, "'The Book of Nature' and Early Modern Science," in *The Book of Nature in Early Modern and Modern History*, ed. Klaas Van Berkel and Arie Johan Vanderjagt (Leuven: Peeters, 2006), 1–26 would be a very competent example pertinent to this period. He cites Calvinist Girolamo Zanchi immediately, a figure I comment on shortly.

54. B. A. Gerrish, "The Reformation and the Rise of Modern Science: Luther, Calvin and Copernicus," in *Calvin and Science*, ed. Richard C. Gamble (New York: Garland, 1992), 170.

55. Young, *John Calvin*, 159.

ing him for not being Copernican would be like blaming our great-grandparents for not believing in climate change in their teenage years. Calvin's attitude to Copernicanism per se is not all that important.

Yet Calvin's general attitude to external sources of knowledge per se may be helpful. The fact that his stance on Copernicanism is difficult to isolate is a function of his caution about taking scientific positions. Genesis commentaries up to his time had often digressed deeply into what was known or thought to be known about a vast range of topics in natural philosophy (what we would call science) and beyond; Genesis 1 in particular seemed so global as to embrace, notionally, every possible area of knowledge.[56] So it is notable that Calvin regards this as outside his brief and even his expertise. In tackling the thorny issue of "waters above" the heavens in Genesis 1:6, Calvin articulates as a principle operative across the entire Genesis narrative, "all that is treated here is the visible form of the world."[57] That is why he understands these waters to simply mean clouds.

Calvin continues here, "Anyone who wants to learn astronomy [*astrologia*] and other obscure arts can do that elsewhere." Now the term *astrologia* rolls together ideas we would associate with both astrology and astronomy, making Calvin's caution understandable. His attitude emerges more clearly as he addresses the place of astronomy/astrology in discussing the luminaries of the fourth day. He accepts the conclusion of "astronomers" that Saturn is in fact larger than the moon and explains why Moses's description instead foregrounds the moon. "Moses wrote in a popular style things which, without instruction, all ordinary persons[58] . . . are able to understand . . . because he was ordained a teacher as well of the unlearned . . . as of the learned."[59] His God-given mission demanded that he must speak in a way that the average person might understand.

Does this render scientific study illegitimate? Not at all. Despite the risks of the superstitious side of astrology, which Calvin elsewhere rebuts, "this study is not

56. See esp. Arnold Ledgerwood Williams, *The Common Expositor: An Account of the Commentaries on Genesis 1527–1633* (Chapel Hill: University of North Carolina Press, 1948), 3–4, 9, 13, 174–76, 257–68. Examples are abundant, but the Renaissance Genesis commentary of polymath Marine Mersenne takes until column 799 just to begin commenting on Gen. 1:2: Marine Mersenne, *Quaestiones celeberrimae in Genesim* (Paris: Cramoisy, 1623); Stanley Jaki, *Genesis 1 through the Ages*, 2nd ed. (Royal Oak, MI: Real View, 1998), 170–71.

57. CO 23.18. My translation. Compare King, *Genesis*, 79.

58. The original term is *idiotae*, whose meaning was not as derogatory as it sounds now, proving that you cannot interpret everything etymologically.

59. King, *Genesis*, 86–87.

to be reprobated [disapproved], nor this science to be condemned" just because some people judge whatever they do not understand, "for astronomy is not only pleasant, but also very useful . . . this art unfolds the admirable wisdom of God." Astronomers are free to continue in "their more exalted knowledge," but Moses was free to be God's mouthpiece to all people, great and small. Therefore, Calvin is free to remain a biblical commentator rather than a popularizer of science, and ordinary people can look up at the moon at night and give glory to God.[60]

Even by acknowledging the apparent discrepancy over the magnitude of these heavenly bodies, as Manetsch points out, "the reformer is implicitly affirming the value of extrabiblical knowledge in the task of scriptural interpretation."[61] He can affirm the value of the study of nature as a noble enterprise, because it is virtually a form of theological study if done with the right attitude. Randall Zachman points out that Calvin loves the night sky as a setting where nature as the theater of God's glory is clearly evident.[62] The intellectual elite are free to investigate it and can prove facts about it "by conclusive reasons,"[63] yet the everyday person is fully able to glorify God in it without needing to consult the experts. Calvin has little time for "experts" who use their knowledge to mock the things of God, but he does not reject natural philosophy in principle.

The Potential of Calvin's Accommodation Principle

Does the fact that Calvin did not use his accommodation principle in relation to the literary frame of the creation week itself mean that we cannot? We have seen that Calvin did not use his accommodation principle to deny either the literal nature of the creation week or its truthfulness or reliability.[64] Yet Calvin's accommodation

60. King, *Genesis*, 86–87.
61. Manetsch, "Problems with the Patriarchs," 13.
62. Zachman, *Reconsidering John Calvin*, 16–17; Schreiner, *Theater of His Glory*, 111–14.
63. King, *Genesis*, 86.
64. Manetsch, "Problems with the Patriarchs," 8, 13; and Greene-McCreight, *Ad Litteram*, 130; contra Young and Stearley, *Bible, Rocks and Time*, 182; Sparks, *God's Word in Human Words*, 245; J. B. Rogers and Donald K. McKim, eds., *The Authority and Interpretation of the Bible: An Historical Approach* (San Francisco: Harper and Row, 1979), 109–11. However, note the most testing examples discussed by David F. Wright, "Calvin's Accommodating God," in *Calvinus Sincerioris Religionis Vindex: Calvin as Protector of the Purer Religion*, ed. Wilhelm Neuser and Brian Armstrong (Kirksville, MO: Sixteenth Century

principle helped him defend the appropriateness of contested biblical texts against critics (the apologetic edge) and ease the struggles of Christians over such texts (the pastoral edge).[65] Given the pastoral and apologetic challenge that Genesis 1:1–2:3 can represent for many modern Christians, has the time come to apply his accommodation principle to the weekly format of Genesis 1:1–2:3 and regard it as a literary schema meant to structure creation's description but not to measure the time it took? Or does that remain "too violent a cavil," playing too fast and loose with the "plain sense" of Scripture and so risking its clarity for the ordinary, uneducated reader?

Christian philosopher Peter van Inwagen notes the necessity for the Genesis account to be applicable and comprehensible in various places to various people, if God is to successfully communicate creation truth to humans through it.[66] This is a tough task for any origins story, yet comparison with its ancient Near Eastern rivals reveals how well Genesis 1 suits this role. This tremendous need for versatility demands that God thoroughly employ accommodation in expressing the truths of creation evenhandedly to diverse human audiences across the ages. And starting life as an ancient document, Genesis 1 inevitably employs ancient literary devices. If the weekly framework is one of those devices, we would need to show that through internal and contextual evidence rather than simply applying accommodation as a tool of convenience. That is not the primary task here, but I have assembled evidence previously that a six plus seventh unit sequence is a familiar literary tool in the ancient Near East and the Old Testament for portraying sequential events with a climax.[67]

Calvin also retains some communicative space between Scripture and the "book of nature." Francis Watson draws from Calvin that "we are to study astron-

---

Journal, 1997), 7–12; and David F. Wright, "Accommodation and Barbarity in John Calvin's Old Testament Commentaries," in *Understanding Poets and Prophets: Essays in Honour of G. W. Anderson*, ed. Graeme Auld (Sheffield: Sheffield University Press, 1993), 413–27.

65. Ford Lewis Battles, "God Was Accommodating Himself to Human Capacity," in *Readings in Calvin's Theology*, ed. Donald K. McKim (Grand Rapids: Baker, 1977), 29.

66. Peter van Inwagen, "Genesis and Evolution," in *Reasoned Faith: Essays in Philosophical Theology*, ed. Eleonore Stump (Ithaca, NY: Cornell University Press, 1993), 103–8.

67. *DOC*, 13 and n. 42, where I list the primary evidence. See S. E. Loewenstamm, "The Seven-Day Unit in Ugaritic Epic Literature," *Israel Exploration Journal* 15 (1965): 122–33; Robert Gordis, "The Heptad as an Element of Biblical and Rabbinic Style," *Journal of Biblical Literature* 62.1 (1943): 18–21; W. M. W. Roth, "The Numerical Sequence X/X+1 in the Old Testament," *VT* 12 (1962): 300–303.

omy to gain one kind of truth and scripture to gain another. The two truths both derive from God . . . and yet they are incommensurable," representing heavenly and earthly orientations in turn. "Owing to this incommensurability of perspective, Calvin does *not* propose to harmonize the scriptural and the astronomical accounts."[68] We stand warned not to try to make Scripture beat science at its own game, following Brer Rabbit into his briar patch.

Yet this is not an issue of entirely different kinds of truth; that smacks too much of Stephen Jay Gould's well-known "nonoverlapping magisteria" (NOMA) stance on the relationship of science and religion, a rather patronizing stance that subtly prohibits religion from commenting on anything in the "real" (i.e., physical) world.[69] Scripture and scientific discourse sometimes address the same topics, not least the working of the heavens.

However, Calvin's judicious comments remind us that Scripture and science speak about their shared subject matter in quite different ways, being driven by quite different communicative purposes, and are tailored to the needs of different audiences. Even the terms need nuancing, as they are not of the same type. Scripture is a source, while science is not a source but a social-epistemological construct that interprets nature or creation, the latter being the source. We need not elaborate further here. We take from Calvin the lesson of admitting not two different *truths* here so much as two different *discourses* that are not suitable to simply place side by side so that one text may prooftext or veto the other.

Calvin might add that the degeneracy of the human heart means that to perceive true things about God through nature, the "truest truths" in nature, the light of Scripture and the ministry of the Spirit will be necessary. "The noetic effect of sin is gradually corrected when the soul is reordered so that once again the cosmos can serve as a 'stage,' 'theater,' or 'book' from which believers are encouraged to learn about their Creator."[70]

68. Watson, "Genesis before Darwin," 25–26.

69. Stephen Jay Gould, "Nonoverlapping Magisteria," in *Leonardo's Mountain of Clams and the Diet of Worms* (New York: Bantam, 1998), 269–83; Stephen Jay Gould, "Nonoverlapping Magisteria: Science and Religion Are Not in Conflict, for Their Teachings Occupy Distinctly Different Domains," *Natural History* 106.3 (1997): 16–22. An immense literature follows.

70. Schreiner, *Theater of His Glory*, 107.

Did Calvin Leave the Door Open for Evolution?

In a famous article written for the *Princeton Theological Review* in 1915, the larger-than-life pillar of Presbyterianism, B. B. Warfield, famous for his defense of biblical inerrancy, holds that Calvin's creation exposition in his *Institutes* and *Commentary on Genesis* effectively "teaches a doctrine of evolution," although he "doubtless had no theory whatever of evolution."[71] What could this mean? Warfield argues that Calvin restricts the true sense of the word "to create" (Heb. *bārā'*; Gen. 1:1, 20, 27; 2:3; 5:1; 6:7) purely to acts of creation out of nothing (familiar in the Latin phrase *ex nihilo*). The equivalent term used in these texts in the Vulgate is *creo*, the verb behind our own word "create." Warfield then notices the careful way that Calvin limits the use of this Latin term and thus its Hebrew antecedent to *ex nihilo* creation in *Institutes* 1.14.20. The text says, "From this history [in Genesis] we shall learn that God by the power of his Word and Spirit created [*creasse*] heaven and earth out of nothing [*ex nihilo*]; that thereupon he brought forth [*produxisse*][72] living beings and inanimate things of every kind."[73] Warfield also draws attention to the part of Calvin's *Commentary on Genesis* that concerns Genesis 1:21, since the Genesis text there employs *bārā'* for the creation of fish and birds on day five of creation, and this might seem to violate this principle. Calvin thinks the term "create" here has in view the original creation of their constituent matter on day one of creation along with its formation into living species on day five.[74] This continues to restrict the definition of "create" to creation out of nothing.

The implication Warfield found for evolution is that the making of various kinds of creatures after day one of creation moves nearer to the theological category of providence, or that in the works of days two through six creation and providence

---

71. B. B. Warfield, "Calvin's Doctrine of the Creation," in *Calvin and Calvinism* (Oxford: Oxford University Press, 1931), 305; original publication B. B. Warfield, "Calvin's Doctrine of the Creation," *Princeton Theological Review* 13 (1915): 190–255.

72. For the grammarians, both of these forms are perfect active infinitives of their respective lexemes.

73. Translation from Battles; Latin text from CO 2:131. Warfield, "Calvin's Doctrine of the Creation," 300.

74. King, *Genesis*, 89. Warfield, "Calvin's Doctrine of the Creation," 301–2.

overlap, although Warfield treads carefully here.[75] God remains the primary cause of "all forms of life, vegetable and animal alike," but they arise from "second causes as to their proximate account." "All that is not immediately produced out of nothing is therefore not created—but evolved," continues Warfield, before adding that Calvin's "doctrine of evolution is entirely unfruitful" thanks to being restricted to the tight limits of "six natural days." To provide a true nexus with evolution, "it was requisite that these six days should be lengthened out into six periods—six ages of growth of the world."[76] This marks out Warfield as a day-age or periodic-day concordist at this point and illustrates the sway of evolutionary theory (although not the Darwinist variety) at this early stage of the twentieth century.

The remaining question for our present purposes is whether Warfield reads Calvin right here or falls into the temptation of recruiting Calvin to buttress his own modern convictions about origins and Bible-science harmonization. In a thorough review article, John Murray examines the passages Warfield studied, finding the *Institutes* texts inconclusive and emphasizing Calvin's conclusion to his discussion of "creation" in Genesis 1:21: despite the sea creatures (specifically the *tannînim* or "large sea creatures") only having received *form* on day five—their basic substance having already been created "in the beginning"—"'creation' is nevertheless a term used truly with respect to the whole and the parts."[77] Murray adds that Calvin actually uses the term "create" of specific creative events, such as vegetation on day three and the sun and moon on day four, in an earlier passage in the *Commentary* where he treats Genesis 1:11. Moreover, Calvin denies there that the earth, despite being used as an instrument of God on day three ("let the earth bring forth"), has any inherent power or potentiality to contribute until God empowers it.[78]

The outcome of this debate is that Calvin proves to have a persistent preference for limiting the word "create" to *ex nihilo* creation, but does at times use the term more broadly than this. Murray demonstrates that despite having used

75. Drawing the theological distinction between creation and providence is a heavily freighted issue on its own, and Warfield, while emphasizing the strength of Calvin's doctrine of providence, is not willing to say, and knows he would not be true to Calvin to say, that Calvin transfers days two through six of the creation week into the sphere of providence.

76. Warfield, "Calvin's Doctrine of the Creation," 303–6.

77. John Murray, "Calvin's Doctrine of Creation," *WTJ* 17 (1954): 33–34. Warfield, to his credit, includes this potentially inconvenient line in his own explanation.

78. King, *Genesis*, 82; Murray, "Calvin's Doctrine of Creation," 36–41.

the terms "seed" and "fountain" to describe the original matter created in Genesis 1:1, Calvin's strong emphasis on the inertness and lack of potential of this matter yields a creation teaching that is not very amenable to evolutionary creation, which really demands that God initially infuse creation with tremendous potential for self-development.[79] Now Warfield himself, thanks to his conservative Presbyterian credentials, represents a late star recruit in the creation debates, and so the battle rages over Warfield's own stance on evolution, particularly as it emerges in this article.[80] Warfield himself strongly advocates evolution here; he finds in Calvin's works on creation a conceptual door just slightly ajar.

THE HIGH TIDE OF SIX-DAY CREATION AT THE TURN OF THE SEVENTEENTH CENTURY

Calvin's Genesis commentary was first published in 1554. In my final chapter I will present the view of six-day creation presented in the Westminster Confession of 1646. If we look beyond the Westminster Confession to the 1651 English translation of an important seventeenth-century work by the Czech philosopher Johann Amos Comenius, *Naturall Philosophie Reformed by Divine Light*—important because it arguably represented the high-tide mark in English publications seeking to offer a complete philosophy from Christian Scripture with the aid of reason—nearly a century intervenes between Calvin and these writings. Comenius's publication capped off a century-long effort by European scholars of every stripe to reform knowledge just as Christendom had, in some sense, been reformed under the influence of Luther, Calvin, and others.[81]

It is hard to express how powerfully Genesis 1 seized the imagination of European thinkers during this period and powered a rather frenzied new push to

---

79. Stauffer, "Luther et Calvin," 78. Stauffer gingerly awards the contest to Murray.

80. D. N. Livingstone, "B. B. Warfield, the Theory of Evolution and Early Fundamentalism," *Evangelical Quarterly* 58 (1986): 69–86; D. N. Livingstone and Mark Noll, "B. B. Warfield (1851–1921): A Biblical Inerrantist as Evolutionist," *Isis* 91 (2000): 283–304; Fred G. Zaspel, "B. B. Warfield on Creation and Evolution," *Themelios* 35 (2010): 198–211; Fred G. Zaspel, "Additional Note: B. B. Warfield Did Not Endorse Theistic Evolution as It Is Understood Today," in *Theistic Evolution: A Scientific, Philosophical, and Theological Critique*, ed. J. P. Moreland et al. (Wheaton, IL: Crossway, 2017), 953–72.

81. Esp. Ann Blair, "Mosaic Physics and the Search for a Pious Natural Philosophy in the Late Renaissance," *Isis* 91.1 (2000): 37–47.

understand the world, stimulated by vigorous study of classical sources and discoveries from the New World in the West and later the Far East as well as of Scripture. Study of Genesis 1 could be distributed into six general genres that in practice often tended to blend:[82]

1. Exegetical works (i.e., biblical commentary), the focus of Williams's *The Common Expositor*.
2. Confessional works, as in theological works such as *loci communes*, "commonplaces," and confessions of faith.
3. Natural-philosophical works emphasizing the physical realm, which acquired the title "Mosaic physics."
4. Mystical or metaphysical works: esoteric efforts that regarded Genesis as a cryptic key to hidden reality.
5. Historical or chronological works, specifically universal histories that began with the creation week and biblical chronologies focused on the refinement of dating details.
6. Literary works: poetic hexaemeral epics that revived the late classical form of these works and culminated in Milton's *Paradise Lost*.

All are fascinating and all demonstrate how many thinkers on either side of 1600 had their imaginations captured by Genesis 1 and other seminal biblical texts.[83] Francis Bacon in *New Atlantis* (1626) could imagine a College of the Six Days' Works established "for the finding out of the true nature of all things," despite warning in *New Organon* (1620) of the folly of trying to found a whole philosophical system on Genesis 1.[84]

Blair identifies a long-recognized distinction in works of "Mosaic philosophy" or "Mosaic physics" between those more mystical ones "who read the Bible

---

82. Most of these points receive further comment and references in chapter 10. See immediately below on point 3 regarding Mosaic physics.

83. Blair, "Mosaic Physics," 33–35, 42, 45, 52, 57–58; Aza Goudriaan, "Creation, Mosaic Physics, Copernicanism, and Divine Accommodation," in *Reformed Orthodoxy and Philosophy, 1625–1750* (Leiden: Brill, 2006), 85–86, 104–13; David S. Sytsma, "Calvin, Daneau, and Physica Mosaica: Neglected Continuities at the Origins of an Early Modern Tradition," *Church History and Religious Culture* 95.4 (2015): 457–59.

84. Francis Bacon, "The New Atlantis," in *Ideal Commonwealths*, ed. Henry Morley (London: Colonial Press, 1901), 119; Blair, "Mosaic Physics," 42.

through layers of allegory" and literalist approaches.[85] This is important because those taking a literal approach tended also to take the six days of creation literally in their philosophical discourses. The key figure in the latter category was Lambert Daneau (ca. 1530–1595), whom Goudriaan names as "consistently credited with initiating [the] tradition of Mosaic physics" and whom he portrays as a true interpretive heir of his teacher John Calvin.[86] The next most important for the retention of literal days was probably Italian Calvinist Girolamo Zanchi (1516–1590). We will shortly discover how their retention of this literal approach influenced ongoing Genesis interpretation.

85. Blair, "Mosaic Physics," 36–37.
86. Sytsma, "Calvin, Daneau, and Physica Mosaica," 458–59, 462–76; Blair, "Mosaic Physics," 43–45, 52.

Chapter Ten

FROM THE WESTMINSTER CONFESSION
TO JOHN WESLEY

Here we find ourselves in a predicament. Just as Reformation-era commentary on Genesis begins to integrate a growing flood of learning from external sources into the global cognitive framework seemingly offered by Genesis 1, we begin to taper our study toward a conclusion.[1] This is because it is here that the list of Christian thinkers of recognized authority for recruitment in creation-related disputes wanes. There are many treatments of Genesis that remain of interest, but fewer and fewer that have garnered the kind of recognition granted to an Augustine, Aquinas, Luther, or Calvin.[2]

The century or so between the death of Martin Luther (1546) and the Westminster Confession was unusually prolific in terms of commentaries and other writings on Genesis. Writers of various Christian persuasions were putting forth their best efforts to expound Genesis and bring it into conversation with knowledge from Christian tradition, linguistics, natural data, and other sources. We have seen the best-known examples among the Reformers, Luther and Calvin, but Genesis had attracted significant literary attention from other Reformers even prior to Luther's Genesis lectures. Another well-known Reformer, Huldrych

---

1. One of my PhD supervisors, Philip Almond, considered the seventeenth century as the time when "things get really interesting": see Philip C. Almond, *Adam and Eve in Seventeenth-Century Thought* (Cambridge: Cambridge University Press, 1999).

2. Some in the seventeenth and eighteenth centuries and omitted here appear in *DOC*, 104–219.

Zwingli, began an expository teaching series known as the "Zurich Prophecy" in 1525 with Genesis 1, and the notes from these Genesis sessions had been published by the time of his premature death in 1531.[3] Zwingli was part of a movement of students of biblical Hebrew that became Protestants and produced Genesis commentaries of high linguistic caliber.

After the publication of Zwingli's brief notes, works on Genesis by Conrad Pellican (1533), Johann Oecolampadius (1536), and Wolfgang Capito (1539) followed, as did those by continental Reformers like Wolfgang Musculus (1554), Jean Mercier/Mercerus (1570), and the Italian Peter Martyr Vermigli (posthumous, 1579).[4] Catholic scholarship on Genesis, too, was reaching a crest. We have mentioned the significant Genesis work of Cardinal Cajetan (1531) and Calvin uses the works of Agostino Steuco from around the same time (1529, 1535).[5] Shortly would follow what Jaki terms "the three major commentaries on Genesis 1 produced at the height of the Counter-Reformation": Jesuits Benito Pereyra (Pererius) (1589), Francisco Suarez (ca. 1616) and Denis of Petau (Petavius) (1644).[6]

All this only touches the tip of the iceberg, for we are on the verge of the seventeenth century, the great "century of the Bible,"[7] when each rapidly expanding

---

3. Sophie Kessler Mesguich, "Early Christian Hebraists," *HB/OT* 2:420–22.

4. Mesguich, "Early Christian Hebraists," 264–68; R. Gerald Hobbs, "Pluriformity of Early Reformation Scriptural Interpretation," *HB/OT* 2:453–87; Peter Opitz, "The Exegetical and Hermeneutical Work of John Oecolampadius, Huldrych Zwingli and John Calvin," *HB/OT* 2:407–27; Otto Zöckler, *Geschichte der Beziehungen zwischen Theologie und Naturwissenschaft: Mit besonderer Rücksicht auf Schöpfungsgeschichte* (Gütersloh: Bertelsmann, 1877), 1:690–701.

5. R. Stauffer, "L'exégèse de Genèse 1/1–3 chez Luther et Calvin," in *Interprètes de la Bible: Études sur les réformateurs du XVIe siècle*, ed. R. Stauffer (Paris: Beauchesne, 1982), 73–75.

6. Benedictus Pererius Valentinus, *Commentariorium et disputationum in Genesim, tomi quatuor, continentes historiam Mosis ab exordio mundi* (Cologne: Hierat, 1601); Francisco Suarez, "Tractatus de Opere Sex Dierum," in *Francisci Suarez opera omnia*, ed. D. M. André (Paris: Vivès, 1856), 3:1–460; Dionysius Petavius, "De sex primorum mundi dierum opificio," in *Dogmata theologica Dionysii Petavii* (Paris: Vivès, 1866), 4:123–508; For details about dating, see Arnold Ledgerwood Williams, *The Common Expositor: An Account of the Commentaries on Genesis 1527–1633* (Chapel Hill: University of North Carolina Press, 1948), 273; Stanley Jaki, *Genesis 1 through the Ages*, 2nd ed. (Royal Oak, MI: Real View Books, 1998), 160–68. See below on Pereyra (Pererius).

7. A twist on the title from J.-R. Armogathe, ed., *Le grand siècle et la Bible*, La bible de tous les temp 6 (Paris: Beauchesne, 1989).

sphere of knowledge would be brought into conversation with the biblical text. Geography, politics, history, chronology, and the stirrings of geology would all be expounded in connection with Scripture. Much of this intellectual and spiritual ferment would take place in mainland Europe, and this literature we must regretfully leave untouched in that it remains unrecruited in the debates we have in view.

The Westminster Confession of Faith

Our narrowing of focus is necessitated by the spell over present-day creation debate literature that is held by a single document: the Westminster Confession of Faith, completed December 4, 1646.[8] It is something of a quirk of history that makes this document so important and still so contested. It is the defining theological document for worldwide Presbyterianism and the doctrinal standard to which would-be ministers in some Presbyterian denominations must still subscribe.[9] Unlike most other denominations' doctrinal standards, the Confession happens to retain Calvin's wording about the timing of creation, "in the space of six days." It was subsequently reproduced in several confessional offshoots: the congregationalist Savoy Declaration (1658), the second London Baptist Confession of Faith (1689) and its near-identical offshoot, the Philadelphia Confession of Faith (1742).[10] When would-be Presbyterian ministers in certain US Presbyterian denominations signal their agreement with the Westminster Confession as

8. Rowland S. Ward, *A Short Introduction to the Westminster Assembly and Its Work*, 2nd ed. (Lansvale: Tulip, 2019), 22.

9. As a non-American and non-Presbyterian, I understand this to be true at least of the Presbyterian Church in America and the Orthodox Presbyterian Church, but evidently not the mainline Presbyterian Church USA. For an easy introduction to the scene, see Joe Carter, "How to Tell the Difference between Presbyterian Denominations," The Gospel Coalition, June 9, 2021, https://www.thegospelcoalition.org/article/tell-difference-pres byterian-denominations/.

10. There is a helpful comparison table for these four documents online at James N. Anderson and Don Lowe, "A Tabular Comparison of the 1646 Westminster Confession of Faith, the 1658 Savoy Declaration of Faith, the 1677/1689 London Baptist Confession of Faith and the 1742 Philadelphia Confession of Faith," Analogical Thoughts, 2007, https://www.proginosko.com/docs/wcf_sdfo_lbcf.html#SDFO4. A simpler phrase, "in six days," is found in the Mennonite Dordrecht Confession (1632): https://gameo.org/in dex.php?title=Dordrecht_Confession_of_Faith_(Mennonite,_1632). See Louis Lavallee, "Creeds and the Six Creation Days," *Impact* 235 (1993), http://www.icr.org/article/364/.

the creedal standard of their church, the question arises what it means to assent to the clause about creation "in the space of six days." For this reason, the Westminster Divines are subject to a special version of the recruitment phenomenon we have discussed, as articles fly back and forth trying to claim various Westminster Divines either as literal interpreters or else, largely arguing from silence, representing a more flexible interpretation of the creation week.

Turning to the Confession, let us note the wording of section 4.1 on creation in the updated version offered at the time of writing by the Evangelical Presbyterian Church: "In the beginning it pleased God the Father, Son, and Holy Spirit to create the world out of nothing in order to reveal the glory of his eternal power, wisdom, and goodness. He made everything in the world, visible and invisible, in the space of six days, and it was very good."[11]

The pivotal phrase "in the space of six days" has a clear precedent in Calvin's *Commentary on Genesis*, where Calvin had defended a literal creation week:

> Here the error of those is manifestly refuted, who maintain that the world was made in a moment. It is too violent a cavil to contend that Moses distributes the work which God perfected at once into six days, for the mere purpose of conveying instruction. Let us rather conclude that God himself took the space of six days [*sex dierum spatium*], for the purpose of accommodating his works to the capacity of men.[12]

Back in chapter 9, I translated the nearest equivalent wording in Calvin's *Institutes* "Moses reports that God's work was completed not in a moment, but in six days" (1.14.2). The Latin reads *non uno momento, sed sex diebus absolutum fuisse Dei opus*, provided here for the sake of the comparison following.

Now Joel Beeke rightly points to medieval precedents for "space of six days" language, notably, Bonaventure's commentary on the *Sentences* of Peter Lombard.[13] More relevant is the wording of *Sentences* 2.12.1 concerning creation, where

---

11. https://epc.org/wp-content/uploads/Files/1-Who-We-Are/B-About-The-EPC/WCF-ModernEnglish.pdf.

12. John Calvin, *Genesis*, ed. J. King, The Geneva Series of Commentaries (London: Banner of Truth, 1965), 78; Latin text in CO 23:18.

13. Joel R. Beeke, "What Did the Reformers Believe about the Age of the Earth?," in *The New Answers Book 4*, ed. Ken Ham (Green Forest, AR: Master Books, 2013), 102. Bonaventure, *Sententiae in IV libris distinctae*, ed. I. C. Brady, Spicilegium Bonaventuri-

Lombard clarifies that God "did not form" the classical four elements, earth, water, air, and fire "simultaneously, as it pleased some of the Fathers [to hold], but at intervals of time and in the course of six days [*intervalla temporum ac sex volumina dierum*]." Shortly afterward in 2.12.2 we read that against Augustine's opinion of an instantaneous creation, others preferred to hold that "at intervals over six days [*intervalla sex dierum*], the kinds of different corporal things were formed . . . according to their proper classes."[14]

Following Calvin, we find related wording features in a number of Reformed writings. The first is from a figure identified by David Sytsma as the fountainhead of "Mosaic physics," Lambert Daneau, who "began his journey as a theologian at Geneva in 1560 under the tutelage of Calvin" and took Calvin as "his own theological model for scriptural interpretation."[15] Daneau clearly retains a literal six creation days in his Latin original, although the conclusion to the 1578 English edition is more explicit in referring to "the *space* of those six dayes."[16] (Note that the Spanish Jesuit scholar Pereyra [Pererius] in *Commentariorium et disputationum in Genesim* [1589] also asserted creation "part by part in a period of six days [*spatio sex dierum*]."[17])

Another protégé of Calvin, Girolamo Zanchi, in his posthumously published *De operibus Dei intra spacium sex dierum creatis opus* (1591), an encyclopedic work

---

anum 4–5 (Grottaferrata: Editiones Collegium S. Bonaventurae ad Claras Aquas, 1971), fol. 62v. This is visible in Lombard's text in this image, surrounded by Bonaventure's commentary in Latin (frequently abbreviated). An easier source to check is that following.

14. Peter Lombard, *The Sentences. Book 2: On Creation*, trans. Giulio Silano, vol. 2, Mediaeval Sources in Translation 43 (Toronto: Pontifical Institute of Mediaeval Studies, 2007), 49–50.

15. David S. Sytsma, "Calvin, Daneau, and Physica Mosaica: Neglected Continuities at the Origins of an Early Modern Tradition," *Church History and Religious Culture* 95.4 (2015): 459.

16. Latin edition: Lambertus Danaeus, *Physica Christiana* (1576; repr. Geneva: Vignon, 1602), 156–58, 180–181 (= chs. 37, 45). English edition: Lambert Daneau, *The Wonderfull Woorkmanship of the World* (London: Andrew Maunsell, 1578), 86–87, and see 73–75.

17. Pererius Valentinus, *Commentariorium et disputationum in Genesim*, 7, with further statements 79–82; I found this clear and early statement about the literal days via Ivan Malara, "Galileo: Creation and Cosmogony. A Study on the Interplay between Galileo's Science of Motion and the Creation Theme" (PhD diss., Università degli Studi di Milano/Gent Universiteit, 2019), 105.

of "Mosaic physics," has the "space of six days" cemented into its title.[18] His earlier theological work *De religione Christiana fides* (1585), one of his last living publications, prominently featured the same phrase. In the 1599 English translation of this work, *Confession of Christian Religion*, clause 5.1 begins, "We believe, that God the Father, by the Sonne, together with the holie ghost, in the space of sixe daies created of nothing all things visible and invisible."[19] Specifically confessional in structure and purpose,[20] *De religione Christiana fides* features several additional elements lacking in the creation clause of another potential model, James Ussher's Irish Articles of 1615:[21] a Trinitarian formula, creation from nothing, the assessment of all creation as very good, and a purpose to glorify God.[22] The Irish Articles simply read: "In the beginning of time, when no creature had any being, God, by his word alone, in the space of six days, created all things, and afterwards, by his providence, doth continue, propagate, and order them according to his own will."[23]

Cursory comparison of the Westminster Confession against Zanchi's *De religione Christiana fides* reveals a parallel structure up to this point, save for the omission of a section Zanchi has on the power of God preceding the one on creation. This accounts for how the Westminster Confession's section 4 can still correspond to Zanchi's section 5. Given that "Zanchi was a pivotal figure in the consolidation

18. Hieronymus Zanchius, *De operibus Dei intra spacium sex dierum creatis opus* (Neustadt: Harnisii, 1591). On his relationship to Calvin, see Roelf Theodoor te Velde, "'Soberly and Skillfully': John Calvin and Jerome Zanchi (1516–1590) as Proponents of Reformed Doctrine," *Church History and Religious Culture* 91.1–2 (2011): 59–62.

19. Girolamo Zanchi, *H. Zanchius, His Confession of Christian Religion* (Cambridge: Legat, 1599), 21.

20. Christopher J. Burchill, "Girolamo Zanchi: Portrait of a Reformed Theologian and His Work," *The Sixteenth Century Journal* 15.2 (1984): 205 and n. 108.

21. Ward, *Short Introduction*, 83; Jan Rohls, *Reformed Confessions: Theology from Zurich to Barmen*, trans. John Hoffmeyer (Louisville: Westminster John Knox, 1998), 26; Harrison Perkins, "The Westminster Assembly's Probable Appropriation of James Ussher," *Scottish Bulletin of Evangelical Theology* 37.1 (2019): 45–63.

22. Girolamo Zanchi, *De religione Christiana fides* (Neustadt Palatinorum: Harnisius, 1601), 75. See now the critical edition: Girolamo Zanchi, *Girolamo Zanchi, De religione Christiana fides – Confession of Christian Religion*, ed. Luca Baschera and Christian Moser, 2 vols. (Leiden: Brill, 2007). This edition includes the 1599 English text published alongside the Latin.

23. See article 18 in Philip Schaff, *The Creeds of Christendom* (Grand Rapids: Baker, 1966), 3:529.

of the Reformed tradition during the last half of the sixteenth century," with his confessional work published in both Latin and English before 1600, this treatise might represent the primary model for this part of the Confession.[24]

It is certainly possible to identify Reformed figures utilizing the "space of six days" wording, including Cambridge-educated Puritan Nicholas Gibbens in his 1601 Genesis commentary or William Perkins, "early English Puritanism's premier theologian," in his 1616 work on the Apostles' Creed.[25] Perkins's important pupil, William Ames, whose *Marrow of Theology* (*Medulla theologica*) (1634) also offered a model of confessional theology for Assembly delegates, likewise perpetuates the phrase.[26] We are reminded, though, not to search too far afield for antecedents for the Westminster phrasing by the explicit quotation from Calvinist bishop Gervase Babington back in 1592: "And lastly, in what time, or how many dayes did God create all things, in six dayes sayeth the Scripture . . . *Non uno momento, sed sex dierum spatio.*"[27] The italics in Babington's work indicate a quotation from a secondary source, but it is unattributed. While I have not found identical wording to this point, this looks most like a mashup of Calvin's *Institutes* 1.14.2, "*non uno momento, sed sex diebus absolutum fuisse Dei opus,*" with "*sex dierum spatium*" from his Genesis commentary.

---

24. Quote from J. L. Farthing, "Zanchi, Jerome (1516–1590)," *HHMBI*, 248. See also Velde, "'Soberly and Skillfully,'" 59–61. This latter suggestion by Richard Muller appears in Beeke, "Reformers," 107–9.

25. Nicholas Gibbens, *Questions and Disputations concerning the Holy Scripture* (London: Kyngston, 1601), 45; see G. Lloyd Jones, *The Discovery of Hebrew in Tudor England: A Third Language* (Manchester: Manchester University Press, 1983), 156 for biographical information. William Perkins, *An Exposition of the Symbole or Creed of the Apostles, according to the Tenour of the Scripture, and the Consent of Orthodoxe Fathers of the Church*, in *The Workes of That Famous and Worthy Minister of Christ, in the Universitie of Cambridge, Mr. William Perkins* (London: Legatt, 1616), 1:143; Donald K. McKim, "Perkins, William (1558–1602)," *HHMBI*, 234; Robert Letham, "'In the Space of Six Days': The Days of Creation from Origen to the Westminster Assembly," *WTJ* 61.2 (1999): 170–71; David W. Hall, "What Was the View of the Westminster Assembly Divines on the Creation Days?," in *Did God Create in Six Days?*, ed. J. A. Pipa Jr. and D. W. Hall, 2nd ed. (White Hall, WV: Tolle Lege, 2005), 50–51.

26. William Ames, *The Marrow of Theology*, trans. John Dykstra Eusden (Grand Rapids: Baker, 1997), 102; Allen Stanton, "William Ames and the Westminster Assembly," *The Confessional Presbyterian* 14 (2018): 51–62.

27. Gervase Babington, *Certaine Plaine, Briefe and Comfortable Notes upon Everie Chapter of Genesis* (London: Charde, 1592), fol. 6, par. 7.

This is not surprising. John Leith points to "the pervasive printing of Calvin's works in English" during this period. "Between 1548 and 1600 no other writer had nearly so many publications in English."[28] "By the 1580s he outsold all other Protestant reformers combined," adds Bruce Gordon.[29] Many pre-1600 editions of the *Institutes*, detailed by Gordon, and of his commentaries, including that on Genesis, may be readily found in Google Books. Westminster delegates did not really need a model for the "space of six days" wording used in clause 4.1 of the Confession other than Calvin, although they existed, as I have shown. "The delegates to the Westminster Assembly closely scrutinized the *Institutes* on crucial matters," while plainly drawing on prior confessional models such as Ames's *Medulla*, Ussher's Irish Articles, and Zanchi's *De religione Christiana fides*.[30]

Two related questions arise here: (1) Does this statement in the Westminster Confession oblige the present-day subscriber to take it literally; and (2) Do we know whether the Westminster Divines themselves were thinking in literal terms of actual, twenty-four-hour days when they endorsed it? The former question I leave to others.[31] The latter is hotly contested, for example, in the debate between Presbyterians David Hall and William Barker, where Hall makes the case that they have straightforward days in mind while Barker denies that this is a clear fact for all Assembly delegates.[32] There are some awful examples of recruitment on Hall's

28. John H. Leith, *Assembly at Westminster: Reformed Theology in the Making* (Atlanta: Knox, 1973), 40.

29. Bruce Gordon, *John Calvin's Institutes of the Christian Religion: A Biography* (Princeton: Princeton University Press, 2016), 57.

30. Gordon, *John Calvin's Institutes*, 48–67.

31. E.g. J. V. Fesko, "The Days of Creation and Confession Subscription in the OPC," *WTJ* 63 (2001): 235–49; J. V. Fesko, "The Legacy of Old School Confession Subscription in the OPC," *JETS* 46.4 (2003): 673–98.

32. Hall, "Westminster Assembly Divines," 44–45; David W. Hall, "The Evolution of Mythology: Classic Creation Survives as the Fittest Among Its Critics," in *Did God Create in Six Days?*, ed. J. A. Pipa Jr. and D. W. Hall (White Hall, WV: Tolle Lege, 2005), 283–94; William S. Barker, "The Westminster Assembly on the Days of Creation: A Reply to David W. Hall," *WTJ* 62.1 (2000): 113–20; David W. Hall, "A Brief Overview of the Exegesis of Genesis 1–11: Luther to Lyell," in *Coming to Grips with Genesis: Biblical Authority and the Age of the Earth*, ed. Terry Mortenson and Thane H. Ury (Green Forest, AR: Master Books, 2008), 60–71; Gregg R. Allison, "Theistic Evolution Is Incompatible with Historical Christian Doctrine," in *Theistic Evolution: A Scientific, Philosophical, and Theological Critique*, ed. J. P. Moreland et al. (Wheaton, IL: Crossway, 2017), 949 n. 69;

part: "At worst, the score is 18-0 or 15-0 or 9-0 or 8-0; at best, it is 21-0" and "we feel safer standing with Luther, Calvin, Ambrose, the Westminster Divines, and the long history of the church."[33] Yet it remains highly unlikely in my view that the Westminster Confession or those Westminster delegates who refer to the issue in their writings meant anything other than literal days of the week by the term, "the space of six days," so Hall's assessment of these figures seems justified. At this point in the flow of intellectual history, there is no other interpretive option that grants the days actual, chronological "space," which seems to be the point of the Confession's wording here. A day-age understanding that each creation day represents a longer period of time does not have a clearly worked-out model until Isaac Newton's student William Whiston late in the century. While some debate what William Ames meant by his version of the six-day phrase *sex dierum interstitiis succendentes* in his *Medulla theologica*, with the pressure to find geological "deep time" within the Genesis creation week yet to develop, I am skeptical that he meant to offer an "intermittent day" model of the creation week.[34] I understand his *interstitiis* as essentially synonymous with *spatio* or Pererius's *intervalla*.

So the argument concerning creation and time at this point was whether the creative work of God involved time, or whether instead the appearance of time in the creation week was a cipher or figure for a different kind of information, as touched on below. The members of the Westminster Assembly seem to have been of one mind, at least in the Confession, in rejecting such a view. Yet there is more to the story than denying any alternatives to Calvin besides Augustine. Alternatives to a literal creation week that would evolve beyond Augustine's minority view were already on the horizon.

Ross and Archer in *The Genesis Debate: Three Views on the Days of Creation*, ed. David Hagopian (Mission Viejo, CA: Crux, 2001), 69.

33. Quotes from Hall, "Westminster Assembly Divines," 54, and Hall, "Evolution of Mythology," 301, respectively.

34. Regarding the debate, see Ames, *Marrow of Theology*, 102; C. John Collins, "How Old Is the Earth? Anthropomorphic Days in Genesis 1:1–2:3," *Presbyterion* 20 (1994): 114 n. 21; Letham, "Space of Six Days," 172; Hall, "Evolution of Mythology," 283–85. See Charlton Thomas Lewis et al., eds., *A Latin Dictionary: Founded on Andrews' Edition of Freund's Latin Dictionary* (Oxford: Clarendon, 1879), 986. In the example text for the meaning "Of time, an interval," which is Martianus Capella's *De nuptiis Philologiae et Mercurii* (*On the Marriage of Philology and Mercury*)—the classic late antique work on the seven liberal arts—the word *interstitium* (in 6.601) describes the part of a day illuminated by the sun and is used in parallel construction with *spatium*.

NO ALTERNATIVE VIEW?

It is not true to say adamantly, "There was no 'alternative view' until the nineteenth century, after the beginning of the warfare between science and Christianity," and, "Prior to that, the only choices were Augustine or Westminster."[35] At the time of the Westminster Assembly, there existed diverse undercurrents of more radical thought that sought alternate sources of knowledge and alternate ways to interpret Scripture, including the Genesis creation narrative. As I hinted in chapter 9, we could think of these alternatives as existing on a spectrum between traditional Renaissance Platonism and a more radical mystical/Hermetic/gnostic viewpoint. Richard Popkin, thinking of a contrast between two existing philosophical options, "Cartesian rationalism and British empiricism," strives to awaken historians of science to a "third force" of avant-garde thinkers who responded to the threat of thoroughgoing skepticism by combining "elements of empirical and rationalist thought with theosophic speculations and Millenarian interpretation of Scripture."[36] Popkin's third stream is related to our third option for interpretation of Genesis 1 beside a literal, temporal creation week and Augustinian instantaneous creation.

One does not have to read too far in sixteenth and seventeenth century works on Genesis before encountering this stream, and sometimes its take on Genesis borders on incomprehensibility until we come to terms with a very different, neognostic way of looking at the world and at Scripture. At the more extreme end, people read Genesis in a bizarre, mystical manner as a code revealing the hidden make-up of reality—as an esoteric text. The extremely idiosyncratic nature of these readings meant that they were never comprehensible and durable enough to become orthodox interpretations but were quite influential in the century up to Comenius's *Divine Light* (1651), our chosen endpoint in chapter 9 for the widespread intellectual employment of Genesis 1 in the reform of knowledge. These mystical or quasi-scientific writers still esteemed and analyzed early Genesis as one

35. Duncan and Hall in Hagopian, *Genesis Debate*, 105; Hall, "Evolution of Mythology," 294. The "warfare" terminology here almost certainly comes from Andrew Dickson White, *A History of the Warfare of Science with Theology in Christendom*, 2 vols. (New York: Appleton, 1896), which Hall cites elsewhere and not always critically enough, e.g., Hagopian, *Genesis Debate*, 23, 114, 116.

36. Richard H. Popkin, "The Third Force in Seventeenth-Century Thought: Scepticism, Science and Millenarianism," in *The Third Force in Seventeenth-Century Thought*, ed. Richard H. Popkin (Leiden: Brill, 1992), 90–91.

of the divine and magical texts that could reveal ultimate truth.[37] It is now widely recognized that this stream of thought contributed significantly to the development of modern science; we recall that even Newton's concept of gravity, with its action exerted at a distance, looked to many peers like belief in magic.[38]

The more mystical variety of Genesis interpretations remains essentially unknown in creation debates, but by the time the Westminster Assembly was beginning, we find the simpler, Platonic version of this alternative expressed modestly and clearly with respect to its impact on interpreting the creation week:

> Some believe there went not a minute to the world's creation, nor shall there go to its destruction, those six dayes so punctually described, make not to them one moment, but rather seem to manifest the method and Idea of the great work of the intellect of God, than the manner how he proceeded in its operation.[39]

Anticipated by Marsilio Ficino (1463–1494) and the already mentioned John Colet,[40] the Cambridge Platonist Henry More in his *Conjectura Cabbalistica* (1653) links the timeless creation week of Augustinian/Platonic/kabbalistic views and the possibility of creation *in a different span of time*.

37. Allen G. Debus, *The Chemical Philosophy: Paracelsian Science and Medicine in the Sixteenth and Seventeenth Centuries* (Mineola, NY: Dover, 1977), 78, 125, 226, 318, 477; Michael T. Walton, "Genesis and Chemistry in the Sixteenth Century," in *Reading the Book of Nature: The Other Side of the Scientific Revolution*, ed. Allen G. Debus and Michael Thomson Walton (Kirksville, MO: Truman State University Press, 1998), 1–14; Michael T. Walton, *Genesis and the Chemical Philosophy: True Christian Science in the Sixteenth and Seventeenth Centuries* (Brooklyn: AMS Press, 2011); Peter J. Forshaw, "Vitriolic Reactions: Orthodox Responses to the Alchemical Exegesis of Genesis," in *The Word and the World*, ed. Kevin Killeen and Peter J. Forshaw (Basingstoke: Macmillan, 2007), 111–36; Peter J. Forshaw, "The Genesis of Christian Kabbalah: Early Modern Speculations on the Work of Creation," in *Hidden Truths from Eden: Esoteric Readings of Genesis 1–3*, ed. Caroline Vander Stichele and Susanne Scholz (Atlanta: SBL Press, 2014), 121–44; *DOC*, 123–28. Key figures include Jacob Böhme, Jacob Brocardus, and Robert Fludd. Works named as or referred to as Paracelsian, Hermeticist, gnostic, or kabbalistic belong in this general category.
38. E.g., Charles Webster, *From Paracelsus to Newton: Magic and the Making of Modern Science* (Cambridge: Cambridge University Press, 1982), 1–11.
39. Thomas Browne, *Religio Medici the Fourth Edition, Corrected and Amended* (London: Crook, 1656), 97. For the Latin original, see Thomas Browne, *Religio, Medici* (Leiden: Hackius, 1644), 143–44.
40. *DOC*, 95–99.

You are to understand that these *Six numbers*, or *days*, do not signify any order of time, but the nature of the things that were said to be made in them. But for any thing in *Moses* his *Philosophick Cabbala*, all might be made at once, or in such periods of time, as is most suitable to the nature of the things themselves.[41]

A position of this flexibility on the creation days might have been in the view of the Westminster Divines and encouraged their retention of what was already a well-established set phrase in Calvinist tradition, "space of six days," in order to stave off Platonist as well as Augustinian timeless interpretations of Genesis 1.[42] Yet when investigation of nature, especially fossils, by savants such as early members of the Royal Society like John Ray, seemed to reveal that nature, too, had a complex past history, hints like Henry More's at a chronological but nonliteral creation week would reappear as a harmonizing possibility.[43]

DIVERGING INTERPRETATIONS:
THE CENTURY FOLLOWING WESTMINSTER (1650–1750)

Who can hope to trace a century of intellectual history in a paragraph? Before we touch on John Wesley, the last Christian figure cited as an authority on creation with any regularity, I will nevertheless sum up some further trends in this period relating to interpretation of early Genesis.

Encyclopedic Genesis Commentary

The Reformation's new focus on Scripture and its democratization, along with the Renaissance flight back *ad fontes* to the literary source and a late medieval flourishing of Hebrew scholarship, had produced a burst of Genesis commentary. This followed a medieval genre called mirror literature that attempted to embrace

41. Henry More, *Conjectura Cabbalistica* (London: Flesher, 1653), 148.

42. Barker, "Westminster Assembly," 115; Hall, "Evolution of Mythology," 293 n. 51.

43. John Ray, *Three Physico-Theological Discourses* (London: Smith, 1693), unpaginated section following 162; Edmund Halley, "An Attempt to Find the Age of the World by the Saltness of the Sea," in *The Philosophical Transactions (from the Year 1700 to the Year 1720) Abridg'd and Dispos'd under General Heads. Vol. V. containing Part I. The Anatomical and Medical Papers, Part II. The Philological and Miscellaneous Papers*, ed. Henry Jones (London: Strahan, 1721), 216–19 (paper delivered in 1715).

all that was known of the world into an encyclopedia that might use Genesis 1 as its structuring tool, as Dominican Vincent of Beauvais had done with *Speculum quadriplex* in around 1240. Some Genesis commentaries grew to enormous size as they utilized the generic categories of Genesis 1 to catalogue every fact accessible to "natural philosophy." Catholic scholar Marin Mersenne took this tack in his 1623 *Quaestiones celeberrimae in Genesim*. Others were not creating natural-philosophical compendia but shared the sense of the profundity of the early chapters of Genesis as an avenue to foundational truth, whether theological, spiritual, or natural. The Genesis commentaries of leading Catholic and Protestant scholars were at the pinnacle of Renaissance learning.

This confluence of knowledge in Genesis interpretation waned greatly after 1650. The desire to find meaning about God through creation continued, "only its expression is usually to be found outside commentaries on Genesis."[44]

Creation Epics

Literary treatments of Genesis themes, specifically hexaemeral ones, and explorations of the six days of creation in poetry and plays were also a noteworthy feature of Renaissance culture and peaked in the century straddling 1600. This long tradition, derived from late classical times, saw versified renditions of creation according to the Genesis text. It persisted through the medieval period to revive in Guillaume de Salluste Du Bartas's *La Sepmaine, ou Création* (1578) and then most famously in John Milton's *Paradise Lost* (1667), the spectacular swan song of the genre, after which quality tapered and interest waned.[45] *Paradise Lost* shows potential influence from the Dutch Arminian theological sphere and ultimately from precedents in the patristic period, especially the Cappadocians, that speculated about an angelic drama preceding the human story in Genesis. Hence the already fallen status of Satan and the prehuman existence of evil in *Paradise Lost* books 1–6, as well as the earth's formation from an original chaos in book 7, an ancient

<hr>

44. Williams, *Common Expositor*, 263–64, and see all of 255–68; Jaki, *Genesis 1*, 160–71.
45. W. Kirkconnell, ed., *The Celestial Cycle* (New York: Gordian, 1967); J. M. Evans, *"Paradise Lost" and the Genesis Tradition* (Oxford: Clarendon, 1968); Leland Ryken, "Paradise Lost and Its Biblical Epic Models," in *Milton and Scriptural Tradition*, ed. James H. Sims and Leland Ryken (Columbia, MO: University of Missouri Press, 1984), 43–81; G. Banderier, "A 'Fortunate Phoenix'? Renaissance and Death of the Hexameron (1578–1615)," *Neuphilologische Mitteilungen* 102.3 (2001): 251–67.

idea often entwined with interpretation of Genesis 1:1–3 throughout the history of exegesis. *Paradise Lost* might have represented the culmination of the tradition of the hexaemeral literary epic poem, but the century now in view in this chapter, 1650–1750, would see numerous treatments of Genesis that found room for increasing signs of terrestrial development in the short compass of Genesis 1:2.[46]

Biblical Chronology and Universal History

These intertwined approaches also had roots going back to the patristic period. Biblical chronology worked with date information supplied in Scripture to correctly frame the chronology of history. Motives might range from seeking the date of creation to anticipating the parousia of Christ, correctly framing church history or calculating the correct date for Easter. Universal history was the practice of trying to account for known history, integrating all sources, biblical and extrabiblical, while beginning that history from the earliest point possible—in some famous cases, from the day of creation. These twin genres survived the medieval period to be taken up in Renaissance Europe and experienced a vigorous life well into the eighteenth century, when Enlightenment freethinkers increasingly questioned their biblical constraints.

The most famous English biblical chronologist, James Ussher, had a considerable influence on the Westminster Confession, as we have seen. Sometimes pilloried as representing a churchly ignorance that controlled the center columns of King James Bibles for far too long, recent historians recognize today why efforts like his *Annals of the Old Testament* (1658), apologetic as its motives are, made good sense as integrative scholarship in their environment.[47] An anonymous universal history appearing in serial form, *An Universal History from the Earliest Account of Time to the Present* (1736–1768), was still capable in the middle of the "century of Enlightenment" of becoming "the most widely circulated subscriber support publication in the eighteenth century with the sole exception of [Denis Diderot's] *Encyclopédie*."[48]

46. Simon Patrick, *A Commentary on the First Book of Moses, Called Genesis* (London: Chiswell, 1695), 4–11 is one example.

47. James Barr, "Why the World Was Created in 4004 BC: Archbishop Ussher and Biblical Chronology," *Bulletin of the John Rylands Library* 67 (1985): 575–608.

48. *An Universal History, from the Earliest Account of Time to the Present*, 2nd ed., 20 vols. (London: Symon, 1740); Tamara Griggs, "Universal History from Counter-Reformation to Enlightenment," *Modern Intellectual History* 4 (2007): 228–29; A. T.

Earth-Origin Theories

The use of early Genesis to help form a picture of the origin of the physical world that took natural discoveries (and philosophical speculations, mystical writings, etc.) into account experienced a striking phase of popularity in this same century, sharing this basic frame of an emergence from chaos and leaving room for natural processes to unfold in that chaos's ordering. That the cosmos could form from an original chaos by natural processes was a classical concept, seen in Hesiod's *Theogony* from the late eighth century BCE and Ovid's *Metamorphoses* from the earliest years of the Christian era. There was a naturalistic Epicurean version also.

This concept persisted in medieval times, as in the work of Thierry of Chartres.[49] It was explored afresh in the Renaissance, rebooted for example by the famous French philosopher Descartes in *The World (Le Monde)* (1650). Descartes proposed that once God impels the chaotic matter into motion, even if he does nothing more to influence the chaos, "the laws of nature are sufficient to cause the parts of this chaos to disentangle themselves and arrange themselves in such a good order that they will have the form of a most perfect world."[50] Descartes's cosmogony, quite radical and risky in its time, helped to prompt a genre called "world-making" in its day by its critics, or "theories of the earth" (or geotheories)[51] in more recent times.[52]

The three most famous British earth theories were those of Thomas Burnet (Latin: 1681–1689; English: 1684–1690), John Woodward (1695) and William

---

Grafton, "Joseph Scaliger and Historical Chronology: The Rise and Fall of a Discipline," *History and Theory* 14 (1975): 156–85; Scott Mandelbrote, "'The Doors Shall Fly Open': Chronology and Biblical Interpretation in England, c. 1630–c. 1730," in *The Oxford Handbook of the Bible in Early Modern England, c. 1530–1700*, ed. Kevin Killeen, Helen Smith, and Rachel Willie (Oxford: Oxford University Press, 2015), 176–95. I spend more time on Ussher and John Lightfoot's *Chronicle of the Times* (1647) in *DOC*, 138–44.

49. Thierry of Chartres, "Tractatus de sex dierum operibus," in *Commentaries on Boethius by Thierry of Chartres and His School*, ed. N. M. Häring (Toronto: Pontifical Institute of Medieval Studies, 1971), 555–62.

50. René Descartes, *The World and Other Writings*, trans. and ed. Stephen Gaukroger, Cambridge Texts in the History of Philosophy (Cambridge: Cambridge University Press, 1998), 23; William Poole, *The World Makers* (Oxford: Lang, 2010), 15–25.

51. Martin J. S. Rudwick, *Bursting the Limits of Time: The Reconstruction of Geohistory in the Age of Revolution* (Chicago: University of Chicago Press, 2005), 133–58.

52. K. V. Magruder, "Theories of the Earth from Descartes to Cuvier: Natural Order and Historical Contingency in a Contested Textual Tradition" (PhD diss., University of Oklahoma, 2000).

Whiston (1696). Burnet owed more to Cartesian and even Stoic principles than biblical ones but retained a seven-part symbolic schema. Woodward sought to base his earth theory on the flood of Noah, while Whiston relied on a Newtonian schema where each creation day lasted a year. Discussion abounded and translations penetrated every corner of the European continent, while famous continental thinkers such as Gottfried Leibniz and Louis de Buffon also contributed to the conversation.[53] Buffon, a leading eighteenth-century French naturalist, would both conclude the first phase of this development with his *Theorie de la Terre* (1749) and begin to reinvent it with *Les Époques de la Nature* (1780), along with a range of other thinkers in France, Germany, Italy, and beyond.[54]

Other thinkers, however, reacted strongly against the hubris and speculation involved in creating cosmogonic systems of this kind; "world-makers" was not a compliment![55] Thinkers of "scientific" stripe often steered away from hypotheses about origins to the task of systematic description and classification of the natural world.[56] A good example is Carl Linnaeus, the inventor of our botanic classification system with *Philosophia botanica* (1755), although he did defend the "diminishing ocean" model of the earth's primordial history on the side.[57] The dominant world picture was static, so ironically, the task of natural history was not historical at all, but descriptive and taxonomic.[58] "Natural philosophy" was distinct from natural history in that it "sought to explain causation," but still in a more ontological than historical manner.[59]

Natural Theology

Another important field during 1650–1750 was natural theology, an enterprise that "drew the culminating reflections of natural philosophy into a larger con-

---

53. Rhoda Rappaport, *When Geologists Were Historians 1665–1750* (Ithaca, NY: Cornell University Press, 1997); Poole, *World Makers*, 55–74; Magruder, "Theories of the Earth."

54. Ezio Vaccari, "European Views on Terrestrial Chronology from Descartes to the Mid-Eighteenth Century," in *The Age of the Earth from 4004 BC to AD 2002*, ed. C. L. E. Lewis and Simon J. Knell, GS Special Publications 190 (London: Geological Society, 2001), 30–34.

55. Poole, *World Makers*, xvi–xvii.

56. Noting that "science" appeared as a term and concept in the nineteenth century.

57. Carl Linnaeus, *Oratio de telluris habitabilis incremento* (Leiden: Haak, 1744).

58. Sara Joan Miles, "From Being to Becoming: Science and Theology in the Eighteenth Century," *PSCF* 43.4 (1991): 215–23.

59. Rudwick, *Bursting the Limits of Time*, 52–54, esp. 58.

versation about what could *theoretically* be known about God apart from special revelation."[60] Deism and skepticism in the later sixteenth and early seventeenth centuries drove natural theology into a strongly apologetic mode that sought to confirm the teachings of Christian theology on the common ground of natural and social phenomena[61]—a burden ultimately too great for natural philosophy to bear, says John Brooke.[62] A late, prominent example of natural theology in Britain was William Paley's *Natural Theology* (1802), which would prove to be a foil for Charles Darwin's evolutionary theory, although some Christian readers might still find reasons to sympathize with Paley. Meanwhile, the collecting, cataloguing, and studying movement that was natural history would yet have its heyday in the mid-nineteenth century.[63]

Awareness of these genres, some representing lines of investigation that sought to reconcile some emerging field of knowledge with Genesis, will help us to decide what it was that John Wesley was trying to do in his own scientific compendium, and why he attempts little by way of integrating Genesis with an explanation of the world's physical origins as the theories of the earth had done.[64]

WHAT ABOUT JOHN WESLEY?

Having begun at the Reformed end of the Protestant spectrum with the Westminster Confession, whose wording about the six days of creation still has ramifications for some trainee Presbyterian ministers to this day, we now venture out to the Arminian/Wesleyan/Methodist wing to touch on the legacy and importance of John Wesley (1703–1791). He is the last figure of Christian

---

60. Randy L. Maddox, "John Wesley's Precedent for Theological Engagement with the Natural Sciences," *Wesleyan Theological Journal* 44.1 (2009): 38.

61. Henning Graf Reventlow, *The Authority of the Bible and the Rise of the Modern World* (Philadelphia: Fortress, 1985), 289–353.

62. J. H. Brooke, *Science and Religion: Some Historical Perspectives*, Cambridge History of Science (Cambridge: Cambridge University Press, 1991), 265.

63. R. J. Berry, "John Ray: Father of Natural Historians," *Science & Christian Belief* 13.1 (2001): 25–27.

64. John Wesley, *A Survey of the Wisdom of God in the Creation: Or a Compendium of Natural Philosophy* (Bristol: Pine, 1763), 2:20–25, 39. His reactions to Burnet and adoption of Woodward's ideas are sometimes implicit. He accepts a cometary sideswipe as the cause of the flood on 39, a concept from Whiston's *New Theory* (1696).

interpretive history who is cited as an authoritative precedent in regard to the Genesis creation texts in the context of the creation debates I have surveyed. There is an interesting Presbyterian-Methodist distinction here. The defining reference point concerning creation for the Reformed wing is initially a person, John Calvin, and ends up being a creed, the Westminster Confession, while Wesleyan attitudes to creation find their primary reference point in the person of John Wesley himself.

Wesley is a frustrating figure for the purpose of recruitment to the cause either for or against literal creation days. He shows little interest in the topic. Several creationist writers confess that Wesley "never wrote extensively on creation or the Flood," but in his work of natural philosophy, *A Survey of the Wisdom of God in the Creation* (1763), "stated his belief that the various rock strata were 'doubtless formed by the general Deluge.'" "In several published sermons," our sources continue in striking unison, "he repeatedly emphasized that the original creation was perfect, without any moral or physical evil (such as earthquakes, volcanoes, diseases, weeds or animal death), which both came into the world after man sinned."[65]

These opinions and a short, traditional biblical chronology of four thousand years from creation to the New Testament era are indeed the opinions Wesley expresses in the passages cited from the *Survey*.[66] A fuller quotation from Wesley's *Explanatory Notes upon the Old Testament* (1765) appears in Thane Ury's survey related to the origin of evil:

> The evening and the morning were the sixth day – So that in six days God made the world. We are not to think but that God could have made the world in an instant: but he did it in six days, that he might shew himself a free agent, doing his own work, both in his own way, and in his own time; that his wis-

---

65. Terrence J. Mortenson, *The Great Turning Point: The Church's Catastrophic Mistake on Geology – Before Darwin* (Green Forest, AR: Master Books, 2004), 42; Jonathan D. Sarfati, *Refuting Compromise* (Green Forest, AR: Master Books, 2004), 130; Hall, "Brief Overview," 73 n. 97, 74. Mortenson is the source of the wording.

66. The diluvialism in the style of John Woodward (1665–1722) appears in Wesley, *Survey*, 2:22. The 4,000-year chronology appears on 227 as our three authors indicate. Schofield lists six English editions and three American editions of the work without ruling out that there were others: Robert E. Schofield, "John Wesley and Science in 18th Century England," *Isis* 44.4 (1953): 336.

dom, power and goodness, might appear to us, and be meditated upon by us, the more distinctly; and that he might set us an example of working six days, and resting the seventh.[67]

Even in the context of the 1760s in England, as for the 1640s, the literal intention of the explanation does not require questioning in my view. Early probing of the possibility of deep time up to and around 1700 in Britain had actually subsided in this period.[68] Even when Wesley refers earlier in the commentary to "this gradual proceeding," he simply means across six days rather than instantaneously.[69] Ury notes next that Wesley follows a traditional chronology when dating the flood "1656 years from the creation."[70] Forster and Marston, hoping otherwise for a broader viewpoint, allow that in his eighteenth-century context, Wesley "could not really be blamed for still believing that the world was 6,000 years old."[71] Indeed, at the time, this remained by far the most common view in England, even though more adventurous thinkers had begun to explore alternatives. Darrel Falk, however (followed closely by Giberson and Collins), finds in Wesley's comments on the Eden narrative in Genesis 2 some interpretive leeway. Wesley allows for phenomenological (and perhaps typological) language in this part of Genesis: "The inspired penman . . . describes things by their outward sensible appearances, and leaves us, by further discoveries of the divine light, to be led into the understanding of the mysteries couched under them."[72] There is a

67. John Wesley, *Explanatory Notes on the Old Testament*, 3 vols. (Bristol: Pine, 1765), 1:9; Thane H. Ury, "Luther, Calvin, and Wesley on the Genesis of Natural Evil: Recovering Lost Rubrics for Defending a Very Good Creation," in *Coming to Grips with Genesis: Biblical Authority and the Age of the Earth*, ed. Terry Mortenson and Thane H. Ury (Green Forest, AR: Master Books, 2008), 408.

68. Gordon Davies speaks of a period of relapse in the natural sciences affecting such efforts over the period 1700–1760: Gordon L. Davies, *The Earth in Decay: A History of British Geomorphology, 1578–1878* (London: Macdonald, 1968), 92–97.

69. Wesley, *Explanatory Notes*, 1:3.

70. Wesley, *Explanatory Notes*, 1:34.

71. Roger Forster and Paul Marston, *Reason, Science and Faith* (Crowborough: Monarch, 1999), 218.

72. Wesley, *Explanatory Notes*, 1:11. Darrel Falk, *Coming to Peace with Science: Bridging the Worlds between Faith and Biology* (Downers Grove, IL: InterVarsity Press, 2004), 35; Karl W. Giberson and Francis S. Collins, *The Language of Science and Faith* (Downers Grove, IL: InterVarsity Press, 2011), 75–76.

hint here of a hermeneutic that transcends the literal and relates to the spiritual insight he said was needed to perceive the glory of God in nature.[73]

So, Wesley says little about the creation week or even the deluge, and what he does say is literal and traditional. He still falls victim to trite recruitment, better justified on the literal side yet trite all the same. "Luther, Calvin and Wesley" are trotted out by Ury, albeit with relevant theological comments.[74] Yet this is hardly relevant to the problem of the evidence of the fossil record.[75] For Falk the trio is Augustine, Calvin, and Wesley, and later, neatly inverted, Wesley, Calvin and Augustine.[76]

In fact, superficial recruitment or superior dismissal of Wesley are not new phenomena in his reception. Andrew Dickson White chose Wesley as one of his main targets as he sought to demolish the supposed deadening influence of religion on science: "There arose in the eighteenth century, to aid the subjection of science to theology, three men of extraordinary power—John Wesley, Adam Clarke, and Richard Watson."[77] Subsequently, Wesley sympathizers sought to salvage his reputation by showing that he had anticipated evolutionary theory a century before Darwin.[78]

The target of such derision or else, in connection with evolution, mistaken praise is normally not Wesley's *Explanatory Notes* but his *Survey of the Wisdom of God in Creation* (1763), a "Compendium of Natural Philosophy" as the subtitle announces.[79] Why not call it a natural theology? Wesley does in fact see his treatise as standing in line with recognized natural theologies of John Ray, William Derham, and others from either side of 1700. Randy Maddox argues that the difference is that Wesley largely avoided natural theology's overtly apol-

73. Mark H. Mann, "Wesley and the Two Books: John Wesley, Natural Philosophy, and Christian Faith," in *Connecting Faith and Science: Philosophical and Theological Inquiries*, ed. Matthew Hill and William Curtis Holzen (Claremont, CA: Claremont Press, 2017), 20–22.

74. Ury, "Luther, Calvin, and Wesley," 401, 403, 421–22.

75. Ury, "Luther, Calvin, and Wesley," 402.

76. Falk, *Coming to Peace with Science*, 36, 60.

77. White, *Warfare of Science*, 1:220; John W. Haas, "John Wesley's Views on Science and Christianity: An Examination of the Charge of Antiscience," *Church History* 63.3 (1994): 379.

78. Maddox, "John Wesley's Precedent," 24–28.

79. On the numerous editions of the work, see Mann, "Wesley and the Two Books," 11 n. 1; and esp. Schofield, "John Wesley and Science," 336.

ogetic agenda that was geared to proving God's existence and attributes from every corner of creation. Wesley remains content instead to display the "power, wisdom and goodness" of God in creation using concrete examples.[80] Yet on the basis of Wesley's disavowal of explaining causes in favor of simply describing the wonderful phenomena of the world,[81] and in light of Rudwick's careful argument concerning the difference between the causal task of natural philosophy and the descriptive role of natural history according to eighteenth-century definitions,[82] I wonder whether Wesley actually provides us with a natural *history* directed to the glory of God more than a natural philosophy. The work is brimful of unfeigned fascination with the phenomena of the world, more than enough to refute any charge of anti-scientism.[83]

Two very competent analyses of what was wrong with falsely polarized receptions of Wesley's legacy with respect to science will set the compass for the culmination of my entire argument. Let me conclude this chapter with the first. Maddox adroitly summarizes the problem this way:

> The lesson ... was that both the earlier dismissals and the sweeping panegyrics lacked balance and nuance. They were not sufficiently aware of the specific options in the engagement of theology and natural science, or of the various factors influencing choices between these options—in Wesley's time or in their own. Accordingly, they "read" Wesley anachronistically as exemplifying current positions which they either rejected or championed. An essential resource in guarding against such misreading is careful historical-contextual study of Wesley's writings on science topics.[84]

Maddox rightly notes in the following pages that our concept of "science" is of nineteenth-century origin and cannot accurately be applied to eighteenth-century figures such as Wesley without qualification.[85]

80. Wesley, *Survey*, 1:iii, vi; Maddox, "John Wesley's Precedent," 38–43; Mann, "Wesley and the Two Books," 19.
81. Wesley, *Survey*, 1:v. Reading the body of the work indeed shows it to be dominantly descriptive.
82. Rudwick, *Bursting the Limits of Time*, 58.
83. Haas, "John Wesley's Views," 391.
84. Maddox, "John Wesley's Precedent," 28.
85. Maddox, "John Wesley's Precedent," 30–35; Peter Harrison, "'Science' and 'Religion': Constructing the Boundaries," *Journal of Religion* 86.1 (2006): 81–91.

The overarching problem identified by Maddox lies at the base of many superficial recruitment exercises:

> One assumption shared by both the dismissals of Wesley's precedent and the idealized appeals to him as a forerunner at the turn to the twentieth century was confidence in the superiority of their own *modern* view; Wesley was worth considering only to the degree that he agreed with that view ... [as] a prescient precursor of current positions.[86]

Until we read ancient writers with motivations that transcend the quest for self-confirmation, our understanding of them will often be shallow and deficient.

---

86. Maddox, "John Wesley's Precedent," 37.

Conclusion

On Revisiting, Not Recruiting, the Ancients

How do writers on the history of interpretation or reception history of the creation week of Genesis, operating in the context of creation debates, come to such contradictory conclusions? Denis Alexander, content with having lined up Philo, Origen, and Augustine in the first edition of *Creation or Evolution: Do We Have to Choose?*, drew the sweeping conclusion,

> A figurative understanding of Genesis 1 was the dominant approach to the text among both Jewish and Christian commentators until at least into the fourteenth century, and it is not until the twentieth century, with the rise of modernist interpretations of the text, that one finds a growing trend to interpret the passage as if it were written in the language of modern science.[1]

Adjustments to this paragraph in his second edition suggest that he might have sensed a little overreach here. For example, he now speaks of "a figurative and theological understanding," although "theological" as a label for patristic hermeneutics is too all-inclusive to be very helpful.[2] On the other wing we find this even less moderate summation from Hall and Duncan:[3]

---

1. Denis Alexander, *Creation or Evolution: Do We Have to Choose?* (Oxford: Monarch, 2008), 157.
2. Denis Alexander, *Creation or Evolution: Do We Have to Choose?*, 2nd ed. (Oxford: Monarch, 2014), 185.
3. The material attributed to Hall and Duncan in this volume closely resembles mate-

Ambrose is as definite as any Church father on the subject [of literal creation days]! Moreover, Augustine and others never repudiated Ambrose's quite literal scheme. That attempt would not come until the twentieth century. . . . These new views have been carefully devised to fit presupposed concepts more in keeping with the altered landscapes of scientific dogma. There was no "alternative view" until the nineteenth century, after the beginning of the warfare between science and Christianity.[4]

Such opposing stances cannot both be true. In an article cautioning against the simplistic nature of appropriation of the so-called Alexandrian-Antiochene interpretive dispute in the early church, Donald Fairbairn aptly warns against

study[ing] Antiochene literal exegesis basically in order to pat ourselves on the backs and say, "See, even in the early church there were people doing exegesis the way we do it, so it must be right." . . . In such a case, we would really be doing nothing more than bolstering our own belief that we are doing exegesis correctly, and . . . giving our own methods a bit of . . . "historical authority," that is, the sanction of a long-standing pedigree. American scholar R. L. Wilken . . . writes that the history of exegesis is usually brought forth only to serve the needs of the present-day exegete. . . . Very little modern study of patristic exegesis by biblical scholars and theologians actually starts with . . . a humble, teachable attitude. Most such scholarship is simply an attempt to give historical authority to our own methods.[5]

We saw earlier that John Thompson complained that "historical figures are pressed into service as proxies for present-day conflicts."[6] It is put very simply by Craig Allert: "we cannot simply parachute into the context of the Fathers and disregard it by plucking out quotations that appear to support our conclusions."[7]

---

rial contributed by Hall alone in similar writings, raising the question of how substantial Duncan's contribution actually was.

4. In "The 24-Hour Reply," in *The Genesis Debate: Three Views on the Days of Creation*, ed. David Hagopian (Mission Viejo, CA: Crux, 2001), 102, 105.

5. Donald Fairbairn, "Patristic Exegesis and Theology: The Cart and the Horse," *WTJ* 69.1 (2007): 5–6.

6. John Thompson, "Introduction to Genesis 1–11," in *Genesis 1–11*, ed. John Thompson, RCS 1 (Downers Grove, IL: InterVarsity Press, 2012), xlvi.

7. Craig D. Allert, *Early Christian Readings of Genesis One: Patristic Exegesis and Literal Interpretation* (Downers Grove, IL: InterVarsity Press, 2018), 158.

By now, this chorus of protest should have alerted us that there is a problem with superficial recruitment of leading Christian interpreters of the history of the church, like student captains alternately choosing their fellow school students to form opposing basketball teams, starting with the most athletic ones and working down. If you are like me, that whole process is something you are trying to forget. Let us not duplicate it with respect to the history of Christian exegesis.

As promised late in the last chapter, Laura Felleman's warnings about method in the utilization of Wesley's legacy will serve us well in transitioning from how *not* to appropriate the great interpreters of the Christian past to how we can do it better. Felleman surveys the naively positive reception of Wesley by those wanting to prove that Wesley had anticipated evolutionary theory.[8] Her critique of that erroneous reception is facilitated by a steady engagement with an important admonitory essay that I introduced originally, Quentin Skinner's "Meaning and Understanding in the History of Ideas" (1969). This work is already half a century old, yet its continued relevance and necessity are demonstrated by the evidence gathered in this book for continued indulgence in the historiographic errors he highlights. Felleman lists them out for us in relation to appropriation of Wesley:[9]

- Anachronism: Wesley is recruited as a supporter of a form of biological evolution that really did not yet exist. Some interpreters mistook his articulation of the "great chain of being," drawn from Charles Bonnet (1720–1793), for belief in a historical development of organic forms.[10]
- The "mythology of coherence": that a writer's ideas were fully coherent and consistent across time and different writings, and so explicable in terms of a single, unifying idea.
- The "mythology of prolepsis," which "occurs whenever a work is used to address a contemporary problem without first considering the original intentions of the author in producing the work."

8. Laura Bartels Felleman, "John Wesley's Survey of the Wisdom of God in Creation: A Methodological Inquiry," *PSCF* 58.1 (2006): 68–69.

9. Felleman, "John Wesley's Survey," 69–70.

10. A. Lovejoy, *The Great Chain of Being* (Cambridge: Harvard University Press, 1936); Daniel J. Wilson, "Lovejoy's the Great Chain of Being after Fifty Years," *Journal of the History of Ideas* 48.2 (1987): 187–206; J. H. Brooke, *Science and Religion: Some Historical Perspectives*, Cambridge History of Science (Cambridge: Cambridge University Press, 1991), 227.

- The "mythology of parochialism," which overlooks what is alien (or simply not understood, and therefore invisible) in the thinking of the writer concerned, producing an impression of "misleading familiarity."

Felleman then refers to Skinner's call back to a focus on "the rhetorical intention of a historical document." Author intention is not popular in the domain of the philosophy of language, but the reality remains that such a thing as "communicative intention" exists, or else writers and speakers would never correct a listener's understanding of their meaning. So it remains important to carefully investigate not just how a text agrees with our existing ideas, but what that writer was trying to do in the context of his or her own times. We can break down the task of understanding thus:

- *Content*: This seems the most obvious area of mastery, but how often do we see ancient works, whose size and complexity can sometimes be intimidating, cherry-picked for isolated passages offering tantalizing supporting evidence? This is very tempting on account of our time and workload pressures and the sheer difficulty of the task of mastering the whole. But how can we really claim to have understood a writer's point if we have only read 1 percent or even 0.1 percent of the work? At that scale, the task has hardly begun. The same applies when we thoughtlessly reproduce the historical research of another writer with barely any mental processing on our own part; this is the worst kind of prooftexting.
- *Genre*: We cannot correctly interpret a text, biblical or historical, if we have mentally miscatalogued it, since our preconception of a text's genre greatly affects the way we mentally decode its content. Felleman argues that Wesley's *Survey* cannot be rightly understood as other than a work of natural philosophy.[11] Since this genre no longer exists as such, this requires a return to the period to understand what such a genre of writing would entail with the help of astute secondary literature.
- *Historical context*: What was happening at the time of writing in political or social or economic terms? What was the social role of the writer, and to what sort of reader was his book marketed? Was the writer politically connected

---

11. Felleman, "John Wesley's Survey," 71.

and involved in the great events of the time, or an outcast or exile, member of a migration to a new land or a missionary enterprise?

- *Intellectual and literary context*: This is critical—to try to understand the available ideas of the time, and thus the immediate context for what the writer wants to say. I would suggest that until we experience the shock of the unfamiliar in any source more than about a century old and have scratched our heads wondering why it was necessary to assert this or that, or even what it means, we have probably not read it carefully enough. Felleman speaks of the necessity of a thorough intertextual reading involving, in the case of Wesley, reading the other natural-philosophical works he edited or read and even checking the changes between different editions of his works.[12]

- *Communicative intention* in biographical context: As discussed above, do we seek to discover what the writer was really trying to get across in the circumstances of their time? What exactly did the work mean to the writer? What were the motives for undertaking it? Was it a product of youthful exuberance or wise old age? What was its intended audience? What was the desired impact on that readership in terms of change of opinion or practical behavior? Did it meet a need or correct an error? How was it received?

- *Theological-spiritual context and value*: This would incorporate church history but also the history of theology, that is, how the piece fits into the development of the church's knowledge of God and exercise of Christian trusting and living. The original motivation for the reading effort of many Christian readers would have begun here, and it would be a shame to let this fall from view. What was it that we learned of spiritual truth at the end of the day? What did we learn about how to read our own Bibles well?

What is the overall impression of such a checklist? One impression is of the amount of sheer hard work it takes to do such research. Who can find the time, energy, and practical resources to permit a study of this scale? Practically speaking, in a manifestation of "body life" in the body of Christ, we will need to divide our labor and utilize existing learning and scholarship rather than imagine that we can reinvent the wheel ourselves (with all the rookie errors this entails, like lone churches reinventing overseas aid ventures or their own schools and universities). This is, after all, why scholars specialize.

12. Felleman, "John Wesley's Survey," 72–73.

We can limit what we attempt to do. For example, we may decide to really understand (by thorough firsthand reading!) a single writing or group of writings by one author properly, and then use judicious reading of high quality secondary sources to fast-track our grasp of the contexts that allow that writing to make sense. Firsthand reading is greatly helped where an editor introduces the work to us and footnotes significant points. Quality secondary sources abound, too. One example I have often used and enjoyed is the comprehensive, multivolume work edited by Magna Sæbø, *Hebrew Bible, Old Testament: The History of Its Interpretation*. There is an ocean vast and deep of contextual discovery in such a work. If access to a serious library is an issue, a handbook like Gerald Bray's *Biblical Interpretation Past and Present* will at least represent a place to start.[13]

These are some methodological pointers for the exploration of the thinking of historical Christian interpreters. What do we learn through this study not just about good and bad ways of undertaking such exploration but about the record of past figures who thought about creation?

Paul Blowers explains the title and thrust of his work on the patristic theology of creation, *Drama of the Divine Economy*, like this. Reflecting Kevin Vanhoozer, *The Drama of Doctrine* (2005), he emphasizes that the patristic Christian view of history was as a divine drama conducted by God with its center in Christ: "I have consistently claimed that, more than philosophical cosmology or cosmogony, the 'drama of the divine economy' decisively shaped the doctrine of creation in the early church."[14] Even when early fathers wrote in literal terms about creation, it does not take much reading to see that they were not asking the questions of Genesis that we often ask. Understanding the origin of the physical world, for instance, is a rather low priority for them compared to understanding the deep ontology of the cosmos or the centrality of Christ in that ontology. They by and large were not interested in the kinds of historical scientific questions that sometimes loom large for us. Their quest was to understand the saving purposes of God in history. In Genesis 1, at the very conception point of that history, they discovered the power of God, power that could summarize superclusters of superclusters of galaxies as, oh yes, "and the stars" (Gen. 1:16) but be thrilled with the crafting of

---

13. Gerald Bray, *Biblical Interpretation: Past and Present* (Downers Grove, IL: Inter-Varsity Press, 1996).

14. Paul M. Blowers, *Drama of the Divine Economy: Creator and Creation in Early Christian Theology and Piety*, OECS (Oxford: Oxford University Press, 2012), 373.

life. They discovered the wisdom of God creating a world by distinguishing one thing from another, frustrating entropy with exquisite order; they discovered the goodness of God that prepared a home world because he wished to know, and birth, and love, another. God wished for new life other than his own. God made a world good for thriving and living and bid life, and bid us, to thrive.

Now I do not think that we can simply go back to a patristic faith, however the evangelical rediscovery of the faith of the early church turns out. The Renaissance, the Reformation, the Enlightenment, modernity, and postmodernity—whatever replaces these traditional historical labels now or in future discussion, the world is changed. Christians must wrestle with all the changes these epochs brought. In some ways the Christian writings of the seventeenth or eighteenth centuries that wrestled with some of the most serious of these changes are just as important to read as those of the church fathers. Where Genesis is concerned, the same is true for the nineteenth and early twentieth centuries, when the gap theory and day-age theories were diligently tried as ways of harmonizing biblical and scientific origins and, I think, proved inadequate, not sufficiently recognizing the differences between biblical and scientific modes of explaining beginnings. But I am certain that we can never understand our current position as Christians in our time and present cultures if we do not discover how we got here. The explorer who looks around at the environment and suddenly feels lost must retrace her steps to discover where the journey has taken her. As in those ancestry programs on television with their subjects in weeping epiphanies, we can understand our present if we can understand our past—by revisiting, not recruiting, the ancients.

Glossary

CONCORDISM The enterprise of reconciling the Genesis creation narratives and facts or theories about the natural world.

COSMOGONY An account of the physical origin of the world.

DAY-AGE INTERPRETATION A specific concordist theory that interprets the days of the creation week of Genesis as referring to ages of prehuman history (i.e., geological eras). Also called the periodic day interpretation.

FRAMEWORK HYPOTHESIS The interpretation of the creation week of Genesis as a symmetrical poetic or teaching device helping to structure and communicate ideas about creation, not meant to be taken literally.

HELLENISM/HELLENISTIC Referring to the diaspora Greek culture that arose in the eastern Mediterranean region in the wake of the conquests of Alexander the Great. Hellenistic Judaism is Greek-influenced Jewish culture.

HERMENEUTIC(AL) Concerning interpretation of texts, often biblical interpretation.

HEXA(E)MERON, HEXA(E)MERAL The narrative of the six days of creation in Genesis 1 or a commentary or poetic treatment of it. I use the Greek spelling featuring the central 'e'.

HISTORIOGRAPHY The theory of researching and reporting history.

PATRISTIC Relating to the period of the church fathers, from apostolic times up to about 600 CE.

YOUNG EARTH CREATIONISM A literal interpretation of the creation week of Genesis 1 in conjunction with early biblical genealogies and date notices that results in the understanding that the earth or even the cosmos is in the order of 10,000 years old or less.

Bibliography

Abelard, Peter. "Expositio in hexameron." PL 178:731–84.

Aertsen, Jan A. "Aquinas's Philosophy in Its Historical Setting." Pages 12–37 in *The Cambridge Companion to Aquinas*. Edited by Norman Kretzmann and Eleonore Stump. Cambridge: Cambridge University Press, 1993.

Albert the Great. *Summa theologiae pars secunda*. Vol. 32 of *B. Alberti Magni opera omnia*. Paris: Vivès, 1895.

Alexander, Denis. *Creation or Evolution: Do We Have to Choose?* Oxford: Monarch, 2008.

———. *Creation or Evolution: Do We Have to Choose?* 2nd ed. Oxford: Monarch, 2014.

Alexandre, Monique. *Le commencement du livre Genèse I–V: La version grecque de la Septente et sa réception*. Christianisme Antique 3. Paris: Beauchesne, 1988.

Allen, Pauline, and Wendy Mayer. *John Chrysostom*. London: Routledge, 2002.

Allert, Craig D. *Early Christian Readings of Genesis One: Patristic Exegesis and Literal Interpretation*. Downers Grove, IL: InterVarsity Press, 2018.

———. *Revelation, Truth, Canon and Interpretation: Studies in Justin Martyr's Dialogue with Trypho*. Leiden: Brill, 2002.

Almond, Philip C. *Adam and Eve in Seventeenth-Century Thought*. Cambridge: Cambridge University Press, 1999.

Althaus, Paul. *The Theology of Martin Luther*. Philadelphia: Fortress, 1966.

Amar, Joseph P. "Christianity at the Crossroads: The Legacy of Ephrem the Syrian." *Religion & Literature* 43.2 (2011): 1–21.

Ambrose. *Hexameron, Paradise, and Cain and Abel*. Translated by John J. Savage. FC 42. Washington, DC: Catholic University of America Press, 1961.

Ames, William. *The Marrow of Theology*. Translated by John Dykstra Eusden. Grand Rapids: Baker, 1997.

Anonymous. *An Universal History, from the Earliest Account of Time to the Present*. 2nd ed. 20 vols. London: Symon, 1740.

Anselm. *Systematische Sentenzen*. Edited by Franz Johannes Plazidus Bliemetzrieder. Beiträge zur Geschichte der Philosophie des Mittelalters 18. Münster: Aschendorffschen, 1919.

———. "Why God Became Man." Pages 100–183 in *A Scholastic Miscellany: Anselm to Ockham*. Edited by Eugene R. Fairweather. Translated by E. Prout. The Library of Christian Classics. Philadelphia: Westminster, 1982.

Aquinas, Thomas. *Scriptum super Libros Sententiarum*. 10 vols. Bologna: Edizioni Studio Domenicano, 2000.

———. *Summa contra Gentiles, 2: Book Two: Creation*. Translated by James F. Anderson. Notre Dame: University of Notre Dame Press, 1976.

———. *Summa Theologiae: Latin Text and English Translation*. Translated and edited by Thomas Gilby and T. C. O'Brien et al. 61 vols. London: Blackfriars, 1964–1973.

Archambault, Paul. "The Ages of Man and the Ages of the World. A Study of Two Traditions." *Revue des Études Augustiniennes* 12 (1966): 193–228.

Arko, Alenka. "Between Literal and Allegorical Exegesis: The Cappadocian Fathers on *Hexaemeron*." *Lateranum* 79.2 (2013): 485–502.

Armogathe, J.-R., ed. *Le grand siècle et la Bible*. La Bible de Tous les Temp 6. Paris: Beauchesne, 1989.

Armstrong, G. T. *Die Genesis in der alten Kirche: Die drei Kirchenväter, Justinus, Irenäus, Tertullian*. Beiträge zur Geschichte der biblischen Hermeneutik 4. Tübingen: Mohr, 1962.

Arnold of Bonneval. "De operibus sex dierum." PL 189:1513–70.

Augustine. *City of God. Volumes I–VII*. LCL 411–17. Cambridge: Harvard University Press, 1957–72.

———. *Confessions*. Translated by Henry Chadwick. Oxford: Oxford University Press, 1991.

———. *De Civitate Dei: The City of God*. Edited by P. G. Walsh. Aris & Phillips Classical Texts. Cambridge: Oxbow, 2005.

———. *De civitate Dei libri XXII. Vol. I. Lib. I—XIII*. Edited by Bernhard Dombart and Alfonsus Kalb. 3rd ed. Leipzig: Teubner, 1921.

———. *Eighty-Three Different Questions*. Translated by David Mosher. FC 70. Washington, DC: Catholic University of America Press, 1977.

———. *Letters. Vol. IV (165–203)*. Translated by Sister Wilfrid Parsons. FC 30. New York: Fathers of the Church, 1955.

———. *The Literal Meaning of Genesis*. Edited by John Hammond Taylor. 2 vols. ACW 41. New York: Newman, 1982.

———. *On Genesis*. Edited by John E. Rotelle. Translated by Edmund Hill. The Works of Saint Augustine 1/13. Hyde Park, NY: New City, 2002.

———. *On Genesis: Two Books on Genesis against the Manichees and On the Literal Interpretation of Genesis; An Unfinished Book*. Translated by Roland J. Teske. FC 84. Washington, DC: Catholic University of America Press, 1991.

———. *Psalms*. Translated by Scholastica Hebgin and Felicitas Corrigan. 2 vols. London: Longmans, Green, 1960.

———. *Sermons on the Liturgical Seasons*. Edited by Mary Sarah Muldowney. FC 38. Washington, DC: Catholic University of America Press, 2010.

Babcock, William S., ed. *Tyconius: The Book of Rules*. Atlanta: Scholars Press, 1989.

Babington, Gervase. *Certaine Plaine, Briefe and Comfortable Notes upon Everie Chapter of Genesis*. London: Charde, 1592.

Backus, I., ed. *The Reception of the Church Fathers in the West*. 2 vols. Leiden: Brill, 1997.

Bacon, Francis. "The New Atlantis." Pages 103–40 in *Ideal Commonwealths*. Edited by Henry Morley. London: The Colonial Press, 1901.

Banderier, G. "A 'Fortunate Phoenix'? Renaissance and Death of the Hexameron (1578–1615)." *Neuphilologische Mitteilungen* 102.3 (2001): 251–67.

Barker, William S. "The Westminster Assembly on the Days of Creation: A Reply to David W. Hall." *WTJ* 62.1 (2000): 113–20.

Barr, James. "Luther and Biblical Chronology." *Bulletin of the John Rylands Library* 72 (1990): 51–67.

———. "Pre-Scientific Chronology: The Bible and the Origin of the World." *Proceedings of the American Philosophical Society* 143 (1999): 379–87.

———. "Why the World Was Created in 4004 BC: Archbishop Ussher and Biblical Chronology." *Bulletin of the John Rylands Library* 67 (1985): 575–608.

Basil of Caesarea. *Homélies sur l'Hexaéméron*. Translated by Stanislas Giet. 2nd ed. SC 26. Paris: Cerf, 1968.

———. *Homilien zum Hexaemeron*. Edited by Emmanuel Amand de Mendieta and Stig Y. Rudberg. GCS(NF) 2. Berlin: Akademie, 1997.

———. "On the Hexaemeron." Pages 3–150 in *Exegetic Homilies*. Edited by Agnes Clare Way. FC 46. Washington, DC: Catholic University of America Press, 1963. IA.

———. *Sur l'origine de l'homme: (Hom. 10. et 11. de l'Hexaéméron)*. Edited by Alexis Smets and Michel van Esbroeck. SC 160. Paris: Cerf, 1970.

Barton, Stephen C., and David Wilkinson, eds. *Reading Genesis after Darwin*. Oxford: Oxford University Press, 2009.

Batten, Don, ed. *The Answers Book: Updated and Expanded*. Acacia Ridge: Answers in Genesis, 1999.

———. "Genesis Means What It Says: Basil (AD 329–379)." September 1, 1994. https://answersingenesis.org/genesis/genesis-means-what-it-says-basil-ad-329-379/.

Battles, Ford Lewis. "God Was Accommodating Himself to Human Capacity." Pages 19–38 in *Readings in Calvin's Theology*. Edited by Donald K. McKim. Grand Rapids: Baker, 1977.

Bede. *On Genesis*. Translated by Calvin Kendall. Translated Texts for Historians 48. Liverpool: Liverpool University Press, 2008.

———. *On the Nature of Things and On Times*. Edited by Calvin B. Kendall and Faith Wallis. Liverpool: Liverpool University Press, 2010.

Beeke, Joel R. "What Did the Reformers Believe about the Age of the Earth?" Pages 101–10 in *The New Answers Book 4*. Edited by Ken Ham. Green Forest, AR: Master Books, 2013.

Bellitto, Christopher M. *The General Councils: A History of the Twenty-One General Councils from Nicaea to Vatican II*. Mahwah, NJ: Paulist, 2002.

Berry, R. J. "John Ray: Father of Natural Historians." *Science & Christian Belief* 13.1 (2001): 25–38.

Birdsall, J. N. "Josephus Flavius (A.D. 37–Post 100)." *NIDCC*, 549.

Blair, Ann. "Mosaic Physics and the Search for a Pious Natural Philosophy in the Late Renaissance." *Isis* 91.1 (2000): 32–58.

Blocher, Henri. *In the Beginning*. Edited by David G. Preston. Downers Grove, IL: InterVarsity Press, 1984.

Blowers, Paul M. "Creation." Pages 513–24 in *The Oxford Handbook of Early Christian Biblical Interpretation*. Edited by Paul M. Blowers and Peter W. Martens. Oxford: Oxford University Press, 2019.

———. *Drama of the Divine Economy: Creator and Creation in Early Christian Theology and Piety.* OECS. Oxford: Oxford University Press, 2012.

———. "Entering 'This Sublime and Blessed Amphitheatre': Contemplation of Nature and Interpretation of the Bible in the Patristic Period." Pages 1:147–76 in *Nature and Scripture in the Abrahamic Religions: Up to 1700.* Edited by Jitse M. van der Meer and Scott Mandelbrote. Brill's Series in Church History 36. Leiden: Brill, 2008.

Boersma, Hans. *Heavenly Participation: The Weaving of a Sacramental Tapestry.* Grand Rapids: Eerdmans, 2011.

———. *Scripture as Real Presence: Sacramental Exegesis in the Early Church.* Grand Rapids: Baker Academic, 2017.

Bonaventure. *Collations on the Six Days.* Translated by J. de Vinck. Paterson, NJ: St Anthony Guild Press, 1970.

———. *Sententiae in IV Libris Distinctae.* Edited by I. C. Brady. Spicilegium Bonaventurianum 4–5. Grottaferrata: Editiones Collegium S. Bonaventurae ad Claras Aquas, 1971.

Bonner, Gerald. "Augustine and Millenarianism." Pages 235–54 in *The Making of Orthodoxy: Essays in Honour of Henry Chadwick.* Edited by Rowan Williams. Cambridge: Cambridge University Press, 1989.

———. "Augustine as Biblical Scholar." Pages 541–63 in *From the Beginnings to Jerome.* Vol. 1 of *Cambridge History of the Bible,* edited by P. R. Ackroyd and C. F. Evans. Cambridge: Cambridge University Press, 1970.

———. *St Augustine of Hippo: Life and Controversies.* London: SCM, 1963.

Bonwetsch, G. Nathanael. *Die Theologie des Methodius von Olympus.* Abhandlungen der Königlichen Gesellschaft der Wissenschaften zu Göttingen. Philologisch-Historische Klasse. Neue Folge 7. Berlin: Weidmannsche, 1903.

Bornkamm, H. *Luther and the Old Testament.* Edited by Victor I. Gruhn. Translated by Eric W. Gritsch and Ruth C. Gritsch. Philadelphia: Fortress, 1969.

Bouteneff, Peter C. *Beginnings: Ancient Christian Readings of the Biblical Creation Narratives.* Grand Rapids: Baker Academic, 2008.

Bradley, James E., and Richard A. Muller. *Church History: An Introduction to Research Methods and Resources.* 2nd ed. Grand Rapids: Eerdmans, 2016.

Bray, Gerald. *Biblical Interpretation: Past and Present.* Downers Grove, IL: InterVarsity Press, 1996.

Brecht, Martin. *Martin Luther: The Preservation of the Church, 1532–1546.* Minneapolis: Fortress, 1993.

Bright, Pamela. *The Book of Rules of Tyconius: Its Purpose and Inner Logic*. University of Notre Dame Press, 1988.

Bril, Alexander. "Plato and the Sympotic Form in the Symposium of St Methodius of Olympus." *ZAC* 9.2 (2005): 279–302.

Brocardus, Jacobus. *Mystica et prophetica libri Geneseos interpretatio*. Leyden: Batavorum, 1575.

Brooke, J. H. *Science and Religion: Some Historical Perspectives*. Cambridge History of Science. Cambridge: Cambridge University Press, 1991.

Brown, Andrew. "Basil: Philosophical Literacy Meets Biblical Literalism?" *ZAC* 26.1 (2022): 95–106.

———. "Hexaemeron." *Brill Encyclopedia of Early Christianity Online*. Leiden: Brill, 2021. http://dx.doi.org/10.1163/2589-7993_EECO_SIM_00001554.

Brown, Jeannine K. "Creation's Renewal in the Gospel of John." *CBQ* 72.2 (2010): 275–90.

Browne, Thomas. *Religio, Medici*. Leiden: Hackius, 1644.

———. *Religio Medici the Fourth Edition, Corrected and Amended*. London: Crook, 1656.

Buonaiuti, Ernesto. "The Ethics and Eschatology of Methodius of Olympus." *HTR* 14.3 (1921): 255–66.

Burchill, Christopher J. "Girolamo Zanchi: Portrait of a Reformed Theologian and His Work." *The Sixteenth Century Journal* 15.2 (1984): 185–207.

Buschart, W. David, and Kent Eilers. *Theology as Retrieval: Receiving the Past, Renewing the Church*. Downers Grove, IL: IVP Academic, 2015.

Butterfield, Herbert. *The Whig Interpretation of History*. London: Bell and Sons, 1931.

Cajetan, Thomas de Vio. *In Quinque Libros Mosis, iuxta sensum literalem, Commentarii: et primum in Genesim*. Vol. 1 of *Opera omnia quotquot in Sacrae Scripturae expositionem reperiuntur*. Rome, 1531. Repr. Hildesheim: Olms, 2005.

Calvin, John. *Genesis*. Edited by J. King. The Geneva Series of Commentaries. London: Banner of Truth, 1965.

———. *Institutes of the Christian Religion*. Edited by John T. McNeill. Translated by Ford Lewis Battles. Library of Christian Classics. Louisville: Westminster John Knox, 1960.

———. *Institutes of the Christian Religion*. Translated by Henry Beveridge. Grand Rapids: Eerdmans, 1989.

———. *Sermons on Genesis, Chapters 1:1–11:4: Forty-Nine Sermons Delivered in Ge-*

neva, *between 4 September 1559 and 23 January 1560.* Translated by Rob Roy McGregor. Edinburgh: Banner of Truth, 2009.

———. *Sermons sur la Genèse, chapitres 1.1–11.4.* Edited by Max Engammare. Supplementa Calviniana 11.1. Neukirchen-Vluyn: Neukirchener Verlag, 2000.

Cantor, Petrus. *Glossae super Genesim. Prologus et capitula 1–3.* Translated by Agneta Sylwan. Studia Graeca et Latina Gothoburgensia 55. Göteborg: Acta Universitatis Gothoburgensis, 1992.

Carmichael, Calum M. *The Story of Creation: Its Origin and Its Interpretation in Philo and the Fourth Gospel.* Ithaca, NY: Cornell University Press, 1996.

Carroll, William E. "Aquinas and Contemporary Cosmology: Creation and Beginnings." *Science & Christian Belief* 24.1 (2012): 5–18.

———. "Aquinas and the Big Bang." *First Things* 97 (1999): 18–20.

Carter, Craig A. *Interpreting Scripture with the Great Tradition: Recovering the Genius of Premodern Exegesis.* Grand Rapids: Baker, 2018.

Chadwick, Henry. "Augustine." Pages 85–87 in *Dictionary of Biblical Interpretation.* Edited by John H. Hayes. Nashville: Abingdon, 1999.

———. "The Early Christian Community." Pages 21–61 in *The Oxford Illustrated History of Christianity.* Edited by John McManners. Oxford: Oxford University Press, 1990.

Charles, J. Daryl, ed. *Reading Genesis 1–2: An Evangelical Conversation.* Peabody, MA: Hendrickson, 2013.

Childs, B. S. *The Struggle to Understand Isaiah as Christian Scripture.* Grand Rapids: Eerdmans, 2004.

Christian, W. A. "Augustine on the Creation of the World." *HTR* 46 (1953): 1–25.

Chrysostom, John. *Homilies on Genesis 1–17.* Translated by R. C. Hill. FC 74. Washington, DC: Catholic University of America Press, 1985.

Clement of Alexandria. *Stromata Buch I–VI.* Edited by Otto Stählin, Ludwig Früchtel, and Ursula Treu. 4th ed. GCS. Berlin: Akademie, 1985.

Cohen, Jeremy. *Be Fertile and Increase, Fill the Earth and Master It: The Ancient and Medieval Career of a Biblical Text.* Ithaca, NY; London: Cornell University Press, 1989.

Colet, John. *Letters to Radulphus on the Mosaic Account of Creation: Together with Other Treatises.* London: Bell, 1876.

Colie, Rosalie L. *Light and Enlightenment: A Study of the Cambridge Platonists and the Dutch Arminians.* Cambridge: Cambridge University Press, 1957.

Colish, Marcia L. *Peter Lombard.* 2 vols. Leiden: Brill, 1994.

Collini, Stefan. "The Identity of Intellectual History." Pages 7–18 in *A Companion to Intellectual History,* edited by Richard Whatmore and Brian Young. Chichester: Wiley, 2015.

Collins, C. John. *Genesis 1–4: A Linguistic, Literary, and Theological Commentary.* Phillipsburg, NJ: P&R, 2006.

———. "How Old Is the Earth? Anthropomorphic Days in Genesis 1:1–2:3." *Presbyterion* 20 (1994): 109–30.

Collins, Francis. *The Language of God: A Scientist Presents Evidence for Belief.* New York: Free Press, 2006.

Congar, Yves M.-J. "Le thème de Dieu-créateur et les explications de l'Hexaméron dans la tradition chrétienne." Pages 1:189–222 in *L'Homme devant Dieu: Melanges offerts au Père Henri de Lubac.* Theologie 56–58. Paris: Aubier, 1963.

Conte, Gian Biagio. *Stealing the Club from Hercules: On Imitation in Latin Poetry.* Berlin: de Gruyter, 2017.

Copleston, Frederick, SJ. *A History of Philosophy.* 11 vols. Mahwah, NJ: Paulist, 1946–2003.

Cosmas (Indicopleustes). *Christianikē Topographia: The Christian Topography of Cosmas, an Egyptian Monk.* Edited by J. W. McCrindle. London: Franklin, 1897.

Costache, Doru. "Approaching an Apology for the Hexaemeron." *Phronema* 27.2 (2012): 53–81.

———. "Making Sense of the World: Theology and Science in St Gregory of Nyssa's An Apology for the Hexaemeron." *Phronema* 28.1 (2013): 1–29.

Courcelle, Pierre. *Recherches sur les Confessions de saint Augustin.* Paris: Boccard, 1968.

Crouzel, Henri. *Origen.* Translated by A. S. Worrall. Edinburgh: T&T Clark, 1989.

Daley, Brian. *The Hope of the Early Church: A Handbook of Patristic Eschatology.* Grand Rapids: Baker Academic, 2010.

Danaeu, Lambert. *Physica Christiana.* 2 vols. Geneva: Vignon, 1602.

———. *The Wonderfull Woorkmanship of the World.* London: Maunsell, 1578.

Daniélou, Jean. *From Shadow to Reality: Studies in the Biblical Typology of the Fathers.* Translated by W. Hubbard. London: Burns and Oates, 1960.

———. *The Theology of Jewish Christianity.* Translated by John A. Baker. London: Darton, Longman and Todd, 1964.

———. "La typologie millénariste de la semaine dans le Christianisme primitif." *VC* 2.1 (1948): 1–16.

Darby, Peter. *Bede and the End of Time.* London: Routledge, 2016.

Davies, Gordon L. *The Earth in Decay: A History of British Geomorphology, 1578–1878*. London: Macdonald, 1968.

Dean, James M. *The World Grown Old in Later Medieval Literature*. Cambridge: Medieval Academy of America, 1997.

Debus, Allen G. *The Chemical Philosophy: Paracelsian Science and Medicine in the Sixteenth and Seventeenth Centuries*. 2 vols. Mineola, NY: Dover, 1977.

DeMarco, David C. "The Presentation and Reception of Basil's *Homiliae in Hexaemeron* in Gregory's *In Hexaemeron*." *ZAC* 17.2 (2013): 332–52.

Dembski, William. *The End of Christianity*. Nashville: B&H, 2009.

Descartes, René. *The World and Other Writings*. Translated and edited by Stephen Gaukroger. Cambridge Texts in the History of Philosophy. Cambridge: Cambridge University Press, 1998.

Dickson, John P. "The Genesis of Everything: An Historical Account of the Bible's Opening Chapter." *ISCAST Online Journal* 4 (2008): 1–18.

Drever, Matthew. "Image, Identity, and Embodiment: Augustine's Interpretation of the Human Person in Genesis 1–2." Pages 117–28 in *Genesis and Christian Theology*. Edited by Nathan MacDonald, Mark W. Elliott, and Grant Macaskill. Grand Rapids: Eerdmans, 2012.

Dulaey, Martine. "A quelle date Augustin a-t-il pris ses distances vis-à-vis du millénarisme?" *Revue des Études Augustiniennes* 46 (2000): 31–60.

Dunbar, David G. "The Delay of the Parousia in Hippolytus." *VC* 37.4 (1983): 313–27.

Dunn, James D. G. *Neither Jew nor Greek*. Vol. 3 of *Christianity in the Making*. Grand Rapids: Eerdmans, 2015.

Earnshaw, Rebekah. *Creator and Creation according to Calvin on Genesis*. Reformed Historical Theology 64. Göttingen: Vandenhoeck & Ruprecht, 2020.

Elliott, Paul. *Creation and Literary Re-Creation: Ambrose's Use of Philo in the Hexaemeral Letters*. Gorgias Studies in Early Christianity and Patristics 72. Piscataway, NJ: Gorgias, 2019.

Ephrem the Syrian. *Hymns*. Edited by Kathleen McVey. Mahwah, NJ: Paulist, 1989.

———. *Selected Prose Works*. Edited by Kathleen E. McVey. Translated by Edward G. Mathews and Joseph P. Amar. FC 91. Washington, DC: Catholic University of America Press, 1994.

Episcopius, Simon. *Institutiones theologicae, privatis lectionibus Amstelodami traditae*. Edited by Étienne de Courcelles. Amsterdam: Blaeu, 1650.

Eusebius of Caesarea. *The History of the Church: A New Translation*. Translated by Jeremy M. Schott. Berkeley: University of California Press, 2019.

Evans, Craig A., Joel N. Lohr, and David L. Petersen, eds. *The Book of Genesis: Composition, Reception, and Interpretation.* VTSup 152. Leiden: Brill, 2012.

Evans, Gillian R. *The Language and Logic of the Bible.* 2 vols. Cambridge: Cambridge University Press, 1984–85.

Evans, J. M. *"Paradise Lost" and the Genesis Tradition.* Oxford: Clarendon, 1968.

Fairbairn, Donald. "Patristic Exegesis and Theology: The Cart and the Horse." *WTJ* 69.1 (2007): 1–19.

Falk, Darrel. *Coming to Peace with Science: Bridging the Worlds between Faith and Biology.* Downers Grove, IL: InterVarsity Press, 2004.

Farrar, F. W. *History of Interpretation.* London: Macmillan, 1886.

Féghali, Paul. "Les premiers jours de la création: commentaire de GN 1,1–2, 4 par Saint Ephrem." *Parole de l'Orient* 13 (1986): 3–30.

Felleman, Laura Bartels. "John Wesley's Survey of the Wisdom of God in Creation: A Methodological Inquiry." *Perspectives on Science and Christian Faith* 58.1 (2006): 68–73.

Ferguson, John. *Clement of Alexandria.* New York: Twayne, 1974.

Fergusson, David. *Creation.* Guides to Theology. Grand Rapids: Eerdmans, 2014.

Fesko, J. V. "The Days of Creation and Confession Subscription in the OPC." *WTJ* 63 (2001): 235–49.

———. "The Legacy of Old School Confession Subscription in the OPC." *JETS* 46.4 (2003): 673–98.

Fishbane, Michael A. *Biblical Interpretation in Ancient Israel.* Oxford: Clarendon Press, 1985.

———. *Biblical Text and Texture: A Literary Reading of Selected Texts.* Oxford: Oneworld, 1998.

Fogleman, Alex. "'Since Those Days All Things Have Progressed for the Better': Tradition, Progress, and Creation in Ambrose of Milan." *HTR* 113.4 (2020): 440–59.

Folliet, Georges. "La typologie du sabbat chez saint Augustin. Son interprétation millénariste entre 389 et 400." *Revue d'Etudes Augustiniennes et Patristiques* 2.3–4 (1956): 371–90.

Forshaw, Peter J. "The Genesis of Christian Kabbalah: Early Modern Speculations on the Work of Creation." Pages 121–44 in *Hidden Truths from Eden: Esoteric Readings of Genesis 1–3.* Edited by Caroline Vander Stichele and Susanne Scholz. Atlanta: SBL Press, 2014.

———. "Vitriolic Reactions: Orthodox Responses to the Alchemical Exegesis of Genesis." Pages 111–36 in *The Word and the World*. Edited by Kevin Killeen and Peter J. Forshaw. Basingstoke: Macmillan, 2007.

Forster, Roger, and Paul Marston. *Reason, Science and Faith*. Crowborough: Monarch, 1999.

Fredriksen, Paula. "Apocalypse and Redemption in Early Christianity: From John of Patmos to Augustine of Hippo." *VC* 45.2 (1991): 151–83.

Frishman, Judith, and Lucas van Rompay, eds. *Book of Genesis in Jewish and Oriental Christian Interpretation: A Collection of Essays*. Leuven: Peeters, 1997.

Froehlich, Karlfried. "'Take Up and Read': Basics of Augustine's Biblical Interpretation." *Interpretation* 58.1 (2004): 5–16.

Froehlich, Karlfried, and Margaret T. Gibson, eds. *Biblia Latina cum Glossa Ordinaria: Facsimile Reprint of the Editio Princeps Adolph Rusch of Strassburg 1480/81*. Turnhout: Brepols, 1992.

Furry, Timothy J. *Allegorizing History: The Venerable Bede, Figural Exegesis and Historical Theory*. Cambridge: Clarke, 2014.

———. "Time, Text, & Creation: The Venerable Bede on Genesis 1." Henry Center for Theological Understanding (blog). May 24, 2017. http://henrycenter.tiu .edu/2017/05/time-text-creation-the-venerable-bede-on-genesis-1/.

Furseth, Inger, and Pål Repstad. *An Introduction to the Sociology of Religion: Classical and Contemporary Perspectives*. Aldershot: Ashgate, 2006.

Geisler, Norman. *Thomas Aquinas: An Evangelical Appraisal*. Eugene, OR: Wipf and Stock, 2003.

George, Timothy. *Reading Scripture with the Reformers*. Downers Grove, IL: InterVarsity Press, 2011.

Gerrish, B. A. "The Reformation and the Rise of Modern Science: Luther, Calvin and Copernicus." Pages 163–78 in *Calvin and Science*. Edited by Richard C. Gamble. New York: Garland, 1992.

Gibbens, Nicholas. *Questions and Disputations concerning the Holy Scripture*. London: Kyngston, 1601.

Giberson, Karl W., and Francis S. Collins. *The Language of Science and Faith*. Downers Grove, IL: InterVarsity Press, 2011.

Giere, Samuel D. "A New Glimpse of Day One: An Intertextual History of Genesis 1.1–5 in Hebrew and Greek Texts up to 200 CE." PhD diss., The University of St. Andrews, 2007.

———. *A New Glimpse of Day One: Intertextuality, History of Interpretation, and Genesis 1.1–5*. BZNW 172. Berlin: de Gruyter, 2009.

Gillingham, Susan. "Biblical Studies on Holiday? A Personal View of Reception History." Pages 17–30 in *Reception History and Biblical Studies: Theory and Practice*. Edited by Emma England and William John Lyons. London: Bloomsbury, 2015.

Gilson, E. *History of Christian Philosophy in the Middle Ages*. New York: Random House, 1955.

Gordis, Robert. "The Heptad as an Element of Biblical and Rabbinic Style." *Journal of Biblical Literature* 62.1 (1943): 17–26.

Gordon, Bruce. *John Calvin's Institutes of the Christian Religion: A Biography*. Princeton: Princeton University Press, 2016.

Goudriaan, Aza. "Creation, Mosaic Physics, Copernicanism, and Divine Accommodation." Pages 85–141 in *Reformed Orthodoxy and Philosophy, 1625–1750*. Leiden: Brill, 2006.

Gould, Stephen Jay. "Nonoverlapping Magisteria." Pages 269–83 in *Leonardo's Mountain of Clams and the Diet of Worms*. New York: Bantam, 1998.

———. "Nonoverlapping Magisteria: Science and Religion Are Not in Conflict, for Their Teachings Occupy Distinctly Different Domains." *Natural History* 106.3 (1997): 16–22.

———. *Rocks of Ages: Science and Religion in the Fullness of Life*. New York: Ballantine, 1999.

Grafton, A. T. "Joseph Scaliger and Historical Chronology: The Rise and Fall of a Discipline." *History and Theory* 14 (1975): 156–85.

Grant, Edward. *Planets, Stars, and Orbs: The Medieval Cosmos, 1200–1687*. Cambridge: Cambridge University Press, 1996.

Grant, Robert M. *Irenaeus of Lyons*. Early Christian Fathers. London: Routledge, 1997.

Greene-McCreight, K. E. *Ad Litteram: How Augustine, Calvin, and Barth Read the "Plain Sense" of Genesis 1–3*. Issues in Systematic Theology 5. Frankfurt am Main: Lang, 1999.

Greenwood, Kyle R., ed. *Since the Beginning: Interpreting Genesis 1 and 2 through the Ages*. Grand Rapids: Baker Academic, 2018.

Gregersen, Niels Henrik. "Grace in Nature and History: Luther's Doctrine of Creation Revisited." *Dialog: A Journal of Theology* 44.1 (2005): 19–29.

Gregory, Frederick. *Nature Lost? Natural Science and the German Theological Traditions of the Nineteenth Century*. Cambridge: Harvard University Press, 1992.

Gregory of Nazianzus. *Gregory of Nazianzus*. Edited and translated by Brian E. Daley. Early Christian Fathers. London: Routledge, 2006.

Gregory the Great. *Moralia in Iob libri XXIII–XXXV*. Edited by M. Adriaen. CCSL 143B. Turnhout: Brepols, 1985.

Gregory of Nyssa. *In Hexaemeron*. Vol. 1 of *Opera Exegetica in Genesim:*. Edited by Hubertus R. Drobner. Gregorii Nysseni Opera 4.1. Leiden: Brill, 2009.

———. *Über das Sechstagewerk*. Edited by Franz Xavier, Peter Wirth, and Wilhelm Gessel Risch. Stuttgart: Hiersemann, 1999.

Griffith, Sidney. "Syriac/Antiochene Exegesis in Saint Ephrem's Teaching Songs *De Paradiso*: The 'Types of Paradise' in the 'Treasury of Revelations.'" Pages 27–52 in *Syriac and Antiochian Exegesis and Biblical Theology for the 3rd Millennium*. Edited by Robert D. Miller. Piscataway, NJ: Gorgias Press, 2008.

Griggs, Tamara. "Universal History from Counter-Reformation to Enlightenment." *Modern Intellectual History* 4 (2007): 219–47.

Gross, Charlotte. "Twelfth-Century Concepts of Time: Three Reinterpretations of Augustine's Doctrine of Creation Simul." *Journal of the History of Philosophy* 23.3 (1985): 325–38.

Haarsma, Deborah B., and Loren D. Haarsma. *Origins: Christian Perspectives on Creation, Evolution, and Intelligent Design*. 2nd ed. Grand Rapids: Faith Alive, 2011.

Haas, John W. "John Wesley's Views on Science and Christianity: An Examination of the Charge of Antiscience." *Church History* 63.3 (1994): 378–92.

Hagopian, David, ed. *The Genesis Debate: Three Views on the Days of Creation*. Mission Viejo, CA: Crux, 2001.

Hall, Christopher A. *Learning Theology with the Church Fathers*. Downers Grove, IL: InterVarsity Press, 2002.

———. *Reading Scripture with the Church Fathers*. Downers Grove, IL: InterVarsity Press, 1998.

Halley, Edmund. "An Attempt to Find the Age of the World by the Saltness of the Sea." Pages 216–19 in *The Philosophical Transactions (from the Year 1700 to the Year 1720) Abridg'd and Dispos'd under General Heads. Vol. V. containing Part I. The Anatomical and Medical Papers, Part II. The Philological and Miscellaneous Papers*. Edited by Henry Jones. London: Strahan, 1721.

Hallo, W. W., and K. L. Younger, eds. *The Context of Scripture*. 4 vols. Leiden: Brill, 1997–2018.

Halsall, Paul. "Medieval Sourcebook: Twelfth Ecumenical Council: Lateran IV 1215." Internet History Sourcebooks Project. 1996. https://sourcebooks.fordham .edu/halsall/basis/lateran4.asp.

Halton, Charles, ed. *Genesis: History, Fiction, or Neither: Three Views on the Bible's Earliest Chapters.* Grand Rapids: Zondervan, 2015.

Hannam, James. *God's Philosophers: How the Medieval World Laid the Foundations of Modern Science.* London: Icon, 2009.

Hanson, R. P. C. *Allegory and Event: A Study of the Sources and Significance of Origen's Interpretation of Scripture.* London: SCM, 1959.

Harding, E. M. "Origenist Crises." Pages 162–67 in *The SCM Press A-Z of Origen.* Edited by John Anthony McGuckin. London: SCM, 2006.

Harris, Joshua Lee. "Terms of the Divine Art: Aquinas on Creation." Henry Center for Theological Understanding (blog). June 7, 2017. http://henrycenter.tiu .edu/2017/06/terms-of-the-divine-art-aquinas-on-creation/.

Harrison, Nonna Verna, ed. *St. Basil the Great on the Human Condition.* Popular Patristics 30. Crestwood, NY: St Vladimir's Seminary Press, 2005.

Harrison, Peter. *The Bible, Protestantism, and the Rise of Natural Science.* Cambridge: Cambridge University Press, 1998.

———. "'The Book of Nature' and Early Modern Science." Pages 1–26 in *The Book of Nature in Early Modern and Modern History.* Edited by Klaas Van Berkel and Arie Johan Vanderjagt. Leuven: Peeters, 2006.

———. "'Science' and 'Religion': Constructing the Boundaries." *Journal of Religion* 86.1 (2006): 81–106.

Harvey, Susan Ashbrook, and David G. Hunter, eds. *The Oxford Handbook of Early Christian Studies.* Oxford: Oxford University Press, 2008.

Heidel, A. *The Gilgamesh Epic and Old Testament Parallels.* 2nd ed. Chicago: University of Chicago Press, 1949.

Heine, Ronald E. *Reading the Old Testament with the Ancient Church.* Evangelical Ressourcement. Grand Rapids: Baker Academic, 2007.

Henke, Rainer. *Basilius und Ambrosius über das Sechstagewerk: Eine vergleiche Studie.* Chrēsis. Basel: Schwabe, 2000.

Hermans, Albert. "Le pseudo-Barnabé est-il millénariste?" *Ephemerides Theologicae Lovanienses* 35.4 (1959): 849–76.

Hess, Richard S. "God and Origins: Interpreting the Early Chapters of Genesis." Pages 86–98 in *Darwin, Creation and the Fall: Theological Challenges.* Edited by R. J. Berry and T. A. Noble. Downers Grove, IL: InterVarsity Press, 2009.

Hidal, Sten. *Interpretatio Syriaca. Interpretatio Syriaca: Die Kommentare des heiligen Ephräm des Syrers zu Genesis und Exodus mit besonderer Berücksichtigung ihrer auslegungsgeschichtlichen Stellung.* Translated by Christiane Boehncke Sjoberg. Coniectanea Biblica: Old Testament Series 6. Lund: Gleerup, 1974.

Hiestand, Gerald. "'And Behold It Was Very Good': St. Irenaeus' Doctrine of Creation." *Bulletin of Ecclesial Theology* 6.1 (2019): 1–27.

Hilary of Poitiers. *Opera. Part IV: Tractatus Mysteriorum, etc.* Edited by Alfred Feder. CSEL 65. Vienna: Tempsky, 1916.

———. *The Trinity.* Translated by Stephen McKenna. FC 25. Washington, DC: Catholic University of America Press, 1968.

Hilbrands, Walter. "Die Länge der Schöpfungstage. Eine exegetische und rezeptionsgeschichtliche Untersuchung von Yom („Tag") in Gen 1,1–2,3." *Biblische Notizen* 149 (2011): 3–12.

Hildebrand, Stephen M. *Basil of Caesarea.* Foundations of Theological Exegesis and Christian Spirituality. Grand Rapids: Baker Academic, 2014.

———. *The Trinitarian Theology of Basil of Caesarea: A Synthesis of Greek Thought and Biblical Truth.* Washington, DC: Catholic University of America Press, 2007.

Hill, Charles E. *Regnum Caelorum: Patterns of Millennial Thought in Early Christianity.* 2nd ed. Grand Rapids: Eerdmans, 2001.

Hippolytus. *Commentaire sur Daniel.* Translated by M. Lefèvre. SC 14. Paris: Cerf, 1947.

Hoek, A. van den. *Clement of Alexandria and His Use of Philo in the Stromateis.* Leiden: Brill, 1988.

Holladay, William L., ed. *A Concise Hebrew and Aramaic Lexicon of the Old Testament.* Grand Rapids: Eerdmans, 1988.

Holland, Richard A., Jr., and Benjamin K. Forrest. *Good Arguments: Making Your Case in Writing and Public Speaking.* Grand Rapids: Baker Academic, 2017.

Holmes, Michael W., ed. *The Apostolic Fathers.* Rev. ed. Grand Rapids: Baker, 1999.

Holsinger-Friesen, Thomas. *Irenaeus and Genesis: A Study of Competition in Early Christian Hermeneutics.* Journal of Theological Interpretation Supplements 1. Winona Lake, IN: Eisenbrauns, 2009.

Honorius of Autun. "Hexaemeron." PL 172:253–66.

Horbury, William. "Old Testament Interpretation in the Writings of the Church Fathers." Pages 727–87 in *Mikra: Text, Translation, Reading and Interpretation of the Hebrew Bible in Ancient Judaism and Early Christianity.* Edited by Martin Jan Mulder. Assen: Van Gorcum, 1990.

Howard-Snyder, Frances, Daniel Howard-Snyder, and Ryan Wasserman. *The Power of Logic*. 5th ed. New York: McGraw-Hill Education, 2012.

Howell, Kenneth J. "Natural Knowledge and Textual Meaning in Augustine's Interpretation of Genesis: The Three Functions of Natural Philosophy." Pages 1:117–45 in *Nature and Scripture in the Abrahamic Religions: Up to 1700*. Edited by Jitse M. van der Meer, Scott Mandelbrote. Brill's Series in Church History 36. Leiden: Brill, 2008.

Hughes, Jeremy. *Secrets of the Times: Myth and History in Biblical Chronology*. JSOT-Sup 66. Sheffield: Sheffield Academic, 1990.

Hull, Edward. *The Timechart History of the World*. Edited by David Gibbons. Chippenham: Third Millennium, 2016.

Hunt, Rosa Maria. "The Self-Enclosing God: John Chrysostom and Ephrem Syrus on Divine Self-Limitation as Gift of Love in Genesis 1–3." PhD diss., Vrije Universiteit Amsterdam, 2015.

Inwagen, Peter van. "Genesis and Evolution." Pages 93–127 in *Reasoned Faith: Essays in Philosophical Theology*. Edited by Eleonore Stump. Ithaca, NY: Cornell University Press, 1993.

Irenaeus (Bishop of Lyon). *Contre les hérésies*. Edited and translated by Adelin Rousseau, Louis Doutreleau, and Charles A. Mercier. SC 100, 152–53, 210–11, 263–64, 293–94. Paris: Cerf, 1965–1982.

Isidore of Seville. "Chronicon. English Translation." Translated by Kenneth B. Wolf. 2004. http://www.ccel.org/ccel/pearse/morefathers/files/isidore_chronicon _01_trans.htm.

Jacobsen, Anders-Christian. "The Importance of Genesis 1–3 in the Theology of Irenaeus." *ZAC* 8.2 (2004): 299–316.

Jacobsen, Anders Lund. "Genesis 1–3 as Source for the Anthropology of Origen." *VC* 62.3 (2008): 213–32.

Jaki, Stanley. *Genesis 1 through the Ages*. 2nd ed. Royal Oak, MI: Real View, 1998.

John of Damascus. *Writings*. Translated by F. H. Chase. FC 37. Washington, DC: Catholic University of America Press, 1958.

Jones, G. Lloyd. *The Discovery of Hebrew in Tudor England: A Third Language*. Manchester: Manchester University Press, 1983.

Josephus, Flavius. *Jewish Antiquities Books I–IV*. Translated by Henry St J. Thackeray. LCL 242. Cambridge: Harvard University Press, 1995.

———. *Jewish Antiquities Books XVIII–XIX*. Translated and edited by Louis H. Feldman. LCL 433. Cambridge: Harvard University Press, 2000.

Julius Africanus. "Chronica." Pages 2:238–309 in *Reliquiae Sacrae*. Edited by M. J. Routh. Oxford: E Typographeo Academico, 1846.

———. *Chronographiae: The Extant Fragments*. Edited by Martin Wallraff and William Adler. Berlin: de Gruyter, 2007.

Justin Martyr. *Apologiae pro Christianis. Dialogus cum Tryphone*. Edited by Miroslav Marcovich. Patristische Texte und Studien. Berlin: de Gruyter, 2005.

———. *Dialogue with Trypho*. Edited by Michael Slusser. Translated by Thomas B. Falls and Thomas P. Halton. Selections from the Fathers of the Church 3. Washington, DC: Catholic University of America Press, 2003.

Kaiser, Denis. "'He Spake and It Was Done': Luther's Creation Theology and His 1535 Lectures on Genesis 1:1–2:4." *Journal of the Adventist Theological Society* 24.2 (2013): 116–36.

Karamanolis, George. "Gregory of Nyssa." In *Brill Encyclopedia of Early Christianity Online*. Leiden: Brill, 2018. http://dx.doi.org/10.1163/2589-7993_EECO_SIM_00001480.

Kelly, Douglas F. *Creation and Change: Genesis 1.1–2.4 in the Light of Changing Scientific Paradigms*. Fearn: Mentor, 1997.

Kelly, J. N. D. *Golden Mouth: The Story of John Chrysostom – Ascetic, Preacher, Bishop*. Ithaca, NY: Cornell University Press, 1998.

Kim, Yoon Kyung. *Augustine's Changing Interpretations of Genesis 1–3: From De Genesi Contra Manichaeos to De Genesi Ad Litteram*. Lewiston, NY: Edwin Mellen Press, 2006.

Kirkconnell, W., ed. *The Celestial Cycle*. New York: Gordian, 1967.

Kline, Meredith G. "Space and Time in the Genesis Cosmogony." *Perspectives on Science and Christian Faith* 48.1 (1996): 2–15.

Knight, Mark. "Wirkungsgeschichte, Reception History, Reception Theory." *JSNT* 33.2 (2010): 137–46.

Köckert, Charlotte. *Christliche Kosmologie und kaiserzeitliche Philosophie: Die Auslegung des Schöpfungsberichtes bei Origenes, Basilius und Gregor von Nyssa vor dem Hintergrund kaiserzeitlicher Timaeus-Interpretation*. STAC 56. Tübingen: Mohr Siebeck, 2009.

Kreeft, Peter. *Summa of the Summa: The Essential Philosophical Passages of the Summa Theologica*. San Francisco: Ignatius, 1990.

Kretzmann, Norman, and Eleonore Stump, eds. *The Cambridge Companion to Aquinas*. Cambridge: Cambridge University Press, 1993.

Kronholm, T. *Motifs from Genesis I–XI in the Genuine Hymns of Ephrem the Syrian with Particular Reference to the Influence of Jewish Exegetical Tradition.* Coniectanea Biblica Old Testament Series 11. Lund: Gleerup, 1978.

Ku, John Baptist. "Interpreting Genesis 1 with the Fathers of the Church." Thomistic Evolution (blog). http://www.thomisticevolution.org/disputed-questions/interpreting-genesis-1-with-the-fathers-of-the-church/.

Kulikovsky, Andrew. *Creation, Fall, Restoration: A Biblical Theology of Creation.* Fearn: Mentor, 2009.

Lactantius. *Divinae institutiones et Epitome divinarum institutionum.* Edited by Samuel Brandt. CSEL 19. Vienna: Tempsky, 1890.

———. *Divinarum institutionum libri septem.* Edited by Eberhard Heck and Antonie Wlosok. 4 vols. Bibliotheca Scriptorum Graecorum et Romanorum Teubneriana. Berlin: de Gruyter, 2011.

———. *The Divine Institutes. Books I–VII.* Translated by Mary Francis McDonald. FC 49. Washington, DC: Catholic University of America Press, 1955.

Lampe, G. W. H. *Patristic Greek Lexicon.* Oxford: Clarendon, 1961.

Lampe, G. W. H., and K. J. Woollcombe, eds. *Essays on Typology.* London: SCM, 1957.

Landes, Richard Allen. "Lest the Millennium Be Fulfilled: Apocalyptic Expectations and the Pattern of Western Chronography 100–800 CE." Pages 137–211 in *Use and Abuse of Eschatology in the Middle Ages.* Edited by Werner Verbeke, Daniel Verhelst, and Andries Welkenhuysen. Leuven: Leuven University Press, 1988.

Lane, Anthony N. S. *John Calvin: Student of the Church Fathers.* Edinburgh: T&T Clark, 1999.

Lavallee, Louis. "Creeds and the Six Creation Days." *Impact* 235 (1993). http://www.icr.org/article/364/.

Lavery, Jonathan, William Hughes, and Katheryn Doran. *Critical Thinking, Sixth Edition: An Introduction to the Basic Skills.* Peterborough: Broadview, 2009.

Leith, John H. *Assembly at Westminster: Reformed Theology in the Making.* Atlanta: Knox, 1973.

Lennox, John. *Seven Days That Divide the World: The Beginning according to Genesis and Science.* Grand Rapids: Zondervan, 2011.

Letham, Robert. "'In the Space of Six Days': The Days of Creation from Origen to the Westminster Assembly." *WTJ* 61.2 (1999): 149–74.

Lewis, Jack P. "The Days of Creation: An Historical Survey of Interpretation." *JETS* 32 (1989): 433–55.

Lewis, James R. "How Religions Appeal to the Authority of Science." Pages 21–40 in

Handbook of Religion and the Authority of Science. Edited by Olav Hammer and James R. Lewis. Leiden: Brill, 2010.

Lewis, Tayler. *The Six Days of Creation; or, The Scriptural Cosmology, with the Ancient Idea of Time-Worlds, in Distinction from Worlds in Space*. Schenectady, NY: Van Debogert, 1855.

Liddell, H. G., and Robert Scott, eds. *An Intermediate Greek-English Lexicon*. Oxford: Clarendon, 1889.

Lieb, Michael, Emma Mason, and Jonathan Rowland, eds. *The Oxford Handbook of the Reception History of the Bible*. Oxford: Oxford University Press, 2006.

Lim, Richard. "The Politics of Interpretation in Basil of Caesarea's Hexaemeron." *VC* 44 (1990): 351–70.

Limborch, Philipp van. *Theologia Christiana ad praxin pietatis ac promotionem pacis Christianae unice directa*. Amsterdam: Wetstenium, 1686.

Linnaeus, Carl. *Oratio de telluris habitabilis incremento*. Leiden: Haak, 1744.

Livingstone, D. N. "B. B. Warfield, the Theory of Evolution and Early Fundamentalism." *Evangelical Quarterly* 58 (1986): 69–83.

Livingstone, D. N., and Mark Noll. "B. B. Warfield (1851–1921): A Biblical Inerrantist as Evolutionist." *Isis* 91 (2000): 283–304.

Loewenstamm, S. E. "The Seven-Day Unit in Ugaritic Epic Literature." *Israel Exploration Journal* 15 (1965): 122–33.

Lombard, Peter. *The Sentences. Book 2: On Creation*. Translated by Giulio Silano. Mediaeval Sources in Translation 43. Toronto: Pontifical Institute of Mediaeval Studies, 2007.

Loughlin, Stephen J. *Aquinas' Summa Theologiae: A Reader's Guide*. London: T&T Clark, 2010.

Louth, Andrew, ed. *Genesis 1–11*. Ancient Christian Commentary on Scripture. Downers Grove, IL: InterVarsity Press, 2001.

Lovejoy, A. *The Great Chain of Being*. Cambridge: Harvard University Press, 1936.

Luneau, Auguste. *L'histoire du salut chez les pères de l'église: La doctrine des âges du monde*. Paris: Beauchesne, 1964.

Luther, Martin. *Genesisvorlesung*. WA 42.

———. *Lectures on Genesis Chapters 1–5*. Translated by George V. Schick. LW 1.

———. *Luther's Large Catechism*. Edited by Friedemann Hebart. Adelaide: Lutheran Publishing House, 1983.

———. *Sermons on the Gospel of St. John*. LW 22.

———. "A Simple Way to Pray, 1535." LW 43:187–212.

———. "Supputatio annorum mundi." WA 53:1–184.

———. *Über das erste Buch Mose.* WA 24.

———. *What Luther Says: An Anthology.* Edited by Ewald M. Plass. 3 vols. St. Louis: Concordia, 1959.

Maddox, Randy L. "John Wesley's Precedent for Theological Engagement with the Natural Sciences." *Wesleyan Theological Journal* 44.1 (2009): 23–54.

Magruder, K. V. "Theories of the Earth from Descartes to Cuvier: Natural Order and Historical Contingency in a Contested Textual Tradition." PhD diss., University of Oklahoma, 2000.

Malara, Ivan. "Galileo: Creation and Cosmogony. A Study on the Interplay between Galileo's Science of Motion and the Creation Theme." PhD diss., Università degli Studi di Milano/Gent Universiteit, 2019.

Mandelbrote, Scott. "'The Doors Shall Fly Open': Chronology and Biblical Interpretation in England, c. 1630–c. 1730." Pages 176–95 in *The Oxford Handbook of the Bible in Early Modern England, c. 1530–1700.* Edited by Kevin Killeen, Helen Smith, and Rachel Willie. Oxford: Oxford University Press, 2015.

Manetsch, Scott M. "Problems with the Patriarchs: John Calvin's Interpretation of Difficult Passages in Genesis." *WTJ* 67.1 (2005): 1–21.

Mangenot, E. "Hexaméron." *DTC* 6:2325–54.

Mann, Mark H. "Wesley and the Two Books: John Wesley, Natural Philosophy, and Christian Faith." Page 11–30 in *Connecting Faith and Science: Philosophical and Theological Inquiries.* Edited by Matthew Hill and William Curtis Holzen. Claremont, CA: Claremont Press, 2017.

Mansi, Johannes Dominicus, ed. *Sacrorum Conciliorum nova et amplissima Collectio.* Florence: Antonium Zatta, 1759–1798.

Margerie, Bertrand de. *Augustine.* Vol. 3 of *An Introduction to the History of Exegesis.* Petersham, MA: Saint Bede's, 1991.

Markus, R. A. "Marius Victorinus and Augustine." *CHLGEMP*, 331–419.

———. *Saeculum: History and Society in the Theology of St. Augustine.* Cambridge: Cambridge University Press, 1970.

Marmodoro, Anna. "Gregory of Nyssa on the Creation of the World." Pages 94–110 in *Creation and Causation in Late Antiquity.* Edited by Anna Marmodoro and Brian D. Prince. Cambridge: Cambridge University Press, 2015.

Martens, Peter W. "Origen's Doctrine of Pre-Existence and the Opening Chapters of Genesis." *ZAC* 16.3 (2012): 516–49.

―――. "Revisiting the Allegory/Typology Distinction: The Case of Origen." *JECS* 16.3 (2008): 283–317.

Mateo-Seco, Lucas Francisco, and Giulio Maspero, eds. *The Brill Dictionary of Gregory of Nyssa*. Leiden: Brill, 2010.

Mattox, Mickey L. "Faith in Creation: Martin Luther's Sermons on Genesis 1." *Trinity Journal* 39.2 (2018): 199–219.

―――. "Martin Luther: Student of the Creation." Henry Center for Theological Understanding (blog). June 14, 2017. http://henrycenter.tiu.edu/2017/06/martin-luther-student-of-the-creation/.

Maxfield, John A. *Luther's Lectures on Genesis and the Formation of Evangelical Identity*. Sixteenth Century Essays & Studies 80. Kirksville, MO: Truman State University Press, 2008.

―――. "Martin Luther's Swan Song: Luther's Students, Melanchthon, and the Publication of the Lectures on Genesis (1544–1554)." *Lutherjahrbuch* 81 (2014): 224–48.

May, G. *Creatio Ex Nihilo: The Doctrine of Creation out of Nothing in Early Christian Thought*. Edinburgh: T&T Clark, 1995.

Mayeski, Marie A. "Catholic Theology and the History of Exegesis." *Theological Studies* 62.1 (2001): 140–53.

―――. "Early Medieval Exegesis: Gregory I to the Twelfth Century." *AHBI* 2:86–112.

McGinn, Bernard. "Augustine's Attack on Apocalypticism." *Nova et Vetera* 16.3 (2018): 775–96.

―――. "Turning Points in Early Christian Apocalypse Exegesis." Pages 81–105 in *Apocalyptic Thought in Early Christianity*. Edited by Robert J. Daly. Grand Rapids: Baker Academic, 2009.

McInerny, Ralph, ed. *Thomas Aquinas: Selected Writings*. London: Penguin, 1998.

McMullin, Ernan. "Darwin and the Other Christian Tradition." *Zygon: Journal of Religion & Science* 46.2 (2011): 291–316.

McVey, Kathleen. "The Use of Stoic Cosmogony in Theophilus of Antioch's Hexaemeron." Pages 32–58 in *Biblical Hermeneutics in Historical Perspective: Studies in Honor of Karlfried Froehlich on His Sixtieth Birthday*. Edited by Mark S. Burrows and Paul Rorem. Grand Rapids: Eerdmans, 1991.

Meinhold, Peter. *Die Genesisvorlesung Luthers und ihre Herausgeber*. Forschungen zur Kirchen- und Geistesgeschichte 8. Stuttgart: Kohlhammer, 1936.

Mejzner, Mirosław. "Methodius: Millenarist or Anti-Millenarist." Pages 63–84 in

Methodius of Olympus. State of the Art and New Perspectives. Edited by Katharina Bracht. Berlin: de Gruyter, 2017.

Mersenne, Marine. *Quaestiones celeberrimae in Genesim*. Paris: Cramoisy, 1623.

Methodius of Olympus. "De creatis." Pages 491–500 in *Methodius*. Edited by G. Nathanael Bonwetsch. GCS 27. Leipzig: Hinrichs, 1917.

————. *Le Banquet*. Translated by H. Musurillo and V.-H. Debidour. SC 95. Paris: Cerf, 1963.

————. "Symposion." Pages 1–142 in *Methodius*. Edited by G. Nathanael Bonwetsch. GCS 27. Leipzig: Hinrichs, 1917.

————. *The Symposium: A Treatise on Chastity*. Translated by Herbert Musurillo. ACW 27. Westminster, MD: Newman, 1958.

Metzger, B. M., ed. *The Oxford Annotated Apocrypha*. Exp. ed. Oxford: Oxford University Press, 1977.

Meyer, Lester. "Luther in the Garden of Eden: His Commentary on Genesis 1–3." *Word & World* 4.4 (1984): 430–36.

Miles, Sara Joan. "From Being to Becoming: Science and Theology in the Eighteenth Century." *Perspectives on Science and Christian Faith* 43.4 (1991): 215–23.

Mitchell, Margaret M., Frances M. Young, and K. Scott Bowie, eds. *Origins to Constantine*. Vol. 1 of *The Cambridge History of Christianity*. Cambridge: Cambridge University Press, 2006.

Momigliano, Arnaldo. "The Origins of Universal History." Page 133–48 in *The Poet and the Historian: Essays in Literary and Historical Biblical Criticism*. Edited by R. E. Friedman. Chico, CA: Scholars, 1983.

More, Henry. *Conjectura Cabbalistica*. London: Flesher, 1653.

Moreland, J. P., Stephen C. Meyer, Christopher Shaw, Wayne Grudem, and Ann K. Gauger, eds. *Theistic Evolution: A Scientific, Philosophical, and Theological Critique*. Wheaton, IL: Crossway, 2017.

Morris, Henry M. *The Genesis Record: A Scientific and Devotional Commentary on the Book of Beginnings*. Grand Rapids: Baker, 1976.

Mortenson, Terrence J. *The Great Turning Point: The Church's Catastrophic Mistake on Geology – Before Darwin*. Green Forest, AR: Master Books, 2004.

Mortenson, Terry, and Thane H. Ury, eds. *Coming to Grips with Genesis: Biblical Authority and the Age of the Earth*. Green Forest, AR: Master Books, 2008.

Mulder, M. J., ed. *Mikra: Text, Translation, Reading and Interpretation of the Hebrew Bible in Ancient Judaism and Early Christianity*. Assen: Van Gorcum, 1988.

Muller, R. A., and J. L. Thompson, eds. *Biblical Interpretation in the Era of the Reformation: Essays Presented to David C. Steinmetz in Honor of His Sixtieth Birthday.* Grand Rapids: Eerdmans, 1996.

Muller, Richard A. "Reflections on Persistent Whiggism and Its Antidotes in the Study of Sixteenth- and Seventeenth-Century Intellectual History." Pages 134–53 in *Seeing Things Their Way: Intellectual History and the Return of Religion.* Edited by Alister Chapman, John Coffey, and Brad Stephan Gregory. Notre Dame: University of Notre Dame Press, 2009.

Murray, John. "Calvin's Doctrine of Creation." *WTJ* 17 (1954): 21–43.

Napel, E. ten. "Some Remarks on the Hexaemeral Literature in Syriac." Pages 57–69 in *IV Symposium Syriacum 1984: Literary Genres in Syriac Literature (Groningen – Oosterhesselen 10–12 September 1984).* Edited by H. W. J. Drijvers, R. Lavenant, C. Molenburg, and G. J. Reinink. Orientalia Christiana Analecta 229. Rome: Pontificium Institutum Studiorum Orientalium, 1987.

Narsai of Nisibis. "On the Expression, 'In the Beginning,' and Concerning the Existence of God." Pages 203–22 in *Biblical Interpretation.* Edited by J. W. Trigg. Message of the Fathers of the Church 9. Wilmington, DE: Glazier, 1988.

Nassif, Bradley. "Antiochene Θεωρία in John Chrysostom's Exegesis." Pages 49–67 in *Ancient & Postmodern Christianity: Paleo-Orthodoxy in the 21st Century: Essays in Honor of Thomas C. Oden.* Downers Grove, IL: InterVarsity Press, 2002.

———. "Introduction." Pages 1–4 in *The School of Antioch: Biblical Theology and the Church in Syria.* Edited by Vahan S. Hovhanessian. New York: Lang, 2016.

Nelson, Paul, and John Mark Reynolds. "Young Earth Creationism." Pages 39–102 in *Three Views on Creation and Evolution.* Edited by J. P. Moreland and J. M. Reynolds. Grand Rapids: Zondervan, 1999.

Nicholson, Oliver P. "The Source of the Dates in Lactantius' 'Divine Institutes.'" *Journal of Theological Studies* 36.2 (1985): 291–310.

O'Brien, Carl. "St Basil's Explanation of Creation." Pages 194–224 in *The Actuality of St. Basil the Great.* Edited by G. Hällström. Turku: Åbo Akademi University Press, 2011.

Oecolampadius, Johann. *An Exposition of Genesis.* Edited by Mickey Leland Mattox. Reformation Texts with Translation 13. Milwaukee: Marquette University Press, 2013.

Origen. *Contra Celsum.* Translated by Henry Chadwick. Cambridge: Cambridge University Press, 1953.

————. *Homilies on Genesis and Exodus*. Translated by Ronald E. Heine. FC 71. Washington, DC: Catholic University of America Press, 1981.

————. *On First Principles*. Edited by Paul Koetschau. Translated by George William Butterworth. Gloucester, MA: Smith, 1973.

Ortlund, Gavin. *Retrieving Augustine's Doctrine of Creation: Ancient Wisdom for Current Controversy*. Downers Grove, IL: InterVarsity Press, 2020.

————. *Theological Retrieval for Evangelicals: Why We Need Our Past to Have a Future*. Wheaton, IL: Crossway, 2019.

Osborn, Ronald E. *Death before the Fall: Biblical Literalism and the Problem of Animal Suffering*. Downers Grove, IL: IVP Academic, 2014.

Pak, Sujin. "Pre-Modern Readings of Genesis 1, Part 1." BioLogos. October 9, 2012. http://biologos.org/blogs/archive/pre-modern-readings-of-genesis-1-part-1.

Parris, David P. *Reading the Bible with Giants*. London: Paternoster, 2006.

————. *Reception Theory and Biblical Hermeneutics*. Eugene, OR: Pickwick, 2009.

Parsons, Stuart E. *Ancient Apologetic Exegesis: Introducing and Recovering Theophilus's World*. Cambridge: Clarke, 2015.

————. "Coherence, Rhetoric, and Scripture in Theophilus of Antioch's Ad Autolycum." *The Greek Orthodox Theological Review* 53.1–4 (2008): 155–222.

————. "Very Early Trinitarian Expressions." *Tyndale Bulletin* 65.1 (2014): 141–52.

Patrick, Simon. *A Commentary on the First Book of Moses, Called Genesis*. London: Chiswell, 1695.

Patterson, L. G. *Methodius of Olympus: Divine Sovereignty, Human Freedom, and Life in Christ*. Washington, DC: Catholic University Press of America, 1997.

Pererius Valentinus, Benedictus. *Commentariorium et disputationum in Genesim, tomi quatuor, continentes historiam Mosis ab exordio mundi*. Cologne: Hierat, 1601.

Perkins, Harrison. "The Westminster Assembly's Probable Appropriation of James Ussher." *Scottish Bulletin of Evangelical Theology* 37.1 (2019): 45–63.

Perkins, William. *An Exposition of the Symbole or Creed of the Apostles, according to the Tenour of the Scripture, and the Consent of Orthodoxe Fathers of the Church*. Vol. 1 of *The Workes of That Famous and Worthy Minister of Christ, in the Universitie of Cambridge, Mr. William Perkins*. London: Legatt, 1616.

Petavius, Dionysius. "De sex primorum mundi dierum opificio." Pages 4:123–508 in *Dogmata theologica Dionysii Petavii*. Paris: Vivès, 1866.

Petersen, Rodney L. "Reformed Worldviews and the Exegesis of the Apocalypse." Pages 242–59 in *Aspects of Reforming: Theology and Practice in Sixteenth*

Century Europe. Edited by Michael Parsons. Milton Keynes: Authentic Media, 2014.

Philo. *On the Creation of the Cosmos according to Moses*. Edited by David T. Runia. Philo of Alexandria Commentary Series. Leiden: Brill, 2001.

Pierce, Alexander H. "Reconsidering Ambrose's Reception of Basil's Homiliae in Hexaemeron: The Lasting Legacy of Origen." *ZAC* 23.3 (2019): 414–44.

Pipa, J. A., Jr., and D. W. Hall, eds. *Did God Create in Six Days?* 2nd ed. White Hall, WV: Tolle Lege, 2005.

Poole, William. *The World Makers*. Oxford: Lang, 2010.

Popkin, Richard H. *History of Scepticism from Erasmus to Spinoza*. Berkeley: University of California Press, 1979.

———, ed. "The Third Force in Seventeenth-Century Thought: Scepticism, Science and Millenarianism." Pages 90–119 in *The Third Force in Seventeenth-Century Thought*. Leiden: Brill, 1992.

Poythress, Vern S. *Interpreting Eden: A Guide to Faithfully Reading and Understanding Genesis 1–3*. Wheaton, IL: Crossway, 2019.

———. "A Misunderstanding of Calvin's Interpretation of Genesis 1:6–8 and 1:5 and Its Implications for Ideas of Accommodation." *WTJ* 76.1 (2014): 157–66.

Presley, Stephen O. *The Intertextual Reception of Genesis 1–3 in Irenaeus of Lyons*. BAC 8. Leiden: Brill, 2015.

Quasten, J. *Patrology*. Vol. 3 of *The Golden Age of Greek Patristic Literature*. Westminster: Newman, 1960.

Ramm, B. *The Christian View of Science and Scripture*. Exeter: Paternoster, 1955.

Rappaport, Rhoda. *When Geologists Were Historians 1665–1750*. Ithaca, NY: Cornell University Press, 1997.

Rasmussen, Adam. *Genesis and Cosmos: Basil and Origen on Genesis 1 and Cosmology*. BAC 14. Boston: Brill, 2019.

Rau, Gerald. *Mapping the Origins Debate*. Downers Grove, IL: IVP Academic, 2012.

Ray, John. *Three Physico-Theological Discourses*. London: Smith, 1693.

Reimann, Henry W. "Luther on Creation: A Study in Theocentric Theology." *Concordia Theological Monthly* 24.1 (1953): 26–40.

Reventlow, Henning Graf. *The Authority of the Bible and the Rise of the Modern World*. Philadelphia: Fortress, 1985.

Rieger, Reinhold. "Lateran Councils." Pages 7:336–38 in *Religion Past and Present*. Edited by Hans Dieter Betz, Don S. Browning, Bernd Janowski, and Eberhard Jüngel. 4th ed. Leiden: Brill, 2010.

Robbins, F. *The Hexaemeral Literature: A Study of the Greek and Latin Commentaries in Genesis*. Chicago: University of Chicago Press, 1912.

Roberts, Jonathan, and Christopher Rowland. "Introduction." *JSNT* 33.2 (2010): 131–36.

Rogers, J. B., and Donald K. McKim, eds. *The Authority and Interpretation of the Bible: An Historical Approach*. San Francisco: Harper and Row, 1979.

Rogers, Rick. "Theophilus of Antioch." *The Expository Times* 120.5 (2009): 214–24.

Rohls, Jan. *Reformed Confessions: Theology from Zurich to Barmen*. Translated by John Hoffmeyer. Westminster John Knox, 1998.

Rosemann, Philipp W. *Peter Lombard*. Oxford: Oxford University Press, 2004.

Ross, Hugh. *Creation and Time*. Colorado Springs, CO: Navpress, 1994.

————. *The Fingerprint of God: Recent Scientific Discoveries Reveal the Unmistakable Identity of the Creator*. Orange, CA: Promise, 1989.

————. *A Matter of Days: Resolving a Creation Controversy*. Colorado Springs, CO: Navpress, 2004.

Roth, W. M. W. "The Numerical Sequence X/X+1 in the Old Testament." *VT* 12 (1962): 300–311.

Rousseau, O. "La typologie augustinienne de l'Hexaemeron et la théologie du temps." *Maison-Dieu* 65 (1961): 80–95.

Rousseau, Philip. *Basil of Caesarea*. Transformation of the Classical Heritage 20. Berkeley: University of California Press, 1994.

————. "Human Nature and Its Material Setting in Basil of Caesarea's Sermons on the Creation." *Heythrop Journal* 49.2 (2008): 222–39.

Rowland, Beryl. "The Relationship of St. Basil's Hexaemeron to the Physiologus." Pages 489–98 in *Epopée animale, fable, fabliau: Actes du IVe. Colloque de la Société Internationale Renardienne (Evreux, 7–11 Septembre 1981)*. Edited by G. Bianciotto and Michel Salvat. Cahiers d'études Médiévales. Paris: Publications de L'Université de Rouen, 1984.

Rudwick, Martin J. S. *Bursting the Limits of Time: The Reconstruction of Geohistory in the Age of Revolution*. Chicago: University of Chicago Press, 2005.

Runia, David T. *Philo in Early Christian Literature*. Assen: Van Gorcum, 1993.

Rupert of Deutz. *De sancta Trinitate et operibus eius*. Edited by Rhabanus Haacke. 4 vols. Corpus Christianorum Continuatio Mediaevalis 21–24. Turnhout: Brepols, 1971.

Russell, Jeffrey B. *Inventing the Flat Earth*. New York: Praeger, 1991.

Ryken, Leland. "Paradise Lost and Its Biblical Epic Models." Pages 43–81 in *Milton and Scriptural Tradition*. Columbia, MO: University of Missouri Press, 1984.

Saak, Eric Leland. *Luther and the Reformation of the Later Middle Ages*. Cambridge: Cambridge University Press, 2017.

Sandwell, Isabella. "How to Teach Genesis 1:1–19: John Chrysostom and Basil of Caesarea on the Creation of the World." *JECS* 19.4 (2011): 539–64.

Sarfati, Jonathan D. *Refuting Compromise*. Green Forest, AR: Master Books, 2004.

Sarisky, Darren. "Who Can Listen to Sermons on Genesis: Theological Exegesis and Theological Anthropology in Basil of Caesarea's Hexaemeron Homilies." Studia Patristica 67 (2013): 13–24.

Sawyer, John F. A. "The Role of Reception Theory, Reader-Response Criticism and/or Impact History in the Study of the Bible: Definition and Evaluation." Paper presented at the Society of Biblical Literature Annual Meeting, San Antonio, Texas, 2004.

Schaff, Philip. *The Creeds of Christendom*. 3 vols. Grand Rapids: Baker, 1966.

Schieder, Rolf. "Authority. II. History and Theology." Pages 1:519–20 in *Religion Past and Present*. Edited by Hans Dieter Betz, Don S. Browning, Bernd Janowski, and Eberhard Jüngel. 4th ed. Leiden: Brill, 1998.

Schmidt, Roderich. "Aetates Mundi: Die Weltalter als Gliederungsprinzip der Geschichte." *Zeitschrift für Kirchengeschichte* 67.3 (1955): 288–317.

Schofield, Robert E. "John Wesley and Science in 18th Century England." *Isis* 44.4 (1953): 331–40.

Schowalter, Daniel N. "Churches in Context: The Jesus Movement in the Roman World." Pages 388–419 in *The Oxford History of the Biblical World*. Edited by Michael D. Coogan. Oxford: Oxford University Press, 2001.

Schreiner, Susan E. *The Theater of His Glory: Nature and the Natural Order in the Thought of John Calvin*. Grand Rapids: Baker Academic, 2001.

Schwanke, Johannes. "Luther on Creation." *Lutheran Quarterly* 16.4 (2002): 1–20.

———. "Martin Luther's Theology of Creation." *International Journal of Systematic Theology* 18.4 (2016): 399–413.

Schwarte, K.-H. *Die Vorgeschichte der augustinischen Weltalterlehre*. Bonn: Habelt, 1966.

Schwarz, Hans. "Creation." Pages 176–79 in *Dictionary of Luther and the Lutheran Traditions*. Edited by Mark A. Granquist, Mary Jane Haemig, Robert Kolb, Mark C. Mattes, and Jonathan Strom. Grand Rapids: Baker Academic, 2017.

Schweitzer, Cameron. "Finding the Typical in the Literal: Augustine's Typological Exegesis in His Literal Commentary on Genesis." *Puritan Reformed Journal* 13.2 (2021): 35–53.

Scott, Mark. "Origen: Decoding Genesis." Henry Center for Theological Understanding (blog). April 26, 2017. http://henrycenter.tiu.edu/2017/04/origen -decoding-genesis/.

Seely, Paul H. "The First Four Days of Genesis in Concordist Theory and in Biblical Context." *Perspectives on Science and Christian Faith* 49 (1997): 85–95.

Severian of Gabala. "Homilies on Creation and Fall." Pages 1–94 in *Commentaries on Genesis 1–3*. Edited by Robert C. Hill, Michael Glerup, and Gerald L. Bray. Ancient Christian Texts. Downers Grove, IL: InterVarsity Press, 2010.

Simonetti, Manilo. "Allegory-Typology." Pages 86–87 in *Encyclopedia of Ancient Christianity*. Edited by A. di Berardino. Cambridge: Institutum Patristicum Augustinianum, 2014.

———. *Biblical Interpretation in the Early Church: An Historical Introduction to Patristic Exegesis*. Translated by J. A. Hughes. Edinburgh: T&T Clark, 1994.

Skinner, Quentin. "Meaning and Understanding in the History of Ideas." *History and Theory* 8.1 (1969): 3–53.

Smalley, Beryl. *The Study of the Bible in the Middle Ages*. Oxford: Blackwell, 1952.

Smith, Christopher R. "Chiliasm and Recapitulation in the Theology of Ireneus." *VC* 48.4 (1994): 313–31.

Smith, Jonathan Z. "Ages of the World." Pages 1:128–33 in *The Encyclopedia of Religion*. Edited by Mircea Eliade. New York: Macmillan, 1987.

Sorabji, Richard. *Time, Creation, and the Continuum: Theories in Antiquity and the Early Middle Ages*. London: Duckworth, 1983.

Sparks, Kenton L. *God's Word in Human Words: An Evangelical Appropriation of Critical Biblical Scholarship*. Grand Rapids: Baker, 2008.

Stanton, Allen. "William Ames and the Westminster Assembly." *The Confessional Presbyterian* 14 (2018): 51–62.

Stauffer, R. "L'exégèse de Genèse 1/1–3 chez Luther et Calvin." Pages 59–85 in *Interprètes de la Bible: Études sur les réformateurs du XVIe siècle*. Edited by R. Stauffer. Paris: Beauchesne, 1982.

Steenberg, Matthew. *Irenaeus on Creation: The Cosmic Christ and the Saga of Redemption*. VCSup 91. Leiden: Brill, 2008.

Stenmark, Mikael. *How to Relate Science and Religion: A Multidimensional Model*. Grand Rapids: Eerdmans, 2004.

Sterling, E. S. "Philo." Pages 789–93 in *Dictionary of New Testament Background*. Edited by Craig A. Evans and Stanley E. Porter. Downers Grove, IL: Inter-Varsity Press, 2000.

Suarez, Francisco. "Tractatus de opere sex dierum." Pages 3:1–460 in *Francisci Suarez opera omnia*. Edited by D. M. André. Paris: Vivès, 1856.

Swift, Louis J. "Basil and Ambrose on the Six Days of Creation." *Augustinianum* 21.2 (1981): 317–28.

Sytsma, David S. "Calvin, Daneau, and Physica Mosaica: Neglected Continuities at the Origins of an Early Modern Tradition." *Church History and Religious Culture* 95.4 (2015): 457–76.

Tarazi, Paul Nadim. "Exegesis for John Chrysostom: Preaching and Teaching the Bible." Pages 5–17 in *The School of Antioch: Biblical Theology and the Church in Syria*. Edited by Vahan S. Hovhanessian. New York: Lang, 2016.

Tatian and Theophilus of Antioch. *Tatiani Oratio ad Graecos / Theophili Antiocheni ad Autolycum*. Edited by Miroslav Marcovich. Patristische Texte und Studien 43. Berlin: de Gruyter, 1995.

Tertullian. *Contre Marcion*. Translated by René Braun. 3 vols. SC 365, 368, 399. Paris: Cerf, 1994.

Teske, Roland J. "Origen and St Augustine's First Commentary on Genesis." Pages 179–85 in *Origeniana Quinta*. Leuven: Leuven University Press, 1992.

Theodoret of Cyrrhus. *Questions on the Octateuch*. Translated by R. C. Hill. Library of Early Christianity. Washington, DC: Catholic University Press of America, 2006.

Theophilus of Antioch. *Ad Autolycum*. Translated by Robert M. Grant. Oxford: Clarendon, 1970.

Thierry of Chartres. "Tractatus de sex dierum operibus." Pages 553–75 in *Commentaries on Boethius by Thierry of Chartres and His School*. Edited by N. M. Häring. Toronto: Pontifical Institute of Medieval Studies, 1971.

Thompson, John L. *Reading the Bible with the Dead: What You Can Learn from the History of Exegesis That You Can't Learn from Exegesis Alone*. Grand Rapids: Eerdmans, 2007.

Thompson, John, ed. *Genesis 1–11*. RCS 1. Downers Grove, IL: InterVarsity Press, 2012.

Tobin, Thomas H. *The Creation of Man: Philo and the History of Intepretation*. Catholic Biblical Quarterly Monograph Series 14. Washington, DC: Catholic Biblical Association, 1983.

————. "Interpretations of Creation in Philo of Alexandria." Pages 108–28 in *Creation in the Biblical Traditions*. Edited by Richard J. Clifford and John J. Collins. Washington, DC: Catholic Biblical Association of America, 1992.

Trigg, Joseph Wilson, ed. *Biblical Interpretation*. Message of the Fathers of the Church 9. Wilmington, DE: Glazier, 1988.

————. "Introduction." Pages i–xxv in *Allegory and Event: A Study of the Sources and Significance of Origen's Interpretation of Scripture*. Louisville: Westminster John Knox, 2002.

Trompf, Garry W. *The Idea of Historical Recurrence in Western Thought: From Antiquity to the Reformation*. Berkeley: University of California Press, 1979.

Trueman, Carl R. *Histories and Fallacies: Problems Faced in the Writing of History*. Wheaton, IL: Crossway, 2010.

Ussher, James. *The Annals of the Old Testament. From the Beginning of the World*. London: Tyler, 1658.

Vaccari, Ezio. "European Views on Terrestrial Chronology from Descartes to the Mid-Eighteenth Century." Pages 25–38 in *The Age of the Earth from 4004 BC to AD 2002*. Edited by C. L. E. Lewis and Simon J. Knell. GS Special Publications 190. London: Geological Society, 2001.

Van Bebber, Mark, and Paul S. Taylor. *Creation and Time: A Report on the Progressive Creationist Book by Hugh Ross*. Mesa, AZ: Eden Productions, 1994.

Van Fleteren, Frederick. "Principles of Augustine's Hermeneutic: An Overview." Pages 1–32 in *Augustine: Biblical Exegete*. Edited by Frederick Van Fleteren and Joseph C. Schnaubelt. New York: Lang, 2001.

Van Fleteren, Frederick, and Joseph C. Schnaubelt, eds. *Augustine: "Second Founder of the Faith."* Collectanea Augustiniana. New York: Lang, 1990.

Van Seters, John. "Creative Imitation in the Hebrew Bible." *Studies in Religion/Sciences Religieuses* 29.4 (2000): 395–409.

————. *Studies in the History, Literature and Religion of Biblical Israel*. Vol. 1 of *Changing Perspectives*. New York: Routledge, 2014.

Van Til, H. J. "Basil, Augustine and the Doctrine of Creation's Functional Integrity." *Science & Christian Belief* 8 (1996): 21–38.

Vannier, M. A. "Le rôle de l'hexaéméron dans l'interprétation augustinienne de la création." *Revue des Sciences philosophiques et theologiques* 71.4 (1987): 537–47.

Velde, Roelf Theodoor te. "'Soberly and Skillfully': John Calvin and Jerome Zanchi (1516–1590) as Proponents of Reformed Doctrine." *Church History and Religious Culture* 91.1–2 (2011): 59–71.

Vermes, Geza. *The Complete Dead Sea Scrolls in English*. London: Penguin, 2004.

Victorinus of Petau. "De fabrica mundi." Pages 3–9 in *Victorini Episcopi Petavionensis opera*. Edited by Johannes Haussleiter. CSEL 49. Vienna: Tempsky, 1916.

———. "A Fragment on the Creation of the World." Pages 388–93 in *The Writings of Quintus Sept. Flor. Tertullianus: Vol. 3, with the Extant Works of Victorianus and Commodianus*, Ante-Nicene Christian Library 18. Translated by Robert Ernest Wallis. Edinburgh: T&T Clark, 1870.

Wallraff, Martin. "The Beginnings of Christian Universal History. From Tatian to Julius Africanus." *ZAC* 14.3 (2011): 540–55.

Walton, John H. *The Lost World of Genesis One: Ancient Cosmology and the Origins Debate*. Downers Grove, IL: IVP Academic, 2009.

Walton, Michael T. "Genesis and Chemistry in the Sixteenth Century." Pages 1–14 in *Reading the Book of Nature: The Other Side of the Scientific Revolution*. Edited by Allen G. Debus and Michael Thomson Walton. Kirksville, MO: Truman State University Press, 1998.

———. *Genesis and the Chemical Philosophy: True Christian Science in the Sixteenth and Seventeenth Centuries*. Brooklyn: AMS Press, 2011.

Ward, Rowland S. *A Short Introduction to the Westminster Assembly and Its Work*. 2nd ed. Lansvale: Tulip, 2019.

Warfield, B. B. "Calvin's Doctrine of the Creation." Pages 287–349 in *Calvin and Calvinism*. Oxford: Oxford University Press, 1931.

———. "Calvin's Doctrine of the Creation." *Princeton Theological Review* 13 (1915): 190–255.

Webber, Robert. *Ancient-Future Faith*. Grand Rapids: Baker, 1999.

Webster, Charles. *From Paracelsus to Newton: Magic and the Making of Modern Science*. Cambridge: Cambridge University Press, 1982.

Webster, John. "Theologies of Retrieval." Pages 549–95 in *The Oxford Handbook to Systematic Theology*. Edited by John Webster, Kathryn Tanner, and Iain Torrance. Oxford: Oxford University Press, 2008.

Weinfeld, Moshe. "Sabbath, Temple, and the Enthronement of the Lord: The Problem of the Sitz im Leben of Genesis 1:1–2:3." Pages 501–12 in *Melanges bibliques et orientaux en l'honneur de M. Henri Cazelles*, edited by André Caquot and Mathias Delcor, 501–12. Kevelaer: Butzon and Bercker, 1981.

Welker, M. "Creation, Big Bang or the Work of Seven Days?" *Theology Today* 52.27 (1995): 173–87.

Wesley, John. *Explanatory Notes on the Old Testament*. 3 vols. Bristol: Pine, 1765.

————. *A Survey of the Wisdom of God in the Creation: Or a Compendium of Natural Philosophy*. 2 vols. Bristol: Pine, 1763.

Wessinger, Catherine, ed. *The Oxford Handbook of Millennialism*. Oxford: Oxford University Press, 2016.

West, David, Tony Woodman, and Anthony John Woodman, eds. *Creative Imitation and Latin Literature*. Cambridge: Cambridge University Press, 1979.

Westerholm, Stephen, and Martin Westerholm. *Reading Sacred Scripture: Voices from the History of Biblical Interpretation*. Grand Rapids: Eerdmans, 2016.

Wevers, John W., ed. *Genesis*. Septuaginta Vetus Testamentum Graecum 1. Göttingen: Vandenhoeck & Ruprecht, 1974.

White, Andrew Dickson. *A History of the Warfare of Science with Theology in Christendom*. 2 vols. New York: Appleton, 1896.

Whitford, David M. *Luther: A Guide for the Perplexed*. London: T&T Clark, 2011.

Wickes, Jeffrey. "Ephrem's Interpretation of Genesis." *St. Vladimir's Theological Quarterly* 52.1 (2008): 45–65.

Wikenhauser, A. "Weltwoche und tausendjähriges Reich." *Theologische Quartalschrift* 127 (1947): 399–417.

Williams, Arnold Ledgerwood. *The Common Expositor: An Account of the Commentaries on Genesis 1527–1633*. Chapel Hill: University of North Carolina Press, 1948.

Williams, Daniel. H. *Evangelicals and Tradition: The Formative Influence of the Early Church*. Evangelical Ressourcement. Grand Rapids: Baker Academic, 2005.

————. *Retrieving the Tradition and Renewing Evangelicalism: A Primer for Suspicious Protestants*. Grand Rapids: Eerdmans, 1999.

————. *Tradition, Scripture, and Interpretation: A Sourcebook of the Ancient Church*. Grand Rapids: Baker Academic, 2006.

Williams, Rowan. "Creation." *ATTA*, 251–54.

Williams, Thomas. "Biblical Interpretation." Pages 59–70 in *The Cambridge Companion to Augustine*. Edited by David Vincent Meconi and Eleonore Stump. Cambridge: Cambridge University Press, 2001.

Wilson, Daniel J. "Lovejoy's the Great Chain of Being after Fifty Years." *Journal of the History of Ideas* 48.2 (1987): 187–206.

Winden, J. C. M. van. "Hexaemeron." *RAC* 14:1250–69.

Woodbridge, John D. *Biblical Authority: A Critique of the Rogers/McKim Proposal*. Grand Rapids: Zondervan, 1982.

Wright, David F. "Accommodation and Barbarity in John Calvin's Old Testament Commentaries." Pages 413–27 in *Understanding Poets and Prophets: Essays in Honour of G. W. Anderson*. Edited by Graeme Auld. Sheffield: Sheffield University Press, 1993.

———. "Calvin's Accommodating God." Pages 3–20 in *Calvinus Sincerioris Religionis Vindex: Calvin as Protector of the Purer Religion*. Edited by Wilhelm Neuser and Brian Armstrong. Kirksville, MO: Sixteenth Century Journal Pub, 1997.

Yarchin, W. *A History of Biblical Interpretation: A Reader*. Peabody, MA: Hendrickson, 2004.

Young, Davis A. *John Calvin and the Natural World*. Lanham, MD: University Press of America, 2007.

Young, Davis A., and Ralph Stearley. *The Bible, Rocks and Time: Geological Evidence for the Age of the Earth*. Downers Grove, IL: InterVarsity Press, 2008.

Young, Frances M. *Biblical Exegesis and the Formation of Christian Culture*. Cambridge: Cambridge University Press, 1997.

———. *Exegesis and Theology in Early Christianity*. Farnham: Ashgate, 2012.

Zachman, Randall C. "Calvin as Commentator on Genesis." Pages 53–84 in *Calvin and the Bible*. Edited by Donald K. McKim. Cambridge: Cambridge University Press, 2006.

———. *Reconsidering John Calvin*. Cambridge: Cambridge University Press, 2012.

Zahlten, Johannes. *Creatio Mundi: Darstellungen der sechs Schöpfungstage und naturwissenschaftliches Weltbild im Mittelalter*. Geschichte und Politik 13. Stuttgart: Klett-Cotta, 1979.

Zanchi, Girolamo. *De operibus Dei intra spacium sex dierum creatis opus*. Neustadt: Harnisii, 1591.

———. *De religione Christiana fides*. Neustadt Palatinorum: Harnisius, 1601.

———. *De religione Christiana fides – Confession of Christian Religion*. Edited by Luca Baschera and Christian Moser. 2 vols. Leiden: Brill, 2007.

———. *H. Zanchius, His Confession of Christian Religion*. Cambridge: Legat, 1599.

Zaspel, Fred G. "B. B. Warfield on Creation and Evolution." *Themelios* 35 (2010): 198–211.

Zincone, S. "Hexaemeron." Page 1:380 in *Encyclopedia of the Early Church*. Edited by A. di Berardino, translated by Adrian Walford. Cambridge: Clarke, 1993.

Zöckler, Otto. "Creation and Preservation of the World." Pages 3:298–304 in *The*

New Schaff-Herzog Encyclopedia of Religious Knowledge. Edited by Samuel Macauley Jackson. Grand Rapids: Baker, 1963.

————. *Geschichte der Beziehungen zwischen Theologie und Naturwissenschaft: Mit besonderer Rücksicht auf Schöpfungsgeschichte.* 2 vols. Gütersloh: Bertelsmann, 1877–79.

Zuiddam, Benno. "Does Genesis Allow Any Scientific Theory of Origin?—A Response to JP Dickson." *Journal of Creation* 26.1 (2012): 106–15.

Index of Authors

Index of Subjects

Abelard, Peter, 179, 190, 192, 201; *Yes and No (Sic et non)*, 192

Abraham, 29, 32n26, 67, 73, 89, 92, 95, 98; Abrahamic covenant, 88

accommodation, divine, 125, 163, 169–70, 171, 196, 227, 229, 238, 242–44, 249–51, 261

Adam, 32, 62, 65, 70, 72, 73, 81, 89, 92, 96, 115, 173, 174, 180, 181, 227, 228, 229, 237

adornment (*ornatio*), 65, 111, 156, 187, 188, 196, 209, 245

Africa, 89, 91, 161, 163

age of the earth/world, 42, 65, 83, 86, 89, 94–95, 147, 180–82, 185, 188, 189, 198, 220–21, 225, 228, 235–36, 246–47, 275, 276; world grown old (*senectus mundi*), 95, 98, 223–24, 235. *See also* chronology, biblical or world

age(s) of the world. *See* history, historiography: periodization of; world-week historical typology (or ages of the world)

air, element of, 35, 134, 187, 202, 262

Albert the Great, 190, 199

Alcuin of York, 193

Alexandria, Egypt, 24, 29, 38, 39, 43, 44, 49, 72, 119

Alexandrians, Alexandrian biblical interpretation, 50, 51, 73, 76, 103–6, 114, 116, 119, 281

Ambrose, patron of Origen, 43

Ambrose of Milan, 43, 51, 52, 119, 129, 137, 142, 145, 150, 151–58, 162, 166, 167, 179, 189, 203, 233, 242, 266, 281; *Hexameron*, 142, 150, 152–58, 179

Ames, William, 264, 265, 266; *Medulla theologica/Marrow of Theology*, 264, 265, 266

anachronism, 113, 198, 220, 278, 282

ancient Near East: cosmology, 244; literature, 24, 251

angels, 17, 45, 48, 63, 134, 168–72, 180–82, 189, 194, 200, 203, 207, 208, 209, 225, 226, 227, 228, 243; angelic history and fall prior to human creation, 181, 228, 231, 270; Augustine's theory of angelic knowledge of creation, 165, 167, 169–71, 175, 177, 182, 190, 197, 209, 225

animals, 17, 26, 36, 80, 115, 133, 136, 137, 138, 146, 148, 171, 173, 174, 183, 187, 203, 209, 212, 253, 254, 275

bates, 4, 8, 14, 19, 231, 233, 234, 245, 258, 269, 275, 281; sociology of, 10–11

Autolycus, 107, 108, 110

Babington, Gervase, 246

Babylon, 92, 95, 181

Bacon, Francis, 256; *New Atlantis*, 256; *New Organon*, 256

baptism, 49, 152, 162

Bardesanes (Bardaisan), 115, 118

Bar Kokhba rebellion, 38, 61

Basil (the Great) of Caesarea, 1, 50, 106, 107, 115, 118, 119, 122, 125–26, 127–58, 162, 168, 179, 184, 187, 188, 189, 197, 204, 205, 226, 227, 233, 242; *Homilies on the Hexaemeron*, 115, 126, 128–48, 150, 151–54, 168; *Homilies on the Psalms*, 135; *Philocalia*, 46, 134, 135n27

Bede, the Venerable, 74, 100, 186–89, 193, 194, 196, 223; *On Times*, 74, 100

beginning of the world, time, creation, etc., 28, 33, 48, 52, 57–58, 106, 114, 118, 121, 140–42, 144, 145, 148, 154, 156, 175, 176, 177, 200–201, 205–6, 228, 254, 261, 263, 286. *See also* Christ, Jesus: as the "beginning"

biblical studies, 12, 13, 16, 150

biology, 159, 173, 177, 282

birds, 26, 115, 132, 146, 174, 207, 253

bishop, role of, 38, 63n34, 69, 76, 78, 107, 120, 127, 129, 134, 151–52, 162, 166, 191, 246, 264

Bonaventure, 213, 261–62; *Collations on the Six Days*, 213

Bossuet, Jacques-Bénigne, 100

Brocardus, Jacob, 221, 268n37

Browne, Sir Thomas, 240

Budde, J. F., 151; *Elementa Philosophiae Theoretica*, 151

Buffon, Louis de, 101, 273; *Les Époques de la Nature*, 101, 273; *Theorie de la Terre*, 273

Burnet, Thomas, 100–101, 272–73, 274n64; *Sacred Theory of the Earth*, 101

Byzantine culture, history, persons, 44, 72, 81, 148

Caesarea in Cappadocia, 127

Caesarea Palestina, 39, 43, 49

Cajetan, Tommaso de Vio, 179, 222, 239, 259

Calvin, John, 1–2, 5, 6, 10, 18, 125, 178, 183, 215, 225n38, 231–57, 258–62, 263n18, 264–69, 275, 277; *Commentary on Genesis*, 232, 237–38, 242–44, 253, 254, 255, 261, 264, 265; *Institutes of the Christian Religion*, 232, 234, 236–37, 241–42, 245, 253, 254, 261, 264, 265; *Sermons on Genesis*, 232, 238

Capito, Wolfgang, 259

Cappadocia, 127

Cappadocian fathers, 50, 120, 127, 145, 152, 168, 228, 270

Cartesianism, 273

Carthage, 76, 161

Cassian, John, 137

cathedral schools: Chartres, 192; Notre Dame, 191

Catholic(ism), Catholic scholarship, 2, 15, 163, 164, 186, 193, 200, 259, 270

cause, causation, 115, 141, 156, 158, 169, 173, 174, 188, 205, 220, 225, 254, 272, 273, 278; God as First Cause, 205, 220, 225, 254; secondary causes, 220, 254

celestial bodies or realm. *See* heaven(s), sky

chaos, primordial, 270, 272

chiliasm. *See* millennium, millenarian(ism)

Christ, Jesus, 4, 28, 32, 35, 44, 45, 58, 59, 61, 63, 66, 70, 71, 77, 94, 138, 151, 162, 176, 213, 224, 229, 285; advent, or arrival of, 70, 71, 72, 73, 74, 85, 88, 92, 95, 100n99, 224; as the "beginning," 141,

days," in literal exposition of Gen. 1, 83,
238, 242, 260–66, 269; as twenty-four
hours long, 115, 116, 130, 142–43, 145,
147, 155–58, 168, 188, 193, 195, 202, 209,
211–12, 229, 245, 265. *See also* sun, the:
days before the; sun, the: light before
the
Decius, 43, 44, 75
"deep time," 42, 100, 147, 228, 266, 276
Demetrius, bishop of Alexandria, 38, 39
Denis of Petau (Petavius), 259
Derham, William, 277
Descartes, René, 272, 273; *The World (Le
Monde)*, 272
development in nature, 150, 158, 173,
175, 212, 228, 241, 255, 271, 282. *See also*
potential or propensity for further
development in creation
devil (or Satan) and demons, 45, 55n6,
270
Diderot, Denis, *Encyclopédie*, 271
Didymus the Blind, 50, 152
Diocletian (r. 284–305), 75, 82; and persecution, 75, 76, 82, 85n32, 87
Diodore of Tarsus, 106, 135, 162
distinction or differentiation, as work of
creation days one–three. *See* creation
week, general: "forming and filling"
(or distinction/differentiation and ornamentation) schema
divine action in the world, 182, 214, 220,
241
Dominican order, 199, 206, 270
Du Bartas, Guillaume de Salluste, 270; *La
Sepmaine, ou Creation*, 270

earth: as a globe, 186, 246; history of,
100, 212, 228; as one of the classical
four elements, 131, 202, 262. *See also*
flat-earth belief; old earth; young-earth
(or young world) concepts, young-earth
creationism

Eastern Roman Empire, 38, 82, 120. *See
also* Byzantine culture, history, persons;
Rome, Roman Empire, Roman administration, Roman culture
Eden, Eden narrative, 36, 41n55, 47–48,
62, 115, 117, 165, 166, 170, 173, 226, 276
Edessa, 113, 114
education, educator, 49, 50, 82, 108, 122,
126, 128, 129, 133, 134, 141, 150, 151, 160,
161, 191, 264
Egypt, Egyptian, 24, 39, 43, 44, 50, 97,
181; captivity in, 234. *See also* exodus of
Israel from Egypt
eighth day of eternity, 58, 92, 94, 117, 144,
157
elements, material, esp. in four-element
theory, 31, 50, 51, 80, 118, 129, 131, 141,
147, 150, 155–56, 187, 202, 203, 262
Eleutherus, 64
emanation, emanationism, 45, 134, 203,
207
emperor worship, 61, 75
empirical approach, empiricism, 8–9, 170,
188, 242, 250, 267, 269
English translations or editions, 16, 62,
64, 87, 120, 141, 144, 149, 180, 185, 193,
219, 232, 237n22, 255, 262, 263, 264, 265,
272, 275n66
Enlightenment, 15, 186, 271, 286
Ephrem the Syrian, 106, 107, 113–19, 120;
Commentary on Genesis, 114–16, 119;
Hymns on Paradise, 117; *Hymns on the
Nativity*, 117–18
Epicureanism, 182, 228, 272
Epiphanius of Salamis, 44, 135, 167;
Panarion, 135
Episcopius, Simon, 228
epistemology, 241, 252. *See also* knowledge
eschatology, 28, 30, 41, 53, 58, 64, 66,
68–69, 71, 83, 86, 87, 89, 92, 106,
137, 157, 224. *See also* millennium,
millenarian(ism)

eternal, world as, 156, 158, 197, 203, 205, 225, 228

eternal realm. *See* ideal, intelligible, or no-etic world/realm or its "ideas" (intellectual models of things in Platonic sense)

eternity, eternal future, 51, 58, 66, 88, 92, 93, 94, 117, 144–45, 147, 157, 166, 235, 238; eternity of God, 142, 147, 166, 168, 200, 208, 213, 261; eternity of the world plan or its idea(s), 52, 171, 173

Europe(an), 15, 185, 186, 190, 199, 213, 224, 255, 260, 271, 273

Eusebius of Caesarea, 27, 38, 43, 72, 73–74, 76, 84, 85n32, 94–95, 99, 100, 107; *Ecclesiastical History*, 38, 43, 73, 107; Eusebian chronology of history, 73–74, 94–95, 99, 100

Eustathius. *See* Pseudo-Eustathius

Evagrius of Pontus, 44

evangelical churches, Christianity, scholarship, 2–3, 4, 7, 193, 197n43, 286

Evangelical Presbyterian Church, 261

Eve, 173, 174, 180, 227, 228, 229

evening, 47, 92, 98, 116, 123, 142, 143, 163, 164, 170, 176, 209, 212, 226, 245, 275

evil, 55n6, 83, 111, 207, 218, 270, 275

evolution, evolutionism, 7, 124, 159, 185, 212, 253–55, 274, 277, 282; theistic, 124, 159, 212

exegesis, biblical, 3, 12, 47, 50, 64, 89, 134, 136, 140, 141, 142, 152, 153, 162, 163, 178, 179, 190, 197, 211, 213, 216, 228, 232, 237n22, 244, 248, 256, 271, 281–82. *See also* interpretation, biblical (biblical meaning)

exile: Jewish, in Babylon, 95, 97; as punishment, 51, 120

existence: as contingent, 205, 210; of God, 166, 213, 278; personal, 219, 241; on a spiritual plane, 73, 84; of the visible cosmos, 34–35, 104, 142, 155, 205, 213, 219, 223

exodus of Israel from Egypt, 85n35, 97

exposition, expository, 70, 109, 111, 112, 114, 119, 121, 122, 128, 145, 148, 154, 162, 165, 184, 196, 213, 224, 232, 253, 259. *See also* commentary

Ezekiel, 62, 63

Fall, the, 66, 231, 241, 275; through Adam's action of eating fruit, 62, 65, 96

Ficino, Marsilio, 268

Fifth Ecumenical Council, in Constantinople (553 CE), 44

fire, element of, 115, 150, 202, 224, 262

"firmament" (*'rāqia'*) or expanse, created on second day, 35, 36, 47, 51, 116, 131, 174, 175, 187, 208, 244

fish and other sea creatures, 32, 80, 131, 133, 137, 138, 146, 207, 253, 254

flat-earth belief, 86, 116

flood (Genesis), 1, 25–26, 28, 92, 221, 246, 247, 273, 275, 276, 277

forms of created entities (in hylomorphic theory), 33, 35, 36, 52, 103, 111, 165, 170, 187, 194, 195, 212, 254; realized in material objects and beings, 34, 36, 180, 195, 212. *See* matter and the material elements

fossils, 116, 269, 277

Fourth Lateran Council, 191, 200

framework hypothesis, 20, 33, 34, 37, 170, 171, 182, 185, 188, 198, 204, 240, 243, 251

Galileo, Galilei, 1, 5, 8

gap (or ruin-restitution) theory, 20, 286

genealogy, genealogies, biblical, 28, 95, 97, 234

"generative principles," Augustinian (or stoic) concept, 149n85, 168, 172–74, 177, 180, 188, 203, 212

Genesis and science. *See* science and religion/theology/Christianity/Bible/Scripture/Genesis

Index of Subjects

Hilary of Poitiers, 51–52, 87–88, 94, 97, 153, 225, 229; *Commentary on Matthew*, 87–88; *On the Trinity*, 51; *Tractatus Mysteriorum*, 87

Hippo, North Africa, 165, 166

Hippolytus of Rome, 69–72, 73, 84, 96–97, 99, 108, 129, 162; *Chronicon*, 72, 96; *Commentary on Daniel*, 69–71

historical theology, 12, 13, 16

history, historiography, 2, 11–12, 16–20, 21, 27, 38, 53, 59, 64, 68, 73, 76, 80, 85, 88, 90, 91, 124, 145, 175, 176, 178, 180, 185, 222, 224, 256, 282–85; biblical, 29, 73, 85, 104, 246; consciousness of, 125, 168; dispensational schemas, 27, 90, 97, 101; historical distance or foreignness, 6, 18, 40, 42, 124, 147; human, 53, 55, 67, 102, 158, 227; natural, 246, 273, 274, 278; periodization of, 55, 57, 63, 66, 70–71, 85, 86, 88, 97–98, 99–102; philosophy of, 83, 90, 145; prehuman, 54, 67, 81, 102, 181–82, 212, 270; theology of, 66, 87, 90, 91, 99, 101–2; triumphalist (or "Whiggish"), 17, 233; universal, 68, 256, 271. *See also* chronology, biblical or world; church history; context: historical; earth: history of; redemption history; world-week historical typology (or ages of the world)

history of ideas, 16–17, 282

Holy Spirit (or Holy Ghost), 30, 45, 104, 123, 133–34, 176, 200, 214, 226–27, 229, 243, 252, 253, 261

Holy Week, 152, 162. *See also* Lent, Christian festival

Homer, 133

homily. *See* preaching; sermon, homily

Honorius of Autun (Augustodunesis), 190, 196, 201; *Hexaemeron*, 196

Hugh of St. Victor, 192, 193, 195, 196, 214n114; *On the Sacraments of the Christian Faith*, 192

humanity: creation of, 28, 35, 47, 110, 112, 115, 132, 148, 162, 173, 174, 180, 181, 194, 200, 203, 208, 217, 218–19, 234; as embodied, 81, 200, 218; as fallen, 99, 170; human life, 9, 47, 98, 131, 132, 137, 154, 213–14, 217, 218–19; as image of God, 28, 35, 79, 165; as individually created, 214, 218, 219, 223, 240; senses of, physical, 34, 103, 218, 226, 236; theology of (anthropology), 44, 64, 83–84, 161, 194, 208. *See also* rational powers; reason(ing), human; soul, human

hymns, songs, 113, 114, 116–18; *Madrashē*, Syriac hymn form, 117

ideal, intelligible, or noetic world/realm or its "ideas" (intellectual models of things in Platonic sense), 33, 34–37, 40–41, 46–47, 49, 52, 103, 111, 131, 142, 147, 165, 168, 170, 173, 175, 182, 187, 194, 197

intellectual: context, culture, climate, 6, 17, 18, 20, 22, 24, 32, 34, 37, 39, 42, 44, 87, 101, 108, 199, 214, 260, 284; intellectual history, 16–18, 20, 21, 177, 185, 266, 269

intellectuals, 115, 130, 150, 160, 161, 228, 243, 250

intelligible world. *See* ideal, intelligible, or noetic world/realm or its "ideas" (intellectual models of things in Platonic sense)

intention, communicative, in a text, 18, 30, 138, 282–83, 284

interpretation, biblical (biblical meaning), 3, 11, 12, 16, 22, 44, 49–50, 78, 89, 90, 97, 160, 166, 167, 178, 230; allegorical, 30, 31–32, 38, 50, 79, 104–6, 112, 114, 118, 119, 132–39, 143, 150, 152, 153, 154, 157, 162, 164, 176, 193, 222, 226, 227, 229, 239, 257; anagogical, 137; analogical, 164; christological, 41, 51, 103, 139, 177, 229; figurative, 31n25, 32, 47–48, 97, 101, 103–6, 118, 137, 138, 164, 165, 176, 179, 196, 240; Jewish, 20n53, 59, 138;

335

143, 145, 147, 148, 149, 150, 154, 166, 172,
177, 178, 180, 184, 197, 199, 204, 205, 206,
208, 210, 212, 213, 225, 230, 255, 256, 257,
267, 272, 283, 285; Greek, 39, 109, 133;
Hellenistic, 24, 30; history of, 12, 16, 21,
149; natural or physical, 21, 49, 129–30,
133, 134, 137, 140, 177, 178, 236, 249–50,
256, 270, 272–74, 275, 277, 278, 283, 284.
See also Aristotelianism or Aristotelian
philosophy; history, historiography:
philosophy of; Mosaic physics or philosophy; Plato, Platonism, Neoplatonism;
Pythagorean philosophy; stoicism
Photius, 81
physical world, sphere, form, 6, 7, 31, 33,
34–36, 39, 45, 46, 47, 49, 52, 66, 67,
76, 81, 91, 103–4, 116, 125, 128, 129, 130,
131, 136, 139, 142, 145, 147, 150, 157, 165,
168, 170, 173, 175, 180, 185, 188, 195, 196,
200, 204, 206, 209, 213, 220, 227, 241,
243, 247, 252, 256, 272, 274, 275, 285; as
visible, 34, 40, 49, 101, 175, 176, 207. *See
also* creation, doctrine or theology of:
visible or invisible aspects of
Physiologus, 138
plan, divine, 52, 53, 55, 166, 171, 175
planet(s), 31, 56, 112, 243n41. *See also*
star(s)
plants, 17, 36, 131, 133, 136, 137, 146, 148,
155, 172, 174, 203, 209, 212. *See also*
vegetation, creation of
Plato, Platonism, Neoplatonism, 34–35,
36, 37, 40, 42, 44, 49, 52, 78, 104, 129,
134, 144, 162, 165, 168, 170, 173, 177, 184,
192, 199, 203, 207n91, 214, 240, 244,
268–69; *Symposium,* 78; *Timaeus,* 129
poetry, 113, 114, 116, 118, 256, 270
politics, 31, 76, 81, 82, 120, 151, 260,
283–84; church politics, 44, 120, 127
polytheism, 44, 91, 108, 109, 111
potential or propensity for further development in creation, 174, 175, 180, 212,

217, 254–55, 272. *See also* development
in nature
power of God, 33, 40, 52, 80, 92, 111, 123,
124, 146, 165, 168, 200, 202, 214, 220,
229, 237, 241, 253, 263, 285; "power,
wisdom and goodness of God," 242, 261,
275–76, 278
praise of God, 92, 117, 118, 137, 170, 175,
219, 245. *See also* worship of God
preaching, 49, 120, 121, 128, 129, 153, 162,
167, 216, 238. *See also* sermon
Presbyterian Church in America, 260n9
Presbyterian Church USA, 260n9
Presbyterians and Presbyterianism, 2, 253,
255, 260–61, 265, 274, 275
priest, priesthood, 2, 39, 43n67, 121, 152,
154, 165
process, creation as, 41, 80, 123, 182, 184;
atemporal, 103, 157–58, 166; involving
development or growth, 202, 214,
219–20, 229, 240–41, 272; within a
literal creation week, 219, 229, 237, 242
prooftexting. *See* "recruitment" of ancient
biblical interpreters: prooftexting of
such figures
prophecy, in Scripture, 107, 109, 111
prose, 116
Protestants and Protestantism, 2, 177, 178,
186, 189, 193, 197, 231, 233, 259, 265, 270,
274
providence and care, 53, 67, 109, 136, 137,
188, 244, 253–54, 263
Pseudo-Dionysius, 199
Pseudo-Eustathius, 72–73, 152, 168; *Hexaemeron,* 73
Puritan(ism), 2, 264
Pythagorean philosophy, 144, 184

rabbinic literature, tradition, 38, 56. *See
also* Judaism
rational beings, 141, 176
Ray, John, 269, 277

Index of Scripture